9

Pittsburgh Series in Bibliography

Pittsburgh Series in Bibliography

RING W. LARDNER

Ring W. Lardner

A DESCRIPTIVE BIBLIOGRAPHY

Matthew J. Bruccoli *and*
Richard Layman

UNIVERSITY OF
PITTSBURGH PRESS
1976

Copyright © 1976, University of Pittsburgh Press
All rights reserved
Feffer and Simons, Inc., London
Manufactured in the United States of America

Library of Congress Cataloging in Publication Data

Bruccoli, Matthew Joseph, birth date
  Ring W. Lardner: a descriptive bibliography.

  (Pittsburgh series in bibliography)
  Includes index.
  1. Lardner, Ring Wilmer, 1885–1933—Bibliography.
I. Layman, Richard, birth date   joint author.
II. Series.
Z8483.93.B78   [PS3523.A7]   016.818'52   75–9126
ISBN 0–8229–3306–3

To Ring W. Lardner, Jr.

Contents

Acknowledgments

A N Y good bibliography is a collaboration between the names on the title page and all the librarians, researchers, collectors, dealers, and others who assisted the compilers. Most of our helpers are listed here in alphabetical order, and we can only insist that this book would have been impossible without their help: Virginia Ashley, Jeanne Bennett, Linda Berry, Beverly Boyer, Mary Bruccoli, T. A. J. Burnett, William R. Cagle, Alexander Clark, C. E. Frazer Clark, Jr., Louise Craft, Joseph Cross, Claudia Drum, Margaret Duggan, Mrs. Ben Hamilton (Hampton Books), Albertha Jacob, Henry Kisor, Jeffrey Layman, Nancy Layman, Charles S. Longley, Charles W. Mann, George Monteiro, Robert Nance, Neal J. Ney, Elizabeth Pugh, Wanda Randall, Jean Rhyne, R. L. Samsell, Seven Gables Bookshop, Stuart Sherman, Scottie Fitzgerald Smith, Howard Webb, Joyce Werner, Thomas Wittenberg.

Richard Taylor, University of South Carolina Information Service, did all of the photographic work cheerfully and competently.

Many people from the University of South Carolina have been helpful. Dean Bruce Nelson, Dean H. Willard Davis, Dean John C. Guilds, the late Dr. John Welsh, Head of the Department of English, and Dr. William Nolte, Head of the Department of English— all provided crucial assistance. The University Center for Cultural Development, under the directorship of Dr. Bert Dillon, provided two research grants. Dr.

John Kimmey, Department of English, provided a
travel grant for Layman.

The staffs of the Boston Public Library, the Brown
University Library, The Library of Congress, the Lilly
Library of Indiana University, the Princeton University Library, the Theatre Division of the Library and
Museum for the Performing Arts at Lincoln Center,
The Newberry Library, the Chicago Historical Society,
the McKissick Library of the University of South Carolina, and the British Museum were particularly helpful among the many institutions which were of assistance.

They who type also serve: Ruth B. Lalka, Debbie
Phillips, and Linda Watts.

Introduction

P UBLICATION is the essential act of scholarship, but all bibliographies are works in progress.

The present volume came about this way: In the summer of 1973 Bruccoli prepared a working draft for Sections A, B, and C of a Lardner bibliography and put his then-graduate-research-assistant Layman to work on checking it. Layman displayed so much aptitude for the assignment that a collaboration seemed obligatory—with Bruccoli primarily responsible for the books and Layman for the magazines, newspapers, and syndications. In the winter of 1973–1974 we sought the assistance of Ring W. Lardner, Jr., who generously allowed us the freedom of his father's papers. As will be seen from the entries, some of the items listed in this bibliography are known only through unique copies in Mr. Lardner's possession. Hence the dedication.

FORMAT

Section A lists chronologically all books, pamphlets, and broadsides wholly or substantially by Lardner— including all printings of all editions in English. At the end of this section there is an AA supplemental list of collections of Lardner's writing. The numbering system for Section A designates the edition and printing for each entry. Thus for *You Know Me Al, A 4.1.b* indicates that it is the fourth book published by Lardner, and that the entry describes the first edition (1), second printing (b). States are designated by inferior numbers—thus A $17.1.a_2$ is the second state of the first printing of the first edition of *What of It?* Issues are indicated by asterisks—thus A $21.1.c^{**}$ is the English (second) issue of the third printing of the first edition of *Round Up*.

Section B lists chronologically all separately published pieces of sheet music with lyrics and/or music by Lardner. Only sheet music offered for sale is included; professional musicians' copies have been omitted.

Section C lists chronologically all titles in which material by Lardner appears for the first time in a book or pamphlet. Items that were previously unpublished are so stipulated. The first printings only of these items are described. It was difficult to set policy for Section C because there are memoirs that quote —or seem to quote—recollected conversations with Lardner or parts of his letters. Therefore, Section C entries have been restricted to the first book publication of material that was clearly written by Lardner. There is a supplemental CC section for borderline items, and this group is admittedly selective.

Section D lists chronologically all first appearances of Lardner's work in magazines. This section augments previously published inventories of Lardner's magazine contributions.[1] Those magazine contributions which were previously published in newspapers

---

1. The inventories consulted appear in Howard W. Webb, Jr., "Ring Lardner's Conflict and Reconciliation with American Society" (Ph.D. diss., University of Iowa, 1953); Robert H. Goldsmith, "Ring W. Lardner: A Checklist," *Bulletin of Bibliography*, 21 (December 1954), 104–106; Donald Elder, *Ring Lardner* (New York: Doubleday, 1956); Walton R. Patrick, *Ring Lardner* (New York: Twayne, 1963); and Clifford M. Caruthers, *Ring Around Max* (DeKalb: Northern Illinois University Press, 1973).

are not listed in this section but are indicated in the footnotes to entries in Section E.

Section E lists all first newspaper appearances of Lardner's work. Items are listed chronologically, except that all appearances of a column are grouped together, followed by other articles which appeared in the same newspaper during the run of that column. For instance, from 1913 to 1919 Lardner wrote the column "In the Wake of the News" for the *Chicago Tribune*. During the same period, he also covered special sports events for the *Tribune*. The coverage of the special events is listed chronologically after the last "In the Wake of the News" column. It seemed preferable to violate chronology in these cases in order to preserve the grouping for the columns.

The syndicated column—usually referred to as "Ring Lardner's Weekly Letter" (1919–1927)—has been listed as it appeared in the *San Francisco Examiner*.[2] Appendix 1 lists other newspapers which are known to have subscribed to this column. Lardner did not write the headlines for the columns, nor are the headlines consistent in subscribing newspapers. The *San Francisco Examiner* was chosen as the newspaper of reference because of its availability. The syndicated column "A Night Letter from Ring Lardner" is listed as it appeared in the *Chicago Tribune*. Since this column was syndicated by the Bell Syndi-

---

2. It cannot be assumed that there is a linear relationship between the column text submitted by Lardner to the Bell Syndicate and the newspaper appearances of that column. Lardner's text probably radiated several forms resulting from the various ways the syndicate distributed it. A subscribing newspaper may have received Lardner's column by mail, telegraph, or messenger. The column may have been sent as a typescript, a mimeographed dispatch, a galley proof, or a mat. No accurate text for Lardner's syndicated work can be established until it has been determined how the Bell Syndicate distributed it.

cate in association with the *New York Daily News–
Chicago Tribune* Syndicate, the *Chicago Tribune* was
almost certainly a "home" for the column. Lardner's
syndicated comic strip, "You Know Me Al" (1922–
1925), is recorded according to its appearances in the
Milwaukee Journal. The *Journal* is used because it
ran the complete comic strip and is available on
microfilm. Early in 1928 the Bell Syndicate re-released
a series of previously published Lardner columns and
articles. This series included selections from the
"Weekly Letter," previously unsyndicated newspaper
columns, and magazine articles—edited to disguise
anachronisms. Two hundred forty-one mimeographed
dispatches of this series have been located (see Appendix 2).

It is a flaw of this bibliography that it does not attempt to list every subsequent appearance of each
item in Sections D and E. A bibliography should provide evidence for tracing the development of an author's career in terms of the circulation of his work.
This statement has particular application to Lardner,
whose readership existed mostly among the non-book-
reading public. But there just was no room for the
information.

Section F lists chronologically movie scripts wholly
or partially written by Lardner, as well as adaptations
in which he had no hand.

Section G lists chronologically Lardner's known
work for dramatic production, whether published or
unpublished. Included are full-length plays written
by Lardner in collaboration, sketches by Lardner
which were parts of revues, and music or lyrics written
by Lardner for musicals. If the item was published, it
is also listed in the appropriate section.

Section H lists chronologically interviews with
Lardner and is almost certainly incomplete. A few
entries lack page numbers. These entries were made

on the basis of newspaper clippings held by Ring W. Lardner, Jr., and the newspapers have not been located.

Section I lists chronologically blurbs by Lardner on dust jackets of books by other authors.

Appendix 1 lists newspapers that subscribed to Lardner's syndicated "Weekly Letter," 1919–1927.

Appendix 2 describes the Bell Syndicate re-releases of Lardner material from 1928 to 1933.

Appendix 3 lists the principal works about Lardner.

TERMS AND METHODS

Edition. All the copies of a book printed from a single setting of type—including all reprintings from standing type, from plates, or by photo-offset processes.

Printing. All the copies of a book printed at one time (without removing the type or plates from the press).

States. States occur only within single printings and are created by an alteration not affecting the conditions of issue to *some* copies of a given printing (by stop-press correction or cancellation of leaves). The only states for Lardner occur in *What of It?* (A 17), where some copies of the first printing have two leaves canceled and tipped in to correct a mispagination.

Issue. Issues occur only within single printings and are created by an alteration affecting the conditions of publication or sale to *some* copies of a given printing (usually a title-page alteration). The only issues for Lardner occur in *Round Up* (A 21), where some of the sheets of the American third printing were bound with a special preliminary gathering having an English title page.

Edition, printing, state, and *issue* have been re-

stricted to the sheets of the book. Binding or dust-
jacket variants have no bearing on these terms.[3] Binding variants in this bibliography are treated simply
as binding variants. No attempt has been made to
assign priority for binding variants; however, it can be
assumed that the deposit copies at The Library of Congress and The British Museum are early copies.

State and *issue* are the most abused terms in the
vocabulary of bibliographical description. Many cata-
loguers use them interchangeably as well as ignorant-
ly. Much would be gained for the profession of bibliography by the consistent and precise usage of these
terms. *State* is easy to use correctly, but *issue* is more
troublesome. Some able bibliographers prefer to define *issue* in terms of publication or distribution, rather than of type pedigree. They argue that a new issue
results whenever a complete printing is introduced
into a publisher's series or whenever a complete printing is released by a new publisher. Under this usage
the reprinting of the Scribners plates for *Round Up*
(A 21) by the Modern Library would constitute the
"Modern Library issue." This usage would also be
applicable to the English so-called "cheap editions,"
which are not editions but remainder sheets in a
cheap binding (see *The Love Nest* [A 19] and *Gullible's Travels* [A 5]). Here again, these bibliographers
would employ *issue:* "cheap issue" or "remainder issue." Nonetheless, because the damage to bibliographical accuracy resulting from the idiosyncratic
usage of *issue* has been so great, we have elected to
treat the term conservatively. It may well be that a

---

3. This statement holds for twentieth-century publishing.
It is not possible to be so dogmatic for nineteenth-century
publishing, when parts of a printing were marketed in different formats—e.g., cloth, paper, and two-in-one bindings. In
such cases it is difficult to avoid calling the different bindings
issues because they do represent a deliberate attempt to alter
the condition of publication.

new term is needed to cover the cases when plates are leased to a new publisher—that is, when a complete printing is published by a different publisher than the one who first made the plates. In *F. Scott Fitzgerald: A Descriptive Bibliography* (1972) Bruccoli suggested that *printing-issue* might serve in these cases, but the term has not gained currency.

The form of entry for first English editions or printings is somewhat condensed from the full form provided for American editions.

Dust jackets for Section A entries have been described in detail because they are part of the original publication effort and sometimes provide information about how the book was marketed. There is, of course, no certainty that a jacket now on a copy of a book was always on it.

For binding-cloth designations we have used the method proposed by Tanselle;[4] most of these cloth grains are illustrated in Jacob Blanck, ed., *The Bibliography of American Literature* (New Haven: Yale University Press, 1955–).

Color specifications are taken from the *ISCC-NBS Color Name Charts Illustrated with Centroid Colors* (National Bureau of Standards).[5] A color designation holds for subsequent lines unless a color change is stipulated.

The spines of bindings or dust jackets are printed horizontally unless otherwise stipulated. The reader

4. G. Thomas Tanselle, "The Specifications of Binding Cloth," *The Library*, 21 (September 1966), 246–247.

5. G. Thomas Tanselle, "A System of Color Identification for Bibliographical Description," *Studies in Bibliography*, 20 (1967), 203–204. The compilers feel that the use of the Centroid designations gives a false sense of precision. Oxidation and fading make precise color description difficult, if not impossible. In any case, color identification by the Centroid system is inexact. Bruccoli's admission that he is color-blind in *F. Scott Fitzgerald: A Descriptive Bibliography* (1972) elicited comment from reviewers. He is still color-blind, but Layman is not.

is to assume that vertically printed spines read from top to bottom, unless otherwise stipulated.

In the descriptions of title pages, bindings, and dust jackets, the color of the lettering is always black, unless otherwise stipulated. The style of type is roman, unless otherwise stipulated.

The term *perfect binding* refers to books in which the pages are held together with adhesive along the back edge after the folds have been trimmed off—for example, most paperbacks.

Dates provided within brackets do not appear on the title page. Usually—but not invariably—they are taken from the copyright page.

The descriptions do not include leaf thickness or sheet bulk because there is no case for Lardner in which these measurements are required to differentiate printings.

Locations are given in the National Union Catalogue symbols—with these exceptions:

BM: British Museum
LC: Library of Congress
Lilly: Lilly Library, Indiana University
MJB: Collection of Matthew J. Bruccoli
RL: Collection of Richard Layman
RLS: Collection of R. L. Samsell, Burbank, Calif.
RWL Jr: Collection of Ring W. Lardner, Jr.

The Scribners code is provided for printings in which it appears. The first letter in this code designates the printing (or what Scribners regards as a new printing); the digits indicate month and year of printing; and the bracketed letter or letters indicate the printer. Thus *A-1.63* [*Col*] signifies that the book is the first printing, that it was printed in January 1963, and that it was printed by the Colonial Press.

Lardner's publishers prepared salesmen's dummies and advance review copies of his books, but we have not seen any.

For paperbacks, the serial number provided is that of the first printing. Paperback publishers normally change the serial number in later printings, but this information has not been noted in this bibliography.

It is desirable in bibliographical description to avoid end-of-line hyphens in transcriptions. Because of word lengths and a measured line, however, it is impossible to satisfy this requirement. End-of-line hyphens have been avoided wherever possible, and always where a hyphen would create ambiguity.

A bibliography is outdated the day it goes to the printer. Addenda and corrigenda are earnestly solicited.

The University of South Carolina
5 October 1974

A. Separate Publications

All books, pamphlets, and broadsides wholly or substantially by Lardner—including all printings of all editions in English, arranged chronologically. At the end of Section A there is an AA supplemental list of collections of Lardner's work.

A 1 ZANZIBAR
Only printing (1903)

ZANZIBAR

A COMIC OPERA IN TWO ACTS

**BOOK BY
HARRY SCHMIDT**

**LYRICS AND MUSIC BY
RING LARDNER**

AS FIRST PERFORMED BY THE AMERICAN MINSTRELS
AT THE NILES OPERA HOUSE, APRIL 14, 1903

FRED D. COOK, PUBLISHER
NILES, MICHIGAN

A 1: 9⅛" x 6⅛"

Unpaged: Fourteen leaves printed on rectos.

[1]^{14}

Contents: leaf 1: title; leaf 2: cast; leaves 3–11: text and lyrics, headed '*Zanzibar* | [rule] | *Act 1* | [rule]'; leaves 12–14: blank.

Typography and paper: 10 point on 12, type unidentified. 9¼" (7⅜") x 6⅛". No running heads. Coated paper.

Binding: Dark gray (266) wrappers. Front goldstamped: 'ZANZIBAR | A COMIC OPERA IN TWO ACTS | BOOK BY HARRY SCHMIDT | LYRICS AND MUSIC BY | RING LARDNER'. All edges trimmed.

Publication: Number of copies and price unknown. Presumably published April 1903.

Printing: Printing by Fred D. Cook, a Niles job printer.

Location: RWL Jr.

Note: The program for *Zanzibar* includes nothing signed by Lardner. Cover title: '[all the following within single-rule frame] ZANZIBAR | [type decoration within double-rules frame] | [following three lines within double-rules frame] Produced April 14, 1903 | at the Opera House in | Niles, Michigan, by the | [type decoration within double-rules frame] | American Minstrels'. Locations: RWL Jr., Fort St. Joseph Museum.
The program provides the "Argument of Zanzibar":

The story opens just after the death of the Sultan of Zanzibar. His son and successor, Seyyid Barghash, has been educated in foreign countries and is expected home to take the throne. Shylock and Padlock, whose former homes were in Buchanan, Mich., appear as valets to two young New Yorkers. Shylock is mistaken for the young Sultan. He at once assumes the throne, but being better acquainted with American government, he changes his title to Mayor, appoints Padlock City Clerk and the members of his court aldermen. In the second act the real Sultan appears and adds complications to the plot. Shylock explains that he was merely keeping the throne warm for the Sultan, and all ends happily.

Lardner had the role of Shylock.

Front wrapper of A 1

A 2   MARCH 6TH, 1914   THE HOME COMING
Only printing (1914)

A 2: 7½" x 10⅜"

This book is in every sense a souvenir of the occasion, and under no
conditions for sale.

COMPILED BY
R. W. LARDNER and EDWARD G. HEEMAN
CHICAGO, ILLINOIS

The pictures, writings, songs, cartoons and other matter were contributed
or are used by permission of the parties whose names
appear with the same.

Copyrighted, 1914, by Edward G. Heeman

[1–2] 3 [4] 5–64

[1–4]⁸

Contents: p. 1: title; p. 2: copyright; pp. 3–4: 'FOREWORD |
By R. W. Lardner'; pp. 5–64: text. "He's a Good Old Scout," pp.
56–57, by Ring Lardner and Aubrey Stauffer.

Typography and paper: 10 point on 12, Cheltenham. 7½″ x
10⅜″. No running heads. Coated wove paper.

Binding: Reddish brown suede. Front goldstamped: 'THE HOME
COMING | [baseball]'. All edges trimmed.

No dust jacket.

Publication: Unknown number of copies. Not for sale. Published
3 March 1914. Copyright 3 March 1914. Copyright #A362776.

Printing: Typesetting and printing by Blakely Printing Co.,
Chicago; binding by Brock & Rankin, Chicago.

Note: This volume was a collaborative effort in which Lardner
participated.

Locations: ICH, LC (rebound; deposit-stamp MAR-6 1914).

Binding (front) of A 2

A 3 BIB BALLADS
Only printing (1915)

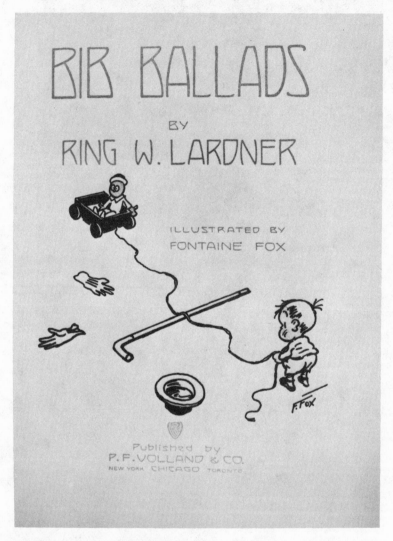

A 3: lettered in light olive gray (112), except 'F. Fox' in black (267); drawing in black with deep reddish orange (36) wagon and moderate reddish orange (37) faces; 8½″ x 6″

Unpaged: [1–64]

[1–4]⁸

Contents: p. 1: half title; p. 2: copyright; p. 3: title; p. 4: blank; p. 5: 'FOREWORD'; p. 6: illustration; pp. 7–63: text, beginning 'Good-By Bill'; p. 64: blank.

Paper: 8¾″ x 6″. Running heads: '[light olive gray (112)] BIB BALLADS'. Wove paper.

Binding: Deep yellow brown (75) S (diagonal fine-ribbed) or B cloth (linen). Front goldstamped: 'BIB BALLADS | [baby with spoon and white bib] | [bowl] | RING W. LARDNER'. Strong brown (55) endpapers. Top edge gilt. All edges trimmed.

No dust jacket. Published in two-piece medium yellow brown (77) cardboard box. Goldstamped on front of lid with same lettering and illustration as book cover. Goldstamped on bottom edge of lid: 'BIB BALLADS—RING W. LARDNER'.

Publication: Unknown number of copies. 50¢. Published 10 July 1915. Copyright 10 July 1915. Copyright #A406743.

Printing: Printing by Faithorn Co., Chicago; plates by Acme Co., Chicago; binding by Brock & Rankin, Chicago.

Note 1:   Copies have been seen with or without a work-up between 'U.' and 'S.' in the copyright notice.

Note 2:   All poems in *Bib Ballads* first appeared in "In the Wake of the News." See Section E. All selections are first book appearances. "Foreword" previously unpublished.

Locations: ICN (S cloth), MJB (S cloth, boxed; B cloth), PSt (B cloth); RL (S cloth).

Binding (front) of A 3

A 4 YOU KNOW ME AL

A 4.1.a
First edition, first printing (1916)

YOU KNOW ME AL

A Busher's Letters

BY

RING W. LARDNER

NEW YORK
GEORGE H. DORAN COMPANY

A 4.1.a: 7⅜″ x 5″

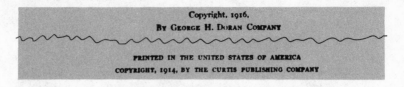

[i–iv] [1–8] 9–247 [248–252]

[1–16]⁸

Contents: pp. i–iv: blank; p. 1: half title; p. 2: blank; p. 3: title;
p. 4: copyright; p. 5: 'CONTENTS'; p. 6: blank; p. 7: half title;
p. 8: blank; pp. 9–247: text, headed 'YOU KNOW ME | AL |
CHAPTER I | A BUSHER'S LETTERS HOME'; pp. 248–252:
blank.

Typography and Paper: 11 point on 14, Original Old Style.
5³⁄₁₆″ (5⁷⁄₁₆″) x 3⁵⁄₁₆″. Twenty-seven lines per page. Running
heads: rectos, chapter titles; versos, 'YOU KNOW ME AL'. Wove
paper.

Binding: Deep reddish orange (36) V cloth (smooth). Front
goldstamped: 'YOU KNOW | ME AL | RING W. LARDNER |
[black drawing of head in baseball cap against gold background,
all within single-rule black frame].' Spine goldstamped: 'YOU |
KNOW | ME | AL | [three squares] | LARDNER | DORAN'. White
wove endpapers. All edges trimmed.
    Also presumed remainder binding in deep yellow (85) V cloth,
stamped in black.

Dust jacket: White paper printed predominantly in black.
Front: '[following two lines in orange] *A Busher's Letters* | [rule] |
YOU KNOW | ME AL | RING W. LARDNER | [head of baseball
player on orange background within single-rule frame] | [orange
device] [three lines in black] | [orange device] [five lines in black]
| [orange rule] | GEORGE H. DORAN COMPANY *Publishers* New
York'. Spine: 'YOU | KNOW | ME | AL | – – – | LARDNER | [Doran
seal] | DORAN'. Back: '*NOVELS of MARK* | [rule] | [ads for
twelve novels] | [rule] | GEORGE H. DORAN COMPANY
Publishers New York'. Front and back flaps: blank.

Publication: Unknown number of copies of the first printing.
$1.25. Published 29 July 1916. Copyright 29 July 1916. Copyright
#A437048.

Printing: Printing and plates by J. J. Little & Ives Co., New
York; binding by H. Wolff, New York.

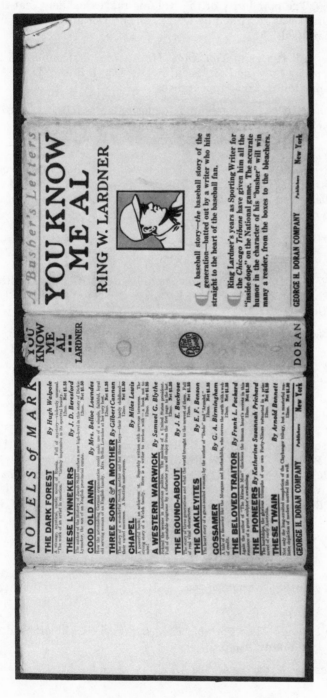

Dust jacket for A 4.1.a

Note 1:   The popularity of this volume makes it likely that the first edition was reprinted by Doran, but no Doran reprints have been identified.

Note 2:   All stories in *You Know Me Al* were first published in *The Saturday Evening Post.* See D 2, D 4, D 5, D 8, D 9, D 10. All selections are first book appearances.

Locations: ICN, LC (rebound; deposit-stamp JUL 31 1916), Lilly (yellow binding), MJB, RLS (dj; review copy).

A 4.1.b
Second printing: New York: Scribners, 1925. Reprinted from the Doran plates, with new 'PREFACE' by Lardner, pp. v–vi. Republished 10 April 1925. Noted in three bindings of uniform set; see AA 1 for note on uniform bindings.

A 4.2
Second edition

RING W. LARDNER | You Know Me Al | A BUSHER'S LETTERS | CLEVELAND AND NEW YORK [tower device] | THE WORLD PUBLISHING COMPANY

Published May 1945. Reprinted July 1945 and February 1946.

A 4.3.a
Third edition, first printing

[all the following within double-rules frame] [to the left of a vertical rule] PUBLISHED BY ARRANGEMENT WITH | CHARLES SCRIBNER'S SONS, NEW YORK | COPYRIGHT, 1916, 1925, | BY CHARLES SCRIBNER'S SONS | COPYRIGHT, 1914, | BY THE CURTIS PUBLISHING COMPANY | [to the right of vertical rule] YOU KNOW ME | AL | A Busher's Letters | *By* | RING W. LARDNER | *Editions for the Armed Services, Inc.* | A NON-PROFIT ORGANIZATION ESTABLISHED BY | THE COUNCIL ON BOOKS IN WARTIME, NEW YORK

1944. #J278.

A 4.3.b
Second printing: 1946? #782.

A 4.4
Fourth edition: *The Portable Ring Lardner*, ed. Gilbert Seldes. New York: Viking, 1946.

Includes *You Know Me Al.* See AA 4.

A 4.5
Fifth edition

YOU KNOW ME AL | [script] A Busher's Letters | *By RING W. LARDNER* | CHARLES SCRIBNER'S SONS | *New York*

1960.

A-2.60 [V].

Introduction by John Lardner.

A 4.6
Sixth edition: *The Ring Lardner Reader*, ed. Maxwell Geismar. New York: Scribners, [1963].

Includes *You Know Me Al*. See AA 9.

A 5 GULLIBLE'S TRAVELS, ETC.

A 5.1.a
First edition, first printing (1917)

Gullible's Travels, Etc.

By
RING W. LARDNER

Author of
You Know Me, Al, etc.

Illustrated by
MAY WILSON PRESTON

INDIANAPOLIS
THE BOBBS-MERRILL COMPANY
PUBLISHERS

A 5.1.a: 7⅜" x 5"

[i–viii] 1–35 [36] 37–155 [156] 157–207 [208] 209–255 [256]

[1–16]⁸ [17]⁴. Glossy frontispiece with protective tissue tipped in facing title page.

Contents: p. i: half title; p. ii: blank; p. iii: title; p. iv: copyright; p. v: 'CONTENTS'; p. vi: blank; p. vii: half title; p. viii: blank; pp. 1–256: text, headed 'Gullible's Travels, Etc. | CARMEN'.
   Five stories. "Carmen," "Three Kings and a Pair," "Gullible's Travels," "The Water Cure," "Three Without, Doubled."

Typography and paper: 12 point on 16, Scotch. 5³⁄₁₆″ (5¹¹⁄₁₆″) x 3⁵⁄₁₆″. Twenty-three lines per page. Running heads: rectos, chapter titles; versos, 'GULLIBLE'S TRAVELS, ETC.' Wove paper.

Binding: Dark blue (183) V cloth (smooth) or dark blue (183) T cloth (bold-ribbed). Front: '[yellowish white (92)] Gullible's | Travels | Etc. | Ring W. Lardner'. Spine: '[yellowish white (92)] Gulli= | ble's | Travels | Etc. | [rule] | Lardner | Bobbs | Merrill'. Pictorial endpapers by May Wilson Preston. All edges trimmed.

Dust jacket: Not seen.

Publication: Unknown number of copies of the first printing. $1.25. Published 10 February 1917. Copyright 10 February 1917. Copyright #A45549.

Printing: Printing by Braunworth & Co., Brooklyn; plates by Hollenbeck Press, Indianapolis; binding by Braunworth.

Note 1:   Publisher's dummy described in L. W. Currey Catalogue, 23 (Winter 1973), #630.

Note 2:   All stories in *Gullible's Travels, Etc.* were first published in *The Saturday Evening Post.* See D 28, D 29, D 34, D 36, D 39. All selections are first book appearances.

Note 3:   Incomplete sales records from the Bobbs-Merrill archives at the Lilly Library indicate sales of 3788 copies and 100 copies of an unidentified "Canadian edition" for the period ending 30 June 1917.

Locations: LC (T cloth; deposit-stamp FEB 14 1917), MJB (V cloth; T cloth), RL (T cloth).

Promotional cards

Bulletin No. 1

WE WAS playin' rummy over to Hatch's, and Hatch must of fell in a bed of four-leaf clovers on his way home the night before, because he plays rummy like he does everything else; but this night I refer to you couldn't beat him, and besides him havin' all the luck my Missus played like she'd been bought off, so when we come to settle up we was plain seven and a half out. You know who paid it. So Hatch says:

"They must be some game you can play."

from

Gullible's Travels
By Ring W. Lardner

Promotional card for A 5.1.a: 4¼" x 5½"

Six promotional cards were distributed for *Gullible's Travels, Etc.*, by the publisher, each with an excerpt from the book: *Bulletin No. 1* (1.1-11), *Bulletin No. 2* (7.5-13), *Bulletin No. 3* (91.4-13), *Bulletin No. 4* (103.3-15), *Bulletin No. 5* (220.17-23; 221.1-4), *Bulletin No. 6* (239.8-16).

Stiff white coated cards, printed on rectos in shades of light gray olive (109) to dark gray olive (111).

Note: In a letter to Lardner dated 10 March 1917, H. H. Howland refers to a second printing of these cards which corrects the title on the lower left-hand corner to read *Gullible's Travels, Etc.*

Locations: Lilly, MJB.

A 5.1.b
Second printing: New York: Scribners, 1925. Reprinted from the Bobbs-Merrill plates with a new 'PREFACE' by Lardner, pp. v–vi. Republished 10 April 1925. Noted in three bindings of uniform set; see AA 1 for note on uniform bindings.

A 5.1.c
Only English printing, from American plates (1926)

GULLIBLE'S
TRAVELS, Etc.

BY

RING W. LARDNER

CHATTO & WINDUS
LONDON

A 5.1.c: 7 7/16″ x 4 15/16″

[a–b] [i–iv] v–vi [vii–x] 1–35 [36] 37–155 [156] 157–207 [208] 209–255 [256]

[1]^6 [2–17]^8

Copyright page: 'PUBLISHED 1926 | PRINTED IN GREAT BRITAIN | ALL | RIGHTS RESERVED'.

Contents: pp. a–b: blank; p. i: half title; p. ii: blank; p. iii: title; p. iv: copyright; pp. v–vi: 'PREFACE', signed 'R. W. L.'; p. vii: 'CONTENTS'; p. viii: blank; p. ix: half title; p. x: blank; pp. 1–256: text, headed 'Gullible's Travels, Etc. | CARMEN'; p. 256: 'BRISTOL: BURLEIGH LTD., AT THE BURLEIGH PRESS'.

Paper: Wove.

Binding: Dark yellowish green (137) V cloth (smooth). Front and back have blindstamped single-rule frame. Spine goldstamped: '[triple rules] | GULLIBLE'S TRAVELS | · | RING W. | LARDNER | CHATTO & WINDUS | [triple rules]'. White wove endpapers. Top and fore edges trimmed. Top edge stained green.

Dust jacket: Not seen.

Publication: 1,500 of copies of the only English printing. 7s. 6d. Published April 1926.

Locations: BM (deposit-stamp 5 MAY 26), Lilly, RL.

Cheap binding: London: Chatto & Windus, [1926?]. Almost certainly remainder binding in dark red (16) paper-covered boards. Location: MJB.

A 5.2
Second edition

RING W. LARDNER | *Gullible's* | *Travels,* | *Etc.* | INTRODUCTION BY JOSEPHINE HERBST | CHICAGO AND LONDON | THE UNIVERSITY OF CHICAGO PRESS

1965

Also published in paperback as Phoenix Book P252.

A 6 MY FOUR WEEKS IN FRANCE
Only printing (1918)

MY FOUR WEEKS IN FRANCE

By

RING W. LARDNER

AUTHOR OF

Gullible's Travels, Etc.

ILLUSTRATED BY

WALLACE MORGAN

INDIANAPOLIS
THE BOBBS-MERRILL COMPANY
PUBLISHERS

A 6: 7⅜″ x 4⅞″

[1–8] 9–187 [188–192]

[1–12]⁸. Six glossy illustrations tipped in.

Contents: p. 1: half title; p. 2: blank; p. 3: title; p. 4: copyright; p. 5: 'CONTENTS'; p. 6: blank; p. 7: half title; p. 8: blank; pp. 9–187: text, headed 'MY FOUR WEEKS IN | FRANCE | I | DODGING SUBMARINES TO COVER THE | BIGGEST GAME OF ALL'; p. 188: blank; pp. 189–192: free and paste-down endpapers.

Typography and paper: 11 point on 17, Scotch. 5⅛″ (5½″) x 3³⁄₁₆″. Twenty-three lines per page. Running heads: rectos and versos, 'MY FOUR WEEKS IN FRANCE'. Wove paper.

Binding: Dark purplish blue (201) boards (imitation V cloth [smooth]), stamped in dark reddish orange (36). Front: '[all within single-rule frame] MY FOUR WEEKS | [triangle] IN FRANCE [triangle] | RING W. LARDNER'. Spine: 'MY | FOUR | WEEKS | IN | FRANCE | LARDNER | BOBBS | MERRILL'. Also pale green (149) V cloth (smooth) stamped in yellowish white (92), and dark bluish gray (192) V cloth stamped in yellowish white (92). White wove sized endpapers. All edges trimmed.

Dust jacket: Off-white paper. Front: '[all within red single-rule frame] [black] MY FOUR WEEKS | [triangle] IN FRANCE [triangle] | RING W. LARDNER | [red drawing of soldier and civilian, signed by W. Morgan] | [red] LAUGH WITH LARDNER | [black] In times like these we thank Heaven for a sense | of humor and for the man that makes us use it. | Mr. Lardner went to Paris and to the Front and | came right back again. But he saw what no man | in the trenches ever saw, and he wrote about it as | no author of a war book ever wrote before.' Spine: '[black] MY | FOUR | WEEKS | IN | FRANCE | LARDNER | PRICE | $1.25 Net | [red circle with ad for war savings stamps] | [black] BOBBS | MERRILL'. Back has mailing instructions. Front flap has mailing label. Back flap: blank.

Publication: Unknown number of copies of the only printing. $1.25. Published 18 May 1918. Copyright 18 May 1918. Copyright #A499108.

Dust jacket for A 6

Printing: Printing by Braunworth & Co., Brooklyn; plates by Hollenbeck Press, Indianapolis; binding by Braunworth.

Note 1:   Serialized (eight parts) in *Collier's* as "A Reporter's Diary," 29 September 1917 to 19 January 1918. See D 48. All selections are first book appearances.

Note 2:   Chapter 2 of *My Four Weeks in France* is included in *A Cavalcade of Collier's,* ed. Kenneth McArdle (New York: Barnes, [1959]) as "A Reporter's Diary."

Locations: ICN (gray cloth), LC (two copies in gray cloth; deposit-stamp MAY 25 1918), MJB (blue boards with dj; gray cloth with dj; green cloth), RL (green cloth).

A 7 TREAT 'EM ROUGH

A 7.1.a.
Only edition, first printing (1918)

TREAT 'EM ROUGH

LETTERS FROM
JACK THE KAISER KILLER

By

RING W. LARDNER
AUTHOR OF
My Four Weeks in France, Gullible's Travels, Etc.

ILLUSTRATED BY
FRANK CRERIE

INDIANAPOLIS
THE BOBBS-MERRILL COMPANY
PUBLISHERS

A 7.1.a: 7⅜" x 4 15/16"

[1–8] 9–10 [11–12] 13–20 [21–22] 23–25 [26] 27–28 [29–30] 31
[32] 33–35 [36] 37–40 [41–42] 43 [44] 45–48 [49–50] 51–55 [56]
57–59 [60] 61–62 [63–64] 65–71 [72] 73–74 [75–76] 77–85 [86]
87–88 [89–90] 91–95 [96] 97–98 [99–100] 101–108 [109–110]
111–114 [115–116] 117–121 [122] 123–125 [126] 127–130
[131–132] 133–134 [135 –136] 137 [138] 139–140 [141–142] 143
[144] 145–148 [149–150] 151–154 [155–156] 157 [158] 159–160
[1–10]⁸

Contents: p. 1: blank; p. 2: frontispiece; p. 3: title; p. 4:
copyright; p. 5: illustration; p. 6: blank; p. 7: half title; p. 8:
blank; pp. 9–160: text, headed 'JACK THE KAISER KILLER'.

Typography and paper: 11 point on 13, Scotch. 5³⁄₁₆″ (5½″) x
3³⁄₁₆″. Twenty-nine lines per page. Running heads: rectos, 'JACK
THE KAISER KILLER'; versos, 'TREAT 'EM ROUGH'. Wove
paper.

Binding: Moderate olive (107) V cloth (smooth). Front has
off-white paper label printed in black and deep reddish orange
(36): '[all within orange single-rule frame] [underlined] TREAT
'EM ROUGH | [orange illustration by F.C. of soldier with a bat
swinging at ball that has caricature of Kaiser] | [swash "L"] *Letters*
| [swash "f"] *from* | JACK *the* KAISER KILLER | [swash, orange]
by [roman; orange "R," "W," and "L"; rest in black] RING W.
LARDNER'. Parts of orange frame stamped on cloth visible around
label in various copies. Spine stamped in deep reddish orange
(36): '[within single-rule frame] [first three lines underlined]
TREAT' | EM | ROUGH | [rule] | LARDNER | [within single-rule
frame] BOBBS | MERRILL'. White wove sized endpapers. All edges
trimmed.

Dust jacket: Grayish brown. Front is same as label on front of
binding with addition of top line in red: 'LAUGH *with* LARDNER'.
Spine: '[black lettering within black single-rule frame] [first three
lines underlined] TREAT' | EM | ROUGH | [rule] | LARDNER | [within
black single-rule frame] PRICE | $1⁰⁰ NET | [within black single-
rule frame] BOBBS | MERRILL'. Back has instructions for mailing.
Front flap has mailing label. Back flap has pictorial ad for *Treat
'Em Rough.*

Dust jacket for A 7.1.a

Publication: Unknown number of copies of the first printing. $1.00. Published 18 September 1918. Copyright 18 September 1918. Copyright #A501835.

Printing: Printing, plates, and binding by Braunworth & Co., Brooklyn.

Note: *Treat 'Em Rough* was first published (in three parts) in *The Saturday Evening Post.* See D 52, D 53, D 54. All selections are first book appearances.

Locations: MJB (dj); LC (rebound; deposit-stamp SEP 21 1918), RL.

A 7.1.b
Second printing: Indianapolis: Bobbs-Merrill, [1918]. Adds eighteen-line poem on p. 6: "To R. W. L." by H.H.H. (H. H. Howland).

Location: MJB (dark olive green [126] V cloth [smooth]; light yellowish green [135] V cloth).

A 8 THE REAL DOPE
Only printing (1919)

THE REAL DOPE

By

RING W. LARDNER

AUTHOR OF

GULLIBLE'S TRAVELS, MY FOUR WEEKS IN FRANCE
TREAT 'EM ROUGH, ETC.

ILLUSTRATED BY

MAY WILSON PRESTON

AND

M. L. BLUMENTHAL

INDIANAPOLIS
THE BOBBS-MERRILL COMPANY
PUBLISHERS

A 8: 7⅜" x 4 13/16"

COPYRIGHT 1919
THE BOBBS-MERRILL COMPANY

PRESS OF
BRAUNWORTH & CO.
BOOK MANUFACTURERS
BROOKLYN, N. Y.

[i–vi] 1–186

[1–12]⁸. Five glossy illustrations tipped in.

Contents: p. i: half title; p. ii: blank; p. iii: title; p. iv: copyright; p. v: half title; p. vi: blank; pp. 1–86: text, headed 'THE REAL DOPE | CHAPTER I | AND MANY A STORMY WIND SHALL BLOW'.

Typography and paper: 11 point on 13, Scotch. 5¼″ (5⅝″) x 3³⁄₁₆″. Twenty-nine lines per page. Running heads: rectos, chapter titles; versos, 'THE REAL DOPE'. Wove paper.

Binding: Dark purplish blue (201) boards (imitation B cloth), stamped in deep reddish orange (36). Front: '[all within single-rule frame] THE REAL DOPE | [triangle] | RING W. LARDNER'. Spine: 'THE | REAL | DOPE | [triangle] | LARDNER | BOBBS | MERRILL'. Also strong reddish brown (40) boards, stamped in black. White wove sized endpapers. All edges trimmed.

Dust jacket: White paper. Front: '[all within red single-rule frame] [red] *Laugh with Lardner* | [black] THE REAL DOPE | [triangle] | RING W. LARDNER | Author of TREAT 'EM ROUGH | MY FOUR WEEKS IN FRANCE, ETC. | [illustration of nurse and patient by May Wilson Preston] | *And I wished you could see her look at me Al.*' Spine: 'THE | REAL | DOPE | [triangle] | LARDNER | PRICE | $1.25 Net | BOBBS | MERRILL'. Back cover: twenty-four-line ad for *The Real Dope*. Front flap has blurb for *My Four Weeks in France*. Back flap has blurb for *Treat 'Em Rough*.

Publication: Unknown number of copies of the only printing. $1.25. Published 15 February 1919. Copyright 15 February 1919. Copyright #A511622.

Printing: Printing by Braunworth & Co., Brooklyn; plates by Hollenbeck Press, Indianapolis; binding by Braunworth.

Note: *The Real Dope* was first published (in six parts) in *The Saturday Evening Post.* See D 55, D 56, D 57, D 59, D 60, D 61. All selections are first book appearances.

Locations: ICN (blue boards), LC (blue boards; deposit-stamp
FEB 19 1919), MJB (blue boards with dj; brown boards), RL
(blue boards).

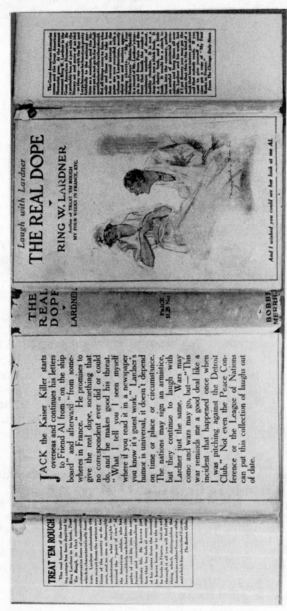

Dust jacket for A 8

A 9 OWN YOUR OWN HOME
Only printing (1919)

OWN YOUR OWN HOME

By RING W. LARDNER

Author of *My Four Weeks in France, The Real Dope, Treat 'Em Rough,* etc.

Illustrated by
FONTAINE FOX

INDIANAPOLIS
THE BOBBS-MERRILL COMPANY
PUBLISHERS

A 9: 7⅜" x 4 15/16"

[i–iv] 1–123 [124]

[1–8]⁸

Contents: p. i: title; p. ii: copyright; p. iii: half title; p. iv: blank; pp. 1–123: text, headed 'OWN YOUR OWN HOME | CHAPTER I | IT'S THE ONLY LIFE'; p. 124: blank.

Typography and Paper: 11 point on 13, Scotch. 5⁵⁄₁₆″ (5¹¹⁄₁₆″) x 3⁵⁄₁₆″. Twenty-eight to thirty lines per page. Running heads: rectos, chapter titles; versos, 'OWN YOUR OWN HOME'. Wove paper.

Binding: Pictorial yellowish white (92) boards. Front: '[all within single-rule frame] [deep reddish orange (36), with double underline] MORE FUN BY | [black, outlined in deep reddish orange] Ring W. Lardner | [black and deep reddish orange drawing] | [black, filled in with deep reddish orange, slanting up] Own Your own Home— | [black] Pictures | [swash] by | [roman] Fontaine Fox'. Spine: '[outlined in black] OWN | YOUR | OWN | HOME | [solid black] LARDNER | $1⁰⁰ | NET | BOBBS | MERRILL'. Back: '[three drawings in deep reddish orange frames] | [deep reddish orange] OWN | YOUR | OWN | HOME | Joys of | Suburban | Life | Seen by | Fontaine Fox'. White wove sized endpapers. All edges trimmed.

Dust jacket: Not seen; possibly not published with jacket.

Publication: 5,000 copies of the only printing. $1.00. Published 7 October 1919. Copyright 7 October 1919. Copyright #A536115.

Printing: Printing by Braunworth & Co., Brooklyn; plates by Hollenbeck Press, Indianapolis; binding by Braunworth.

Note 1: All stories in *Own Your Own Home* were first published in *The Red Book Magazine*. See D 12, D 17, D 20, D 24. All selections are first book appearances.

Note 2: Incomplete sales records from the Bobbs-Merrill archives at the Lilly Library indicate sales of 4,385 copies between September 1919 and June 1920.

Locations: ICN, LC (deposit-stamp OCT 10 1919), MJB, RL.

Binding for A 9

A 10   REGULAR FELLOWS I HAVE MET
Only printing (1919)

Regular Fellows I Have Met

BY
RING W. LARDNER

WITH ILLUSTRATIONS BY REGULAR CARTOONISTS

CHICAGO
1919

A 10: 10½" x 7¾"

Copyright 1919
B. A WILMOT
Chicago

Unpaged: Two hundred leaves printed on rectos; interleaved with tissue.

Possibly not gathered: single leaves glued at back with cloth and sewn through three holes with heavy cord.

Contents: leaf 1: blank; leaf 2: recto, title; verso, copyright; leaf 3: 'FOREWORD'; leaves 4–200: text, beginning with caricature of Lawrence R. Adams, with five-line verse by Lardner.

Typography and paper: Verse printed in 10 point on 12, Italic. No running heads. Wove paper, watermarked: '[script] Strathmore USA'.

Binding: Deep yellowish green (132) suede, with deep yellowish green (132) silk lining. Front goldstamped: 'REGULAR FELLOWS | I HAVE MET | BY RING W. LARDNER'. Top and bottom edges trimmed; front edge deckle.

No dust jacket.

Publication: *Regular Fellows I Have Met* was a subscription book (or mug book) sold to the men included in the text. Unknown number of copies. Price unknown. Published 31 December 1919. Copyright 31 December 1919. Copyright #A561325.

Printing: Printing by Carbery & Reed, Chicago; cuts by Chicago *Herald & Examiner;* binding by A. Landa & Sons, Chicago.

Locations: ICN, MJB.

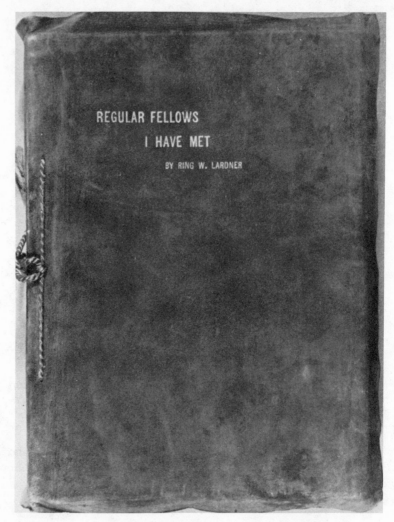

Binding (front) of A 10

A 11 THE YOUNG IMMIGRUNTS

A 11.1
First edition, only printing (1920)

The
Young Immigrunts

By
RING W. LARDNER, Jr.

WITH A PREFACE BY
THE FATHER

Portraits by Gaar Williams

INDIANAPOLIS
THE BOBBS-MERRILL COMPANY
PUBLISHERS

A 11.1: 7¼" x 4¾"

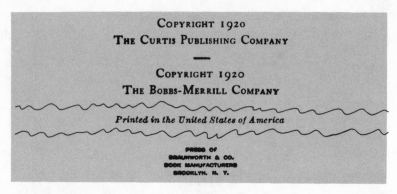

[i–iv] v [vi] vii [viii] ix–x [xi–xii] 13–14 [15–16] 17–20 [21–22]
23–24 [25–26] 27–30 [31–32] 33–34 [35–36] 37–40 [41–42] 43–46
[47–48] 49–52 [53–54] 55–58 [59–60] 61–64 [65–66] 67–68 [69–
70] 71–78 [79–80] 81–82 [83–84] 85–86 [87–88]

[1–5]⁸ [6]⁴

Contents: p. 1: half title; p. ii: frontispiece; p. iii: title; p. iv:
copyright; p. v: 'CONTENTS'; p. vi: illustration; p. vii: 'LIST OF
ILLUSTRATIONS'; p. viii: illustration; pp. ix–x: 'PREFACE'; p.
xi: half title; p. xii: illustration; pp. 13–86: text, headed 'The
Young Immigrunts | CHAPTER 1 | My Parents'; pp. 87–88: blank.

Typography and paper: 12 point on 16, Century Expanded. 4⅞″
(5³⁄₁₆″) x 2¹³⁄₁₆″. Twenty-one lines per page. Running heads:
rectos, chapter titles; versos, 'THE YOUNG IMMIGRUNTS'.
Wove paper.

Binding: Yellowish gray (93) boards printed in black. Front:
'With Preface by the Father | [script] The | [roman] YOUNG |
IMMIGRUNTS | RING W· LARDNER JR· | [silhouettes with
strings]'. Spine and back: continuation of illustrations, signed
by Gaar Williams on back bottom edge. White wove endpapers of
same stock as text. All edges trimmed.

Dust jacket: Gray paper printed in black, with same illustrations
and printing as on the boards. Front and back flaps have ads for
The Young Immigrunts.

Publication: 6,000 copies of the only printing. $1.00. Published
1 May 1920. Copyright 1 May 1920. Copyright #A566903.

Printing: Printing by Braunworth & Co., Brooklyn; plates by
Bookwalter-Ball Co., Indianapolis; binding by Braunworth.

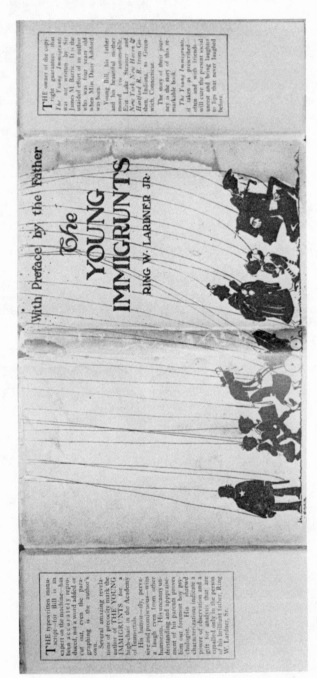

Dust jacket for A 11.1

Note 1:   *The Young Immigrunts* was first published in *The Saturday Evening Post*. See D 67. First book appearance.

Note 2:   *The Young Immigrunts* is a parody of *The Young Visiters* and purports to be the work of Lardner's four-year-old son, Ring, Jr. Although it was obviously written by the senior Ring Lardner, some readers have been fooled. Indeed, *Merle Johnson's American First Editions* makes the error of attributing the book to the boy.

Locations: ICN, LC (deposit-stamp MAY–8 1920), MJB (dj), RLS.

A 11.2
Second edition: What of It?. New York: Scribners, 1925.

The augmented third printing includes *The Young Immigrunts*. See A 17.1.c.

A 11.3
Third edition: *The Portable Ring Lardner*, ed. Gilbert Seldes. New York: Viking, 1946.

Includes *The Young Immigrunts*. See AA 4.

A 11.4
Fourth edition: *The Ring Lardner Reader*, ed. Maxwell Geismar. New York: Scribners, [1963].

Includes *The Young Immigrunts*. See AA 9.

A 12 BELL SYNDICATE BROADSIDE
Only printing (1920?)

A 12: broadside; approx. 18½" x 14"

New York: Bell Syndicate, [1920?].

Broadside, printed on recto only.

Includes Lardner's 22 August 1920 Bell Syndicate "Weekly Letter," "A Ounce of Preventions Is Worth a Pint of Hootch." See
E 3191.

Unknown number of copies distributed for promotional purposes.

Location: RWL Jr.

A 13 SYMPTOMS OF BEING 35

A 13.1
First edition, only printing (1921)

Symptoms of Being 35

By
RING W. LARDNER

SILHOUETTES BY
HELEN E. JACOBY

INDIANAPOLIS
THE BOBBS-MERRILL COMPANY
PUBLISHERS

A 13.1: 7 5/16″ x 4⅞″

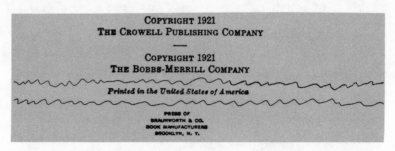

[i–ii] [1–12] 13–16 [17–18] 19–22 [23–24] 25–28 [29–30] 31–32 [33–34] 35–36 [37–38] 39–42 [43–44] 45–48 [49–50] 51–52 [53–62]

[1–4]^8

Contents: pp. i–ii; 1–2: blank; p. 3: half title; p. 4: card page; p. 5: blank; p. 6: illustration and excerpt; p. 7: title; p. 8: copyright; p. 9: prefatory note; p. 10: blank; p. 11: half title; p. 12: blank; pp. 13–53: text, headed 'Symptoms of Being 35'; pp. 54–62: blank.

Typography and paper: 12 point on 16, Modern No. 1. 4⁹⁄₁₆″ (5¹⁄₁₆″) x 2¹³⁄₁₆″. Twenty lines per page. Running heads: rectos and versos, 'SYMPTOMS OF BEING 35'. Wove paper.

Binding: Light greenish gray (154) boards printed predominantly in blackish green (152) with deep reddish orange (36) as noted. Front: '[double rules] | [orange "S"] Symptoms | [swash] of [roman] [orange "B"] Being | [orange, to the right of the preceding two lines] 35 | [orange rule] | RING W. LARDNER | [double rules] | [silhouettes signed by H. E. Jacoby] | To him it was like as if she was | kissing an old cab horse on a bet | for the benefit [swash] of [roman] the Red Cross'. Spine: '[vertically] Lardner: SYMPTOMS OF BEING 35 : BOBBS | MERRILL'. White wove sized endpapers. All edges trimmed.

Dust jacket: Not seen; possibly not published with jacket.

Publication: 4,000 copies of the only printing. 75¢. Published 19 August 1921. Copyright 19 August 1921. Copyright #A622499.

Printing: Printing by Braunworth & Co., Brooklyn; plates by William Mitchell Printing Co., Greenfield, Ind.; binding by Braunworth.

Note 1:   *Symptoms of Being* 35 was first published as "General Symptoms of Being 35" in *The American Magazine.* See D 75. First book appearance.

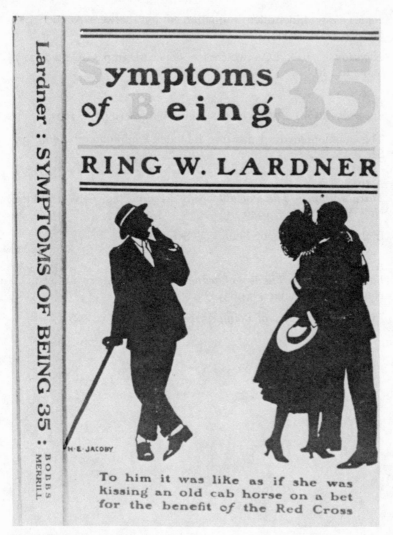

Binding (front and Spine) of A 13.1

Note 2:   A set of promotional cards was distributed for *Symptoms of Being 35* in 1921.[1] None of these cards has been located. See A 5.1.a.

Note 3:   Incomplete sales records from the Bobbs-Merrill archives at the Lilly Library indicate sales of 4,078 copies and 25

---

1. H. H. Howland to Lardner, 5 August 1921, Lilly Library.

copies of an unidentified "Canadian edition" between August 1921
and December 1923.

Locations: ICN, LC (two copies; deposit-stamp AUG 22 1921),
MJB, RL, RLS.

A 13.2
Second edition: What of It?. New York: Scribners, 1925.

The augmented third printing includes *Symptoms of Being 35.*
See A 17.1.c.

A 13.3
Third edition: The Portable Ring Lardner, ed. Gilbert Seldes.
New York: Viking, 1946.

Includes *Symptoms of Being 35.* See AA 4.

A 13.4
Fourth edition: The Ring Lardner Reader, ed. Maxwell Geismar.
New York: Scribners, [1963].

Includes *Symptoms of Being 35.* See AA 9.

A 14 THE BIG TOWN

A 14.1.a
First edition, first printing (1921)

THE BIG TOWN

HOW I AND THE MRS. GO TO NEW YORK
TO SEE LIFE AND GET KATIE A HUSBAND

By
RING W. LARDNER

Illustrations by
MAY WILSON PRESTON

INDIANAPOLIS
THE BOBBS-MERRILL COMPANY
PUBLISHERS

A 14.1.a: 7 5/16″ x 4⅞″

[i–viii] 1–244 [245–248]

[1–16]⁸. Five glossy illustrations tipped in.

Contents: p. i: half title; p. ii: card page; p. iii: title; p. iv: copyright; p. v: 'CONTENTS'; p. vi: blank; p. vii: half title; p. viii: blank; pp. 1–244: text, headed 'THE BIG TOWN | CHAPTER I | QUICK RETURNS'; pp. 245–248: blank.
  Five stories. "Quick Returns," "Ritchey," "Lady Perkins," "Only One," "Katie Wins a Home."

Typography and paper: 12 point on 16, Modern No. 1. 5⅛″ (5½″) x 3³⁄₁₆″. Twenty-two or twenty-three lines per page. Running heads: rectos, chapter titles; versos, 'THE BIG TOWN'. Wove paper.

Binding: Moderate olive green (125) V cloth (smooth) stamped in black (267). Front: '[swash] The [roman] BIG TOWN | [rule] | RING W. LARDNER'. Spine: '[swash] The | [roman] BIG | TOWN | [triangle] | LARDNER | BOBBS | MERRILL'. White wove sized endpapers. All edges trimmed.

Dust jacket: White paper. Front: '[orange] *The* | [black] Big | Town | [orange] *By* | *Ring W. Lardner* | [black and orange illustration of man and woman]'. Spine: '[swash] The | [roman] BIG | TOWN | [triangle] | LARDNER | BOBBS | MERRILL'. Back has ad for *Symptoms of Being 35* and other Lardner titles. Front and back flaps have ads for *The Big Town*.

Publication: 4,000 copies of the first printing. $1.75. Published 29 October 1921. Copyright 29 October 1921. Copyright #A630160.

Printing: Printing by Braunworth & Co., Brooklyn; plates by William Mitchell Printing Co., Greenfield, Ind.; binding by Braunworth.

Note 1:   All stories in *The Big Town* were first published in *The Saturday Evening Post*. See D 68, D 71, D 72, D 73, D 76. All selections are first book appearances.

Dust jacket for A 14.1.a

Note 2:   Incomplete sales records from the Bobbs-Merrill archives at the Lilly Library indicate sales of 3,322 copies and 150 copies of an unidentified "Canadian edition" between October 1921 and December 1923.

Locations: ICN, LC (rebound; deposit-stamp NOV–3 1921), Lilly (dj), MJB (dj), RL, RLS.

A 14.1.b
Second Printing.   New York: Scribners, 1925. Reprinted from Bobbs-Merrill plates, with new 'PREFACE' by Lardner, pp. v–vi. Republished 10 April 1925. Noted in three bindings of uniform set; see AA 1 for note on uniform bindings.

A 14.2
Second edition: *Ring Lardner's Best Stories*, foreword by William McFee. New York: Garden City Publishing Co., [1938].

Includes *The Big Town.* See A 21.1.e, AA 2.

Note: The title page stipulates '*De Luxe Edition*'. Cheap printing —if any—not seen.

A 14.3
Third edition: *The Portable Ring Lardner*, ed. Gilbert Seldes. New York: Viking Press, 1946.

Includes *The Big Town.* See AA 4.

A 14.4
Fourth edition

[swash] The | [roman] BIG TOWN | [illustration of people drinking cocktails] | *How I and the Mrs. go to New York* | *to see life and get Katie a husband* | *by* | RING W. LARDNER | [Bantam seal] | BANTAM BOOKS · NEW YORK

Published March 1949. Bantam #466.

Note: Two chapters of *The Big Town*, "Quick Returns" and "Lady Perkins," are in *The Ring Lardner Reader*, ed. Maxwell Geismar (New York: Scribners, [1963]).

A 15 SAY IT WITH OIL

A 15.1.a
First edition, first printing (1923)

Say It With Oil

A FEW REMARKS
ABOUT WIVES

BY

Ring W. Lardner

Author of
"You Know Me, Al," "Gullible's Travels,"
"The Big Town," etc.

NEW YORK
GEORGE H. DORAN COMPANY

A 15.1.a: 7 5/16" x 4⅞"

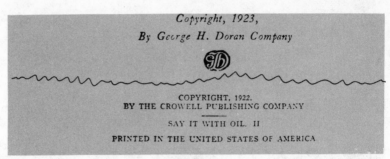

Oil: [i–ii] [1–8] 9–25 [26–28]

Bricks: [1–8] 9–33 [34]

[1–4]⁸

Note: *Say It with Oil* is half of an upside-down book; the other half is Nina Wilcox Putnam's *Say It with Bricks.*

Contents: pp. i–ii: blank; p. 1: half title; p. 2: blank; p. 3: title; p. 4: copyright; p. 5: dedication; p. 6: blank; p. 7: half title; p. 8: blank; pp. 9–25: text, headed '*Say It with Oil*'; p. 26: blank; p. 27: half title for *Say It with Bricks;* p. 28: upside-down half title for *Say It with Oil.*

Typography and paper: 12 point on 15, Caslon. 4¹³⁄₁₆″ (5½″) x 3⅛″. Twenty-two lines per page. Running heads: rectos and versos, '[rule] | *Say It with Oil* | [rule]'. Wove paper.

Binding: Light orange yellow (70) boards printed in deep reddish orange (36). Front: '[script] Say it with | [roman] OIL | RING | LARDNER | [oil can]'. Spine: '[script] Say | it | with | [roman] OIL | RING | LARDNER | [upside down] [script] Say | it | with | [roman] BRICKS | NINA | WILCOX | PUTNAM'. Back: '[upside down] [script] Say it with | [roman] BRICKS | NINA | WILCOX | PUTNAM | [bricks]'. White wove sized endpapers. All edges trimmed.

Dust jacket: White paper printed in black. Front: '[script] Say it with | [roman] OIL | RING | LARDNER | [orange, brown, and gray illustration of man with dipper of oil by B. Cory Kilvert]'. Spine: '[script] Say | it | with | [roman] OIL | RING | LARDNER | [upside down] [script] Say | it | with | [roman] BRICKS | NINA | WILCOX | PUTNAM'. Back: '[upside down] [script] Say it with | [roman] BRICKS | NINA | WILCOX | PUTNAM | [orange, brown, and black illustration of woman with bricks by Kilvert]'. *Oil* flap has ad for *Say It with Oil. Bricks* flap has ad for *Say It with Bricks.*

Dust jacket for A 15.1.a

Publication: Unknown number of copies of the first printing. $1.00. Published 23 March 1923. Copyright 23 March 1923. Copyright #A698882.

Printing: Printing, plates, and binding by Quinn & Boden, Rahway, N.J.

Note: Say It with Oil was first published in *The American Magazine.* See D 88. First book appearance.

Locations: LC (rebound; deposit-stamp MAR 30 '23), MJB (dj).

A 15.1.b
Second printing: New York: Doubleday, Doran, [1923?]. Doran seal removed from copyright page.

A 15.2
Second edition: The Portable Ring Lardner, ed. Gilbert Seldes. New York: Viking Press, 1946.

Includes *Say It with Oil.* See AA 4.

A 15.3
Third edition: The Ring Lardner Reader, ed. Maxwell Geismar. New York: Scribners, [1963].

Includes *Say It with Oil.* See AA 9.

A 16 HOW TO WRITE SHORT STORIES

A 16.1.a
Only edition, first printing (1924)

HOW TO WRITE SHORT STORIES

[WITH SAMPLES]

BY

RING W. LARDNER

NEW YORK · LONDON
CHARLES SCRIBNER'S SONS
MCMXXIV

A 16.1.a: 7½" x 5⅛"

[i–iv] v–x [xi–xii] [1–2] 3–43 [44–46] 47–78 [79–80] 81–111 [112–114] 115–141 [142–144] 145–178 [179–180] 181–216 [217–218] 219–246 [247–248] 249–282 [283–284] 285–316 [317–318] 319–359 [360]

$[1–22]^8 [23]^{10}$

Contents: p. i: half title; p. ii: blank; p. iii: title; p. iv: copyright; pp. v–x: 'PREFACE', signed 'RING LARDNER'; p. xi: 'CONTENTS'; p. xii: blank; p. 1: headnote for "The Facts"; p. 2: blank; pp. 3–359: text, headed 'How to Write Short Stories | I | THE FACTS | I'; p. 360: blank.

   Ten stories.   "The Facts," "Some Like Them Cold," "Alibi Ike," "The Golden Honeymoon," "Champion," "My Roomy," A Caddy's Diary," "A Frame-Up," "Harmony," "Horseshoes." All stories previously published in magazines. See Section D. First book appearances for all stories except "The Golden Honeymoon." See C 9.

Typography and Paper: 11 point on 13, Scotch No. 2. 5¾₆″ (5⅝″) x 3⁵⁄₁₆″. Twenty-nine or thirty lines per page. Running heads: rectos, story titles; versos, 'How to Write Short Stories'. Wove paper.

Binding: Dark grayish green (151) V cloth (smooth). Front goldstamped: facsimile of Lardner's signature. Spine goldstamped: 'HOW | TO WRITE | SHORT | STORIES | [short rule] | RING W. | LARDNER | SCRIBNERS'. White wove coated endpapers. Top and bottom edges trimmed.

Dust jacket: Front: '[black against red background] HOW TO WRITE | SHORT | STORIES | WITH SAMPLES | [swash] By | [roman] RING W. | LARDNER | [black-and-white drawing of crowd of people typing]'. Spine: '[off-white background] [black] HOW | TO WRITE | SHORT | STORIES | [short rule] | [red] RING W. | LARDNER | [black] SCRIBNERS'. Back has twenty-three-line ad for the collection, within red double-rules frame and red top and bottom lines. Front flap has price and spillover from illustration. Back flap: blank.

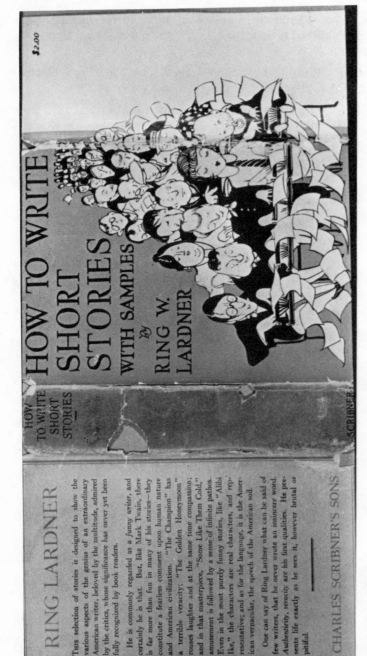

$2.00

HOW TO WRITE
SHORT
STORIES

WITH SAMPLES

By

RING W.
LARDNER

SCRIBNERS

HOW
TO WRITE
SHORT
STORIES

RING LARDNER

This selection of stories is designed to show the various aspects of the genius of an extraordinary American writer, beloved by the multitude, admired by the critics, whose significance has never yet been fully recognized by book readers.

He is commonly regarded as a *funny* writer, and certainly he is that. But, like Mark Twain, there is far more than fun in many of his stories—they constitute a fearless comment upon human nature and American veracity. "The Champion" has a terrible veracity; "The Golden Honeymoon" rouses laughter and at the same time compassion; and in that masterpiece, "Some Like Them Cold," amusement is followed by a sense of infinite pathos. Even in the most purely funny stories, like "Alibi Ike," the characters are real characters, and representative; and as for the language, it is the American vernacular, the speech of the American soil.

One can say of Ring Lardner what can be said of few writers, that he never wrote an insincere word. Authenticity, veracity are his first qualities. He presents life exactly as he sees it, however brutal or pitiful.

CHARLES SCRIBNER'S SONS

Dust jacket for A 16.1.a

Publication: Unknown number of copies of the first printing. $2.00. Published 9 May 1924. Copyright 9 May 1924. Copyright #A793272.

Printing: Printing by Scribner Press (by New York Electro-typing Co.); plates and binding by Scribner Press.

Locations: LC (two copies; deposit-stamp MAY 12 '24), Lilly (dj), MJB (dj).

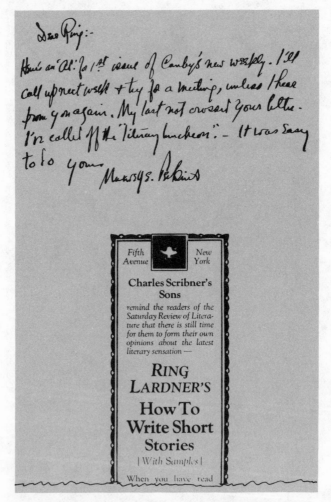

Proof of ad for A 16.1.a in *Saturday Review of Literature*, with previously unpublished note from Maxwell Perkins

A 16.1.b
Second printing. May 1924. Not seen.

A 16.1.c
Third printing. June 1924. Not seen.

A 16.1.d
Fourth printing. July 1924. Not seen.

A 16.1.e
Fifth printing. August 1924. Not seen.

A 16.1.f
Sixth printing. New York: Scribners, 1924. On copyright page: 'Sixth Printing November, 1924'.

A 16.1.g
Seventh ? printing. New York: Scribners, 1925. This printing retains the Scribner Press seal on the copyright page. Noted in three bindings of uniform set; see AA 1 for note on uniform bindings.

A 16.1.h
Only English printing, from American plates (1926)

HOW TO WRITE
SHORT STORIES

[WITH SAMPLES]

BY

RING W. LARDNER

CHATTO & WINDUS

LONDON

A 16.1.h: 7½″ × 4⅞″

Pagination: Same pagination as first printing, except that p. [359] is unnumbered.

Collation: Same collation as first printing.

Copyright page: 'PUBLISHED 1926 | PRINTED IN GREAT BRITAIN | ALL | RIGHTS RESERVED'.

Contents: Same as first printing; ten stories.

Paper: Wove paper.

Binding: Green V cloth (smooth). Blindstamped double-rules frame on front and back. Spine goldstamped: '[triple rules] | HOW | TO WRITE | SHORT | STORIES | RING W. | LARDNER | CHATTO & WINDUS | [triple rules]'.

Dust jacket: Not seen.

Publication: Unknown number of copies of the only English printing. 7s. 6d. Published May 1926.

Printing: p. 359: 'BRISTOL: BURLEIGH LTD., AT THE BURLEIGH PRESS'.

Location: BM (deposit-stamp 5 MAY 26).

Note to A 16:   Two offset reprints reported, but not seen: St. Clair Shores, Mich.: Scholarly Press, 1971; and Havertown, Pa.: R. West, 1973.

A 17 WHAT OF IT?

A 17.1.a₁
Only edition, first printing, first state (1925)

WHAT OF IT
?

BY

RING W. LARDNER

NEW YORK · LONDON
CHARLES SCRIBNER'S SONS
MCMXXV

A 17.1.a₁: 7⅜″ x 5⅛″

[a–b] [i–iv] v–vii [viii] ix–x [1–2] 3–38 [39–40] 41–52 [53–54] 55–73 [74–76] 77–199 201–200 202–220 (pp. 201 and 200 transposed in first state)

[1]⁸ [2]⁴ [3–15]⁸

Contents: p. a: blank; p. b: card page; p. i: half title; p. ii: blank; p. iii: title; p. iv: copyright; pp. v–vii: 'PREFACE'; p. viii: blank; pp. ix–x: 'CONTENTS'; p. 1: 'THE OTHER SIDE'; p. 2: blank; pp. 3–220: text, headed 'T'.

Thirty-one pieces. "The Other Side," "Plays" ("Clemo Uti—'The Water Lilies'," "I. Gaspiri," "Taxidea Americana"), "Bed-Time Stories" ("How to Tell a True Princess," "Cinderella," "Red Riding Hood," "Bluebeard"), "Obiter Dicta" ("'In Conference'," "A Close-up of Domba Splew," "What of It?" "The Big Drought," "In Regards to Geniuses," "Why Authors?" "The Dames," "Lay Off the Thyroid," "The Spulge Nine," "A Visit to the Garrisons," "Sane Olympics," "Welcome to Our Suburb," "Polyglot Bridge," "Business Is Business," "Games for Smart Alecks—I," "Games for Smart Alecks—II," "Tennis by Cable," "Who's It?" "Prohibition," "Segregate the Fats," "Don't Be a Drudge," "That Which We Call a Rose," "Who's Who"). All pieces previously published in magazines or syndicated by the Bell Syndicate. See Sections D and E. All first book appearances.

Typography and paper: 12 point on 15, Scotch No. 2. 5⅛″ (5⅝″) x 3⁵⁄₁₆″. Twenty-five lines per page. Running heads: rectos, story titles; versos, section titles. Wove paper.

Binding: Dark grayish green (151) V cloth (smooth). Front goldstamped: facsimile of Lardner's signature. Spine goldstamped: 'WHAT | OF IT? | [short rule] | RING W. | LARDNER | SCRIBNERS'. White wove sized endpapers. Top edge trimmed.

Dust jacket: Two printings of the dust jacket have been noted; priority undetermined.

   Printing 1.   Front: '[in white circle against light blue background, with cartoon figures] [swash "W"] What [swash "f"] of it? | [swash "R"] Ring W. Lardner'. Spine: '[against white background] WHAT | OF IT ? | RING W. | LARDNER | SCRIBNERS'. Back has photo of Lardner and excerpts from articles on Lardner by Laurence Stallings and Edmund Wilson. Front flap has an ad for *What of It?* and blurbs for *How to Write Short Stories* by H. L. Mencken and the *New York World*. Back flap has ads for *The Big Town, Gullible's Travels,* and *You Know Me Al.*
   Printing 2.'   Front: same as printing 1, except that background color is reddish orange. Spine: '[against white background] WHAT | OF IT? | RING W. | LARDNER | [lamp in relief on black square] | SCRIBNERS'. From the only example seen it is impossible to determine whether the spine, back, and flaps of the reddish orange dust jacket were originally off-white or white that has oxidized to a tannish off-white shade. Back: same as for printing 1. Front flap: same as for printing 1, but with the addition of the price at the top: 'WHAT OF IT? $1.75 | [double rules]'. Back flap: same as for printing 1.

Publication: Unknown number of copies of the first printing. $1.75. Published 10 April 1925. Copyright 10 April 1925. Copyright #A855446.

Printing: Printing by Scribner Press (by New York Electrotyping Co.); plates and binding by Scribner Press.

Locations: LC (deposit-stamp JUN–2 '25), MJB (both dust jackets), RL.

A 17.1.a₂
First printing, second state

[a–b] [i–iv] v–vii [viii] ix–x [1–2] 3–38 [39–40] 41–52 [53–54] 55–73 [74–76] 77–220

[1]⁸ [2]⁴ [3–13]⁸ [14]⁸ (±14₆,₇) [15]⁸

Locations: Lilly, MJB.

Dust jacket for A 17.1.a1

A 17.1.b
Second printing: New York Scribners, 1925.

[a–b] [i–iv] v–vii [viii] ix–x [1–2] 3–38 [39–40] 41–52 [53–54]
55–73 [74–76] 77–220

[1–14]^8 [15]^4

Note: The second printing retains the Scribner Press seal on
the copyright page.

Location: MJB.

A 17.1.c
Third printing (augmented):   New York: Scribners, 1925.

[i–iv] v–vii [viii] ix–x [1–2] 3–38 [39–40] 41–52 [53–54] 55–73
[74–76] 77–220 [221–222] 223–256 [257–258] 259–276 [277–278]

[1–18]^8

The third printing adds *The Young Immigrunts* and *Symptoms
of Being 35.* Retains the Scribner Press seal on the copyright page.
Noted in three bindings of uniform set; see AA 1 for note on
uniform bindings.

Note: The English edition of *The Love Nest* (A 19.2) includes
eighteen pieces from *What of It?*

Location: MJB.

A 18 BELL SYNDICATE FOLIO
Only printing (1925?)

Ring Lardner's Weekly Letter
to
8,000,000 Readers Through the Medium of Such Papers as:

RING LARDNER

JAMES MONTGOMERY FLAGG

Buffalo, N. Y.	COURIER		
Duluth, Minn.	NEWS TRIBUNE		
Portland, Ore.	JOURNAL		
Joplin, Mo.	GLOBE		
Wichita, Kans.	EAGLE		
Los Angeles, Cal.	EXAMINER		
Oklahoma City, Okla.	OKLAHOMAN		
Montreal, Can.	STAR		
Beaumont, Tex.	ENTERPRISE		
Evansville, Ind.	COURIER		
Davenport, Iowa	DEMOCRAT		
Huntington, Ind.	PRESS		
Hartford, Conn.	COURANT		
Cincinnati, Ohio.	COMMERCIAL TRIBUNE		
Terre Haute, Ind.	TRIBUNE		
Charleston, S. C.	NEWS & COURIER		
Shreveport, La.	TIMES		
Toledo, Ohio	TIMES		
Colorado Springs, Colo.	TELEGRAPH		
Richmond, Va.	NEWS LEADER		
Houston, Texas	CHRONICLE		
Little Rock, Ark.	ARKANSAS DEMOCRAT		
Montgomery, Ala.	JOURNAL		
Wilkesbarre, Pa.	TIMES LEADER		
Louisville, Ky.	COURIER JOURNAL		
Denver, Colo.	ROCKY MT. NEWS		
Zanesville, Ohio	TIMES SIGNAL		
Waterbury, Conn.	REPUBLICAN		
Tokio, Japan	JAPAN ADVERTISER		
San Diego, Cal.	UNION		
Seattle, Wash.	POST INTELLIGENCER		
Winnipeg, Can.	FREE PRESS		
Dayton, Ohio	NEWS		
Baltimore, Md.	AMERICAN		
Tarrytown, N. Y.	NEWS		
Pueblo, Colo.	STAR JOURNAL		
New Haven, Conn.	REGISTER		
Bridgeport, Conn.	POST		
Raleigh, N. C.	NEWS & OBSERVER		
Butte, Mont.	MINER		
Wilmington, Del.	STAR		
Fresno, Cal.	REPUBLICAN		
Chattanooga, Tenn.	TIMES		
Philadelphia, Pa.	BULLETIN		
Des Moines, Ia.	REGISTER & TRIBUNE		
Casper, Wyo.	HERALD		
Winston-Salem, N. C.	SENTINEL		
Austin, Texas	AMERICAN		
Wichita Falls, Texas	RECORD NEWS		
Waco, Tex.	NEWS TRIBUNE		
Jacksonville, Fla.	JOURNAL		
Pensacola, Fla.	JOURNAL		
Indianapolis, Ind.	STAR		
Reading, Pa.	TRIBUNE		
San Bernardino, Cal.	SUN		
Canton, Ohio	NEWS		
Miami, Fla	METROPOLIS		
Springfield, Ohio	NEWS		
Columbus, Ga.	ENQUIRER SUN		
Tulsa, Okla.	WORLD		
Enid, Okla.	EAGLE & NEWS		
Yakima, Wash.	HERALD		
Pocatello, Idaho	HERALD		
Huntington W. Va.	HERALD DISPATCH		
Johnson City, Tenn.	CHRONICLE		
Clarksville, Tenn.	LEAF CHRONICLE		
Bethlehem, Pa.	GLOBE		
Muskogee, Okla.	DAILY NEWS		
Wheeling, W. Va.	NEWS		
Scranton, Pa.	TELEGRAM		
Cleveland, Ohio	TIMES		
Hamilton	SPECTATOR		
Boston, Mass.	GLOBE	Chicago, Ill.	HERALD EXAMINER
Pittsburgh, Pa.	GAZETTE TIMES	Detroit, Mich.	NEWS
Ft. Worth, Tex.	STAR TELEGRAM	Jackson, Mich.	NEWS
Nashville, Tenn.	TENNESSEAN	Atlanta, Ga.	JOURNAL
Marion, Ohio	STAR	San Francisco, Cal.	EXAMINER
Elkhart, Ind.	TRUTH	Charlotte, N. C.	NEWS
San Antonio, Tex.	LIGHT	Birmingham, Ala.	NEWS
Asheville, N. C.	CITIZEN	New Orleans, La.	ITEM
St. Paul, Minn.	DISPATCH	Syracuse, N. Y.	HERALD
Kansas City, Mo.	STAR	Washington, D. C.	STAR
Springfield, Mass.	UNION	Rochester, N. Y.	HERALD
Toronto, Can.	STAR WEEKLY	Milwaukee, Wis.	JOURNAL
Omaha, Nebr.	WORLD HERALD	Salt Lake City, Utah	TRIBUNE
New York, N. Y.	AMERICAN	Columbia, S. C.	STATE

WIRE YOUR ORDER!

THE BELL SYNDICATE, Inc. 154 Nassau St., New York, N.Y.

A 18: folio; approx. 15½″ x 10″

Ring Drops Some Souvenir Hints

"Oranges From Florida, So Why Not Corn Fritters From Iowa?" Asks Noted Humorist

By RING LARDNER

To the editor:

One of the most serious problems which the average tourist is up vs. is what to buy in the way of souvenirs to take back to the loved ones at home. A souvenir which is at once handsome, appropriate, useful and at the same time not beyond one's means is something that in bird language might be termed a rara avis.

"One of the Most Serious Problems the Tourist Is Up Vs. Is What To Buy in the Way of Souvenirs."

And a person who has the nag of always selecting such a souvenir is as few and far between as baby steamboat captains.

Personly it is my good fortune to be acquainted with at lease one of these last named geniuses in the person of Mr. Crowninshield the buxom editor of Vanity Fair and wile I realize that this ain't the time of yr. when people are patronizing resorts, still and all I may as well take this opportunity of passing on to the genial reader some of the idears gleaned from the above named gent and others in the hopes that you will remember them next time you go away and they will be helpful in choosing the little mementos you wish to bring back to relatives and friends.

SOMETHING FROM CALIFORNIA

On a recent visit to the tropics Mr. Crowninshield bought for a lady named Rice a kind of a little round mesh bag made of rice pearls which the bag was just about the right size to hold a baseball or a cricket ball or maybe a billiard ball. Aside from the gift being so suitable on acct. of the name of the pearls being the same name as the beneficiary, why the little trinket is also the reverse of a eyesore and if Mrs. Rice ever decides to become a active baseball, cricket or billiard player, the bag will come in very handy as a container of the ball she wishes to convey to the scene of combat. She was recently quoted as saying that she might of got along for 10 or 11 more yrs. without no rice pearl ball carrier but certainly not longer than that.

Mr. Crowninshield bought for the wife of the undersigned a set of 12 articles which they was no name on them to tell what they are for but the Mrs. has came to the conclusion that they are flat-iron holders and can't hardly wait for the day when they will be so many garments in need of pressing that she can use them all at once.

Mean wile she eagerly awaits the postman every A. M. in the hopes that he will bring a invitation to a flatiron party that will enable her to blossom out in full regalia and make the rest of the guests wished they had a acquaintance like Mr. Crowninshield.

A souvenir which the madam recd. from another source some time ago was broughten to her all the way from sunny California and was nothing more or less than a pin cushion made of California redwood. It makes a person shutter to think how many people there are in this country and the Near East that ain't got no friends who has visited California and broughten them back a redwood pin cushion.

THROW IT AT THE DOG

Personly the Mrs. derives a great deal of comfort and consolation from this souvenir and has even told almost total strangers that if she ever does change her mind and begin using a pin cushion, the redwood pin cushion from California will be her first choice. On 1 or 2 occasions they has been visitors in the house who acted for a time like they would take this trinket home with them if she offered it to them but has changed their mind before it come time to go.

It seems to me that it was also from California that somebody another brought us a pine cone about a ft. and a ½ long and ¼ a ft. in diameter which laid around the old home in Niles, Mich., for yrs. and no matter how dark and gloomy the day or how monotonous life may of been to other familys they was always a undercurrent of suspense in our house as to who would be the first to fall over this elegant pine cone and break their neck.

California and Florida may be aptly termed the hot bed of souvenirs as far as this country is concerned and persons who wish to travel only for the sake of buying souvenirs is adviced to concentrate on one of these 2 states. In either one of them you can get a box of grapefruit or a box of oranges which the folks at home will be tickled to death with same on acct. of it coming direct from where it growed whereas if you visited Iowa and sent home a dish of corn fritters your friends would think you are crazy.

No matter what you buy in either of the 2 famous resort states mentioned above it will be highly appreciated, but if you do your touring in other states you have got to be mighty particular. Like for inst. it ain't etiquette to fetch back nothing from Maine except a pillow stuffed with balsam and the piece de resistance from the northern peninsula of Michigan is a hunk of copper ore. Visiters to Wisconsin will do well to specialize in cheese instead of milk and cream as the last named is libel to protest if you half to take it or send it say as far as Texas or North Carolina.

In any of the states boarding on the sea shore what more suitable present for the stay at homes than shells a specially the big curly shells with the pink insides and the sharp point

"They Was Always a Undercurrent of Suspense in Our House as to Who Would Fall Over This Elegant Pine Cone."

that can be used to throw at a dog or somebody that is practicing on a alto horn. Surely these is preferable to either live or dead fish particularly if the tourist intends conveying them home in person.

(1925 By The Bell Syndicate, Inc.)

Ring Conducts Big Rat War

Tries Kindness First and Then Decides on Extermination—Big-Hearted Stranger From Philly Submits Hot Proposition

By RING LARDNER

To the editor:

On acct. of being away most of the winter the undersigned ain't give his readers no Great Neck news for a long wile and it probably seems even longer but any way it is high time that you folks was told what has been going on and am only sorry that they ain't room for me to put in all the items instead of just these few.

My admires will no doubtless recall that in my last report of home doings mentions was made of Ida leaving a piece of pumpkin pie on the top of the ice box one night with instructions to me to not eat same when I come home on acct. of it being flavored with rat poison.

This may of led some of you people to think that possibly our little love nest as I call it might of maybe been infested with members of the rodent tribe. Well friends if that was your guess you certainly hit the nail on the hammer. But it turned out that rats won't touch pie since what the pied piper done to their grand-parents, and the only casualty resulting from the above plot was a harmless little member of the feline species.

A LITERARY RAT

Not only that but when I and the madam returned last month from our sojourn in the sunny southland as it has been aptly styled we was told by Ida and others that the rats had increased in population more than Miami and Los Angeles combined and this we was able to believe that same evening when they begun to resume their night life and we could hear them in the walls hurrying to the various rodent supper clubs.

Well a little thing like rats making a noise in the walls was not going

able wind instruments. But one night I seen one of them in the master bed room as the master was preparing for bed and having been broughten up modest I thought it was about time to protest.

"Rat," I said, "I know you are hiding somewheres within ear shot and I want to appeal to your better nature and ask you and your friends and relatives to get the h—l out of here and move to Bayside or somewheres as I have all ready got enough of a family to feed without you fellows, to say nothing of the housing problem. I don't want to be tough on rats or anybody else but things has reached a pt. where either you or the Lardners has got to leave Great Neck and as we was here first I hope you will take the hint."

Mean wile I was riding into N. Y. city one day and seen a big ad of a exterminator company which promised to clean out rats and other young visiters in 4 hrs. so I wrote down the phone number and waited developments, but the days and nights went by and they was reports coming in every few minutes from different members of the household that he or she had just saw another big rat and speaking about big rats, did anybody ever hear of anybody else seeing a small rat, but any way that was the way matters was when 2 things happened that forced me to action.

One of the pieces of furniture in my room is a portable typewriter which you can carry it around with you when you are traveling and it makes it look like you have got a lot of baggage. Well these here portable typewriters always have a key that you can lock them up with for fear somebody would steal one of your idears and the key is always tied onto the handle of the typewriter case with a ribbon.

"I Had to Sit and Look at Raymond Hitchcock Instead."

to unlock the typewriter and maybe write me a insulting letter in answer to my appeal, but had been frightened off just as they was going to insert the key in the lock.

Now if they's one thing I don't like it is for somebody else to use my typewriter a specially a rat. And on this same day Miss June Walker the actress accepted a invitation to come to dinner and my admires probably is aware, she is about as big as an aspirin tablet so I was scared that if we didn't watch her all the time one of the rodents might walk off with her and we would be in wrong with Equity.

ONE PARROT ENOUGH

So I called up the exterminators and sure enough one of them showed up right away and smeared all the cracks and crannies with the stuff that spells disaster to rats and I bet when they rushed out of the house in search of water they wished they had went when I first warned them and not waited for such a cold miserable day.

Other news of our town is that the new station has now been in use for several weeks and it might be said that it wasn't built any too soon. However it is a very handsome edifice and they have got a big bulletin board in the waiting room and as our line is just a suburban line and the trains is always on time you might say, why they ain't no sense in posting them up on the board and it has been suggested that the board be used to post the names of who all is going on the next train so as you will know whether that is the train you want to take or not.

They's been lots of times when I have got aboard of a train hoping I would set where I could watch Jane Cowl all the way to town and found out that she wasn't on that train and I had to look at Raymond Hitchcock or Jack Hazzard.

And I got 2 letters in the mail the other day and one of them was from a man in Philly who said he had a great title for a story and if I would send him some nominal sum like $50.00 for inst. why he would tell me the title and then I could write the story. I did not reply to this big hearted stranger but I did answer a letter from the Audubon society asking me to become a life member of same which would only cost me a $1000.00. I told them I was already supporting a parrot in the style to which it had been accustomed and felt like this was all I could afford to do at this time for the genus bird.

"One Night I Seen One in the Master Bed Room as the Master Was Preparing for Bed."

to bother a man like I a specially when I could drowned them out with the radio or any one of my numer-

Well, one day I found the key laying on the floor. A rat had chewed the ribbon in 2 probably in a effort

(1925 By The Bell Syndicate, Inc.)

All New Dope On Approaching Customers Given By Ring

Tells How to Sell Nail Clippers to the President, J. W. Davis, Dave Belasco and Magnus Johnson—Great Help to Salesmen

By RING LARDNER

To the editor:

Many books and articles has been written on what is known as the "proper approach" in business and how the nag of always saying the right thing when you first meet people is of supreme importance whether you want to sell them something or merely make a favorable impression on them in a social way. It is a whole lot easier to worm your way into a man's good gracious if you show him right off the reel that you know who he is and talk on some subject which they are interested in.

Like for inst. suppose you was going to try and sell a farm to a man named Mr. Estes who is a bond salesman. If you went up to him and said "Good-morning Mr. Estes how is bonds this morning?" you would have a good deal better chance of doing business with him than as if you was to say "Hellow there Mr. Whats his Name, I forget what business you are in but how about buying a little farm this morning?"

MICHIGAN SOUR MILK

As I say many books and articles has been written on this subject and there is even some books on the market that tells you just what to say to parties in different walks of life like insurance men or carpenters or haberdashers or in fact most any walk of life. However it has been called to my tension by a friend of mine that is on the road for a wholesale sour milk concern that they's a big difference amongst individuals even in the same line of business and a conversation which might interest one undertaker and make him feel friendly towards you might maybe bore another undertaker stiff and spoil whatever chance you have of selling him sour milk or whatever it is you are selling.

This friend recites a personal experience of his own which illustrates the point in question. It seems like he was traveling in the northern peninsula of Michigan where sour milk is one of the stables of life as they use it to clean the dust off their tricycles. Well my friend had a tip that a certain butcher in Houghton was in the market for a large quantity of choice sour milk. This man's name was Black but it was pronounced like the a was left out. He was sick in tired of the butcher business and his ambition was to sell out his butcher shop and devote all his time to marking tennis courts. My friend did not know this, nor did he know about the peculiar pronunciation of the name Black. So he approached the butcher in the following words, "Good-morning Mr. Black. How is meat this morning?" to his astonishment Mr. Black give him a dirty look and had him chased out of the shop. If my friend had said, "Good-morning Mr. Blck. How is tennis courts this morning?" They's no question in anybody's mind but what he could of sold him a plethora of sour milk.

So my friend says that the only real serviceable book or article of instructions along these lines would

"Mr. Black Gave Him a Dirty Look and Chased Him Out of the Shop."

be one that told the name, habits and eccentricities of everybody that a person was libel to meet, but inasmuch as the author of such a book would half to be personly acquainted with practically everybody in the world it ain't likely that such a article or book will be written during our time.

I would probably be the man best fitted to write such a thing as I knew most of the people that is worth knowing, but am sorry to say that my other interests such as getting the rats out of our home and seeing that the madam don't light the fireplace fire in the middle of August keeps me too busy. However I will take time to give a few hints in regards to some of the more prominent of my friends in the hopes that some of my readers may be going to

"HOW IS YOUR HORSE?"

For the sake of clearness and simplicity we will pretend like we have in mind a man named Haffle who is selling finger nail clippers and amongst his prospective clients is President Coolidge. (Any other article may be substituted for finger nail

clippers at the discretion of the reader).

Well, if a person went up to President Coolidge and throwed finesse to the winds and said "Listen Mr. Coolidge your finger nails is too long but here is a little article that will remedy that defect," why you would probably be escorted to the nearest exit by the entire secret service. The proper method which would undoubtedly entrance the President and insure a sale would be as follows: "Good-morning Mr. Coolidge. How is your horse? And speaking about horses reminds me of a man that was very wealthy and had a great many horses but the woman he loved would not have nothing to do with him on acct. of him never cutting his finger nails. Now I am selling a little article, etc."

Or suppose it was J. W. Davis.

"Well Mr. Davis I guess after what happened to you last fall you probably ain't got no presidential bee buzzing in your head no more and speaking about bees that reminds me that I once shook hands with a man that was running for office and his finger nails was so long that I thought a bee had stang me and I would not be surprised but what that was what caused him being defeated. Now I am selling a little article, etc.

Or suppose it was Mr. Belasco.

"Well Mr. Belasco I see they been accusing you of putting on plays that

"Good Morning, Mr. Coolidge. How Is Your Horse?"

have dealing with same and is at a loss in regards to the right entree.

ain't clean. That reminds me of a story about a fella that his finger nails was never clean. Now if he had of kept them short they would not of been so noticeable. I have got a little article, etc."

Or Magnus Johnson.

"Well Mr. Johnson they tell me you are a dirt farmer and speaking about dirt, etc."

(1925 By The Bell Syndicate, Inc.)

THE BELL SYNDICATE, Inc. 154 Nassau St., New York, N. Y.

New York: Bell Syndicate, [1925?].

[1–4]

[1]²

Contents: p. 1: portrait of Lardner by James Montgomery Flagg and list of subscribing papers; p. 2: "Ring Drops Some Souvenir Hints"; p. 3: "Ring Conducts Big Rat War"; p. 4: "All New Dope on Approaching Customers Given by Ring." Reprinted from Bell Syndicate "Weekly Letter." See E 3425, E 3426, E 3430.

Unknown number of copies distributed for promotional purposes.

Location: RWL Jr.

A 19 THE LOVE NEST AND OTHER STORIES

A 19.1
First edition, only printing (1926)

THE LOVE NEST AND OTHER STORIES

BY

RING W. LARDNER

WITH AN INTRODUCTION
BY
SARAH E. SPOOLDRIPPER

NEW YORK
CHARLES SCRIBNER'S SONS
MCMXXVI

A 19.1: 7⅜" x 5¼"

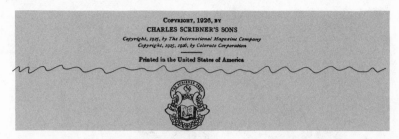

[a–d] [i–iv] v–xvi [xvii–xviii] [1–2] 3–27 [28–30] 31–54 [55–56] 57–79 [80–82] 83–104 [105–106] 107–134 [135–136] 137–160 [161–162] 163–183 [184–186] 187–208 [209–210] 211–232 [233–234]

[1–16]⁸

Contents: pp. a–c: blank; p. d: card page; p. i: half title; p. ii: blank; p. iii: title; p. iv: copyright; pp. v–xvi: 'INTRODUCTION | BY SARAH E. SPOOLDRIPPER'; p. xvii: 'CONTENTS'; p. xviii: blank; p. 1: 'THE LOVE NEST'; p. 2: blank; pp. 3–232: text, headed 'I | THE LOVE NEST'; pp. 233–234: blank.

Nine stories. "The Love Nest," "Haircut," "Zone of Quiet," "Women," "A Day with Conrad Green," "Reunion," "Rhythm," "Mr. and Mrs. Fix-It," "Who Dealt?" All stories previously published in magazines. See Section D. All first book appearances.

Typography and paper: 12 point on 15, Scotch. 5⅛″ (5⅝″) x 3⁵⁄₁₆″. Twenty-five lines per page. Running heads: rectos, story titles; versos, 'The Love Nest'. Wove paper.

Binding: Dark grayish green (151) V cloth (smooth). Front goldstamped: facsimile of Lardner's signature. Spine goldstamped: 'THE LOVE | NEST | [short rule] | RING W. | LARDNER | SCRIBNERS'. White wove endpapers. Top and bottom edges trimmed.

Dust jacket: Off-white paper illustrated on front, back, and spine with orange and black drawings by Margaret Freeman. Front: '[swash "T"] *The* | [roman] LOVE | NEST | *and* | OTHER STORIES | *By* | RING W. LARDNER'. Spine: '[swash "T"] *The* | [roman] LOVE | NEST | *and* | OTHER | STORIES | [decoration] | LARDNER | SCRIBNERS'. Back has ad for *The Love Nest*. Front flap has blurbs for *How to Write Short Stories* by H. L. Mencken and from the *New York World* and an ad for *What of It?* Back flap has ads for *The Big Town, Gullible's Travels,* and *You Know Me Al.*

Dust jacket for A 19.1

Publication: Unknown number of copies of the only printing. $1.75. Published 26 March 1926. Copyright 26 March 1926. Copyright #A891091.

Printing: Printing by Scribner Press; plates by New York Electrotyping Co.; binding by Scribner Press.

Note: The "Introduction by Sarah E. Spooldripper" was written by Lardner.

Locations: LC (deposit-stamp APR 15 1926), Lilly (dj), MJB (dj).

A 19.2
Only English edition (augmented), only printing (1928)

THE LOVE NEST
AND OTHER STORIES

BY
RING W. LARDNER

WITH AN INTRODUCTION
BY
SARAH E. SPOOLDRIPPER

LONDON
PHILIP ALLAN & CO., LTD.
QUALITY HOUSE, GREAT RUSSELL STREET, W.C.1

A 19.2: 7¼" x 4¾"

[1–4] 5–11 [12] 13 [14–16] 17–39 [40–42] 43–63 [64–66] 67–87 [88–90] 91–110 [111–112] 113–132 [133–134] 135–159 [160–162] 163–181 [182–184] 185–262 [263–264] 265–285 [286–288] 289–320

[A] B–I K–U⁸

Copyright page: 'FIRST EDITION 1928 | MADE AND PRINTED IN GREAT BRITAIN BY | M. F. ROBINSON & CO. LTD., AT THE LIBRARY PRESS, LOWESTOFT'.

Contents: p. 1: half title; p. 2: blank; p. 3: title; p. 4: copyright; pp. 5–11: 'INTRODUCTION | BY SARAH E. SPOOLDRIPPER'; p. 12: blank; p. 13: 'CONTENTS'; p. 14: blank; p. 15: 'The Love Nest'; p. 16: blank; pp. 17–320: text, headed 'THE LOVE NEST'.

 Twenty-five stories. "The Love Nest," "Zone of Quiet," "Reunion," "Mr. and Mrs. Fix-It," "Who Dealt?" "A Day with Conrad Green," "Bedtime Stories" ("How to Tell a True Princess," "Cinderella," "Red Riding Hood," "Bluebeard"), "Obiter Dicta" ("Polyglot Bridge," "Business Is Business," " 'In Conference,' " "What of It?" "The Dames," "Sane Olympics," "Welcome to Our Suburb," "Tennis by Cable," "Who's It?" "Prohibition," "Don't Be a Drudge," "That Which We Call a Rose," "Who's Who"), "Haircut," "The Other Side." No first book material. All items in this volume previously appeared in the American edition of either *The Love Nest* (A 19) or *What of It?* (A 17).

Typography and paper: 5⁷⁄₁₆″ (5⅝″) x 3⁵⁄₁₆″. Twenty-eight lines per page. Running heads: rectos, story titles; versos, 'The Love Nest'. Wove paper.

Binding: Dark grayish yellow (91) P cloth (pebble grain). Front has black single-rule frame. Spine: '[rule] | *The Love* | *Nest* | *Ring* | *Lardner* | *Philip Allan* | [rule]'. Also noted in deep red (13) V cloth (smooth) with same stamping. White wove endpapers. All edges trimmed.

Dust jacket: Not seen.

Publication: Unknown number of copies of the only ? printing. 7s. 6d. Published September 1928.

Locations: BM (red; deposit-stamp 11 SEP 28), MJB (grayish yellow and red cloth).

Cheap binding: London: P. Allan, 1930. Not seen; entry based on *The English Catalogue of Books*. Almost certainly remainder binding of 1928 sheets.

A 19.3
Third edition

THE LOVE NEST | and other stories | By Ring Lardner | A
SUPERIOR REPRINT | Published By | The Military Service
Publishing Co. | Harrisburg, Pennsylvania

Published February 1945. #M646. Ten stories; adds "Alibi Ike."

A 19.4
Fourth edition: *The Love Nest.* New York: Bantam, 1948.

#145. Not seen.

A 20 THE STORY OF A WONDER MAN
Only printing (1927)

THE STORY
OF A WONDER MAN

BEING THE AUTOBIOGRAPHY

OF

RING LARDNER

ILLUSTRATED BY MARGARET FREEMAN

NEW YORK
CHARLES SCRIBNER'S SONS
1927

A 20: 7⅜" x 5 3/16"

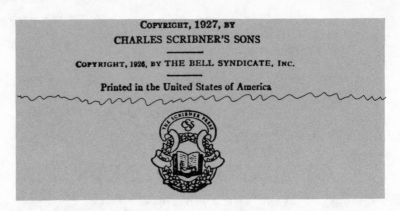

[a–b] [i–iv] v–x 1–32 [33] 34–38 [39] 40–151 [152]

[1]¹⁰ [2–10]⁸

Contents: p. a: blank; p. b: card page; p. i: half title; p. ii: blank; p. iii: title; p. iv: copyright; pp. v–vi: 'Foreword | By Sarah E. Spooldripper'; pp. vii–viii: 'Contents'; pp. ix–x: 'Illustrations'; pp. 1–3: 'Introduction'; pp. 4–151: text, headed 'Chapter 1 | The Birth of a Wonder Man'; p. 152: blank.

Typography and paper: 12 point on 14, No. 61 Cochin. 4¹³⁄₁₆″ (5¼″) x 3⅛″. Twenty-five lines per page. Running heads: rectos, chapter titles; versos, 'THE STORY OF A WONDER MAN'. Wove paper.

Binding: Dark grayish green (151) V cloth (smooth). Front goldstamped: facsimile of Lardner's signature. Spine goldstamped: 'THE | STORY | OF A | WONDER | MAN | BEING THE | AUTOBIOGRAPHY | OF | RING | LARDNER | SCRIBNERS'. White wove sized endpapers. Top and bottom edges trimmed.

Dust jacket: Front, back, and spine have black-and-white drawings by Margaret Freeman against orange background. Front: '[black against off-white panel] THE STORY ["OF" above "A"] OF A WONDER MAN | BEING THE | AUTOBIOGRAPHY | OF | RING LARDNER'. Spine: '[black against white panel] THE | STORY | OF A | WONDER | MAN | BEING THE | AUTO-| BIOGRAPHY | OF | RING | LARDNER | [short rule] | SCRIBNERS'. Back has same printing as front. Front flap has price and ad for *The Story of a Wonder Man*. Back flap has ad for *Scribner's Magazine*.

Dust jacket for A 20

Publication: Unknown number of copies of the only printing. $1.75. Published 18 March 1927. Copyright 18 March 1927. Copyright #A972180.

Printing: Printing, plates, and binding by Scribner Press.

Note 1:   All pieces in *The Story of a Wonder Man* were syndicated under various titles (twenty-seven installments) by the Bell Syndicate. See Section E. All selections are first book appearances.

Note 2:   The "Foreword By Sarah E. Spooldripper" was written by Lardner.

Locations: ICN, LC (two copies; deposit-stamp MAR 25 '27), Lilly (dj), MJB (dj), RL, RLS.

A 21 ROUND UP

A 21.1.a
First edition, first printing (1929)

Round Up

The Stories of

Ring W. Lardner

––––––––––––––––––––

––––––––––––––––––––

NEW YORK
CHARLES SCRIBNER'S SONS
MCMXXIX

A 21.1.a: 7½" x 5¼"

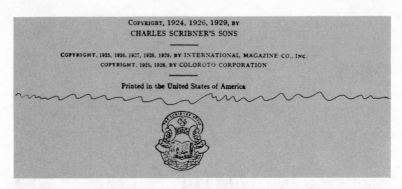

[i–vi] vii–viii [1–2] 3–11 [12] 13–33 [34] 35–63 [64] 65–85 [86] 87–107 [108] 109–127 [128] 129–139 [140] 141–235 [236] 237– 247 [248] 249–281 [282] 283–303 [304] 305–355 [356] 357–373 [374] 375–383 [384] 385–407 [408] 409–417 [418] 419–445 [446] 447–467 [468–472]

[1–15]¹⁶

Contents: p. i: blank; p. ii: card page; p. iii: half title; p. iv: blank; p. v: title; p. vi: copyright; pp. vii–viii: 'CONTENTS'; p. 1: half title; p. 2: blank; pp. 3–467: text, headed 'I | THE MAYSVILLE MINSTREL'; pp. 468–472: blank.

Thirty-five stories. "The Maysville Minstrel,"* "I Can't Breathe,"* Haircut," "Alibi Ike," "Liberty Hall,"* "Zone of Quiet," "Mr. Frisbie,"* "Hurry Kane,"* "Champion," "Contract,"* "Dinner,"* "Women," "A Day with Conrad Green," "Old Folks' Christmas,"* "Harmony," "The Love Nest," "Ex Parte,"* "The Golden Honeymoon," "Now and Then,"* "Horseshoes," "There Are Smiles,"* "Anniversary," "Reunion," "Travelogue," "Who Dealt?" "My Roomy," "Rhythm," "Some Like Them Cold," "Nora,"* "Man Not Overboard,"* "A Caddy's Diary," "Mr. and Mrs. Fix-It," "A Frame-Up," "Sun Cured,"* "The Facts." All stories previously published in magazines. See Section D. First book appearances indicated by asterisks.

Typography and paper: 10 point on 10, Century Expanded. 5⅞" (6⅛") x 3¹³⁄₁₆". Forty-two lines per page. Running heads: rectos, story titles; versos, 'ROUND UP'.

Binding: Dark yellowish green (137) V cloth (smooth). Front goldstamped: facsimile of Lardner's signature. Spine goldstamped: 'ROUND UP | THE STORIES | OF | RING W. | LARDNER | SCRIBNERS'. White wove sized endpapers. Top and bottom edges trimmed.

An Appreciation of "Round Up"
by Carl Van Doren, Editor-in-Chief
of the Literary Guild of America.

"'Round Up,' the collected short stories of Ring W. Lardner, is a characteristically, completely, unmistakably American book. No completely American book. No truly a native product of a native art as can be found in our fiction. To do this with the comic strip, or in the sporting page or the comic strip, or in the vaudeville of America.

"Many readers who have been identified with Ring Lardner still, indeed, associate him with the sporting page and the comic strip from which he may be said to have worked his way. But American art, and it is true that in its earlier instances it tended to confine him to a single character, a half-type here and there, a sport, or, when he dealt with other characters, to put them through much the same paces on occasion after occasion. Like any clown in any comic strip. But so did Mark Twain at the beginning of his career, hunted to another device of sheer comic matter, that of the travelling correspondent making fun both of what he saw and of what he was. As Mark Twain, however, eventually outgrew his formula, so Mr. Lardner has outgrown his. The later stories which he has produced during the past half dozen years are marked by the variety and distinction which journalism can do without but which literature must have if it is to deserve that name in any strict sense.

"This is not to imply that Mr. Lardner has lost the better of his early qualities. He is still as accurate as a dictaphone in reproducing the

(CONTINUED ON BACK PAGE OF JACKET)

ROUND UP
The Stories of
RING W.
LARDNER

ROUND UP
THE STORIES
OF
RING W.
LARDNER

SCRIBNERS

"'Round Up,' the collected short stories of Ring W. Lardner, is a characteristically, completely, unmistakably American book, truly a native product of a native art. Up to the present Mr. Lardner has had two rather distinct audiences: a large popular audience which has read him chiefly for his comedy, and a small, sophisticated one which has read him for his insight. It is time for these two audiences to meet on common ground."
—CARL VAN DOREN,
Editor-in-chief, The Literary Guild.

THE STORIES OF RING LARDNER

Sir James Barrie

"I find, for instance, 'Harmony' a joy as much as 'Some Like Them Cold,' 'The Golden Honeymoon,' and 'Champion.' Congratulations to Ring Lardner. He is the real thing."

Edmund Wilson

"Lardner has imitated nobody and nobody else could reproduce his essence. . . . There is scarcely a single paragraph of Lardner which, in its blending of freshness with irony, does not convey the sense of a distinguished intelligence and an intricate and unique personality. Furthermore, he has achieved, unrivalled, mastery of what has come to be known as the American language. . . . He writes the vernacular like an artist and not merely like a clever journalist. . . . There is nothing artificial or far-fetched about his slang; it is as natural as it is apt. His language is the product of a philologist's ear and a born writer's relish for words."

Harry Hansen

"Ring Lardner's most remarkable quality is the ability to write apparently about only externals, and at the same time to lay bare the souls of these people. He knows them. He writes their language, knows their most intimate thoughts. His stories have the feel of reality about them."

H. L. Mencken

"His stories are superbly adroit and amusing; no other contemporary American, sober or gay, writes better. His imaginary characters are astoundingly real and brilliant. The character he finally sets before us is an astoundingly real as to hide that the effect is indistinguishable from that of life itself."

CHARLES SCRIBNER'S SONS, NEW YORK

---

language spoken by the majority of American. He still catches all the turns of thought of persons who do not really think, and the turns of feeling of persons who feel precisely as their friends and neighbors feel. 'Round Up' is therefore as representative of life in the United States as the crowd at a baseball game. At the same time it presents the back as a picture of an emotion than representation. At point after point it cuts through the surface of things observed and reveals human character working in ways which suggest not merely America but also mankind at large.

"Because Mr. Lardner is extremely funny he lets people think he is extremely comic pretending so well. Yet these two qualities of his work come from the same quality in his mind. It is detached, ironic, congenitally incapable of delusion. What he reports in his stories is what he sees, and he reports it as he sees it. He shows no signs of any effort to turn his materials into comedy. He does not, come to think of it, go out of his way to report the discrepancy which he finds between the men and women they imagine themselves and the men and women they imagine they are and the pretences by which they imagine they live. He merely exhibits such discrepancies in a tireless series of cases and leaves it to his readers to do their own laughing and comprehending.

"Up to the present Mr. Lardner has had two rather distinct audiences. His sharp ear for dialects which has read him chiefly for his comedy, and a small sophisticated one which has read him for his insight. It is time for these two audiences to meet on common ground and to realize that their author has given them trivial and original without being trivial, and original without being esoteric."

—CARL VAN DOREN.

Dust jacket for A 21.1.a

Dust jacket: Yellow background with predominantly black lettering. Front: 'ROUND UP | [reddish brown] the Stories of | [black] RING W. | LARDNER | [reddish brown and black design around eleven-line framed comment by Carl Van Doren]'. Spine: 'ROUND UP | THE STORIES | OF | RING W. | LARDNER | [brown and black design continued from front] | SCRIBNERS'. Back has comments by Sir James Barrie, Edmund Wilson, Harry Hansen, and H. L. Mencken. Front and back flaps have "An Appreciation of 'Round Up' by Carl Van Doren . . . ."

Publication: 20,000 copies of the first printing. $2.50. Published 5 April 1929. Copyright 5 April 1929. Copyright #A7721.

Printing: Printing, plates, and binding by Scribner Press.

Locations: ICN, LC (deposit-stamp APR 26 1929), MJB (dj), RL, RLS.

A 21.1.b
Second printing

ROUND UP | THE STORIES OF | RING W. LARDNER | [rule and black circle with device] | NEW YORK 1929 | [next three lines within circle] THE | LITERARY | GUILD

Retains Scribner Press seal.

Note: Priority, if any, of first and second printings not determined. Possibly published simultaneously. The Literary Guild distributed approximately seventy thousand copies, and there probably were multiple Literary Guild printings.

Location: MJB.

A 21.1.c*
Third printing (American issue): New York: Scribners, 1935. The dust jacket identifies this as 'DOLLAR EDITION'. The copyright page retains Scribner Press seal.

Location: MJB.

A 21.1.c**
Third printing (English issue, 1935)

Round Up
The Stories of
Ring W. Lardner

LONDON
WILLIAMS & NORGATE, Lᴛᴅ.

A 21.1.c**: 7 1/16" x 5"

[iii–vi] vii–viii [1–2] 3–11 [12] 13–33 [34] 35–63 [64] 65–85 [86] 87–107 [108] 109–127 [128] 129–139 [140] 141–235 [236] 237–247 [248] 249–281 [282] 283–303 [304] 305–355 [356] 357–373 [374] 375–383 [384] 385–407 [408] 409–417 [418] 419–445 [446] 447–467 [468]

$[1]^{16}$ (-1_1) $[2-14]^{16}$ $[15]^{16}$ (-15_{15-16})

Note: This English issue is made up from sheets of third printing with special first gathering. Published in England but printed in the United States with integral Williams & Norgate title page.

Copyright page: 'First Published in Gt. Britain . . . 1935 | COPYRIGHT AND PRINTED IN U.S.A.'

Contents: pp. i–ii: excised; p. iii: half title; p. iv: blank; p. v: title; p. vi: copyright; pp. vii–viii: 'CONTENTS'; p. 1: half title; p. 2: blank; pp. 3–467: text, headed 'I | THE MAYSVILLE MINSTREL'; p. 468: blank; pp. 469–472: excised.

Typography and paper: Same as the first printing.

Binding: Deep blue (179) V cloth (smooth). Spine gold-stamped: 'ROUND-UP | THE STORIES | OF | RING W. LARDNER | WILLIAMS & | NORGATE LTD.' Off-white wove endpapers. Top edge stained gray; all edges trimmed.

Dust jacket: Front has four gold bands against white with black lettering: 'ROUND UP | RING LARDNER'S | FAMOUS | STORIES'. Spine has nine bands of white, black, and gold: 'ROUND | UP | RING | LARDNER | WILLIAMS & | NORGATE LTD.' Back has ads for *Neighbours* and *The Winged Bull*. Front flap has ad for *Round Up*. Back flap is blank.

Publication: Unknown number of copies of the English issue. 7s. 6d. Published September 1935.

Locations: BM (deposit-stamp 14 SEP 35), MJB (dj).

A 21.1.d
Fourth printing: The Collected Short Stories of Ring Lardner. New York: Modern Library, [1941].

Reprint of *Round Up*. See AA 3.

A 21.1.e
Fifth printing (augmented): Ring Lardner's Best Stories, foreword by William McFee. New York: Garden City Publishing Co., [1938].

Adds *The Big Town* to the first edition of *Round Up*. See A 14.2, AA 2.

Note: The title page stipulates '*De Luxe Edition*'. Cheap printing —if any—not seen.

A 21.2
Second edition

[all within double-rules frame] [to left of vertical rule] PUBLISHED BY ARRANGEMENT WITH | CHARLES SCRIBNER'S SONS, NEW YORK | *Copyright, 1924, 1926, 1929, by Ellis A. Lardner* | *Copyright, 1925, 1926, 1927, 1928, 1929, by* | *International Magazine Co., Inc.* | *Copyright, 1925, 1926, by Coloroto Corporation* | *Manufactured in the United States of America* | [to right of vertical rule] ROUND UP | *The Stories of* | *Ring W. Lardner* | *Armed Services Editions, Inc.* | A NON-PROFIT ORGANIZATION SPONSORED BY | THE COUNCIL ON BOOKS IN WARTIME, NEW YORK

[c. 1946]. #F–172. Twenty-four stories.
Locations: MJB, RLS.

A 21.3
Third edition: The Best Short Stories | of | RING | LARDNER | *CHARLES SCRIBNER'S SONS · NEW YORK*

1957. A-10.57[v]. Twenty-five stories from *Round Up*. See AA 5.

Reprinted 1974 in cloth and paper (Scribner Library #SL 494).

A 22   STOP ME—IF YOU'VE HEARD THIS ONE
Only Printing (1929)

STOP ME—
IF YOU'VE HEARD
THIS ONE

BY

RING W. LARDNER

An advance printing from the
July, 1929, issue of

COSMOPOLITAN

A 22: 6″ x 4½″

[1] 2–18 [19–20]

[1]¹⁰

Contents: p. 1: title; pp. 2–11: text, headed '[swash] STOP
ME——— | IF YOU'VE | HEARD | THIS ONE'; pp. 12–19: ads for
Cosmopolitan; p. 20: blank.

Typography and paper: 8 point on 9, Goudy Old Style. 4⅝"
(4¹³⁄₁₆") x 3⁵⁄₁₆". Thirty-seven lines per page. No running heads.
Coated wove paper.

Binding: Pale yellow (89) boards with herringbone pattern.
Front: 'STOP ME— | IF YOU'VE HEARD | THIS ONE | BY |
RING W. LARDNER | [decoration]'. Yellow laid endpapers with
herringbone wire lines. All edges trimmed.

Dust jacket: No jacket noted. Probably not distributed in dust
jacket.

Publication: Unknown number of copies distributed in June
1929 as promotional piece for *Hearst's International-Cosmopolitan* magazine. Not for sale. See D 165.

Location: MJB.

A 23 RING LARDNER'S UPROARIOUS NOTES
First edition, first printing (1929)

A 23: cover title, lettered in white against medium blue background;
7 9/16″ x 5 9/16″

[1–4]

[1]²

Contents: p. 1: cover; pp. 2–3: Lardner's notes on members of the cast, with caricatures by Gard; p. 4: "Let George Do It."

Publication: Distributed at the Broadhurst Theatre, New York, during the run of *June Moon* in 1929. Possibly reprinted during the run of the play.

Location: NN (Lincoln Center).

Note: A revised edition was prepared for the road tour of *June Moon*. The only example seen (at NN Lincoln Center) was printed for the Broad Street Theatre, Newark, N.J. It has a variant cover and omits Lardner's notes on the cast, but it includes "Let George Do It." See C 47, D 172, and E 4669 for other appearances of notes on the cast. See E 4667 for another appearance of "Let George Do It."

A 24 JUNE MOON

A 24.1
First edition, only printing (1930)

JUNE MOON
A COMEDY

IN A PROLOGUE AND THREE ACTS

BY
RING LARDNER
AND
GEORGE S. KAUFMAN

CHARLES SCRIBNER'S SONS
NEW YORK ⋅ LONDON
1930

A 24.1: 7½″ x 4¾″

[i–iv] v–vi [vii–xii] [1–2] 3–6 [7] 8–23 [24–26] 27–77 [78–80] 81–136 [137–138] 139–187 [188]

[1–11]⁸ [12]⁴ [13]⁸

Contents: p. i: half title; p. ii: blank; p. iii: title; p. iv: copyright; pp. v–vi: 'FOREWORD'; p. vii: cast; p. viii: blank; p. ix: 'THE SCENES'; p. x: blank; p. xi: 'NOTE' [production and copyright information]; p. xii: blank; p. 1: 'JUNE MOON | [rule] | PROLOGUE'; p. 2: blank; pp. 3–187: text, headed 'JUNE MOON | PROLOGUE'; p. 188: blank.

Typography and paper: 11 point on 13, Scotch. 5⅜″ (5¹¹⁄₁₆″) x 3³⁄₁₆″. Running heads: rectos, acts; versos, 'JUNE MOON'. Wove paper.

Binding: Dark yellowish pink (30) V cloth (smooth). White paper label on spine with black lettering: '[rule] | [short rule] | *June* | *Moon* | [quarter moon] | *Lardner* | *and* | *Kaufman* | [short rule] | [rule] | SCRIBNERS | [rule]'. White wove sized endpapers. Top and bottom edges trimmed.

Dust jacket: Lavender printed in black. Front: '[decorated single-rule frame within larger single-rule frame] JUNE | MOON | *by* | *Ring Lardner* | *and* | *George S. Kaufman* | *A Play in* | *Three Acts* | SCRIBNERS'. Spine: '[rule] | [short rule] | *June* | *Moon* | [quarter moon] | *Lardner* | *and* | *Kaufman* | [short rule] | [rule] | SCRIBNERS | [rule]'. Back has ads for *The Roof, Waterloo Bridge, June Moon,* and *Half Gods.* Front flap has price and ad for *June Moon.* Back flap has ad for *Round Up.*

Publication: Unknown number of copies of the only printing. $2.00. Published 28 March 1930. Copyright application not found. Copyright #D pub. 85990.

Locations: LC (two copies; deposit-stamp APR–1 1930), Lilly (dj), MJB (dj).

Round Up
By Ring W. Lardner

"Lardner," declared John Chamberlain in the New York Times, "is pre-eminently our best short-story writer, and 'Round Up' gives the full measure of his talent."

The same opinion is expressed by Donald Douglas in a review of "Round Up" in the Forum. He is the best short-story writer in sight because he is a reporter with an exquisite gift for observation and a highly literary conscience. He is a humorist only because he is a great deal more than that."

Lewis Mumford, so impressed with this collection of short stories that in his review in the Herald Tribune he declared "the stories brought together in 'Round Up' must be counted among the few that will be readable twenty years hence," endeavored, in the same review, to define the essence of Lardner's charm. He said:

"Out of the formless life of our time he has extracted the boiler-plate of current slang; he has achieved a living speech; out of canned goods and synthetic breakfast foods he has produced, with consummate art, a seven-course dinner. From a hundred dead jokes and banal witticisms and cheap wise cracks he has created a commentary which is as funny to a mature mind as the original repartee seemed to the vulgar."

For Those Who Read Plays

The Roof
By John Galsworthy

Mr. Galsworthy's latest play, in three acts, is a commentary on morals, involving several groups of characters living in a London apartment-house who are driven to the roof of the building by an alarm of fire. Its recent production in London elicited cordial critical response.

Waterloo Bridge
By Robert E. Sherwood

This play, by the former editor of *Life* and the author of "The Road to Rome," concerns a dramatic meeting on Waterloo Bridge during an air raid over London, and the war between desire and wisdom which wages in young hearts.

June Moon
By Ring Lardner and George S. Kaufman

Clever and amusing dialogue in a play that satirizes song-writers and Tin Pan Alley, with an amazing foreword, and Lardner's vivid understanding of the human heart which passes for humor but is really art.

Half Gods
By Sidney Howard

A comedy of manners concerning marriage, in which a happy home is saved by means of a black eye. By the author of "The Silver Cord," "Ned McCobb's Daughter," "Lucky Sam McCarver," and "They Knew What They Wanted."

June Moon
Lardner and Kaufman

SCRIBNERS

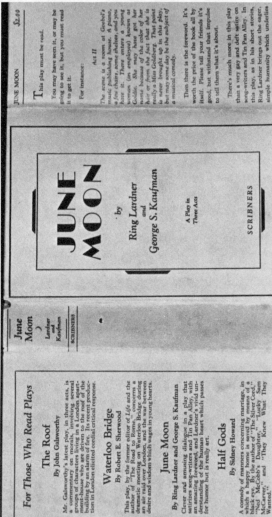

JUNE MOON

by

Ring Lardner
and
George S. Kaufman

A Play in
Three Acts

SCRIBNERS

JUNE MOON $2.00

This play must be read.

You may have seen it, or may be going to see it, but you must read it to get it.

For instance:

Act II

The scene is a room at Goebel's music publishing house. A young man, Fred, comes down stage to have it. There enters a young woman (an employee) known as Goldie. She may have got her name because of the color of her hair or from the fact that she is really a Miss Goldberg. That point is never brought up in this play, but may some day be the subject of a musical comedy.

Then there is the foreword. It's worth the price of the book all by itself. Please tell your friends it's good, but withstand that impulse to tell them what it's about.

There's much more in this play than a very gay and deft satire on song-writers and Tin Pan Alley. In this play, as in his short stories, Ring Lardner brings out the eager, simple humanity which underlies the colloquially spoken.

Dust jacket for A 24.1

A 24.2
Second edition (acting version)

JUNE MOON | *A COMEDY IN A PROLOGUE* | *AND THREE ACTS* | BY | RING LARDNER | AND | GEORGE S. KAUFMAN | COPYRIGHT, 1929, BY RING LARDNER AND GEORGE S. KAUFMAN | COPYRIGHT, 1930, BY CHARLES SCRIBNER'S SONS | COPYRIGHT, 1931 (ACTING EDITION), BY RING LARDNER | AND GEORGE S. KAUFMAN | All Rights Reserved | [twelve-line copyright and production notice] | SAMUEL FRENCH, INC. | 25 WEST 45TH STREET, NEW YORK, N. Y. | FINE ARTS BUILDING, 811 WEST 7TH STREET, | LOS ANGELES, CALIF. | SAMUEL FRENCH, LTD., | 26 SOUTHAMPTON STREET, STRAND, W.C.2, LONDON

Revised acting version; with Lardner's music and lyrics for "Hello, Tokio!" and "Give Our Child a Name," pp. 105–107.

Published 30 January 1931.

Note 1: *June Moon* opened in New York on 9 October 1929 and ran for 273 performances.

Note 2: *June Moon* was abridged in *The Best Plays of 1929–30 and the Yearbook of the Drama in America*, ed. Burns Mantle (New York: Dodd, Mead, 1930), pp. 236–271.

Locations: LC (deposit-stamp MAR 20 1931), MJB.

A 25 LOSE WITH A SMILE
Only printing (1933)

LOSE WITH
A SMILE

By

Ring W. Lardner

NEW YORK

CHARLES SCRIBNER'S SONS

1933

A 25: 7 7/16" x 5"

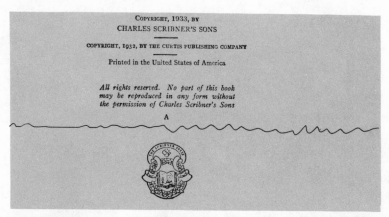

[i–vi] vii–viii [ix–x] 1–83 [84–85] 86–128 [129] 130–142 [143] 144–174

[1–11]⁸ [12]⁴

Contents: p. i: half title; p. ii: card page; p. iii: title; p. iv: copyright; p. v: 'CONTENTS'; p. vi: blank; pp. vii–viii: 'ILLUSTRATIONS'; p. ix: half title; p. x: blank; pp. 1–174: text, headed 'I | ONE HIT, ONE ERROR, ONE | LEFT'.

Typography and paper: 12 point on 16, Old Style No. 1. 5⁵⁄₁₆″ (5⅝″) x 3⅛″. Twenty-four lines per page. No running heads. Wove paper.

Binding: Dark grayish green (151) V cloth (smooth). Front goldstamped: facsimile of Lardner's signature. Spine goldstamped: 'LOSE | WITH A | SMILE | [short rule] | RING W. | LARDNER | SCRIBNERS'. Also strong purplish blue (196) V cloth, stamped in moderate greenish blue (173). White sized endpapers. Top and bottom edges trimmed.

Dust jacket: Front: '[white against green background] LOSE WITH | A SMILE | [black-and-white drawing of man in baseball cap within baseball diamond] | [white] RING LARDNER'. Spine: '[black against green] LOSE | WITH | A | SMILE | [triangular decoration] | RING | LARDNER | SCRIBNERS'. Back quotes William Bolitho on Lardner. Front flap has ad for *Lose with a Smile*. Back flap has ad for *Round Up*.

Publication: Unknown number of copies of the only printing. $1.50. Published 3 March 1933. Copyright 3 March 1933. Copyright #A59801.

Printing: Printing, typesetting, and binding by Scribner Press.

Dust jacket for A 25

Note: All stories in *Lose with a Smile* were first published in *The Saturday Evening Post*. See D 206, D 207, D 208, D 212, D 218. All selections are first book appearances.

Locations: ICN, LC (two copies, both green; deposit-stamp MAR–8 1933), MJB (blue and green bindings; both in dj), RL, RLS.

A 26 FIRST AND LAST

A 26.1.a
Only edition, first printing (1934)

FIRST AND LAST

Ring Lardner

CHARLES SCRIBNER'S SONS
NEW YORK   LONDON
1934

A 26.1.a: 7 7/16" x 5 ¼"

[a–b] [i–iv] v–vi [vii–viii] [1–2] 3–15 [16–20] 21–43 [44–46] 47–80 [81–82] 83–113 [114–116] 117–131 [132–134] 135–148 [149–150] 151–178 [179–180] 181–226 [227–228] 229–246 [247–248] 249–273 [274–276] 277–303 [304–306] 307–320 [321–322] 323–326 [327–328] 329–377 [378]

[1–23]⁸ [24]¹⁰

Contents: pp. a–b: blank; p. i: half title; p. ii: blank; p. iii: title; p. iv: copyright; pp. v–vi: 'PREFACE' by Gilbert Seldes; p. vii: 'CONTENTS'; p. viii: blank; p. 1: 'SYMPTOMS OF BEING 35'; p. 2: unsigned introductory note; pp. 3–377: text, headed 'SYMPTOMS OF BEING 35'; p. 378: blank.

Eighty-four pieces. Symptoms of Being 35, The Young Im-migrunts, "Men and Women" (*Say It with Oil,* "Marriage Made Easy," "Love Letters Made Easy,"* "My Own Beauty Secrets,"* "Knickers for Women,"* "Large Coffee,"* "Old Man Liver"*), "A Variety of Sports" ("A Reporter in Bed,"* "Tips on Horses,"* "How Winners Quit Winners,"* "Salt Water Fishing,"* "The Origin of Football,"* "New Golf Accessories,"* "Miss Sawyer, Champion,"* "The Master Minds"*), "A Yacht Race" ("Disaster,"* "Lost Legs,"* "A Delayed Start,"* "A Perfect Day,"* "The End of It,"* "Years Later"*), "A World's Serious" ("Advance Notice,"* "The First Day,"* "The Second Day,"* "The Third Day,"* "The End"*), "A Prize Fight"* (twelve articles on the Dempsey-Firpo fight), "On Politics" (seven articles on "Disarmament in 1921,"* "The Democrats in 1924,"* "On Prohibition,"* "Both Parties: 1928"*), "A General Commentary" ("On Names,"* "On Chain

Letters,"* "On Jobs,"* "On Newspapers,"* "On Conversation"*),
"Children, Society, and Dogs" ("Visiting Royalty,"* "Table Man-
ners,"* "Opening Remarks,"* "Dogs,"* "Colleges for Cops,"* "A
Bedtime Story"*), "An Infant Industry" ("Off Color,"* "A
Crooner,"* "Running Comment,"* "Night and Day,"* "Fun on the
Air,"* "A Perfect Program"*), "A Few Parodies" ("A Literary
Diary,"* "Your Broadway, Beau, and You Can Have It,"* "Odd's
Bodkins,"* "Dante and ——"*), "Notes on Travel" ("To Nas-
sau,"* "Brief Baedeker"*), "Short Plays" ("Thompson's Vaca-
tion,"* "The Bull Pen,"* "Quadroon,"* "Dinner Bridge," "Cora,
or Fun at a Spa,"* "Abend di Anni Nouveau,"* "Clemo Uti—'The
Water Lilies,' " "I Gaspiri," "Taxidea Americana"). All pieces were
first published in magazines or syndicated by the Bell Syndicate.
See C 18 and Sections D and E. First book appearances indicated
by asterisks.

Typography and paper: 10 point on 10, Century Expanded. 5⅞6″
(6″) x 3½″. Twenty-nine, thirty, and thirty-one lines per page.
Running heads: rectos, section titles; versos, 'FIRST AND LAST'.
Wove paper.

Binding: Moderate bluish green (164) V cloth (smooth). Front:
'[in outline against two dark blue (183) bands] FIRST AND LAST
| RING LARDNER'. Spine: '[in outline against three dark blue
bands] FIRST | AND LAST | RING | LARDNER | SCRIBNERS'.
White wove sized endpapers. Top edge stained blue; top and
bottom edges trimmed.

Dust jacket: Front has *New York Times* comment on Lardner
printed in white on eight blue bands separating lines of black
printing: 'FIRST | and | LAST | RING | LARDNER'. Spine: '[black
on white background separated by eight blue bands] FIRST | and |
LAST | RING | LARDNER | [white] Scribners'. Back has photo
of Lardner and forty-line critical assessment of Lardner and *First
and Last*. Front flap has price and partial contents list of *First and
Last*. Back flap has blurbs from *The New York Times, New York
Evening Post,* and *Hartford Courant* for *Round Up*.

Publication: Unknown number of copies of the first printing.
$2.50. Published 8 June 1934. Copyright 8 June 1934. Copyright
#A72736.

Printing: Printing, typesetting, and binding by the Scribner
Press.

Locations: ICN, LC (two copies; deposit-stamp JUN–8 1934),
MJB (dj), RL, RLS.

Dust jacket for A 26.1.a

A 26.1.b
Second printing: New York: Scribners, 1934.

The copyright page omits the 'A', but retains the Scribner Press
seal.

A 27 RING AROUND MAX
Only edition (1973)

**THE CORRESPONDENCE OF
RING LARDNER & MAX PERKINS**

**Edited by
CLIFFORD M. CARUTHERS**

NORTHERN ILLINOIS UNIVERSITY PRESS
DeKalb, Illinois

A 27: 8 7/16" x 5 7/16"

[i–vi] vii–xxiii [xxiv] 1–192

Perfect binding.

Contents: p. i: half title; p. ii: blank; p. iii: title; p. iv: copyright; p. v: 'CONTENTS'; p. vi: caricature of Lardner; p. vii: 'PREFACE'; p. viii: caricature of Lardner; pp. ix–xxiii: 'FOREWORD'; p. xxiv: caricature of Lardner; pp. 1–192: text, headed 'THE CORRESPONDENCE OF | RING LARDNER | AND | MAXWELL PERKINS'.

Typography and paper: 10 point on 12, Times Roman. 6⁹⁄₁₆″ (7⁵⁄₁₆″) x 3¹¹⁄₁₆″. Thirty-seven lines per page. No running heads. White wove paper.

Binding: Published simultaneously in cloth and paper.
   Cloth. Black (267) V cloth (smooth). Spine goldstamped: '[vertically] Caruthers RING AROUND MAX [NIU Press device]'. White wove endpapers. All edges trimmed.
   Paper. Black paper wrappers. Front: '[Following three lines in vivid red (11) against white background surrounded by a black circle within a white circle] RING | [slanted] AROUND | MAX | [following two lines in white] THE CORRESPONDENCE OF | RING LARDNER & MAX PERKINS | [following two lines in red]

Edited By | CLIFFORD M. CARUTHERS | [following two lines in medium gray (265)] NORTHERN ILLINOIS UNIVERSITY PRESS | DeKalb, Illinois'. Spine: '[vertically] [white] Caruthers [red] RING AROUND MAX [black NIU Press device on white rectangle]'. Inside front and inside rear wrappers illustrated with material from *You Know Me Al* comic strip.

Dust jacket: Front and spine same as wrapper. Back has ad for *The Complete Correspondence of Ring Lardner*. Front flap has ad for *Ring Around Max*. Back flap has photo of Caruthers with biographical note.

Publication: Published simultaneously in cloth and wrappers: 504 copies in cloth; 2,580 copies in wrappers. $8.50 cloth; $5 paper. Published 2 January 1973. Copyright 2 January 1973. Copyright #A426869.

Printing: Composition, printing, and binding by George Banta & Co., Menasha, Wis.

Locations: LC, MJB (cloth and paper).

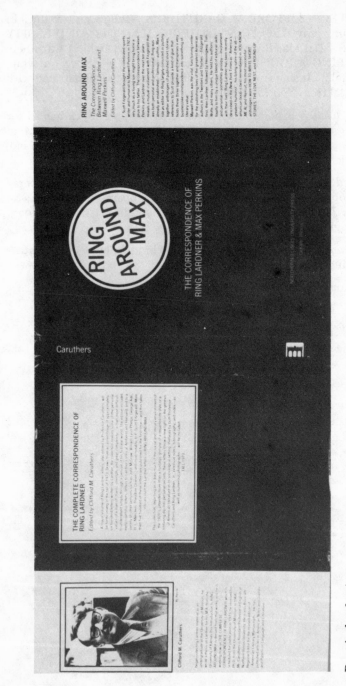

Dust jacket for A 27

A 28 THE LETTER-BOOK
Unlocated (1930–1931)

The United States Copyright Office holds applications for five copyrights in Lardner's name for leaflets with the series title *The Letter-Book,* published by The Letter-Book Co. in Chicago and printed by the Blakely Printing Co. Although the copyright applications indicate that a copy of each of the leaflets was submitted with the application, no copy of any of these five publications has been located.

1. "Let's Pass a Law." 22 December 1930. #AA 59424.
2. "The Crucial Moment." 1 February 1931. #AA 60961.
3. "Just Among Friends." 4 March 1931. #AA 63635.
4. "Derelectus." 1 April 1931. #AA 69616.
5. "Days of Daze." 1 May 1931. #AA 69617.

AA Supplement

Collections

1925

5 vols. New York: Scribners, 1925.

In 1925 Scribners published a five-volume uniform set of Lardner, four of which included a new preface by the author, dated March 1925:

> *The Big Town* (second printing)
> *What of It?* (third printing, augmented)
> *How to Write Short Stories* (seventh ? printing; 1924 preface)
> *Gullible's Travels, Etc.* (second printing)
> *You Know Me Al* (second printing)

Each volume was made from the same sheets used for the regular trade bindings.

Bindings: The uniform set was bound in three different styles: one cloth and two styles of fabrikoid (also called Artcraft leather):
Binding 1. Medium greenish blue (173) V cloth (smooth), goldstamped on spine. See illustration.
Binding 2. Dark blue (183) AR fabrikoid (coarse ribbed morocco), goldstamped and blindstamped on front and spine. See illustration.
Binding 3. Dark purplish blue (201) A fabrikoid (ribbed morocco), goldstamped and blindstamped on front and spine. See illustration.

Note 1: The uniform set was also used as a subscription premium for *Scribner's Magazine.*

Note 2: Perkins to Lardner, 17 February 1925: "I do not know how familiar you are with the way these sets are sold. It is almost altogether by canvassers, though sometimes in part by mail order advertising and is largely in combination with a subscription to the magazine. In view of the expense of collections and of the general machinery of selling, the margin of profit is a very low one, and therefore the terms given to authors are low, and may seem to you at first sight to be extremely so. We are ready to pay you the highest that we pay anyone, as we should do, which is a royalty of 20¢ per set; and this is to be paid according to the printing, and not according to the sale, and the first edition in this case would be 10,000 sets."

Perkins to Lardner, 19 June 1925: "I am sending you a set of the books in what is known as 'The Artcraft Edition' because of the binding. The binding is called Artcraft leather which has at first a certain aroma; but it gets over that after a little. The reason we have this edition is because the binding has a very strong general appeal apparently" (*Ring Around Max,* pp. 54, 72).

AA 1: binding 1 (spine)

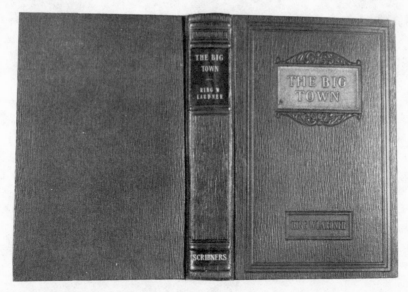

AA 1 : binding 2

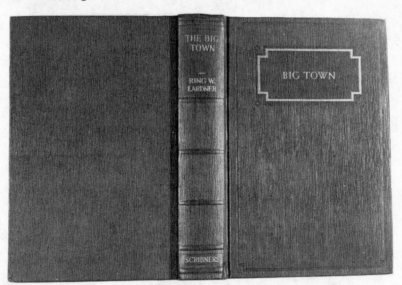

AA 1 : binding 3

AA 2 BEST STORIES
1938

Ring Lardner's | BEST STORIES | [seven lines of type] | With a
Foreword by | WILLIAM McFEE | [printing press] | *DeLuxe
Edition* | GARDEN CITY PUBLISHING CO., INC. | New York

1938. Fifth printing (augmented by *The Big Town*) of *Round Up*.
See A 14.2, A 21.1.e. *No first book material.*

AA 3 COLLECTED SHORT STORIES
1941

[runner with torch] [following five lines within single-rule frame]
The Collected | Short Stories | OF | RING | LARDNER | [below
frame] THE MODERN LIBRARY · NEW YORK

1941. Fourth printing of *Round Up*. See A 21.1.d. *No first book
material.*

AA 4 PORTABLE LARDNER
1946

[first three lines slanted within suitcase] THE PORTABLE | RING
| LARDNER | EDITED AND | WITH AN INTRODUCTION | BY
GILBERT SELDES | NEW YORK 1946 [circular Viking device]
| THE VIKING PRESS

On copyright page: 'Published by The Viking Press in September
1946'.

Contents: You Know Me Al, The Big Town, "Alibi Ike,"
"Rhythm," "Haircut," "Champion," "A Day with Conrad Green,"
"The Love Nest," "The Golden Honeymoon," "Some Like Them
Cold," "A Caddy's Diary," *Gullible's Travels,* "Carmen," *Symptoms
of Being 35,* "A General Commentary" ("On Newspapers," "On
Chain Letters," "On Conversation"), "Men and Women" ("Say
It with Oil," "Marriage Made Easy," "Love Letters Made Easy,"
"Large Coffee"), "A World's Serious" ("Advance Notice," "The
First Day," "The Second Day," "The Third Day," "The End"),
"On Politics" ("Disarmament in 1921," "The Democrats in 1924,"
"On Prohibition"), "Children, Society, and Dogs" ("Visiting
Royalty," "Table Manners," "Opening Remarks," "Dogs"), "An
Infant Industry" ("Off Color," "A Crooner," "Running Comment,"

"Night and Day," "Fun on the Air," "A Perfect Program"), *The Young Immigrunts*, "A Few Parodies" ("A Literary Diary," "Your Broadway, Beau, and You Can Have It," "Odd's Bodkins," "Dante and—"), "Short Plays" ("Thompson's Vacation," "The Bull Pen," "Quadroon," "Dinner Bridge," "Cora, or Fun at a Spa," "Abend di Anni Nouveau," "Clemo Uti—The Water Lilies,'" "I Gaspiri," "Taxidea Americana"). *No first book material.*

Reprinted as *The Indispensable Ring Lardner* (New York: The Book Society, 1950).

AA 5 BEST SHORT STORIES
1957

The Best Short Stories | of | RING LARDNER | *CHARLES SCRIBNER'S SONS • NEW YORK*

1957. A-10.57[v]. Twenty-five stories from *Round Up*. Reprint noted: E-12.63[V]. See A 21.3. *No first book material.*

Reprinted 1974 in cloth and paper (Scribner Library #SL 494).

AA 6 BEST SHORT STORIES
1959

THE BEST SHORT STORIES OF | RING LARDNER | *With an Introduction by* | Alan Ross | 1959 | CHATTO & WINDUS | LONDON

Contents: "Haircut," "Alibi Ike," "Liberty Hall," "Zone of Quiet," "Mr. Frisbie," "Hurry Kane," "Champion," "A Day with Conrad Green," "Old Folks' Christmas," "Harmony," "The Love Nest," "Ex Parte," "The Golden Honeymoon," "Horseshoes," "Anniversary," "Reunion," "Who Dealt?" "My Roomy," "Some Like Them Cold," "A Caddy's Diary," "Mr. and Mrs. Fix-It." *No first book material.*

Reprinted 1974.

AA 7 HAIRCUT
1961

HAIRCUT | AND OTHER STORIES | *by Ring Lardner* | New York | CHARLES SCRIBNER'S SONS

1961.

On copyright page: A-12.61[C].

Scribner Library (#SL 53).

Contents: "Haircut," "I Can't Breathe," "Alibi Ike," "Zone of Quiet," "Champion," "A Day with Conrad Green," "The Love Nest," "The Golden Honeymoon," "Horseshoes," "Some Like Them Cold." *No first book material.*

AA 8 SHUT UP
1962

A Ring Lardner Selection | edited by Babette Rosmond | and Henry Morgan | SHUT UP, HE | EXPLAINED | CHARLES SCRIBNER'S SONS | New York

1962.

On copyright page: A-3.62[V].

Contents: "Introduction by Sarah E. Spooldripper," *The Young Immigrunts, The Big Town*, "Some Short Nonsense Plays" ("The Tridget of Greva," "The Bull Pen," "Quadroon," "Dinner Bridge," "Cora or Fun at a Spa," "Abend di Anni Nouveau," "Clemo Uti— 'The Water Lillies,' " "I Gaspiri 'The Upholsterers,' " "Taxidea Americana"), *June Moon* ("Prologue and Act I"), "A Few Parodies," "Miss Sawyer, Champion," " 'In Conference,' " "A Close-up of Domba Splew," "A Visit to the Garrisons," "Business Is Business," "Here's Ring Lardner's Autobiography,"* "The Perfect Woman,"* "Over the Waves" ("Over the Waves,"* "Heavy Da-Dee Dough Boys,"* "Life of the Boswells,"* " 'Pu-leeze! Mister Hemingway,' "* "The Crucial Game,"* "Herb and Frank Panic 'Em,"* "Lyricists Strike Pay Dirt," "Announcers' Prep School,"* "Some Short-Selling,"* "Rudy in Irate Mood," "The Old Man Shows His Air Mail,"* "We're All Sisters Under the Hide of Me," "Hail to the Chief,"* "The Perfect Radio Program"). Asterisks indicate first book appearances. See C 47.

AA 9 RING LARDNER READER
1963

The | RING LARDNER | *Reader* | Edited by *MAXWELL GEISMAR* | Charles Scribner's Sons *New York*

1963.

On copyright page: A-11.62[H]. Printed in 1962, but published in January 1963.

Reprint noted: B-9.71[C].

Subsequently included in the Scribner Library (#SL 1200). First Scribner Library printing not seen.

Contents: You Know Me Al, Gullible's Travels, "Haircut," "The Maysville Minstrel," "Travelogue," "The Facts," "Anniversary," "Quick Returns," "Lady Parkins," "Three Without, Doubled," "A Visit to the Garrisons," "Some Like Them Cold," "I Can't Breathe," "Zone of Quiet," "Champion," "A Caddy's Diary," "In Conference," "The Love Nest," "A Day with Conrad Green," "Mr. Frisbie," "Sun Cured," "Now and Then," "My Own Beauty Secrets," "The Golden Honeymoon," "Who Dealt?" "Liberty Hall," "Contract," "Old Folks' Christmas," "Ex Parte," *The Young Immigrunts, Symptoms of Being 35,* "Dinner," "There Are Smiles," "Say It with Oil," "Marriage Made Easy," "Table Manners," "Dogs," "Alibi Ike," "My Roomy," "Hurry Kane," "Nora," "Rhythm," "Tips on Horses," "How Winners Quit Winners," "Salt Water Fishing," "The Origin of Football," "New Golf Accessories," "A Yacht Race," "A World's Serious," "Night and Day," "Sane Olympics," "Thompson's Vacation," "Clemo Uti—'The Water Lilies,' " "I. Gaspiri," "Quadroon," "Dinner Bridge," "Cora, or Fun at a Spa," "Abend Di Anni Nouveau," "Taxidea Americana," "How to Tell a True Princess," "Cinderella," "Red Riding Hood," "Bluebeard," "A Bedtime Story," Prefaces ("How to Write Short Stories," "The Love Nest," "The Story of a Wonder Man"), "A Close-Up of Domba Splew," "Don't be a Drudge," "Segregate the Fats," "What of It?" *No first book material.*

AA 10 LOVE NEST
1965

THE LOVE NEST | and Other Stories | *by* | RING LARDNER | *Edited with Notes* | *by* | Tamotsu Nishiyama | & Katsuhiro Jinzaki | THE SIGN OF [seal] A GOOD BOOK | THE EIHŌSHA LTD. | —*Tokyo*—

1965.

Contents: "The Love Nest," "Old Folks' Christmas," "Anniversary," "There Are Smiles," and Japanese notes. *No first book material.*

AA 11 SOME CHAMPIONS

Entry added in proof. See C 58 for complete description.

B. Sheet Music

Describes only sheet music with lyrics or music by Lardner offered for sale. Professional copies for musicians have been omitted.

B 1 "LITTLE PUFF OF SMOKE" "GOODNIGHT"

B 1.1
First Edition, 1910

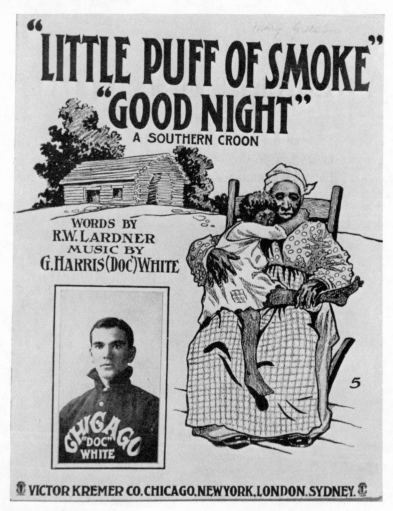

B 1: front cover; 13⅜" x 10⅜"

[1] 2–5 [6]

[1]³ (single leaf inserted in folio)

Copyright notice: p. 2: 'V.K. 1241–3–1 Copyright, 1910, by Victor Kremer Co., Chicago–New York. | International Copyright secured.'

Contents: p. 1: title; pp. 2–5: music and lyrics; p. 6: ads. Noted with variant ads on p. 6 (outside rear cover): "Imam" or "Cherry Leaf Rag."

Paper: Wove paper.

Publication: Number of copies, price, and date of publication unknown. Copyright 13 August 1910. Copyright #E238433.

Note: The variant ads on the outside rear cover possibly indicate separate printings.

Location: MJB (both ads).

B 1.2
Second edition, 1916: Chicago and New York: Harold Rossiter Music Co., [1916].

Location: RL.

B 2 GEE! IT'S A WONDERFUL GAME
  1911

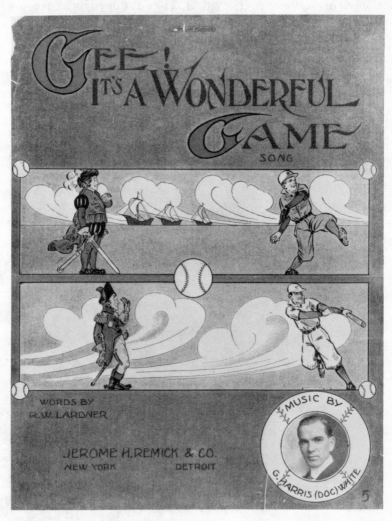

B 2: front cover; 13¾″ x 10¾″

[1] 2–5 [6]

[1]³ (single leaf inserted in folio)

Copyright notice: p. 2: 'Copyright MCMXI by JEROME H. REMICK & Co. | Copyright Canada MCMXI by JEROME H. REMICK & Co. | Propiedad para la Republica Mexicana de Jerome H. Remick & Co., Detroit y New York. Depositada conforme a la ley.'

Contents: p. 1: cover; pp. 2–5: music and lyrics; p. 6: ads for songs. Plate number on pp. 3 and 6: '4501'.

Paper: Coated wove.

Publication: Number of copies, price, and date of publication unknown. Copyright 13 June 1911. Copyright #E258896.

Location: RPB.

B 3 TEDDY YOU'RE A BEAR
1916

B 3: front cover; 13½" x 10¾"

[1] 2–5 [6]

[1]³ (single leaf inserted in folio)

Copyright notice: p. 2: 'Copyrighted 1916 by Jerome H. Remick & Co., New York–Detroit | Performing rights reserved. International copyright secured.'

Contents: p. 1: cover; pp. 2–5: music and lyrics; p. 6: ads for songs. Plate number on pp. 3 and 6: '1593 2'.

Paper: Coated wove.

Publication: Number of copies, price, and date of publication unknown. Copyright 21 June 1916. Copyright #E386816.

Location: RPB.

B 4 OLD BILL BAKER
1916

B 4: front cover; 13⁷⁄₁₆″ x 10⁷⁄₁₆″

[1] 2–5 [6]

[1]³ (single leaf inserted in folio)

Copyright notice: p. 2: '*Copyright MCMXVI by T. B. Harms &
Francis Day & Hunter, N.Y.* | 5431–4   All Rights Reserved.
International Copyright Secured.'

Contents: p. 1: cover; pp. 2–5: music and lyrics; p. 6: ads for
songs.

Paper: Wove paper.

Publication: Number of copies and date of publication unknown. 60¢. Copyright 8 November 1916. Copyright #E392333.

Note: Written for the show *Very Good Eddie* (1916).

Locations: MJB, RPB.

B 5 PROHIBITION BLUES
1919

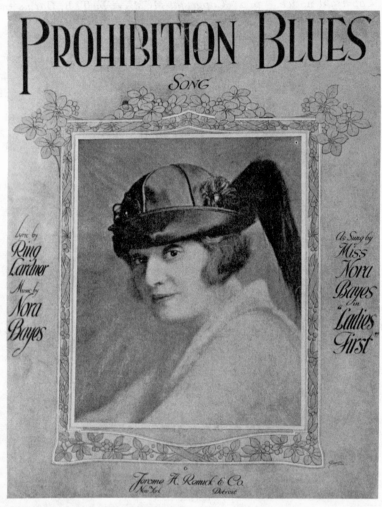

B 5: front cover; 13 11/16" x 10⅝"

[1] 2–5 [6]

[1]³ (single leaf inserted in folio)

Copyright notice: p. 2: 'Copyright MCMXIX by JEROME H. REMICK & CO., Detroit & New York | Copyright, Canada, MCMXIX by Jerome H. Remick & Co. | Propiedad para la Republica Mexicana de Jerome H. Remick & Co., Detroit y New York. Depositada conforme a la ley | 758–4 *Performing Rights Reserved*'.

Contents: p. 1: cover; pp. 2–5: music and lyrics; p. 6: ad. Noted with variant ads on p. 6 (outside rear cover): "I'm Forever Blowing Bubbles" (RPB) or "Operatic And High Class Songs" (MJB).

Paper: Coated wove.

Publication: Number of copies, price, and date of publication unknown. Copyright 30 April 1919. Copyright #E450855.

Note 1: Lardner wrote both the music and lyrics; but the music was credited to Nora Bayes, as was the custom at that time.

Note 2: The variant ads on the outside rear cover possibly indicate separate printings.

Locations: MJB, RPB.

B 6 MONTANA MOON
1929

B 6: front cover; 11⅞″ x 9⅙″

[A] [1–2] 3–5 [6–7]

[1]^4

Copyright notice: p. 2: 'Copyright MCMXXIX by Harms Inc.,
New York | 8401–4   Copyrighted in South America by Harry
Kosarin, Rio de Janeiro | Propiedad Asegurada Para Republica
Argentina Por J. Feliu e Hijos, Buenos Aires | *International
Copyright Secured   Made in U.S.A.   All Rights Reserved*'.

Contents: p. A: cover; p. 1: ads for songs; pp. 2–5: music and
lyrics; p. 6: ads for songs; p. 7: ad for "Sleepy Valley." Plate
number on pp. 2–5: '8401–4'.

Paper: Coated wove.

Publication: Number of copies, price, and date of publication
unknown. Copyright 2 October 1929. Copyright #E pub. 9836.

Location: RPB.

B 7 JUNE MOON
1929

B 7: front cover; 12″ x 9⅛″

[A] [1–2] 3–5 [6–7]

[1]⁴

Copyright notice: p. 2: 'Copyright MCMXXIX by HARMS Inc.,
New York | 8400–4   Copyrighted in South America by Harry
Kosarin, Rio de Janeiro | Propiedad Asegurada Para Republica
Argentina Por J. Feliu e Hijos, Buenos Aires | *International
Copyright Secured   Made in U.S.A.   All Rights Reserved*'.

Contents: p. A: cover; p. 1: ads for songs; pp. 2–5: music and
lyrics; p. 6: ads for songs; p. 7: ad for "Sleepy Valley."

Paper: Coated wove.

Publication: Number of copies, price, and date of publication
unknown. Copyright 2 October 1929. Copyright #E pub. 9835.

Locations: MJB, RPB.

    B 8 BE GOOD TO ME
     1930

Copyright notice: 'Copyright MCMXXX by Vincent Youmans
Inc., Music Publisher, 67 W. 44th St., N.Y.C. | International
Copyright Secured   All Rights Reserved | Copyrighted in South
America for Vincent Youmans Inc. by Harry Kosarin Rio de
Janeiro | Propiedad Asegurada Para Vincent Youmans Inc. en
Republica Argentina por Harry Kosarin Buenos Aires | Propiedad
Asegurada Para Vincent Youmans Inc. en Republica Uruguay
por Harry Kosarin Montevideo'.

Publication: Number of copies, price, and date of publication
unknown. Copyright 20 February 1931. Copyright #E pub. 22415.

Note: Lyrics by Lardner; music by Vincent Youmans. Written
for the show *Smiles* (1930).

Location: RWL Jr (entry based on two pages of sheet music
only). No complete copy located.

B 9 IF I WERE YOU, LOVE
    (I'D JUMP RIGHT IN THE LAKE)
    1930

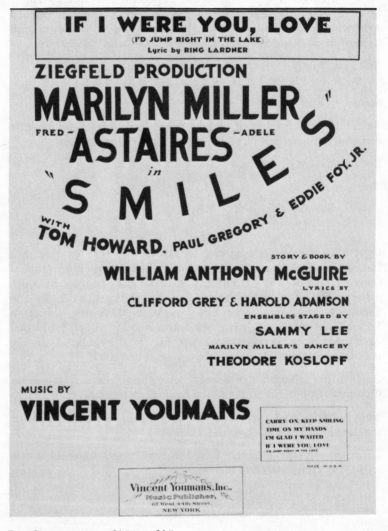

B 9: front cover; 12 ⅜" x 10¼"

[1–2] 3–5 [6]

[1]³ (single leaf inserted in folio)

Copyright notice: p. 3: 'Copyright MCMXXX by Vincent Youmans, Inc., Music Publisher, 67 W. 44th St., N. Y. C. | International Copyright Secured   All Rights Reserved | Copyrighted in South America for Vincent Youmans, Inc. by Harry Kosarin, Rio de Janeiro | Propiedad Asegurada Para Vincent Youmans, Inc. en Republica Argentina por Harry Kosarin, Buenos Aires | Propiedad Asegurada Para Vincent Youmans, Inc. en Republica Uruguay por Harry Kosarin, Montevideo'.

Contents: p. 1: cover; p. 2: ad for "Love Is Like a Song"; pp. 3–5: music and lyrics; p. 6: ad for "Say 'Oui'-Cherie."

Paper: Coated wove.

Publication: Number of copies, price, and date of publication unknown. Copyright 31 December 1930. Copyright #E pub. 22416.

Note: Written for the show *Smiles* (1930).

Location: MJB.

*   *   *

Note 1: According to E 2571, Lardner wrote words and music for "Home, Sweet Home" sung by Bert Williams in the 1917 *Ziegfeld Follies*. Elder (p. 246) provides a subtitle "(That's Where the Real War Is)" and indicates that the song was later recorded. No copyright record or other evidence of publication has been found. In "Insomnia," a stream-of-consciousness sketch written in the first person and seemingly autobiographical, Lardner wrote: "Bert [Williams] sang a song of mine once and I had it published; it was put on phonograph records, too, and I think the total royalties from sheet music and records amounted to $47.50." This song has not been identified.

Note 2: The Lardner papers at The Newberry Library include a contract between Lardner and Harms & Day & Hunter, Music Publishers, dated 18 April 1910, for three songs: "My Old Kentucky Home—Good Night," "I Wonder What My Stomach Thinks of Me," and "Swanie Swanson." No copyright record or other evidence of publication has been found for these songs.

Note 3: The music and lyrics for "Hello Tokio!" and "Give Our Child a Name" are included in the acting version of *June Moon*. See A 24.2.

Note 4:   Lardner contributed three songs to Aubrey Stauffer's 1913 Chicago production *In Allah's Garden:* "Beside the Bonnie Brier Bush," "Lydia Pynkham," "Oh You Fatima Girl." No copies have been located.

Note 5:   Lardner wrote the lyrics for the 1913 version of Nat Mann's "That Old Quartet." No copy has been located.

C. First-Appearance Contributions to Books and Pamphlets

Titles in which material by Lardner appears for the first time in a book or pamphlet, arranged chronologically. Previously unpublished items are so stipulated. Only the first printings for these volumes are described, but English editions are noted. Locations are provided for scarce items only. At the end of Section C there is a CC supplemental list of borderline items.

C 1 FUNNY STORIES
1915

[within single-rule frame] FUNNY STORIES | ABOUT THE | FORD | [drawing of jester] | VOL. II | The Presto Publishing Co. | Hamilton, Ohio

1915.

"Phil and His 4D," pp. 30–35. Previously unpublished.

Locations: ICN, MJB.

C 2 FUNABOUT FORDS
1917

Funabout | Fords | 1917 MODEL | [device] | CHICAGO | THE HOWELL COMPANY | 1917

On copyright page: 'PUBLISHED APRIL, 1917'.

Two Bill/Steve letters, pp. 19–27, from "In the Wake of the News." See E 1951, E 1958.

Location: CLU.

Note: Not to be confused with J. J. White's *Funabout Fords* (Chicago: Howell, 1915), which includes no Lardner material.

C 3 ILLIO
1917

The · 1917 · ILLIO | [tomahawk] | [set into lower right corner of photograph of university building, against peace pipe] PUBLISHED BY | THE JUNIOR | CLASS OF THE | UNIVERSITY | [triangle] OF ILLINOIS [triangle]

"Home-Coming," pp. 431–433. Previously unpublished.

C 4 ST. FRANCIS LOBBYIST
1920

The St. Francis Lobbyist | Edition de Luxe | Published at the
Hotel St. Francis during the National Democratic Convention, |
San Francisco, June 23 to July 6, 1920. | THOS. J. COLEMAN,
Publisher.

A souvenir book made by binding together the twelve issues of
The St. Francis Lobbyist with additional material. "A Tough Luck
Tale of the Turf Told by Ring Lardner," p. 1, and "An Irish Love
Lyric," p. 3—both in issue #7. Possibly also unsigned contribu-
tions. Previously unpublished. See D 69, D 70.

Location: MJB (bound volume and individual issues).

C 5 AMERICAN LANGUAGE
1921

THE | AMERICAN LANGUAGE | [following two lines in red]
An Inquiry into the Development | of English in the United
States | By | H. L. MENCKEN | SECOND EDITION | REVISED AND
ENLARGED | [red Borzoi seal] | NEW YORK | ALFRED · A · KNOPF
| MCMXXI

On copyright page: 'Revised Edition Published December, 1921'.

Cites Lardner as source, p. 276, n. 49; quotes Lardner about
baseball players' use of "everything/anything" and "somethin/
nothin," p. 318, n. 108; short play, "Baseball-American," pp. 392–
393; short play, "Ham-American," pp. 394–395. All previously
unpublished.

Note: The fourth edition of 1938 adds a note on p. 425 in which
Mencken reports a conversation with Lardner.

C 6 CIVILIZATION IN THE UNITED STATES
1922

CIVILIZATION IN THE | UNITED STATES | *AN INQUIRY BY
THIRTY AMERICANS* | EDITED BY HAROLD E. STEARNS |
[device] | NEW YORK | HARCOURT, BRACE AND COMPANY

1922.

"Sport and Play," pp. 457–461. Previously unpublished.

C 7 OUR AMERICAN HUMORISTS
1922

[within double-rules frame] OUR AMERICAN | HUMORISTS |.
BY | THOMAS L. MASSON | AUTHOR OF "HUMOROUS
MASTERPIECES," "BEST STORIES IN THE | WORLD," "DOGS
FROM LIFE," ETC. | [device] | NEW YORK | MOFFAT, YARD
AND COMPANY | 1922

"A Small Vocabulary May Have a Big Kick," pp. 189–192. See
E 3237. "Inside Facts of the Writing Game," pp. 194–196. See
E 3203. Untitled autobiographical note, pp. 206–208.

C 8 TOM MASSON'S ANNUAL
1923

[double-rules black frame within single-rule red frame] Tom
Masson's Annual | for 1923 | *Edited by* | Thomas L. Masson | [red
seal in blindstamped frame] | Garden City New York | Doubleday,
Page & Company | 1923

On copyright page: 'First Edition'.

"How to 'Stork' Big Game," pp. 43–46. See E 3317.

C 9 BEST SHORT STORIES OF 1922
1923

THE | BEST SHORT STORIES | OF 1922 | AND THE |
YEARBOOK OF THE AMERICAN | SHORT STORY | EDITED BY
| EDWARD J. O'BRIEN | [eight lines listing previous volumes in
the series] | [publisher's seal] | BOSTON | SMALL, MAYNARD &
COMPANY | PUBLISHERS

1923.

"The Golden Honeymoon," pp. 242–259. See A 16, D 82.

Toronto: Goodchild, [1923].

C 10 SEVEN LIVELY ARTS

C 10.1
The Seven Lively Arts (1924)

THE SEVEN | LIVELY ARTS | By | *Gilbert Seldes* | [ten italic
lines] | WALTER PATER | [device] | HARPER & BROTHERS
PUBLISHERS | NEW YORK AND LONDON MCMXXIV

On copyright page: 'First Edition'.

Excerpt from "A World's Serious," pp. 114–117. See A 26, E 3624.
Excerpt from "Highbrows Have Nothing on Lardner," pp. 125–
126. See A 26 ("A Literary Diary") and E 3294.

C 10.2
The 7 Lively Arts. New York: Sagamore Press, [1957].

New edition; adds Lardner letter to Seldes, pp. 128–129.

C 11 TOM MASSON'S ANNUAL
1924

[double-rules black frame within single-rule red frame] Tom
Masson's Annual | for 1924 | *Edited by* | Thomas L. Masson | [red
seal in blindstamped frame] | Garden City New York | Doubleday,
Page & Company | 1924

"Snappy Chatter with President," pp. 293–295. See E 3381. "Ring
Investigates Washington Scandal Rumor," pp. 296–299. See
E 3380.

C 12 BARBER SHOP BALLADS
1925

[red] Barber Shop | Ballads | [the following four lines in black
between red, black, and white barber poles] A Book of Close
Harmony | Edited by Sigmund Spaeth | Illustrated by Ellison
Hoover | Foreword by Ring Lardner | [drawing of quartet] | [red]
New York · Simon & Schuster · 1925

On copyright page: 'PUBLISHED IN JULY, 1925.'

"An Introduction by Ring Lardner," pp. 7–10. Previously unpublished.

C 13 BEST SHORT STORIES OF 1925
1926

THE | BEST SHORT STORIES | OF 1925 | AND THE | YEARBOOK OF THE AMERICAN | SHORT STORY | EDITED BY | EDWARD J. O'BRIEN | [seal] | BOSTON | SMALL, MAYNARD & COMPANY | PUBLISHERS

1926.

"Haircut," pp. 174–185. See A 19, D 110.

C 14 LAUGHS
1926

[within single-rule red and double-rules black frames] LAUGHS | *A sovereign remedy for boredom | collected from the four | corners of the earth* | Edited by Thomas L. Masson | [red seal on blind-stamped panel] | Garden City New York | Doubleday, Page & Company | 1926

On copyright page: 'FIRST EDITION'.

"The Art of Keeping Conversation Alive," pp. 53–56. See E 3440.

C 15 BEST SHORT STORIES OF 1926
1926

THE | BEST SHORT STORIES | OF 1926 | AND THE | YEARBOOK OF THE AMERICAN | SHORT STORY | EDITED BY | EDWARD J. O'BRIEN | [triangular seal] | DODD, MEAD AND COMPANY | NEW YORK : : : : 1926

"Travelogue," pp. 185–196. See A 21, D 123.

Also published as *The Best Short Stories of 1926 II: American.* London: Cape, [1926].

C 16 CHARLES SCRIBNER'S SONS PRESENT
1926

CHARLES SCRIBNER'S SONS | PRESENT | [rule] | RING W. LARDNER | [double rules] | IN | THE GOLDEN HONEYMOON | [rule] | AND | HAIRCUT | [double rules] | AMERICAN

BOOKSELLERS | ASSOCIATION | [rule] | ST. LOUIS MAY 13, 1926 | [rule]

Published 13 May 1926.

"Gentlemen, Mr. Lardner!" Previously unpublished.

Note: "The Golden Honeymoon" is reprinted from *How to Write Short Stories;* "Haircut," from *The Love Nest.*

Locations: LC (deposit-stamp MAY 18 '26), MJB.

C 17 MOTLEY MEASURES
1927

Motley Measures | by | Bert Leston Taylor | *With a Foreword by* | *Ring Lardner* | New York [Borzoi device] 1927 | Alfred · A · Knopf

"Foreword," pp. vii–ix. Previously unpublished.

C 18 DUTCH TREAT YEAR BOOK
1927

[within tan frame with four black rules] Year Book | Dutch Treat | Club | [illustration of printer on tan background, signed 'Albert Levering'] | 1927 | *Privately Printed*

New York, 1927.

"Dinner & Bridge," pp. 40–49. Previously unpublished. See A 26, D 131.

Location: MJB.

C 19 BUT——IS IT ART
1927

[red rule] | [black] BUT——IS IT ART | [thick red rule] | [black] PERCY HAMMOND | [red rule] | [black anchor] | [red rule] | [black] GARDEN CITY NEW YORK | DOUBLEDAY, PAGE & COMPANY | [red rule] | [black] 1927

On copyright page: 'FIRST EDITION'.

Letter, pp. 137–138. Previously unpublished.

C 20 MY FAVORITE STORY
1928

My | Favorite Story | [decorated rule] | *By* | Fannie Hurst | Sir Philip Gibbs | Ring W. Lardner | W. Somerset Maugham | Montague Glass | Robert Hichens | [rule] | *With an Introduction* | *by* | Ray Long | *Editor of Cosmopolitan* | [double rule] | 1928 | *NEW YORK*

"Foreword" to "I Can't Breathe," p. 103. Previously unpublished.

Note: This book was probably not for sale, but was distributed as a premium to *Hearst's International-Cosmopolitan* subscribers.

C 21 LITERARY TREASURES OF 1928
1928

[within single-rule frame] Literary | Treasures | *of* | 1928 | *Published by* | Hearst's International-Cosmopolitan | Magazine | *for private distribution only*

"Anniversary," pp. 11–26. See A 21, D 135.

Note: "Old Folks' Christmas" was included in *Literary Treasures of 1929,* but the story was almost certainly collected first in *Round Up* (published 5 April 1929). See A 21.

C 22 STAGE-STRUCK
1930

[within double-rules and single-rule frames] STAGE-STRUCK | JOHN GOLDEN | BY | JOHN GOLDEN | AND | VIOLA BROTHERS SHORE | [seal] | SAMUEL FRENCH | Thos. R. Edwards Managing Director | NEW YORK LOS ANGELES | SAMUEL FRENCH Ltd. LONDON | 1930

Five-line testimonial by Lardner, "Ring Lardner Says," p. xiii. Previously unpublished.

C 23 NOT FOR CHILDREN
1930

NOT | FOR | CHILDREN | Pictures and Verse by | ROLAND YOUNG | [drawing] | WITH AN INTRODUCTION BY RING

LARDNER | DOUBLEDAY, DORAN & COMPANY, INC. |
GARDEN CITY 1930 NEW YORK

On copyright page: 'FIRST EDITION'.

"Introduction": ' "Perhaps it's 'Not for Children,' but it made me
a Young fan." ' Lardner is also quoted on front of dust jacket:
' "CERTAINLY NOT" '. Previously unpublished.

Location: MJB.

C 24 THE TIMID SOUL
1931

The | TIMID SOUL | A pictorial account of the life and times |
of CASPAR MILQUETOAST | [drawing of Milquetoast] | by H.
T. WEBSTER | with an introduction by | RING LARDNER |
[device] | SIMON and SCHUSTER | NEW YORK · 1931

"Introduction." Previously unpublished.

C 25 NEW YORKER SCRAPBOOK
1931

THE NEW YORKER | SCRAPBOOK | [DD ship seal] | DOUBLE-
DAY, DORAN & COMPANY, INC. | GARDEN CITY, NEW
YORK, 1931

On copyright page: 'FIRST EDITION'.

"Sit Still," pp. 349–353. See D 183.

C 26 DUTCH TREAT YEAR BOOK
1932

[green] 1932 | [black-and-white drawing signed 'J.M.F.'] | [green]
CHASES | DIRT | (sic) | OLD DUTCH TREAT | CLEANSER |
[black rule] | [green] THE BOOK | [black] with | [green] NOBODY
NUDE | [black] That is, *nakedly* nude | [rule] | *Printed so
privately, it's a shame* | 7

New York, 1932.

"Too bad we burned this," p. 20. Previously unpublished.

Location: MJB.

C 27 ANDOVER/EXETER
1932

ANDOVER | EXETER | [illustration of two baseball players] | 50¢ | W. | JUNE 11th, 1932

Cover title.

"Baseball Reminiscences of Andover by One Who Has Never Been There," p. 9. Previously unpublished verse.

Locations: RL, RWL Jr.

C 28 BLACKOUTS
1932

[within single-rule frame] [two rules] BLACKOUTS | FOURTEEN REVUE SKETCHES | *Edited by* | *MARJORIE RICE LEVIS* | [device] | *SAMUEL FRENCH* | *New York Los Angeles* | *SAMUEL FRENCH LTD. London* | *1932* | [two rules]

"The Tridget of Greva," pp. 1–9. Previously unpublished. See AA 8.

C 29 BOTTOMS UP
1933

[line of music] | For he's a jol-ly good fel-low | BOTTOMS UP! | [nine-line description of contents] | *Edited by* CLIFFORD LEACH | *Price* 35 *Cents* | [tapered rule] | PUBLISHED BY | PAULL-PIONEER MUSIC CORPORATION | 119 Fifth Avenue, New York City | [five-line copyright notice]

1933.

" '3.2 Blues' or 'Fore (Per Cent by Volume) boding,' " p. [3]. Three-stanza poem.

Location: LC.

Note: Revised printing seen with price raised to 75¢ and address of publisher changed to 1657 Broadway. Lardner's poem is re-titled "Salute to 'Bottoms Up!' " and third stanza is omitted. Location: MJB.

C 30 SIXTH NEW YORKER ALBUM
1933

THE | SIXTH | NEW YORKER | ALBUM | [green drawing of
Eustace Tilley] | WITH A FOREWORD | BY | RING LARDNER |
MCMXXXIII | HARPER & BROTHERS | NEW YORK, N.Y.

"Foreword." Previously unpublished.

C 31 NOTHING CAN REPLACE MUSIC
1933

[thick vertical rule running length of page] | Nothing Can |
Replace Music | *Newspaper Editorials and Comments* | *On Music
and the Radio* | [ASCAP seal] | "*. . . There being no property more
peculiarly a* | *man's own than that which is produced* | *by the
labour of his mind.*"

1933.

"Over The Waves" and "Ricordi to the Rescue," pp. 29–31. See
AA 8, D 209, D 239.

C 32 AMERICAN SPECTATOR YEAR BOOK
1934

The | AMERICAN SPECTATOR | YEAR BOOK | *Edited by* |
George Jean Nathan Sherwood Anderson | Ernest Boyd
James Branch Cabell |Theodore Dreiser Eugene O'Neill |
[Pegasus seal] | FREDERICK A. STOKES COMPANY | NEW
YORK MCXXXIV

"The Lor and the Profits," pp. 75–80. See D 223.

C 33 NEW YORKER BOOK OF VERSE
1935

The NEW YORKER | BOOK OF VERSE | [swash initial capitals]
An Anthology | OF POEMS FIRST PUBLISHED | IN THE NEW

YORKER | 1925–1935 | HARCOURT, BRACE AND COMPANY | NEW YORK

1935.

On copyright page: 'first edition'.

"The Constant Jay," p. 108. See D 111.

C 34   DIARY OF OUR OWN SAMUEL PEPYS
1935

[within a single-rule frame] THE DIARY | OF OUR OWN | SAMUEL PEPYS | 1911–1925 [1926–1934] | [double rules] | [following line within decorative frame] F. P. A. | (FRANKLIN P. ADAMS) | [rule] | *Simon and Schuster* | *New York • 1935*

Two volumes.

Lardner conversation, I, p. 486; letter to F.P.A., II, p. 1175. See E 4676.

C 35   BEDSIDE ESQUIRE
1940

THE BEDSIDE | *ESQUIRE* | *Edited by* | ARNOLD GINGRICH | Editor of *Esquire* | TUDOR PUBLISHING COMPANY | *New York*

1940.

"Greek Tragedy," pp. 221–231. See D 246.

C 36   SPORTS EXTRA
1944

Sports Extra | CLASSICS OF SPORTS REPORTING | *Edited by* STANLEY FRANK | [device] | NEW YORK | A. S. BARNES & COMPANY

1944.

"You Know Him, Pal," pp. 125–128. Bell Syndicate coverage of 1927 World Series reprinted from *The New York World,* 7 October 1927. See E 3682 ("Miss Thoke Fears . . .").

C 37 KICK-OFF!
       1948

KICK-OFF! | [football player] | *Edited by* | ED FITZGERALD |
[Bantam rooster] | BANTAM BOOKS | NEW YORK

1948.

"Eckie," pp. 48–58. See D 222.

Location: MJB.

C 38 TREASURY OF GOLF HUMOR
       1949

A TREASURY OF | GOLF HUMOR | EDITED BY DAVE
STANLEY | *ILLUSTRATED BY COBBLEDICK* | [cartoon of
golfer] | LANTERN PRESS · *PUBLISHERS* · NEW YORK

1949.

"Tee Time," pp. 132–137. See D 167.

Note: Dave Stanley was a pseudonym for David Dachs.

C 39 GREATEST SPORT STORIES
       1953

THE | GREATEST | SPORT | STORIES | FROM THE | [gothic]
Chicago | Tribune | [roman] EDITED BY ARCH WARD | A. S.
BARNES AND COMPANY | NEW YORK

1953.

"In the Wake of the News" (15 August 1914), pp. 131–133; "In
the Wake of the News" (18 April 1915), pp. 141–143; "In the
Wake of the News" (4 May 1917), pp. 145–146. See E 1582,
E 1806, E 2496.

C 40 COLLIER'S GREATEST SPORT STORIES
       1955

Collier's | Greatest | SPORTS | Stories | *Edited by* | TOM MEANY
| A. S. BARNES AND COMPANY · NEW YORK

1955.

John Wheeler, "Ring Lardner," pp. 99–104; "Introduction" by
Lardner and extensively quoted. Lardner, "Pluck and Luck," pp.
104–108. See D 138, D 158.

C 41 RING LARDNER
1956

Ring | Lardner | A BIOGRAPHY BY | DONALD ELDER | [rule] |
DOUBLEDAY & COMPANY, INC. | *Garden City, New York, 1956*

On copyright page: 'First Edition'.

Previously unpublished letters, as well as first book publication
of journalism and other material, throughout.

C 42 WAKE UP THE ECHOES
1956

WAKE UP THE ECHOES | FROM THE SPORTS PAGES OF THE
| NEW YORK HERALD TRIBUNE | Edited by Bob Cooke | Sports
Editor of the New York Herald Tribune | PREFACE BY BOB
CONSIDINE | [rule] | HANOVER HOUSE · GARDEN CITY, N.Y.

1956.

On copyright page: 'First Edition'.

"Grantland Rice Lets Ring Lardner Tell Him About Baseball," p.
234. See E 4616.

C 43 HISTORY OF BASEBALL
1959

[two-page title] ALLISON DANZIG | and | JOE REICHLER | *The
History of* BASEBALL | *Its Great Players, Teams* | *and Managers* |
PRENTICE-HALL, INC. | *Englewood Cliffs, N.J.*

1959.

Poem on Christy Mathewson, p. 186. See E 2223. Comment on
Walter Johnson, p. 189 (unlocated).

C 44 GOOD HOUSEKEEPING TREASURY
1960

[two-page title] [montage of magazine covers, flowers, and writing material on wood-grain desk top; right-hand page:] THE | Good Housekeeping | TREASURY | SELECTED FROM THE COMPLETE FILES | BY DONALD ELDER AND | THE EDITORS OF GOOD HOUSEKEEPING | SIMON AND SCHUSTER 1960

On copyright page: 'FIRST PRINTING'.

"Mamma," pp. 215–218. See D 184.

C 45 I'VE GOT NEWS FOR YOU
1961

I'VE GOT NEWS | FOR YOU | by John Wheeler | E. P. Dutton & Co., Inc. | New York 1961

On copyright page: 'FIRST EDITION'.

"Ring Lardner," pp. 117–138. Quotes conversation, letters, verse, and speech, pp. 82, 281–282. See D 138.

C 46 SCOTT FITZGERALD
1962

SCOTT | FITZGERALD | [line of five type decorations] | *by* ANDREW TURNBULL | CHARLES SCRIBNER'S SONS | *New York*

1962.

On copyright page: 'A.1.61 [V]'.

"To Zelda," p. 143. Seven stanzas of poem. Two stanzas previously published in Arthur Mizener, *The Far Side of Paradise* (Boston: Houghton Mifflin, 1951), pp. 161–162. See C 56 ("To Z.S.F.").

C 47 SHUT UP
1962

A Ring Lardner Selection | edited by Babette Rosmond | and

Henry Morgan | SHUT UP, HE | EXPLAINED | CHARLES
SCRIBNER'S SONS | New York

1962.

On copyright page: 'A-3.62 [V]'.

First book appearances: "Here's Ring Lardner's Autobiography,"
"The Perfect Woman," "Over the Waves," "Heavy Da-Dee Dough
Boys," "Life of the Boswells," " 'Pu-leeze! Mister Hemingway,' "
"The Crucial Game," "Herb and Frank Panic 'Em," "Announcer's
Prep School," "Some Short Selling," "The Old Man Shows His Air
Mail," "Hail to the Chief." See AA 8, E 4746, D 124, D 209, D 210,
D 219, D 220, D 221, D 225, D 227, D 228, D 233, D 235.

C 48 DEADLINES AND MONKEYSHINES
1962

[two-page title] Deadlines & Monkeyshines | [rule] | [all the
following against background of newspaper clippings] The
Fabled World of | Chicago Journalism | John J. | McPhaul |
PRENTICE-HALL, INC. | Englewood Cliffs, N.J.

1962.

Quotes six-line Lardner verse, p. 168. Previous publication
unlocated.

C 49 F. SCOTT FITZGERALD AND
HIS CONTEMPORARIES
1963

F. SCOTT | FITZGERALD *and* | *his contemporaries* | WILLIAM
GOLDHURST | THE WORLD PUBLISHING COMPANY [seal] |
Cleveland and New York

1963.

On copyright page: 'First Edition'.

Letters to Fitzgerald (1925, May 1926, and 27 February 1930),
pp. 113–114. Previously unpublished.

C 50 STAGESTRUCK
1965

STAGESTRUCK: | *The Romance of* | *Alfred Lunt and Lynn Fontanne* | MAURICE ZOLOTOW | [seal] | HARCOURT, BRACE & WORLD, INC. NEW YORK

1965.

On copyright page: 'First edition'.

Untitled verse, pp. 161–163. See E 4654.

London: Heinemann, 1965.

C 51 TIME OF LAUGHTER
1967

THE | TIME | OF | LAUGHTER | *by Corey Ford* | *with a Foreword by* FRANK SULLIVAN | *Little, Brown and Company* · Boston · *Toronto*

1967.

On copyright page: 'FIRST EDITION'.

Opening of "Bugs Baer's Comeback," p. 11. See D 80.

C 52 ILLINOIS PROSE WRITERS
1968

[flowers] | ILLINOIS PROSE | WRITERS A SELECTION | *Edited by* Howard W. Webb, Jr. | Southern Illinois University Press *Carbondale and Edwardsville* | Feffer & Simons, Inc. *London and Amsterdam*

1968.

"Observations on a City Series," pp. 124–127. See E 3098.

C 53 ZELDA
1970

ZELDA | A BIOGRAPHY | [rule] | *by Nancy Milford* | HARPER & ROW, PUBLISHERS | NEW YORK, EVANSTON, and LONDON

1970.

On copyright page: 'FIRST EDITION'.

Excerpt from poem, "A Christmas Wish—and What Came of It,"
p. 96. Previously unpublished. See C 56.

C 54 BASEBALL
1971

BASEBALL | THE GOLDEN AGE · HAROLD SEYMOUR, Ph.D. |
[seal] | NEW YORK · OXFORD UNIVERSITY PRESS · 1971

Quotes Lardner, p. 426. See E 3238.

C 55 BEST IN THE WORLD
1973

THE BEST IN | [gothic] THE WORLD | [following five lines in
gray roman] A Selection of News | and Feature Stories, |
Editorials, Humor, | Poems, and Reviews | from 1921 to 1928 |
[gray rule] | Edited, | with Introductions, by | John K. Hutchens
and George Oppenheimer | THE VIKING PRESS NEW YORK

1973.

"Watch Little Neck," pp. 177–178. See E 3437 ("Ring Reveals
Interview . . ."). "Weather Report," pp. 179–180. See E 3445
("Ring Confused with Thunder Shower . . .").

C 56 THE ROMANTIC EGOISTS
1974

[first three lines in display type] THE | ROMANTIC | EGOISTS |
EDITED BY | MATTHEW J. BRUCCOLI | SCOTTIE
FITZGERALD SMITH | *AND* | JOAN P. KERR | *ART EDITOR* |
MARGARETA F. LYONS | [device] | *CHARLES SCRIBNER'S
SONS* [slash] *NEW YORK*
1974.

Copyright page: '1 3 5 7 . . . 19 MD/C 20 18 16 . . . 2'.

Facsimiles of music manuscript signed by Lardner, p. 103; "A
Christmas Wish—And What Came of It," p. 104; "To Z.S.F."
(eight stanzas), p. 115. See C 53, C 46.

Also limited issue of 500 boxed, numbered copies—simultaneously published with trade issue.

C 57 BABE RUTH
1974

KEN SOBOL | [two gray baseball bats] | BABE RUTH | & | The American Dream | [two gray baseball bats] | Introduction by Dick Schaap | Random House [device] New York

1974.

On copyright page: 'First Edition'.

Excerpts on p. 88 from E 1180 and E 1182. Excerpt on p. 118 from D 187.

C 58 SOME CHAMPIONS
Forthcoming

Some Champions, ed. Matthew J. Bruccoli and Richard Layman. New York: Scribners, 1976.

Twenty-six previously uncollected articles and stories: "Who's Who," "What I Ought to Have Learnt in High School," "What I Don't Know About Horses," "Meet Mr. Howley," "Me, Boy Scout," "Caught in the Draft," "Heap Big Chief," "Chicago's Beau Monde," "Eckie," "Alias James Clarkson," "Some Champions," "Oddities of Bleacher 'Bugs'," "The Cost of Baseball," "Jersey City Gendarmerie, Je T'Aime," "X-Ray," "Call for Mr. Keefe," "Insomnia," "Along Came Ruth," "Battle of the Century," "Mamma," "Second-Act Curtain," "Cured!," "Bob's Birthday," "Poodle," "Widow," "Br'er Rabbit Ball."

All first book appearances, except "Mamma." See C 44.

CC. Supplement

Borderline Items

CC 1 THIS TO THAT
1927

THIS TO THAT | *The Word-Change* | *Book* | By | SHELBY LITTLE | With an Introduction by | RICHARD HENRY LITTLE | [device] | NEW YORK | MINTON, BALCH & COMPANY | 1927

Lardner changes *sober* to *tight*, #150. Previously unpublished.

Location: MJB.

CC 2 TOM MASSON'S BOOK OF WIT & HUMOR
1927

[within single-rule frame] Tom Masson's | Book of | Wit & Humor | [seal] | *by Thomas L. Masson* | J. H. SEARS & COMPANY, Inc. | *Publishers New York*

1927.

Simile attributed to Lardner, p. 207: "Heavy as a grand opera chorus girl."

CC 3 FAVORITE JOKES
1930

[all the following within frame of type devices] FAVORITE JOKES ... | of FAMOUS PEOPLE | WITH AN INTRODUCTION TO EACH CELEBRITY | AS TOLD TO | AND | CONSPICUOUSLY | ILLUSTRATED | *By* | FRANK ERNEST NICHOLSON | FAMOUS JOURNALIST | AND EXPLORER | [seal] | Copyright, 1930 | By | POPULAR BOOK CORP. | *Publishers* | Printed in the United States of America | POPULAR BOOK CORPORATION | 96–98 PARK PLACE - - - - - - - NEW YORK, N. Y. | [outside frame] 1

159

Attributes telegram, joke, and comment to Lardner, pp. 24–25.

Location: MJB.

Note: Different text of telegram printed in *Barbed Wires,* ed. Joyce Denebrink (New York: Simon & Schuster, 1965).

CC 4 VICIOUS CIRCLE
1951

Margaret Case Harriman | [leaf] | The Vicious Circle | THE STORY | OF THE ALGONQUIN ROUND TABLE | *Illustrated by* Al Hirschfield | RINEHART & Co., INC. NEW YORK : TORONTO

1951.

Lardner quoted in anecdotes, pp. 239–241.

CC 5 TUMULT AND SHOUTING
1954

The Tumult | and the Shouting | *My Life in Sport* | by Grantland Rice | A. S. BARNES & COMPANY, NEW YORK

1954.

Reports Lardner conversation, pp. 145, 150, 176, 194–195, 326, 327.

CC 6 AMERICAN TREASURY
1955

[first three lines within single-rule frame decorated with stars] *The* | *American* | *Treasury* | 1455–1955 | SELECTED, ARRANGED, AND EDITED BY | CLIFTON FADIMAN | ASSISTED BY CHARLES VAN DOREN | [torch] | [rule] | *Harper & Brothers, Publishers* | *New York*

1955.

On copyright page: 'FIRST EDITION'.

Comments by Lardner, pp. 252, 270, 949. Previous publications unlocated.

CC 7 BORN IN A BOOKSHOP
1965

[angel head and wings] | [following four lines within frame]
*Born | in a | Bookshop | Chapters from the Chicago Renascence |
by Vincent Starrett* | UNIVERSITY OF OKLAHOMA PRESS:
NORMAN

1965.

On copyright page: 'First edition'.

Reports Lardner conversation, pp. 256–258.

CC 8 RING LARDNER AND PORTRAIT OF FOLLY
1972

TWENTIETH-CENTURY AMERICAN WRITERS | RING
LARDNER | AND | THE PORTRAIT | OF FOLLY | By Maxwell
Geismar | THOMAS Y. CROWELL | *New York*

1972.

On copyright page: First printing indicated by '1 . . . 10'.

Excerpt from possible Lardner interview, pp. 100–101. See H 3.

CC 9 GEORGE S. KAUFMAN
1972

[two-page title] [left-hand page:] [photograph of Kaufman] |
GEORGE S. KAUFMAN | [rule] | NEW YORK *Atheneum* | 1972 |
[photograph of Kaufman] | [right-hand page:] [photograph of
Kaufman] *An Intimate Portrait* | [rule] | by Howard Teichmann |
[photograph of Kaufman]

On copyright page: 'FIRST EDITION'.

Reports Lardner conversation, p. 70.

D. Appearances in Magazines

In Section D cross-references to Lardner's books are given by acronyms rather than by entry numbers:

YKMA	*You Know Me Al* (A 4)
GT	*Gullible's Travels, Etc.* (A 5)
MFW	*My Four Weeks in France* (A 6)
TER	*Treat 'Em Rough* (A 7)
RD	*The Real Dope* (A 8)
OYOH	*Own Your Own Home* (A 9)
YI	*The Young Immigrunts* (A 11)
SB35	*Symptoms of Being 35* (A 13)
BT	*The Big Town* (A 14)
SIWO	*Say It with Oil* (A 15)
HTWSS	*How to Write Short Stories* (A 16)
WOI	*What of It?* (A 17)
LN	*The Love Nest and Other Stories* (A 19)
RU	*Round Up* (A 21)
LWS	*Lose with a Smile* (A 25)
F&L	*First and Last* (A 26)

D 1
"The Cost of Baseball," *Collier's*, 48 (2 March 1912), 28, 30.
Article.

D 2
"A Busher's Letters Home," *The Saturday Evening Post*, 186 (7 March 1914), 6–8, 57–58.
Story. *YKMA*.

D 3
"My Roomy," *The Saturday Evening Post*, 186 (9 May 1914), 17–19, 61–62, 65.
Story. *HTWSS, RU*.

D 4
"The Busher Comes Back," *The Saturday Evening Post*, 186 (23 May 1914), 18–20, 61–62.
Story. *YKMA*.

D 5
"The Busher's Honeymoon," *The Saturday Evening Post*, 187 (11 July 1914), 12–14, 33–34.
Story. *YKMA*.

D 6
"Sick 'Em," *The Saturday Evening Post*, 187 (25 July 1914), 16–18, 33–35.
Story.

D 7
"Horseshoes," *The Saturday Evening Post*, 187 (15 August 1914), 8–10, 44–46.
Story. *HTWSS, RU*.

D 8
"A New Busher Breaks In," *The Saturday Evening Post*, 187 (12 September 1914), 15–17, 53–54.

Story. *YKMA.*

D 9
"The Busher's Kid," *The Saturday Evening Post*, 187 (3 October 1914), 20–22, 53–54.

Story. *YKMA.*

D 10
"The Busher Beats It Hence," *The Saturday Evening Post*, 187 (7 November 1914), 21–23, 38–40.

Story. *YKMA.*

D 11
"Back to Baltimore," *The Red Book Magazine*, 24 (November 1914), 29–41.

Story.

D 12
"Own Your Own Home," *The Red Book Magazine*, 24 (January 1915), 488–500.

Story. *OYOH.*

D 13
"Tour No. 2," *The Saturday Evening Post*, 187 (13 February 1915), 16–18, 41–42; (20 February 1915), 21–23, 41–42.

Story in two parts.

D 14
"The Busher Abroad," *The Saturday Evening Post*, 187 (20 March 1915), 19–21, 57–58; (10 April 1915), 20–22, 73–74; (8 May 1915), 20–22, 65–67; (15 May 1915), 25–27, 77–78.

Story in four parts.

D 15
" 'Braves' Is Right," *The American Magazine*, 79 (March 1915), 19–23, 66–70.

Article.

D 16
"Some Team," *The American Magazine,* 79 (April 1915), 20–24, 80–85,
Article.

D 17
"Welcome to Our City," *The Red Book Magazine,* 25 (May 1915), 29–40.
Story. *OYOH.*

D 18
"Tyrus," *The American Magazine,* 79 (June 1915), 19–23, 78.
Article.

D 19
"The Busher's Welcome Home," *The Saturday Evening Post,* 187 (5 June 1915), 18–20, 52–54.
Story.

D 20
"The Last Laugh," *The Red Book Magazine,* 25 (July 1915), 540–550.
Story. *OYOH.*

D 21
"Alibi Ike," *The Saturday Evening Post,* 188 (31 July 1915), 16–18, 30.
Story. *HTWSS, RU.*

D 22
"Matty," *The American Magazine,* 80 (August 1915), 26–29.
Article.

D 23
"Harmony," *McClure's,* 45 (August 1915), 20–22, 56–57.
Story. *HTWSS, RU.*

D 24
"Uncivil War," *The Red Book Magazine,* 25 (September 1915), 938–949.
Story. *OYOH.*

D 25
"The Poor Simp," *The Saturday Evening Post*, 188 (11 September 1915), 16–18, 61–62.

Story.

D 26
"Where Do You Get That Noise?" *The Saturday Evening Post*, 188 (23 October 1915), 10–12, 40–41.

Story.

D 27
"Oh, You Bonehead!" *The Saturday Evening Post*, 188 (30 October 1915), 16–18, 45–46.

Story.

D 28
"Carmen," *The Saturday Evening Post*, 188 (19 February 1916), 14–15, 36–37.

Story. *GT*.

D 29
"Three Kings and a Pair," *The Saturday Evening Post*, 188 (11 March 1916), 17–19, 57–58.

Story. *GT*.

D 30
"Good for the Soul," *The Saturday Evening Post*, 188 (25 March 1916), 20–23, 78, 81–82.

Story.

D 31
"War Bribes," *The Red Book Magazine*, 26 (April 1916), 1111–1121.

Story.

D 32
"The Crook," *The Saturday Evening Post*, 188 (24 June 1916), 18–20, 52–53.

Story.

D 33
"The Swift Six," *The Red Book Magazine*, 27 (July 1916), 549–560.

Story.

D 34
"Gullible's Travels," *The Saturday Evening Post*, 189 (19 August 1916), 3–6, 31, 34–35, 38.

Story. *GT*.

D 35
"Champion," *Metropolitan*, 44 (October 1916), 14–16, 62–64.

Story. *HTWSS, RU*.

D 36
"The Water Cure," *The Saturday Evening Post*, 189 (14 October 1916), 5–7, 105–106.

Story. *GT*.

D 37
"A One-Man Team." *The Red Book Magazine*, 28 (November 1916), 93–97, 100–103.

Story.

D 38
"The Facts," *Metropolitan*, 45 (January 1917), 7–10, 52–53.

Story. *HTWSS, RU*.

D 39
"Three Without, Doubled," *The Saturday Evening Post*, 189 (13 January 1917), 11–13, 69–70.

Story. *GT*.

D 40
"Tour Y-10," *Metropolitan*, 45 (February 1917), 12–14, 34, 39–40, 42–43.

Story.

D 41

"The Hold-Out," *The Saturday Evening Post*, 189 (24 March 1917), 8–10, 49–50.

Story.

D 42

"Ring Lardner—Himself," *The Saturday Evening Post*, 189 (28 April 1917), 27, 45.

Humorous autobiographical sketch.

D 43

"Fore!" *The Red Book Magazine*, 29 (May 1917), 35–46.

Story.

D 44

"A Friendly Game," *The Saturday Evening Post*, 189 (5 May 1917), 10–12, 53, 55.

Story.

D 45

"Ball-A-Hole," *The Saturday Evening Post*, 189 (12 May 1917), 16–18, 75, 78.

Story.

D 46

"Gas, Oil and Air," *Milestones*, 1 (June 1917), 1–2, 14–15.

Story.

D 47

"The Yellow Kid," *The Saturday Evening Post*, 189 (23 June 1917), 8–10, 69.

Story.

D 48

"A Reporter's Diary," *Collier's*, 60 (29 September 1917), 6–7, 24–25; (13 October 1917), 8–9, 41; (3 November 1917), 8–9, 25–26; (17 November 1917), 8–9, 34; (1 December 1917), 8–9, 33–34; (15 December 1917), 16–17; (12 January 1918), 14–15, 34; (19 January 1918), 18–19.

Article in eight parts. *MFW*.

D 49
"The Last Night," *The Red Book Magazine,* 30 (November 1917),
95–98, 100.

Story.

D 50
"The Clubby Roadster," *The Red Book Magazine,* 30 (February
1918), 61–65, 156.

Story.

D 51
"Call for Mr. Keefe," *The Saturday Evening Post,* 190 (9 March
1918), 3–4, 78, 80, 82.

Story.

D 52
"Jack the Kaiser Killer," *The Saturday Evening Post,* 190 (23
March 1918), 10–11, 43, 45–46.

Story. *TER.*

D 53
"Corporal Punishment," *The Saturday Evening Post,* 190 (13
April 1918), 10–11, 73–74, 77.

Story. *TER.*

D 54
"Purls before Swine," *The Saturday Evening Post,* 190 (8 June
1918), 5–7, 41–42.

Story. *TER.*

D 55
"And Many a Stormy Wind Shall Blow," *The Saturday Evening
Post,* 191 (6 July 1918), 5–7, 63.

Story. *RD.*

D 56
"Private Valentine," *The Saturday Evening Post,* 191 (3 August
1918), 3–4, 28, 30.

Story. *RD.*

D 57
"Strategy and Tragedy," *The Saturday Evening Post*, 191 (31 August 1918), 5–7, 40–41.

Story. *RD*.

D 58
"A Chip of the Old Block," *The Red Book Magazine*, 31 (September 1918), 76–79, 106, 108.

Story.

D 59
"Decorated," *The Saturday Evening Post*, 191 (26 October 1918), 6–7, 46, 49.

Story. *RD*.

D 60
"Sammy Boy," *The Saturday Evening Post*, 191 (21 December 1918), 10–11, 35, 38.

Story. *RD*.

D 61
"Simple Simon," *The Saturday Evening Post*, 191 (25 January 1919), 21–22, 24.

Story. *RD*.

D 62
"The Busher Reënlists," *The Saturday Evening Post*, 191 (19 April 1919), 3–4, 147, 151, 155.

Story.

D 63
"The Battle of Texas," *The Saturday Evening Post*, 191 (24 May 1919), 12–13, 94, 98.

Story.

D 64
"Along Came Ruth," *The Saturday Evening Post*, 192 (26 July 1919), 12–13, 120, 123.

Story.

D 65
"The Courtship of T. Dorgan," *The Saturday Evening Post,* 192
(6 September 1919), 8–9, 173–174, 177.

Story.

D 66
"The Busher Pulls a Mays," *The Saturday Evening Post,* 192 (18
October 1919), 16–17, 182, 185–186.

Story.

D 67
"The Young Immigrunts," *The Saturday Evening Post,* 192 (31
January 1920), 12–13, 77.

Parody travel article. *YI.* Published as by Ring W. Lardner, Jr.,
but by Lardner.

D 68
"Quick Returns," *The Saturday Evening Post,* 192 (27 March
1920), 3–4, 54, 57–58.

Story. *BT.*

D 69
"A Tough Luck Tale of the Turf Told by Ring Lardner," *The St.
Francis Lobbyist,* no. 7 (30 June 1920), 1.

Anecdote. See C 4

D 70
"An Irish Love Lyric," *The St. Francis Lobbyist,* no. 7 (30 June
1920), 3.

Poem. See C 4.

Note: The St. Francis Lobbyist was a souvenir newspaper published by the St. Francis Hotel in San Francisco during the 1920
Democratic National Convention. Twelve numbers were published from 23 June to 6 July 1920. Two signed contributions by
Lardner are in the 30 June issue, but it is possible that there are
unsigned Lardner contributions because the *Lobbyist* was a co-
operative project of the newspapermen at the hotel. These issues
were subsequently published in book form.

D 71
"Beautiful Katie," *The Saturday Evening Post*, 193 (10 July 1920), 14–15, 133, 136, 138.

Story. *BT*.

D 72
"The Battle of Long Island," *The Saturday Evening Post*, 193 (27 November 1920), 12–13, 40, 42, 44.

Story. *BT*.

D 73
"Only One," *The Saturday Evening Post*, 193 (12 February 1921), 5–7, 61–62.

Story. *BT*.

D 74
"What Is the 'American Language'?" *The Bookman*, 53 (March 1921), 81–82.

Book review.

D 75
"General Symptoms of Being 35—Which Is What I Am," *The American Magazine*, 91 (May 1921), 12–13, 56, 58.

Article. *SB35*.

D 76
"The Comic," *The Saturday Evening Post*, 193 (14 May 1921), 12–13, 94, 97–98.

Story. *BT*.

D 77
"A Frame-Up," *The Saturday Evening Post*, 193 (18 June 1921), 14–15, 65, 68, 71.

Story. *HTWSS, RU*.

D 78
"Some Like Them Cold," *The Saturday Evening Post*, 194 (1 October 1921), 17–19, 82.

Story. *HTWSS, RU*.

D 79
"The Battle of the Century," *The Saturday Evening Post,* 194 (29 October 1921), 12, 84–86.

Story.

D 80
"Bugs Baer's Comeback," *Columbia Jester,* 22 (February 1922), 17.

Poem. Partially reprinted in C 51.

D 81
"A Caddy's Diary," *The Saturday Evening Post,* 194 (11 March 1922), 12–13, 108–110.

Story. *HTWSS, RU.*

D 82
"The Golden Honeymoon," *Cosmopolitan,* 73 (July 1922), 59–64.

Story. See C 9. *HTWSS, RU.*

D 83
"The Bull Pen," *Judge,* 82 (29 July 1922), 26–27.

Play.

D 84
"My Week in Cuba," *Cosmopolitan,* 73 (August 1922), 48–51.

Article.

D 85
"You Know Me, Al," *Cosmopolitan,* 73 (September 1922), 82–83.

Miscellany. Partially reprinted in *F&L* ("Thompson's Vacation").

Note: The series of miscellanies in *Cosmopolitan* from September to December 1922 consists of short plays, poems, and parodies appearing together under a single title.

D 86
"For He's a Jolly Good Fellow," *Cosmopolitan,* 73 (October 1922), 80–81.

Miscellany.

D 87
"Let's Go!" *Cosmopolitan,* 73 (November 1922), 80–81.

Miscellany.

D 88
"Say It With Oil," *The American Magazine,* 94 (November 1922),
8–9, 104, 107.

Article. *SIWO.*

D 89
"Little Sunbeams of Success," *Cosmopolitan,* 73 (December
1922), 30–31.

Miscellany.

D 90
"What I Don't Know about Horses," *Trotter and Pacer,* 76 (December 1922), 307.

Article.

D 91
"Not Guilty," *Cosmopolitan,* 74 (January 1923), 80–81.

Play.

D 92
"Bringing Up Children," *Cosmopolitan,* 74 (February 1923), 92–93.

Article.

D 93
"The Dames," *Hearst's International,* 43 (March 1923), 68–69.

Article. *WOI.*

D 94
"Why Authors?" *Hearst's International,* 43 (April 1923), 82–83.

Article. *WOI.*

D 95
"In Regards to Geniuses," *Hearst's International,* 43 (May 1923),
28–29.

Article. *WOI.*

D 96
"The Big Drought," *Hearst's International*, 43 (June 1923), 72–73.
Article. *WOI.*

D 97
"Enoch Arden," *The Bookman*, 57 (June 1923), 404–407.
Parody.

D 98
"Bed-Time Stories (How to Tell a Princess and Bluebeard),"
Hearst's International, 44 (July 1923), 42–43.
Parody. *WOI.*

D 99
"Cinderella," *Hearst's International*, 45 (August 1923), 26–27.
Parody. *WOI.*

D 100
"What I Ought to of Learnt in High School," *The American Magazine*, 96 (November 1923), 10–11, 78, 80, 82.
Autobiographical article.

D 101
"L. Gaspiri [The Upholsterers]," *Chicago Literary Times*, 1 (15 February 1924), 3.
Play. *WOI.*

D 102
"The Lardner Plan," *Life*, 83 (20 March 1924), 9.
Article.

D 103
"A Close-Up of Domba Splew," *Hearst's International*, 45 (June 1924), 74–75.
Parody. *WOI.*

D 104
Grantland Rice, "Who Are the Greatest Athletes?" *Vanity Fair*, 23 (June 1924), 98, 100.
Lardner answers questionnaire on p. 100.

D 105
"What of It?" *Liberty*, 1 (7 June 1924).

Story. *WOI.*

D 106
" 'In Conference,' " *Liberty*, 1 (16 August 1924), 3–4.

Story. *WOI.*

D 107
"A Group of Artists Write Their Own Epitaphs," *Vanity Fair*, 23 (October 1924), 42–43.

Lardner epitaph.

D 108
"Taxidea Americana," *The Wisconsin Literary Magazine*, 24 (December 1924), 1.

Play. *WOI.*

D 109
"The Other Side," *Liberty*, 1 (14 February 1925), 5–6; "The Basque Country" (21 February 1925); "The Riviera" (28 February 1925), 5, 7; "Paris Again and Merrie England" (7 March 1925), 16–17; "Scotland to England to Home" (14 March 1925), 11, 13.

Travel serial in five parts. *WOI.*

D 110
"Haircut," *Liberty*, I (28 March 1925).

Story. See C 13. *LN, RU.*

D 111
"The Constant Jay," *The New Yorker*, 1 (18 April 1925), 20.

Poem. See C 33.

D 112
"Mr. and Mrs. Fix-It," *Liberty*, 2 (9 May 1925), 5–8.

Story. *LN.*

D 113
"Sea Island Sports," *The American Golfer*, 28 (16 May 1925), 12, 34.
Article.

D 114
"What You Will Encounter in Nassau," *The American Golfer*, 28 (30 May 1925), 25, 34.
Article.

D 115
"Cora, or Fun at a Spa," *Vanity Fair*, 24 (June 1925), 42.
Play. *F&L.*

D 116
"Zone of Quiet," *Hearst's International-Cosmopolitan*, 78 (June 1925), 44–48.
Story. *LN, RU.*

D 117
"Women," *Liberty*, 2 (20 June 1925), 5–8.
Story. *LN, RU.*

D 118
"The Love Nest," *Hearst's International-Cosmopolitan*, 79 (August 1925), 53–55, 194–195.
Story. *LN.*

D 119
"A Day with Conrad Green," *Liberty*, 2 (3 October 1925), 5–8.
Story. *LN.*

D 120
"Reunion," *Liberty*, 2 (31 October 1925), 5–9.
Story. *LN, RU.*

D 121
"Who Dealt?" *Hearst's International-Cosmopolitan*, 80 (January 1926), 32–35.
Story. *LN, RU.*

D 122
"Rhythm," *Hearst's International-Cosmopolitan,* 80 (March 1926), 32–35.

Story. *LN, RU.*

D 123
"Travelogue," *Hearst's International-Cosmopolitan,* 80 (May 1926), 36–39, 181.

Story. See C 15.

D 124
"The Ideal Woman," *Vanity Fair,* 26 (August 1926), 52.

Lardner answers questionnaire. See C 47 ("The Perfect Woman").

D 125
"I Can't Breathe," *Hearst's International-Cosmopolitan,* 81 (September 1926), 40–43, 201–202.

Story. *RU.*

D 126
"The Jade Necklace," *Hearst's International-Cosmopolitan,* 81 (November 1926), 28–31.

Story.

D 127
"Sun Cured," *Hearst's International-Cosmopolitan,* 82 (January 1927), 32–35.

Story. *RU.*

D 128
"Hurry Kane," *Hearst's International-Cosmopolitan,* 82 (May 1927), 52–55, 160, 162, 164–166.

Story. *RU.*

D 129
"Then and Now," *Hearst's International-Cosmopolitan,* 82 (June 1927), 66–69, 223.

Story. *RU.*

D 130
"The Spinning Wheel," *Hearst's International-Cosmopolitan*, 83 (July 1927), 106–108, 111.

Story.

D 131
"Dinner Bridge," *The New Republic*, 51 (20 July 1927), 227–229.

Play. See C 18. *F&L*.

D 132
"The Venomous Viper of the Volga," *Hearst's International-Cosmopolitan*, 83 (September 1927), 52–53, 198–202.

Story.

D 133
"Miss Sawyer, Champion," *The New Yorker*, 3 (10 September 1927), 23.

Parody. *F&L*.

D 134
"Man Not Overboard," *Hearst's International-Cosmopolitan*, 83 (November 1927), 50–51, 138, 140, 142.

Story. *RU*.

D 135
"Anniversary," *Hearst's International-Cosmopolitan*, 84 (January 1928).

Story. See C 21. *RU*.

D 136
"Nora," *Hearst's International-Cosmopolitan*, 84 (February 1928), 36–39.

Story. *RU*.

D 137
"Liberty Hall," *Hearst's International-Cosmopolitan*, 84 (March 1928), 64–67, 108, 112.

Story. *RU*.

D 138
John N. Wheeler, "Ring Lardner," *Collier's*, 81 (17 March 1928), 16, 44.

Introduction by Lardner; Wheeler also quotes conversation and correspondence. See C 40; partially reprinted in C 45.

D 139
"The Battle of Palm Beach," *Collier's*, 81 (24 March 1928), 12, 51–52.

Article.

D 140
"There Are Smiles," *Hearst's International-Cosmopolitan*, 84 (April 1928), 32–35, 130.

Story. *RU*.

D 141
"With Rod and Gun," *Collier's*, 81 (7 April 1928), 10, 41.

Article.

D 142
"Mr. Frisbie," *Hearst's International-Cosmopolitan*, 84 (June 1928), 42–45, 122.

Story. *RU*.

D 143
"Laugh, Clown!" *Collier's*, 81 (23 June 1928), 18.

Article.

D 144
"Wedding Day," *Hearst's International-Cosmopolitan*, 85 (July 1928), 66–69.

Story.

D 145
"Dante and — — —," *The New Yorker*, 4 (7 July 1928), 16–17.

Article. *F&L*.

D 146
"The Maysville Minstrel," *Hearst's International-Cosmopolitan,*
85 (September 1928), 64–67.

Story. *RU.*

D 147
"Dinner," *Harper's Bazar,* 63 (September 1928), 70–71, 124,
126.

Story. *RU.*

D 148
"Just Politics," *Collier's,* 82 (1 September 1928), 16–17; (15
September 1928), 12–13.

Article in two parts. Part 2 in *F&L* ("Both Parties: 1928").

D 149
"Can You Keep a Secret?" *Collier's,* 82 (6 October 1928), 20–21.
Article.

D 150
"Ex Parte," *Hearst's International-Cosmopolitan,* 85 (November
1928), 44–45, 155.

Story. *RU.*

D 151
"Old Folks' Xmas," *Hearst's International-Cosmopolitan,* 86 (January 1929), 82–85, 133.

Story. *RU.*

D 152
"Adrift in New York," *Collier's,* 83 (12 January 1929), 15, 43.

Article.

D 153
"With Rope and Gum," *Collier's,* 83 (2 February 1929), 13, 43.

Article.

D 154
"Onward and Upward–," *Collier's,* 83 (16 February 1929), 18, 49.

Article.

D 155
"Absent-Minded Beggar," *Hearst's International-Cosmopolitan*, 86 (March 1929), 70–71, 186, 188–192.

Story.

D 156
"Contract," *Harper's Bazar*, 64 (March 1929), 100–101, 142, 144, 149.

Story. *RU*.

D 157
"The Boy Entertainer," *Collier's*, 83 (2 March 1929), 17, 32.

Article.

D 158
"Pluck and Luck," *Collier's*, 83 (16 March 1929), 13, 74.

Article. See C 40.

D 159
"Paul the Fiddler," *Collier's*, 83 (23 March 1929), 24, 58.

Article.

D 160
Anon., "Introducing Ring W. Lardner," *Wings*, 3 (April 1929), 3.

Quotes, Lardner: "I have no definite method. When I begin a story I have no idea what it is going to be about."

D 161
"Reuben, the Young Artist," *Collier's*, 83 (13 April 1929), 26, 51.

Article.

D 162
"The Keeper of the Bees," *Collier's*, 83 (11 May 1929), 28, 56.

Article.

D 163
"High-rollers," *Hearst's International-Cosmopolitan*, 86 (June 1929), 76–77, 108, 110.

Story.

D 164
"Ringside Seat," *Collier's*, 83 (15 June 1929), 15, 53.

Article.

D 165
"Stop Me—If You've Heard This One," *Hearst's International-Cosmopolitan*, 87 (July 1929), 98–99, 122, 124.

Story. See A 22.

D 166
"Why We Have Left Hands," *Collier's*, 84 (6 July 1929), 13, 55.

Article.

D 167
"Tee Time," *Collier's*, 84 (27 July 1929), 15, 53.

Article. See C 38.

D 168
"Oh, Shoot!" *Collier's*, 84 (10 August 1929), 15, 57.

Article. *F&L* ("On Prohibition").

D 169
"A Nice Quiet Racket," *Collier's*, 84 (31 August 1929), 12, 51.

Article.

D 170
"Pity Is Akin–," *Hearst's International-Cosmopolitan*, 87 (September 1929), 74–75, 161–162.

Story.

D 171
"Bad News for Pitchers," *Collier's*, 84 (14 September 1929), 19, 52.

Article.

D 172a
"Facts About the Players," *The Playgoer*, 1 (22 to 28 September 1929), 2–3.

D 172b
"Who's Who in the Cast," *The New York Magazine Program: The Broadhurst Theatre* (n.d.), pp. 4, 45.

D 172c
"Facts About the Players in 'June Moon'," *The Playgoer*, 6 (17 November 1930), unpaged.

These three items, D 172a, b, and c, are program notes for *June Moon*. See E 4669. Partially reprinted in C 47. See A 23.

D 173
"Large Coffee," *The New Yorker*, 5 (28 September 1929), 26–27.
Article. *F&L.*

D 174
"Any Ice Today Lady?" *Collier's*, 84 (28 September 1929), 18, 63.
Article.

D 175
"Cubs Win World Series," *Collier's*, 84 (12 October 1929), 35, 65.
Article.

D 176
"That Old Sweetheart of Mine," *Hearst's International-Cosmopolitan*, 87 (November 1929), 34–35, 166, 168–169.
Story.

D 177
"Jersey City Gendarmerie, Je T'aime," *The New Yorker*, 5 (2 November 1929), 24–25.
Article.

D 178
"Army Black and Navy Blue," *Collier's*, 84 (30 November 1929), 24, 65.
Article.

D 179
"Great Blessings," *Hearst's International-Cosmopolitan*, 87 (December 1929), 79–81, 132.
Story.

D 180
"Bobby or Bust," *Collier's*, 84 (21 December 1929), 19, 51.

Article.

D 181
George S. Kaufman and Ring Lardner, "This Play's the Thing—June Moon," *Theatre Magazine*, 51 (February 1930), 32–35, 58.

Play.

D 182
"Second-Act Curtain," *Collier's*, 85 (19 April 1930), 10, 64, 66.

Story.

D 183
"Sit Still," *The New Yorker*, 6 (19 April 1930), 17–18.

Article. See C 25.

D 184
"Mamma," *Good Housekeeping*, 90 (June 1930), 52–54, 252.

Story. See C 44.

D 185
"X-Ray," *The New Yorker*, 6 (5 July 1930), 15.

Article.

D 186
"Words and Music," *Good Housekeeping*, 91 (August 1930), 30–33, 173–174.

Story.

D 187
"Br'er Rabbit Ball," *The New Yorker*, 6 (13 September 1930), 61–62, 64–65.

Article. Reprinted in C 58; partially reprinted in C 57.

D 188
"Asleep on the Deep," *The New Yorker*, 6 (4 October 1930), 23–24.

Article. *F&L* ("Years Later").

D 189
" 'Tables for Two'," *The New Yorker*, 6 (18 October 1930), 23–24.
Article.

D 190
"The Higher-Ups," *The New Yorker*, 6 (1 November 1930), 15.
Article.

D 191
"From a Zealous Non-Worker," *The New Yorker*, 6 (29 November 1930), 26–27.
Article.

D 192
"Old Man Liver," *The New Yorker*, 6 (3 January 1931), 17–19.
Article. *F&L.*

D 193
"Cured!" *The Red Book Magazine*, 57 (March 1931), 41–45, 124.
Story.

D 194
"Insomnia," *Hearst's International-Cosmopolitan*, 90 (May 1931), 81–83.
Article.

D 195
"All Quiet on the Eastern Front," *The New Yorker*, 7 (27 June 1931), 14–16.
Article.

D 196
"A Slow Train through Arizona," *Hearst's International-Cosmopolitan*, 91 (September 1931), 86–87.
Article.

D 197
"A Reporter in Bed," *The New Yorker*, 7 (26 September 1931), 61–62.
Article. *F&L.*

D 198
"Meet Mr. Howley," *The Saturday Evening Post*, 204 (14 November 1931), 12, 115.

Autobiographical article.

D 199
"Me, Boy Scout," *The Saturday Evening Post*, 204 (21 November 1931), 5, 101, 102.

Autobiographical article.

D 200
"Quadroon," *The New Yorker*, 7 (19 December 1931), 17–18.

Play. *F&L.*

D 201
"Caught in the Draft," *The Saturday Evening Post*, 204 (9 January 1932), 33, 64.

Autobiographical article.

D 202
"The Master Minds," *The New Yorker*, 7 (16 January 1932), 15–16.

Parody. *F&L.*

D 203
"Heap Big Chief," *The Saturday Evening Post*, 204 (23 January 1932), 28, 68.

Autobiographical article.

D 204
"Chicago's Beau Monde," *The Saturday Evening Post*, 204 (20 February 1932), 31, 88.

Autobiographical article.

D 205
"Alias James Clarkson," *The Saturday Evening Post*, 204 (16 April 1932), 24, 108.

Autobiographical article.

D 206
"One Hit, One Error, One Left," *The Saturday Evening Post*, 204 (23 April 1932), 3–5, 44, 46.

Story. *LWS*.

D 207
"When the Moon Comes over the Mountain," *The Saturday Evening Post*, 204 (7 May 1932), 8–9, 72–73.

Story. *LWS*.

D 208
"Lose with a Smile," *The Saturday Evening Post*, 204 (11 June 1932), 16–17, 86, 88.

Story. *LWS*.

D 209
"Over the Waves," *The New Yorker*, 8 (18 June 1932), 30, 32, 34–36.

Radio review. See C 47.

D 210
"Heavy Da-Dee-Dough Boys," *The New Yorker*, 8 (25 June 1932), 30, 32–35.

Radio review. See C 47.

D 211
"The Truth about Ruth," *The New Yorker*, 8 (2 July 1932), 26–28.

Radio review.

D 212
"Meet Me in St. Louie," *The Saturday Evening Post*, 205 (2 July 1932), 14–15, 30.

Story. *LWS*.

D 213
"The Crooner's Paradise," *The New Yorker*, 8 (16 July 1932), 22, 26–27.

Radio review.

D 214
"Allie Bobs Oop Again," *The New Yorker*, 8 (30 July 1932), 24,
26–27.

Radio review.

D 215
"Holycaust," *The Saturday Evening Post*, 205 (30 July 1932),
12–13, 55, 58.

Story.

D 216
"Deacon Gets Tilt for Tat," *The New Yorker*, 8 (20 August 1932),
26, 28, 30, 32.

Radio review.

D 217
"An Epistle of Paul," *The New Yorker*, 8 (3 September 1932), 30,
32–34.

Radio review.

D 218
"The Ides of June," *The Saturday Evening Post*, 205 (5 September
1932), 12–13, 62–63.

Story. *LWS*.

D 219
"Life of the Boswells," *The New Yorker*, 8 (17 September 1932),
55–58.

Radio review. See C 47.

D 220
"Pu-leeze! Mr. Hemingway," *The New Yorker*, 8 (1 October 1932),
34, 36, 38.

Radio review. See C 47.

D 221
"The Crucial Game," *The New Yorker*, 8 (22 October 1932),
32–34.

Radio review. See C 47.

D 222
"Eckie," *The Saturday Evening Post*, 205 (22 October 1932), 14, 92.

Autobiographical article. See C 37.

D 223
"The Lor and the Profits," *The American Spectator*, 1 (November 1932), 2

Parody. See C 32.

D 224
"Ring Lardner Explaining Why He Will Vote Socialist," *New Leader*, 14 (5 November 1932), 6.

Statement.

D 225
"Herb and Frank Panic 'Em," *The New Yorker*, 8 (5 November 1932), 46–48.

Radio review. See C 47.

D 226
"Lyricists Strike Pay Dirt," *The New Yorker*, 8 (19 November 1932), 45–47.

Radio review. *F&L* ("Off Color").

D 227
"Announcer's Prep School," *The New Yorker*, 8 (3 December 1932), 30–31.

Radio review. See C 47.

D 228
"Some Short-Selling," *The New Yorker*, 8 (17 December 1932), 64–65.

Radio review. See C 47.

D 229
"Ring In! (Two Weeks Late)," *The New Yorker*, 8 (14 January 1933), 50–51.

Radio review.

D 230
"Rudy in Irate Mood," *The New Yorker*, 8 (4 February 1933), 45–46.

Radio review. *F&L* ("A Crooner").

D 231
"An Infant Industry," *The New Yorker*, 9 (25 February 1933), 57–58.

Radio review.

D 232
"I Am a Fugitive from a National Network," *The New Yorker*, 9 (18 March 1933), 55–57.

Radio review. *F&L* ("Running Comment").

D 233
"The Old Man Shows His Air Mail," *The New Yorker*, 9 (8 April 1933), 63–65.

Radio review. See C 47.

D 234
"We're All Sisters Under the Hide of Me," *The New Yorker*, 9 (6 May 1933), 33–35.

Radio review. *F&L* ("Night and Day").

D 235
"Hail to the Chief," *The New Yorker*, 9 (27 May 1933), 35–37.

Radio review. See C 47.

D 236
"Some Champions," *The Saturday Evening Post*, 205 (3 June 1933), 29.

Autobiographical article.

D 237
"Radio's All-America Team for 1932–1933," *The New Yorker*, 9 (17 June 1933), 39–40.

Radio review.

D 238
"Comics Face Starvation as Gag Men Near Wit's End," *The New Yorker*, 9 (8 July 1933), 41.

Radio review. *F&L* ("Fun on the Air").

D 239
"Ricordi to the Rescue," *The New Yorker*, 9 (5 August 1933), 43–44.

Radio review.

D 240
"The Perfect Radio Program," *The New Yorker*, 9 (26 August 1933), 31–32.

Radio review. *F&L*.

D 241
"Take a Walk," *The American Magazine*, 116 (October 1933), 66–70, 106, 109.

Story.

D 242
"Odd's Bodkins," *The New Yorker*, 9 (7 October 1933), 17–18.

Parody. *F&L*.

D 243
"Bob's Birthday," *The Red Book Magazine*, 62 (November 1933), 36–37, 75.

Story.

D 244
"Poodle," *Delineator*, 124 (January 1934), 8–9, 30, 32–33.

Story.

D 245
"Via the Canal," *New York Sunday News*, 7 January 1934, pp. 66–67.

Story.

D 246
"Greek Tragedy," *Esquire*, 1(February 1934), 18–19, 85, 147.
Story. See C 35.

D 247
Leon Surmelian, "Nitwit Incomparable," *New Movie*, 11 (March 1935), 32, 50.
Letter.

D 248
"Widow," *The Red Book Magazine*, 65 (October 1935), 28–31, 65.
Story.

D 249
"Freedom of the Press," *Pictorial Review*, 37 (November 1935), 14–15, 43–45.
Story.

D 250
"How Are You?" *The Red Book Magazine*, 66 (December 1935), 22–25, 83.
Story.

D 251
"Ring Lardner's 1929 Christmas Card," *The Reader's Digest*, 28 (January 1936), 86.
Poem.

D 252
"Claude Diphthong, Student of Crime," *Ellery Queen's Mystery Magazine*, 24 (August 1954), 54–64.
Story.

D 253
Benjamin Lease, "An Evening at the Scott Fitzgeralds': An Unpublished Letter of Ring Lardner," *English Language Notes*, 8 (September 1970), 40–42.

D 254

Ring Lardner, Jr., "Ring Lardner & Sons," *Esquire*, 77 (March 1972), 98–103, 169–170, 172, 175, 178, 180.

Anecdotes and quotes from previously unpublished Lardner letters.

* * *

Note: Copyright records indicate that Lardner published an article on the White Sox in *Cherry Circle*, 16, no. 11. No copy has been located.

E. Appearances in Newspapers and Syndicated Material

In Section E cross-references to Lardner's books are given by acronyms rather than by entry numbers:

BB   *Bib Ballads* (A 3)
WOI   *What of It?* (A 17)
SWM   *The Story of a Wonder Man* (A 20)
F&L   *First and Last* (A 26)

ADDENDA

The following items were located while this bibliography was in press.

E 4747
"Gullible Pens His Own Review," *Chicago Tribune*, 10 March 1917, p. 7.

E 4748
Joseph Pierson, "Ring Lardner, Joker, Jobbed by French Cops," *Chicago Tribune*, 21 August 1917, p. 1.

Parody interview of Lardner.

E 4749
"E'en War So Grim Refuses to Dim Humor of Him," *Chicago Tribune*, 22 August 1917, p. 1.

E 4750
"Lardner Meets Horrors in the Wake of the War," *Chicago Tribune*, 23 August 1917, p. 1.

E 4751
"Life's One Rule After Another with Parisians," *Chicago Tribune*, 25 August 1917, p. 1.

E 4752
"In the Wake of the War,"

Chicago Tribune, 30 August 1917, p. 3.

E 4753
"Those Germans Can't Seem to Kill Dr. 'Smith,' " *Chicago Tribune*, 12 September 1917, p. 5.

E 4754
Lucy Calhoun, "You Know Me, Al, Pleads Ring in Speeders' Court," *Chicago Tribune*, 18 June 1919, p. 21.

Humorous report of Lardner's trial.

E 4755
"Lardner's Prank in Paris Nearly Costs Jackie Coogan His Curls," (Chicago) *Herald and Examiner*, 29 September 1924.

E 4756
David Condon, "In the Wake of the News," *Chicago Tribune*, 15 October 1958, p. 1, pt. 4.

Quotes Lardner speech.

NILES DAILY STAR
(*1901*)

E 1

"Clever Class Poem," *Niles Daily Star*, 14 June 1901.

Presumably Lardner's first appearance in print.

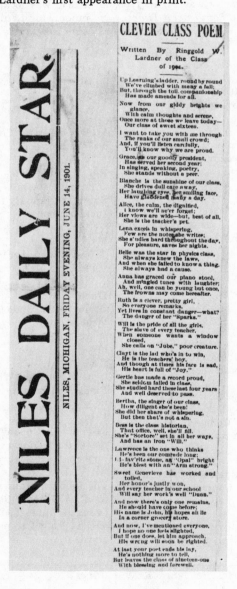

CLEVER CLASS POEM

Written By Ringgold W. Lardner of the Class of 1901.

Up Learning's ladder, round by round
We've climbed with many a fall;
But, through the toil, companionship
Has made amends for all.

Now from our giddy heights we glance,
With calm thoughts and serene—
Once more at those we leave today—
Our class of sweet sixteen.

I want to take you with me through
The ranks of our small crowd;
And, if you'll listen carefully,
You'll know why we are proud.

Grace, as our goodly president,
Has served her second year;
In singing, speaking, poetry,
She stands without a peer.

Blanche is the sunshine of our class,
She drives dull care away,
Her laughing eyes, her smiling face,
Have gladdened many a day.

Alice, the calm, the dignified,
I know we'll ne'er forget;
Her views are wide—but, best of all,
She is the teacher's pet.

Lena excels in whispering,
Few are the notes she writes;
She studies hard throughout the day,
For pleasure, saves her nights.

Belle was the star in physics class,
She always knew the laws,
And when she failed to know a thing,
She always had a cause.

Anna has graced our piano stool,
And mingled tunes with laughter;
Ah, well, one can be young but once,
The frowns may come hereafter.

Ruth is a clever, pretty girl,
So everyone remarks,
Yet lives in constant danger—what?
The danger of her "Sparks."

Will is the pride of all the girls,
The slave of every teacher.
When someone wants a window closed,
She calls on "Jube," poor creature.

Clayt is the lad who's in to win,
He is the teachers' boy,
And though at times his face is sad,
His heart is full of "Joy."

Gertie has made a record proud,
She seldom failed in class,
She studied hard these last four years
And well deserved to pass.

Bertha, the singer of our class,
How diligent she's been!
She did her share of whispering,
But then that's not a sin.

Bess is the class historian,
That office, well, she'll fill.
She's "Sortore" set in all her ways,
And has an iron "Will."

Lawrence is the one who thinks
He's been our comrade long;
His fav'rite stone, an "Opal" bright
He's blest with an "Arm strong."

Sweet Genevieve has worked and toiled,
Her honor's justly won,
And every teacher in our school
Will say her work's well "Dunn."

And now there's only one remains,
He should have come before;
His name is John, his hopes all lie
In a corner grocery store.

And now, I've mentioned everyone,
I hope no one feels slighted,
But if one does, let him approach,
His wrong will soon be righted.

At last your poet ends his lay,
He's nothing more to tell,
But leaves the class of nineteen-one
With blessing and farewell.

(Sidebar vertical text:)

NILES DAILY STAR.

NILES, MICHIGAN, FRIDAY EVENING, JUNE 14, 1901.

SOUTH BEND TIMES
(1905–1907)

From Fall 1905 until November 1907, Lardner was a reporter for the *South Bend Times,* covering general news, court proceedings, society news, theater, and sports. His articles were unsigned. (*Note:* After this bibliography was set in type, an article was located in the 10 January 1906 *South Bend Times,* p. 7, announcing Lardner's association with that paper. He was described as the new sports editor.)

See "Meet Mr. Howley," D 198.

CHICAGO INTER-OCEAN[1]
(1907–1908)

E 2
"Purple Re-Enters the Arena Coyly," 22 December 1907, p. 3, sports section.

E 3
"Mixers Show Best on the Gridiron," 29 December 1907, p. 2, sports section.

E 4
"Colleges to Vote on Length of the Football Season," 4 January 1908, p. 4.

E 5
"Big Nine Passes Seven-Game Rule by Small Margin," 5 January 1908, p. 1, sports section.

E 6
"Michigan Is Made Victim of Plot by 'Big Eight' Colleges," 12 January 1908, p. 1, sports section.

E 7
"Exiled Michigan and Chicago May Resume Contests Next Year," 16 January 1908, p. 4.

E 8
"Nebraska Likely to Replace Wolverines in the Conference," 17 January 1908, p. 7.

E 9
"Conference Awaits Arrival of Stagg," 19 January 1908, p. 2, sports section.

E 10
"Fresh Evidence of Plot Is Revealed," 20 January 1908, p. 9.

E 11
"Calm Settles Upon Conference Waters," 26 January 1908, p. 2, sports section.

E 12
"Austin and Lake Win Semi-Finals," 28 January 1908, p. 4.

E 13
"Twenty-Six Cubs Will Be Taken on Southern Journey," 2 February 1908, p. 1, sports section.

The following four articles (E 14 to E 17) from *Chicago Inter-Ocean* are unsigned but attributable to Ring Lardner. See D 198 and D 199.

---

1. All articles are signed 'R. W. Lardner'.

E 14
"Hyde Park Bests Wendell Philips
on Gridiron, 18 to 6," 17 November 1907, p. 2, sports section.

E 15
"Indians Outclass Maroons," 24
November 1907, p. 2, sports
section.

E 16
"Central Y.M.C.A. Five Meets Yale
Tonight," 25 December 1907, p.
13.

E 17
"Yale Five Beaten by Central
Team," 26 December 1907, p. 9.

CHICAGO EXAMINER
(*1908*)

From February 1908 until November 1908, Lardner was a sports reporter for the *Chicago Examiner*. Beginning in March 1908, he shared the by-line 'James Clarkson'. Clarkson was a convenience by-line for the *Examiner* sports staff, appearing on the work of various members of the department. Though Lardner almost certainly wrote most of the 'James Clarkson' articles between March and November 1908, it is impossible to demonstrate that he wrote all of them.

CHICAGO TRIBUNE[2]
(*1908–1910*)

E 18
"Cubs Frisky in June Sunshine,"
3 March 1909, p. 8.

E 19
"Pfiester Appears in Camp of
Cubs," 4 March 1909, p. 10.

E 20
"Honored Cubs Are 'Bunch of
Stiffs'," 5 March 1909, p. 14.

E 21
"Cubs Work at Furious Clip," 6
March 1909, p. 14.

E 22
"Cubs Break Camp; Go to Hot
Springs," 7 March 1909, p. 1,
pt. 3.

E 23
"Cubs Defy Flood; Work on
Island," 10 March 1909, p. 8.

E 24
"Cubs Stiffened by High Low
Game," 11 March 1909, p. 6.

E 25
"Floods Drive Cubs South," 12
March 1909, p. 10.

E 26
"Cub Squad at Louisville," 13
March 1909, p. 10.

E 27
"Cubs Find Rain in South," 28
March 1909, p. 1, pt. 3.

---

2. All articles are signed 'R. W. Lardner'. Lardner began writing for the *Chicago Tribune* in November 1908, but did not receive a by-line until March 1909.

E 28
"Cubs Pushed to Outdo Turtles,"
29 March 1909, p. 12.

E 29
"Cubs Whitewash Southern
Champs," 30 March 1909, p. 8.

E 30
"Cubs Once More Trim Nashville," 31 March 1909, p. 8.

E 31
"Cubs Put Groove in Plate," 1
April 1909, p. 14.

E 32
"Cubs in April Fool Joke," 2 April
1909, p. 6.

E 33
"Keep on March Through
Georgia," 3 April 1909, p. 8.

E 34
"Absentees Make Cubs' Task
Hard," 4 April 1909, p. 1, pt. 3.

E 35
"First Defeat of Season for Cubs,"
5 April 1909, p. 12.

E 36
"Cubs Take Fall Out of Colonels,"
6 April 1909, p. 12.

E 37
"Cub 'Subs' in Tie with Punchers,"
7 April 1909, p. 14.

E 38
"Cubs Triumph in Comedy Contest," 8 April 1909, p. 8.

E 39
"Cub Recruits Out in Cold," 9
April 1909, p. 8.

E 40
"Cubs Bonus Day Fixed for June
3," 10 April 1909, p. 12.

E 41
"Cubs Win 1 to 0 in Ten Innings,"
11 April 1909, p. 1, pt. 3.

E 42
"Cubs' Last Practice Game," 12
April 1909, p. 12.

E 43
"Chance Cancels Last Dayton
Tilt," 13 April 1909, p. 8.

E 44
"Sox=Keyed Up to Tie Tiger's
Tail," 14 April 1909, p. 11.

E 45
"White Sox Lose First to Tigers,"
15 April 1909, p. 8.

E 46
"Cravath Poles One Over Fence,"
16 April 1909, p. 13.

E 47
"Tigers Bury Sox in Hitting
Melee," 17 April 1909, p. 9.

E 48
"At Last Sox Win; Browns Victims," 18 April 1909, p. 1, pt. 3.

E 49
"Browns Bat Sox Into Last Hole,"
19 April 1909, p. 13.

E 50
"Sky Leaks Tears; White Sox
Loaf," 20 April 1909, p. 8.

E 51
"Sox at Home Seek Pelts of
Tigers," 21 April 1909, p. 8.

E 52
"Soggy Ball Yard Delays Revenge," 22 April 1909, p. 8.

E 53
"Piano Mover Is the 'Candy Kid'," 23 April 1909, p. 12.

E 54
"Tigers Trimmed Again by Smith," 25 April 1909, pp. 1–2, pt. 3.

E 55
"Sox Possess Find in Pitcher Scott," 26 April 1909, p. 10,

E 56
"Lucky First for White Sox Bunch," 27 April 1909, p. 8.

E 57
"Sox Again Trim Brownies, 1 to 0," 28 April 1909, p. 10.

E 58
"Pitcher Walsh Speeding West," 29 April 1909, p. 8.

E 59
"Walsh Here, but Still Unsigned," 30 April 1909, p. 10.

E 60
" 'Commy' Says Sox Will Play Today," 1 May 1909, p. 12.

E 61
"Walsh and Evers Drop Bat for Pen," 2 May 1909, p. 1, pt. 3.

E 62
"Tigers Score Win Over Erring Sox," 3 May 1909, p. 12.

E 63
"Tigers Helpless Before White," 4 May 1909, p. 8.

E 64
"Comedy for Naps; Tragedy for Sox," 5 May 1909, p. 8.

E 65
"Sox Cop Victory by Triple Steal," 6 May 1909, p. 12.

E 66
"Naps Nose Out Sox in Ninth," 7 May 1909, p. 8.

E 67
"Sox Are Happy as the Birds in May," 8 May 1909, p. 8.

E 68
"Lajoie Hammers Smithy to Bench," 9 May 1909, pp. 1–2, pt. 3.

E 69
"Ed Walsh Victor; Jim Scott Loser," 10 May 1909, p. 12.

E 70
"Rain Stops the Champions," 11 May 1909, p. 8.

E 71
"Cubs Given Game in Last Inning," 12 May 1909, p. 12.

E 72
"Heap Big Indian Scalps Bear Cubs," 13 May 1909, p. 8.

E 73
"Cubs Never in It with Big Christy," 14 May 1909, p. 12.

E 74
"Cubs Turn on Foe and Get Revenge," 15 May 1909, p. 8.

E 75
"Tinker Breaks Up the Game," 16 May 1909, p. 1, pt. 3.

E 76
"Cubs Make Most of Day of Rest,"
17 May 1909, p. 12.

E 77
"Ungrateful Cubs Lick Phillies,
8–1," 18 May 1909, p. 8.

E 78
"Cubs Take Third Straight," 19
May 1909, p. 12.

E 79
"Reulbach Hands Game to Quakers," 20 May 1909, p. 8.

E 80
"Game Is Easy for Cubs," 21 May
1909, p. 8.

E 81
"Cubs Gain a Lap on Idle Pirates,"
22 May 1909, p. 8.

E 82
"Day of Rest for Cub Crew," 23
May 1909, p. 1, pt. 3.

E 83
"Lizzies Tie Can to Tails of Cubs,"
24 May 1909, p. 10.

E 84
"Home Run Smash Wins for Cubs,
4–3," 25 May 1909, p. 8.

E 85
"Cubs Again Beat Lumley's
Dodgers," 26 May 1909, p. 8.

E 86
"Third Straight Goes to the Cubs,"
27 May 1909, p. 14.

E 87
"Rest for Dodgers and Cubs," 28
May 1909, p. 8.

E 88
"Cubs Win Hot Exhibition," 29
May 1909, p. 8.

E 89
"Cubs Clout Ball and Win in
11th," 30 May 1909, pp. 1–2, pt. 3.

E 90
"Pirates Rude to Champion Cubs,"
31 May 1909, p. 14.

E 91
"Cubs Break Even, but Feel Joy-
ful," 1 June 1909, p. 9.

E 92
"Cubs Beat Reds in Tenth Inning," 2 June 1909, p. 12.

E 93
"Cubs Calcimined at Racing
Game," 3 June 1909, p. 8.

E 94
"Cubs Given $10,000; Also a Ball
Game," 4 June 1909, p. 12.

E 95
"Sixteen to Share in $10,000
Bonus," 5 June 1909, p. 10.

E 96
Pfiester Puzzle to Murray's Men,"
6 June 1909, pp. 1–2, pt. 3.

E 97
"Brilliant Game a Cub Victory,
1–0," 7 June 1909, p .12.

E 98
"Gates Closed to Expectant Fans,"
8 June 1909, p. 8.

E 99
"Brown Bows to Mighty Christy,"
9 June 1909, p. 12.

E 100
"Mud Halts Cubs; Pirates Climb,"
10 June 1909, p. 8.

E 101
" 'Rube' Marquard Picnic for
Cubs," 11 June 1909, p. 12.

E 102
"Mourning Doves Jar the
Champs," 12 June 1909, p. 8.

E 103
"Cubs Clip Wings of Lowly
Doves," 13 June 1909, pp. 1–2,
pt. 3.

E 104
"Cubs Winners in Vaudeville
Bill," 14 June 1909, p. 10.

E 105
"No Cold Beans on Cubs' Menu
List," 15 June 1909, p. 8.

E 106
"Pennant Hoisted; Victory Follows," 17 June 1909, p. 8.

E 107
"Dodgers Generous to Cubs," 18
June 1909, p. 8.

E 108
"Cubs Slaughter Lowly Super-
bas," 20 June 1909, p. 1, pt. 3.

E 109
"Cubs Keep Kibosh on the
Dodgers," 21 June 1909, p. 10.

E 110
"Cub Army Loses to 'Griff's'
Reds," 24 June 1909, p. 12.

E 111
"Cubs' Park Is Wet; Game Called
Off," 25 June 1909, p. 12.

E 112
"Cubs Beat Reds in Listless
Game," 26 June 1909, p. 12.

E 113
"Cubs Once More Calcimine
Reds," 27 June 1909, p. 1, pt. 3.

E 114
"Six Cub Pitchers in Two Defeats," 28 June 1909, p. 10.

E 115
"Cubs Swoop Down on Enemy
Today," 29 June 1909, p. 12.

E 116
"Close Old Park with Cub Defeat," 30 June 1909, p. 12.

E 117
"Nearly 36,000 See Cubs Bag
Victory," 1 July 1909, p. 10.

E 118
"Cubs Have Feast at Pickle
Works," 2 July 1909, p. 12.

E 119
"Champs Win, 8–0; Drop Other,
4–2," 3 July 1909, p. 12.

E 120
"Cubs Take Final in Easy Man-
ner," 4 July 1909, pp. 1–2, pt. 3.

E 121
"Defeat for Cubs by Cardinals,
3–2," 5 July 1909, p. 6.

E 122
"No Game by Cubs; Rain Mars
Sport," 6 July 1909, p. 16.

E 123
"Champs Winners on Getaway
Day," 7 July 1909, p. 8.

E 124
"World's Champs Beaten Soundly," 8 July 1909, p. 12.

E 125
"Cubs Play Rings Around Phillies," 9 July 1909, p. 6.

E 126
"Crippled Champs Lose to Phillies," 10 July 1909, p. 10.

E 127
"Cubs Slaughter Quaker Pitchers," 11 July 1909, pp. 1–2, pt. 3.

E 128
"Ocean Title Lost by Cubs," 12 July 1909, p. 10.

E 129
"Overall Hurls to Victory," 13 July 1909, p. 8.

E 130
"Doves Are Twice Victims of Cubs," 14 July 1909, p. 8.

E 131
"Cubs Massacre Innocent Doves," 15 July 1909, p. 8.

E 132
"Cubs Fatten on a Diet of Doves," 16 July 1909, p. 10.

E 133
"Kroh's Pitching Beats Doves, 4–1," 17 July 1909, p. 10.

E 134
"Split Best Cubs Get in Brooklyn," 18 July 1909, p. 1, pt. 3.

E 135
"Brown Humbles Artful Dodgers," 20 July 1909, p. 8.

E 136
"Cubs Tie up Game and Lose in Ninth," 21 July 1909, p. 6.

E 137
"Cubs Grab Last from Brooklyn," 22 July 1909, p. 8.

E 138
"Evers Is Elusive, So Cubs Win, 3 to 1," 23 July 1909, p. 10.

E 139
"Rain Stops Champs in Race," 24 July 1909, p. 10.

E 140
" 'Bugs' Is So Wild Cubs Win Easily," 25 July 1909, p. 1, pt. 3.

E 141
"White Sox Land in Washington," 29 July 1909, p. 8.

E 142
"Sox in Hot Games; Win One Victory," 30 July 1909, p. 10.

E 143
"Sox Grab Couple from Tailenders," 31 July 1909, p. 10.

E 144
"Sox Take Opener; Repeat in Second," 1 August 1909, pp. 1–2, pt. 3.

E 145
"Sox Join Seashore Crowd," 2 August 1909, p. 10.

E 146
"Sox Are Anxious to Tackle Enemy," 3 August 1909, p. 8.

E 147
"Sox Fall Twice; Fans Mob Hurst," 4 August 1909, p. 6.

E 148
"Skies Weep Rain; Sox Rest," 5
August 1909, p. 8.

E 149
"White Sox Split with Athletics,"
6 August 1909, p. 10.

E 150
"White Sox Drop Grewsome
Game," 7 August 1909, p. 10.

E 151
"Speed Boys Take Measure of
Sox," 8 August 1909, p. 1, pt. 3.

E 152
"White Sox Rest; Outlook
Gloomy," 9 August 1909, p. 10.

E 153
"Defeat for Sox Comes in Ninth,"
10 August 1909, p. 6.

E 154
"Speed Boys Beat White Sox
Again," 11 August 1909, p. 6.

E 155
"Yanks Find Smith; Sox Lose
Out, 2–1," 12 August 1909, p. 6.

E 156
"Jim Scott Pulls Sox Out of
Ruck," 13 August 1909, p. 10.

E 157
"Walsh Hurls Sox to Triumph,
4–3," 14 August 1909, p. 10.

E 158
"Yankees Aviate and Sox Win,
7–3," 15 August 1909, p. 1, pt. 3.

E 159
"Sox Help Tigers Regain the
Lead," 16 August 1909, p. 10.

E 160
"Rain Stops Sox and Tigers," 17
August 1909, p. 6.

E 161
"Sox Are Favored by Dame Fortune," 18 August 1909, p. 8.

E 162
"Sox Jolt Tigers Into Third Hole,"
19 August 1909, p. 6.

E 163
"Tigers Down Sox in Close 1–0
Game," 20 August 1909, p. 6.

E 164
"Dougherty's Bat Clinches Victory," 22 August 1909, pp. 1–2,
pt. 3.

E 165
"Game of Thrills Lost by the Sox,"
23 August 1909, p. 6.

E 166
"Dougherty's Bat Defeats
Yankees," 24 August 1909, p. 8.

E 167
"Sullies Downed by Speed Boys,"
25 August 1909, p. 8.

E 168
"Speed Boys Play White Sox to
Tie," 26 August 1909, p. 8.

E 169
"White Sox Split with Speed
Boys," 27 August 1909, p. 8.

E 170
"Deluge Prevents Senators' Defeat," 28 August 1909, p. 6.

E 171
"Two Games to Sox; One Is a
Present," 29 August 1909, pp. 1–
2, p. 3.

E 172
"E. Walsh Pitches Sox to Victory," 30 August 1909, p. 10.

E 173
"Athletics Gain; White Sox Lose,"
31 August 1909, p. 8.

E 174
"White Hose Jolt Mackmen's
Hopes," 1 September 1909, p. 10.

E 175
"Sox Crush Hopes of Mackmen,
6 to 2," 2 September 1909, p. 12.

E 176
"Stab by Parent Saves White
Sox," 3 September 1909, p. 12.

E 177
"Sox Win Game by Brilliant
Rally," 4 September 1909, p. 8.

E 178
"Sox Slide Back to Fifth Place,"
5 September 1909, p. 1, pt. 3.

E 179
"Sox Aid the Naps Who Win
Game, 6–1," 6 September 1909, p.
10.

E 180
"Equal Division by Sox and
Naps," 7 September 1909, p. 18.

E 181
"White Sox Show Good in the
Mud," 9 September 1909, p. 14.

E 182
"Victory for Sox Turned Into
Tie," 10 September 1909, p. 14.

E 183
"Road to Defeat Claims the Sox,"
11 September 1909, p. 12.

E 184
"White Sox Twice on the Short
End," 12 September 1909, pp. 1–
2, pt. 3.

E 185
"Sox and Naps Tie for Fourth
Place," 13 September 1909, p. 14.

E 186
"Walsh Lands Sox in Fourth
Place," 14 September 1909, p. 10.

E 187
"Sox and Naps Tie; Game Is
Stopped," 15 September 1909, p.
10.

E 188
"Vengeance Sweet, Saith White
Sox," 16 September 1909, p. 12.

E 189
"Slugging by Sox Brings Victory,"
17 September 1909, p. 14.

E 190
"No Game for Sox in Boston
Town," 18 September 1909, p. 12.

E 191
"First to Our Sox Other to
T'Other," 19 September 1909, p. 1,
pt. 3.

E 192
"White Sox Shiver in Cold Weather," 20 September 1909, p. 12.

E 193
"Red Sox Run Wild; White Sox
Beaten," 21 September 1909, p. 8.

E 194
"Scott Off Form; Yankees Beat
Sox," 22 September 1909, p. 8.

E 195
"Rainbound Sox See Shows," 23
September 1909, p. 14.

E 196
"Sox Boost Yanks at Own Expense," 24 September 1909, p. 8.

E 197
"Punctured Skies Halt White Sox," 25 September 1909, p. 8.

E 198
"Fourth Now Sure for the Sullies," 26 September 1909, pp. 1–2, pt. 3.

E 199
"White Sox Quiet in Capital Town," 27 September 1909, p. 12.

E 200
"Sox at Top Speed Crush Senators," 28 September 1909, p. 12.

E 201
"Sullys Rub It In on the Senators," 29 September 1909, p. 16.

E 202
"Sox Crush Hopes of the Mackmen," 30 September 1909, p. 8.

E 203
"Mackmen's Hopes Blasted by Sox," 1 October 1909, p. 14.

E 204
"Don't Care Game Goes to Sox," 2 October 1909, p. 8.

E 205
"Sox and Tigers Play a Tie," 3 October 1909, p. 1, pt. 3.

E 206
"Windup Game to Champion Tigers," 4 October 1909, p. 12.

E 207
"Dying Champions on Vicious Tear," 5 October 1909, p. 12.

E 208
"Sox Frolic with Rogers Parks, 4–0," 6 October 1909, p. 10.

E 209
"Only One Series Seen by Chicago," 7 October 1909, p. 8.

E 210
"Pittsburg Awake for Once in Life," 8 October 1909, p. 15.

E 211
"Huge Mob of Fans Sees Pirates Win," 9 October 1909, p. 13.

E 212
Entry canceled.

E 213
"Tigers Even Up World's Battle," 10 October 1909, pp. 1–2, pt. 3, section 2.

E 214
"Pirates and Fans Storm Tigertown," 11 October 1909, p. 12.

E 215
"'Game of Thrills Won by Pirates," 12 October 1909, p. 13.

E 216
"Tigers Tie Series; Mullin an Enigma," 13 October 1909, p. 14.

E 217
"Pirates Now Lead in World's Series," 14 October 1909, p. 12.

E 218
"Tigers' 5–4 Victory Costs Three Men," 15 October 1909, p. 8.

E 219
"Tigers Win Out; Pirates Losers," 16 October 1909, p. 12.

E 220
"Pirates Outgame Tigers for
Title," 17 October 1909, pp. 1–2,
pt. 3.

E 221
"Big Games for Locals Today," 19
October 1909, p. 8.

E 222
"Redskin Tames Overall's Cubs,"
20 October 1909, p. 12.

E 223
"Sox Handed Coin by Boss Comiskey," 21 October 1909, p. 8.

E 224
"Foster Argues; Schulte Scores,"
22 October 1909, p. 12.

E 225
"Cubs Trim Giants in Final Game,
1–0," 23 October 1909, p. 14.

E 226
"Allerdice's Toe Beats Marquette,"
24 October 1909, pp. 1–2, pt. 3.

E 227
"Cubs 1910 Champs, Declares
Chance," 28 October 1909, p. 8.

E 228
"Badgers Victors; Purple Scores,"
31 October 1909, pp. 1, 3, pt. 3.

E 229
"American League Favors 140
Games," 3 November 1909, p. 14.

E 230
"Hard Spring Trip for Cubs," 13
November 1909, p. 14.

E 231
"Purple a Meal for Illini," 14 November 1909, p. 2, pt. 3.

E 232
"Hart Turns Down Big League
Job," 16 November 1909, p. 12.

E 233
"Move to Rid Game of Peril," 20
November 1909, p. 12.

E 234
"Wisconsin Plays Maroon to a
Tie," 21 November 1909, pp. 1, 3,
pt. 3.

E 235
"Elect Al Tearney Three Eyes
Head," 23 November 1909, p. 14.

E 236
"Treat in Store for Cuban Fans,"
24 November 1909, p. 14.

E 237
"Ward's Election Will Start War,"
28 November 1909, p. 1, pt. 3.

E 238
"C. W. Murphy Mum on Baseball
War," 30 November 1909, p. 12.

E 239
"Sullivan Plans Clearing House,"
3 December 1909, p. 18.

E 240
"Cobb Tops List of A. L. Sluggers,"
6 December 1909, p. 14.

E 241
"Williams Slated as N. L. Secretary," 8 December 1909, p. 20.

E 242
"Murphy Sure to Vote for J.
Ward," 9 December 1909, p. 16.

E 243
"Clarke to Quit Baseball?" 11 December 1909, p. 10.

E 244
"Johnson Courts War with Rivals," 12 December 1909, p. 1, pt. 3.

E 245
"Stovall May Join Sox," 18 December 1909, p. 10.

E 246
"Baseball Warclouds Vanish," 19 December 1909, p. 1, pt. 3.

E 247
"Finds Hagerman Much in Demand," 22 December 1909, p. 16.

E 248
" 'Jiggs' Has Eyes on Semi-Pro Club," 23 December 1909, p. 12.

E 249
"Bonus Incentive to Cub Twirlers," 24 December 1909, p. 6.

E 250
"Local Fans Spend a Year of Calm," 26 December 1909, pp. 1–2, pt. 3.

E 251
"Herrmann to Meet Murphy," 13 January 1910, p. 10.

E 252
"Isbell's Career as Sox at an End," 21 January 1910, p. 12.

E 253
"Northwest May Not See Sox," 22 January 1910, p. 10.

E 254
"Suggest Changes in Rules," 23 January 1910, pp. 1, 3, pt. 3.

E 255
"Baseball Actors Make 'Hit'," 25 January 1910, p. 12.

E 256
"Pig Feast Makes Duffy Feel Good," 15 February 1910, p. 12.

E 257
"168 Game Schedule for A.A.," 16 February 1910, p. 14.

E 258
"A.L. Moguls Agree on a 20 Year Life," 17 February 1910, p. 12.

E 259
"Cubs Hear Call to Loosen Arms," 20 February 1910, pp. 1, 3, pt. 3.

E 260
"Manager Chance to Resume Helm," 21 February 1910, p. 12.

E 261
"Chance Is Sure of Cubs' Success," 22 February 1910, p. 14.

E 262
"Howard Balks on Sale to Colonels," 23 February 1910, p. 15.

E 263
"Trainload of Sox Leaves for Coast," 26 February 1910, p. 14.

E 264
"Cubs Missing as Train Pulls Out," 27 February 1910, p. 1, pt. 3.

E 265
"West Baden Rude to Chicago Cubs," 28 February 1910, p. 12.

E 266
" 'Lid' On and Off in Camp of Cubs," 1 March 1910, p. 15.

E 267
"Frisky Cubs Get First Workout," 2 March 1910, p. 14.

E 268
"Cubs and Old Sol West Baden
Pals," 3 March 1910, p. 9.

E 269
"City Champs Off for New Orleans," 4 March 1910, p. 12.

E 270
"Cubs Land in Sunny South," 5
March 1910, p. 14.

E 271
"Schulte Victim of Cubs' Hoodoo,"
6 March 1910, pp. 1–2, pt. 3.

E 272
"Cub Youngsters Pluck Pelicans,"
7 March 1910, p. 14.

E 273
"Cub 'Vets' Start Work on
Mound," 8 March 1910, p. 12.

E 274
"Chance's Pet Cubs to Work," 9
March 1910, p. 14.

E 275
"Cub Youngsters Look Good to
P. L.," 10 March 1910, p. 12.

E 276
"Cubs Are Idle as J. Pluvius
Pours," 11 March 1910, p. 14.

E 277
"Sheckard Joins Cub Camp," 12
March 1910, p. 12.

E 278
"Rally in Ninth Gives Cubs
Game," 13 March 1910, pp. 1–2,
pt. 3.

E 279
"Pelican Pitcher Helps Cubs Win,"
14 March 1910, p. 14.

E 280
"Naps Give Cubs Taste of Defeat,"
15 March 1910, p. 12.

E 281
"Naps Find Knapp; Cubs Lose, 8
to 4," 16 March 1910, p. 14.

E 282
"Lajoie's Big Bat Causes Cubs
Woe," 17 March 1910, p. 12.

E 283
"Stack's Benders Hold Naps Safe,"
18 March 1910, p. 18.

E 284
"Final Game Goes to Cleveland
6–1," 19 March 1910, p. 12.

E 285
"Pelicans Battle Cubs 12 Innings,"
20 March 1910, pp. 1–2, pt. 3.

E 286
"Cubs and Pels Go 10 Innings to
Tie," 21 March 1910, p. 12.

E 287
"Real Cubs Land Victory in 11th,"
22 March 1910, p. 14.

E 288
"One Cub 'Fired'; Two Draw
Fines," 23 March 1910, p. 14.

E 289
"Cub Rally in 9th Beats Climbers,"
24 March 1910, p. 14.

E 290
"Too Hot for Cubs in Birmingham," 25 March 1910, p. 14.

E 291
"Cub Kids Awake with Ven-
geance," 26 March 1910, p. 14.

E 292
"Real Cubs Blank Babb's Turtles,"
27 March 1910, pp. 1–2, pt. 3.

E 293
"Cubs Use Pail of Fine Whitewash," 28 March 1910, p. 12.

E 294
"Cubs Win Opener from Nashville," 29 March 1910, p. 12.

E 295
"Cubs Down Volunteers 3–1," 30
March 1910, p. 14.

E 296
"Cubs Are Outhit, but Win by 9 to
2," 31 March 1910, p. 9.

E 297
"Colonels Taste Cub Whitewash,"
1 April 1910, p. 14.

E 298
"King Cole Holds Louisville Safe,"
2 April 1910, p. 11.

E 299
"Luderus' Stick Beats Colonels," 3
April 1910, pp. 1–3, pt. 3.

E 300
"Day Off for Cubs; Rain Inter-
feres," 4 April 1910, p. 10.

E 301
"Beaumont Big Aid in Cub Victory," 5 April 1910, p. 14.

E 302
"Brooklyn Trade Still in Balance,"
6 April 1910, p. 14.

E 303
"Weather Too Bad for Cubs to
Play," 7 April 1910, p. 12.

E 304a
"Carr's Hoosiers Blanked by
Cubs," 8 April 1910, p. 6.

E 304b
"Cubs in Batfest Beat Dayton
Vets," 9 April 1910, p. 6.

E 305
"Cubs Sting Ball; Columbus
Falls," 10 April 1910, p. 1, pt. 3.

E 306
"P. Moran Pitches; Cubs Win in
10th," 11 April 1910, p. 12.

E 307
"Drenched Cubs Beat Toledo 4–1,"
12 April 1910, p. 9.

E 308
"Cubs Finish with a Clean Record," 13 April 1910, p. 12.

E 309
"Overall to Open Against Redlegs," 14 April 1910, p. 9.

E 310
"Reds' Late Rally Shuts Out
Cubs," 15 April 1910, p. 12.

E 311
"Reds Hit Brown; Whip Cubs
Again," 16 April 1910, p. 8.

E 312
"Cubs in Batfest Defeat Redlegs,"
17 April 1910, p. 1, pt. 3.

E 313
"Cubs End Grudge Beating Reds,
9–2," 18 April 1910, p. 10.

E 314
"Cubs in St. Louis; Game Called
Off," 19 April 1910, p. 7.

E 315
"Weeping Skies Keep Cubs Idle,"
20 April 1910, p. 12.

E 316
"Cubs in Bad Fix; Saved by
Clock," 21 April 1910, p. 8.

E 317
"Cubs in Own Yard Show Up
Reds, 6–1," 22 April 1910, p. 8.

E 318
"Skies Pour Aqua on Cubs and
Reds," 23 April 1910, p. 7.

E 319
"Cubs and Reds Bow to Weather,"
24 April 1910, p. 1, pt. 3.

E 320
"Cubs Again Idle; J. Kling Reports," 25 April 1910, p. 10.

E 321
"No Game; Cubs Watch Kling,"
26 April 1910, p. 7.

E 322
"Schulte Springs Rainy Day
Verse," 27 April 1910, p. 9.

E 323
"M'Intire Twirls Cubs to Victory,"
28 April 1910, p. 12.

E 324
"Rescuer Brown Saves Cub
Game," 29 April 1910, p. 8.

E 325
"Cubs Slip When Near Pinnacle,"
30 April 1910, p. 12.

E 326
"Pirates Victors; Cubs Walk
Plank," 1 May 1910, p. 1, pt. 3.

E 327
"Taft Sees Cubs Lose to Pirates,"
3 May 1910, p. 12.

E 328
"Cubs Once More Bow to
Weather," 4 May 1910, p. 12.

E 329
"Pirates Trounce Chance's Cubs,
8–3," 5 May 1910, p. 13.

E 330
"Cubs Take First on Pirate Soil,"
6 May 1910, p. 12.

E 331
"Cubs Dosed with Bitter
Medicine," 7 May 1910, p. 16.

E 332
"Rain Postpones Cub-Pirate
Game," 8 May 1910, p. 1, pt. 3.

E 333
"Flynn's Home Run Whips Cubs,
7 to 4," 9 May 1910, p. 12.

E 334
"Cubs Grab First from Giants,
2–0," 10 May 1910, p. 12.

E 335
"Cubs Victors in Ragtime Battle,"
11 May 1910, p. 14.

E 336
"Cubs Take Third from Giants,
4–3," 12 May 1910, p. 8.

E 337
"Game to Giants Before They Go,"
13 May 1910, p. 8.

E 338
"Pirate Castoff Blanks Cubs 3–0,"
14 May 1910, p. 8.

E 339
"Doves Show Cubs They Can Repeat," 15 May 1910, p. 1, pt. 3.

E 340
"Cub Richie Beats His Former Pals," 16 May 1910, p. 12.

E 341
"Cubs Grab Final from Boston, 4–3," 17 May 1910, p. 12.

E 342
"Cubs' Diamond Watersoaked," 18 May 1910, p. 12.

E 343
"Pfiester's Stick Gives Cubs Game," 19 May 1910, p. 8.

E 344
"Cubs by Victory Push Pittsburg," 20 May 1910, p. 8.

E 345
"Cubs Again Idle; Grounds Too Wet," 21 May 1910, p. 8.

E 346
"Pittsburg Gains; Cubs Idle Again," 22 May 1910, p. 1, pt. 3.

E 347
"Phillies Ducked in Aqueous Game," 23 May 1910, p. 10.

E 348
"Cubs Lose Chance to Worry Pirates," 24 May 1910, p. 8.

E 349
"Cubs Gain a Lap on Idle Pirates," 25 May 1910, p. 12.

E 350
"Cubs Jump Over Pirates in Race," 26 May 1910, p. 12.

E 351
"One Lone Bingle Off Mr. Overall," 27 May 1910, p. 14.

E 352
"Cubs Slaughter Haughty Pirates," 29 May 1910, p. 1, pt. 3.

E 353
"Pirates Victims in 10th Straight," 30 May 1910, p. 14.

E 354
"Cubs Break Even in Holiday Games," 31 May 1910, p. 14.

E 355
"Cubs at Boston to Tackle Doves," 1 June 1910, p. 14.

E 356
"Cubs Rout Doves in Opening Clash," 2 June 1910, p. 12.

E 357
"M'Intire Pitches Cubs to Victory," 3 June 1910, p. 10.

E 358
"Cubs Take Third from Boston, 9–0," 4 June 1910, p. 10.

E 359
"Discard's Swipe Finishes Cubs," 5 June 1910, p. 1, pt. 3.

E 360
"Cubs Frolic with Waterbury Nine," 6 June 1910, p. 12.

E 361
"Cruel Phillies Batter Cubs, 12–2," 7 June 1910, p. 10.

E 362
"Stack Is Traitor; Beats Cubs, 1 to 0," 8 June 1910, p. 10.

E 363
"King Cole Bags Seven in a Row,"
9 June 1910, p. 10.

E 364
"Thrills in Game Won by Cubs,
5–4," 10 June 1910, p. 10.

E 365
"Cubs' Hot Rally Humbles
Giants," 11 June 1910, p. 12.

E 366
"Murphy and Brush Losers," 12
June 1910, p. 1, pt. 3.

E 367
"Cubs Fearless in Haunts of
Giants," 13 June 1910, p. 8.

E 368
"Giants' Miscues Give Cubs
Game," 14 June 1910, p. 12.

E 369
"Cubs Take Three; 'Zim' Earns
Halo," 15 June 1910, p. 12.

E 370
"Cy Barger Star in Cubs' Defeat,"
16 June 1910, p. 10.

E 371
"Sky Spills Aqua; Cubs Take
Rest," 17 June 1910, p. 13.

E 372
"Cubs Win in 13th on a Wild
Pitch," 18 June 1910, p. 12.

E 373
"Infant Cyclone Stops Cub
Game," 19 June 1910, p. 1, pt. 3.

E 374
"Slugging Cubs Beat Reds,
10–3," 20 June 1910, p. 10.

E 375
"Cubs Swat Hard, Beating Reds,
6–4," 21 June 1910, p. 10.

E 376
"Cubs Beat Reds by Squeeze
Play," 22 June 1910, p. 12.

E 377
"Beaumont's Bat Gives Cubs
Game," 23 June 1910, p. 10.

E 378
"Cub 'Subs' Whip Champions,
9–0," 24 June 1910, p. 12.

E 379
"Honus' Big Club Beats Cubs,
6 to 5," 25 June 1910, p. 12.

E 380
"Pirates Trounce Cubs, 8–2,"
26 June 1910, p. 1, pt. 3.

E 381
"Victory to Cubs but It's No
Cinch," 27 June 1910, p. 8.

E 382
"Cubs Get One Hit; Reds Take
Game," 28 June 1910, p. 10.

E 383
"Cubs in Batfest Defeat Reds,
11–1," 29 June 1910, p. 12.

E 384
"Sallee a Puzzle; Cubs Victims,
2–1," 30 June 1910, p. 12.

E 385
"Is St. Louis Heat the Cause?,"
1 July 1910, p. 12.

E 386
"Cardinals Fall Before Brownie,"
2 July 1910, p. 10.

E 387
"Rain Costs Cubs a Game,"
3 July 1910, p. 4, pt. 3.

E 388
"Cubs in One Game Score Victory,
5–3," 4 July 1910, p. 11.

E 389
"White Sox Score Double Victory,"
5 July 1910, p. 14.

E 390
"Browns Whip Sox by Rally in
10th," 6 July 1910, p. 10.

E 391
"Sox' Boots Help Triumph of
Naps," 7 July 1910, p. 12.

E 392
"White Sox, Tired, Reach New
York," 8 July 1910, p. 12.

E 393
"White Sox Start with 13–4
Defeat," 9 July 1910, p. 10.

E 394
"Sox Win 1 Game; Lose the
Other," 10 July 1910, p. 1, pt. 3.

E 395
"Sox Quit Gotham for the
Atlantic," 11 July 1910, p. 8.

E 396
"Yankee Batting Beats White
Sox," 12 July 1910, p. 10.

E 397
"Volter's Willow Beats White
Sox," 13 July 1910, p. 8.

E 398
"Speed Boys Whip White Sox
5 to 1," 14 July 1910, p. 12.

E 399
"White Sox Draw Double Defeat,"
15 July 1910, p. 8.

E 400
"White Sox Lose Seven Straight,"
16 July 1910, p. 8.

E 401
"Duffites Handed One More Defeat," 17 July 1910, p. 1, pt. 3.

E 402
"Rain Saves Coin of Sox Athletes,"
18 July 1910, p. 8.

E 403
"Macks Hand Sox Another
Defeat," 19 July 1910, p. 10.

E 404
"Hose Calcimined; Drop Game
No. 10," 20 July 1910, p. 10.

E 405
"Sox, Going South, Make It 11 in
row," 21 July 1910, p. 10.

E 406
"White Sox Break String of
Losses," 22 July 1910, p. 8.

E 407
"Sox in 6th Place Almost 2
Hours," 23 July 1910, p. 8.

E 408
"Walter Johnson Beats White
Sox," 24 July 1910, p. 1, pt. 3.

E 409
"White Sox Rest in Hot Capital,"
25 July 1910, p. 8.

E 410
"Sox Grab Opener but Lose
Second," 26 July 1910, p. 8.

E 411
"Sox Split Even with Senators,"
27 July 1910, p. 10.

E 412
"Tired White Sox Hit Jungle-
town," 28 July 1910, p. 8.

E 413
"Tigers Down Sox in Shutout
Game," 29 July 1910, p. 8.

E 414
"Sox Get One Hit; Detroit Wins,
1–0," 30 July 1910, p. 7.

E 415
"Champion Tigers Again Defeat
Sox," 31 July 1910, p. 1, pt. 3.

E 416
"Joy, Then Gloom, in Wide
Pickets," 1 August 1910, p. 10.

E 417
"Sox Hand Defeat to Athletics,
6–1," 2 August 1910, p. 10.

E 418
"White Sox Lose to Athletics,
3–2," 3 August 1910, p. 8.

E 419
"Senator Meloan Costs Sox
Game," 4 August 1910, p. 8.

E 420
"Sox Tie Macks in 16 Innings,
0 to 0," 5 August 1910, p. 8.

E 421
"White Sox Trim Nearest Rivals,"
6 August 1910, p. 8.

E 422
"Senators Shove Hose Back a
Peg," 7 August 1910, p. 1, pt. 3.

E 423
"Sox Regain Lap Lost Saturday,"
8 August 1910, p. 14.

E 424
"Fall of Sox, 3 to 2, Before
Senators," 9 August 1910, p. 12.

E 425
"White Sox Check Speed Boys'
Rush," 10 August 1910, p. 14.

E 426
"Sox Jolt Boston in Twelfth, 2–1,"
11 August 1910, p. 10.

E 427
"Big Ed Walsh in Role of a Hero,"
12 August 1910, p. 10.

E 428
"White Sox Again Beat Speed
Boys," 13 August 1910, p. 8.

E 429
"Yanks Blank Sox in Slab Battle,"
14 August 1910, p. 1, pt. 3.

E 430
"Huge Crowd Sees Sox Win and
Lose," 15 August 1910, p. 10.

E 431
"Sox Beat Yanks; Series Even Up,"
16 August 1910, p. 10.

E 432
"Sox Lose Ginger; Yankees Win,
7–1," 17 August 1910, p. 12.

E 433
"White Sox Land in Sleepytown,"
18 August 1910, p. 10.

E 434
"Sox Fall Victim to 'Last Chance',"
19 August 1910, p. 10.

E 435
"Sox Fail to Stop Mackmen's
Rush," 20 August 1910, p. 8.

E 436
"Macks Win Final from White
Sox," 21 August 1910, p. 1, pt. 3.

E 437
"Day Off for Sox in Philadelphia,"
22 August 1910, p. 12.

E 438
"Washington Fans in Riot of
Glee," 23 August 1910, p. 10.

E 439
"Ed. Walsh Bests Walter Johnson," 24 August 1910, p. 8.

E 440
"Senators Upset Duffites in 10th,"
25 August 1910, p. 10.

E 441
"Heavy Slugging Beats Sox 8 to
4," 26 August 1910, p. 10.

E 442
"Sox Game Is Off; Play Two
Today," 27 August 1910, p. 10.

E 443
"Sox Drop First; Second Is Draw,"
28 August 1910, pp. 1–2, pt. 3.

E 444
"Hard Luck Hits Sox on Sea
Trip," 29 August 1910, p. 8.

E 445
"Sox Meet Defeat in Boston
Game," 30 August 1910, p. 10.

E 446
"Sox, Held to Hit, Drop Contest,
4–0," 31 August 1910, p. 10.

E 447
"White Hose Find Smith Easy
Prey," 1 September 1910, p. 12.

E 448
"White Sox Land in Jungle,"
2 September 1910, p. 10.

E 449
"Tigers Find Sox Easy to Defeat,"
3 September 1910, p. 10.

E 450
"Tigers Trim Sox in Short Combat," 4 September 1910, p. 1, pt. 3.

E 451
"White Sox Idle; Rain at Detroit,"
5 September 1910, p. 10.

E 452
"Duffites Divide with Cleveland,"
6 September 1910, p. 14.

E 453
"Sox Break Even in Bargain Bill,"
7 September 1910, p. 10.

E 454
"Cellar Battle Held Up by Mud,"
8 September 1910, p. 10.

E 455
"White Sox Split in Bargain Bill,"
9 September 1910, p. 10.

E 456
"One Game to Sox; Other to
Browns," 10 September 1910,
p. 10.

E 457
"Sox and Browns Divide Twin
Bill," 11 September 1910, pp. 1–2,
pt. 3.

E 458
"Hose Victims of Mullin's Curves,"
12 September 1910, p. 12.

E 459
"Soaked Diamond Balks Sox
Game," 13 September 1910, p. 10.

E 460
"Sox Lose Game, 1–0 to Lucky
Browns," 14 September 1910,
p. 10.

E 461
"Sox Practice on St. Louis
Browns," 15 September 1910,
p. 14.

E 462
"White Sox Beat Speed Boys, 4–2,"
16 September 1910, p. 14.

E 463
"Sox Pass Off Day on Battle
Field," 17 September 1910, p. 10.

E 464
"Start in First Gives Sox Game,"
18 September 1910, p. 1, pt. 3.

E 465
"White Sox Blank Boston Reds,
6–0," 19 September 1910, p. 12.

E 466
"Sox Win 5 in Row; New York
Beaten," 20 September 1910,
p. 12.

E 467
"Hose Put Yanks Out of Running,"
21 September 1910, p. 10.

E 468
"Sox Bag Seventh; Beat Yankees,
6–4," 22 September 1910, p. 10.

E 469
"Rain Stops Sox; Two Games
Today," 24 September 1910, p. 10.

E 470
"Sox Down Macks in Two
Contests," 25 September 1910,
pp. 1–2, pt. 3.

E 471
"Cubs Excel Athletics in Many
Points," 25 September 1910,
p. 2, pt. 3.

E 472
"White Sox Divide with Athletics," 26 September 1910, p. 12.

E 473
"Macks May Play Practice Series,"
27 September 1910, p. 10.

E 474
"Sox Stand Still; Win One, Lose
One," 28 September 1910, p. 10.

E 475
"Johnson Breaks Strike-Out
Mark," 29 September 1910, p. 8.

E 476
"Cubs in Batfest Whip Reds 9 to
6," 2 October 1910, p. 1, pt. 3.

E 477
"Cubs Cinch Flag in National
Race," 3 October 1910, pp. 21–22.

E 478
" 'Zim' Hero at Bat, but Reds Win,
5–3," 4 October 1910, p. 23.

E 479
"Rain Stops Game with Cubs on
Top," 5 October 1910, p. 23.

E 480
"Sheckard First in Batting List,"
6 October 1910, p. 23.

E 481
"Former Champs Cinch for Cubs,"
7 October 1910, p. 21.

E 482
"Brown Is Master of Pirate Crew,"
8 October 1910, pp. 21–22.

E 483
"No Rest Given Cub Hurlers,"
9 October 1910, p. 2, pt. 3.

E 484
"Cubs Cinch Game in Final Session," 10 October 1910, p. 21.

E 485
"West Side Elite Beaten by
Cards," 11 October 1910, p. 21.

E 486
"Battle 10 Rounds to Beat Cards,
4–3," 12 October 1910, p. 21.

E 487
"Cardinals Drop Another to Cubs,"
13 October 1910, p. 19.

E 488
"Cards in Front in This Gallop,"
14 October 1910, p. 23.

E 489
"Cubs Go Tonight to Battle
Macks," 15 October 1910, p. 19.

E 490
"Fans Riot at Evers' Store,"
16 October 1910, p. 2, pt. 3.

E 491
"Big Mob Greets Chance's Stars,"
17 October 1910, p. 21.

E 492
"Every Play in First Pennant
Battle Described in Detail,"
18 October 1910, p. 22.

E 493
"Every Play in Second Pennant
Battle Described in Detail,"
19 October 1910, p. 22.

E 494
" 'Must Win Today' Cry of Cub
Fans," 20 October 1910,
pp. 21–22.

E 495
"Every Play in Third Pennant
Battle Described in Detail,"
21 October 1910, p. 22.

E 496
"Cole Cubs' Hope in Today's
Game," 22 October 1910, p. 19.

E 497
"Every Play in Fourth Pennant
Battle Described in Detail,"
23 October 1910, p. 10, pt. 3.

E 498
"Every Play in Final Pennant
Battle Described in Detail,"
24 October 1910, p. 22.

E 499
"Cubs Get $1,315.78 Each as
Losers," 25 October 1910, p. 10.

E 500
" 'All Star' team May Visit
Japan," 27 October 1910, p. 8.

E 501
"No Game for Cubs at Gunther
Park," 28 October 1910, p. 10.

E 502
"Overall Boasts a Brand New
Arm," 3 November 1910, p. 11.

E 503
"Murphy Denies Meeting Fogel,"
4 November 1910, p. 11.

E 504
"Stahl Will Quit Boston Red
Hose," 5 November 1910, p. 9.

E 505
"Maroons Humble Purdue Team,
14–5," 6 November 1910,
pp. 1–2, pt. 3.

E 506
"Pitching Pals Leave for West,"
9 November 1910, p. 16.

E 507
"Tinker May Play Third Base,"
11 November 1910, p. 11.

E 508
"Cornell Swamps Maroons, 18 to
0," 13 November 1910, pp. 1–2,
pt. 3.

E 509
"Badgers Last for Maroons,"
14 November 1910, p. 13.

E 510
"War Clouds over Baseball
Camps," 16 November 1910, p. 10.

E 511
"Peace Pervades Minor Leagues,"
17 November 1910, p. 10.

E 512
"All Is Serene on Baseball Rialto,"
18 November 1910, p. 13.

E 513
"Evers to Coach Annapolis Team,"
19 November 1910, p. 14.

E 514
"Chicago Victim of Badger Skill,"
20 November 1910, pp. 1–2, pt. 3.

E 515
"A. L. to Meet in Gotham Town,"
22 November 1910, p. 14.

E 516
"Cubs' Old Infield to Be a
Memory?," 27 November 1910,
p. 1, pt. 3.

The following five articles (E 517
to E 521) from the *Chicago Tribune* do not carry Lardner's by-
line but were possibly written by
him since they are about teams
he was covering at the time.

E 517
"Galena Fans See Cubs in
Action," 16 June 1909, p. 14.

E 518
"Sox Meet Macks in Two
Contests," 25 September 1910,
pp. 1–2, pt. 3.

E 519
"White Sox Give Browns Beating,"
30 September 1910, p. 8.

It is doubtful that Lardner wrote
this article.

E 520
"Browns' Errors Give Sox
Victory," 1 October 1910, p. 10.

E 521
"Cubs Grab Last from Pittsburg," 9 October 1910, pp. 1–2,
pt. 3.

THE SPORTING NEWS[3]
"Pullman Pastimes" (1910–1911)

E 522
15 December 1910, p. 2.

E 523
21 December 1910, p. 2.

E 524
28 December 1910, p. 2.

E 525
5 January 1911, p. 3.

E 526
12 January 1911, p. 6.

E 527
19 January 1911, p. 2.

E 528
26 January 1911, p. 3.

E 529
2 February 1911, p. 2.

E 530
9 February 1911, p. 2.

E 531
16 February 1911, p. 2.

BOSTON AMERICAN[4]
(1911)

E 532
"Shean Trade Should Help the
Rustlers," 28 February 1911, p. 8.

E 533
"Veterans Must 'Make Good' for
Rustlers," 1 March 1911, p. 1.

E 534
"Rustlers Are Short of Good
Backstops," 3 March 1911, p. 10.

E 535
"Rustlers Make Ready for Trip to
the South," 4 March 1911, p. 11.

E 536
"Rustlers Start on Hustling Spring
Trip," 5 March 1911, p. 8S.

E 537
"Red Sox Likely to Win Second
Place Rustlers Will Not Be the
Tail-enders," 5 March 1911, p. 8S.

E 538
"Rustlers Get Away for South
Tonight," 6 March 1911, p. 8.

E 539
"Rustlers Are Off to Invade
Georgia," 7 March 1911, p. 9.

E 540
"Rustlers Arrive in Augusta,"
8 March 1911, pp. 1, 12.

E 541
"First Practice for 'Rustlers',"
9 March 1911, pp. 1, 12.

---

3. All articles are signed 'R. W. Lardner'.
4. All articles except one (E 728) are signed 'R. W. Lardner'. The
file of the *Boston American* examined is at the Boston Public Library.

E 542
"Taft to Watch the Rustlers,"
10 March 1911, pp. 1, 12.

E 543
"Rustler Teams in Hot Game,"
11 March 1911, pp. 1, 6.

E 544
"Rustler Colts Beat Out Regulars,"
12 March 1911, p. 7S.

E 545
"Rustlers Almost Get Hofman
Chance Foils Baseball Coup,"
12 March 1911, p. 8S.

E 546
"Rustlers Have a Day of Rest in
Augusta," 13 March 1911, p. 8.

E 547
"Owner Russell Says Rustlers Not
Sold," 14 March 1911, p. 10.

E 548
"Tenney Leads Band Against
Yanigans," 15 March 1911, p. 6.

E 549
"Rustlers Will Play Yankees,"
16 March 1911, p. 11.

E 550
"Taft to See Rustler Game,"
17 March 1911, p. 12.

E 551
"Rustlers Play First Real Game of
Season," 18 March 1911, p. 7.

E 552
"Rustlers Win First Game of Year,
3 to 0," 19 March 1911, p. 5S.

E 553
"Rustlers Begin Live Campaign
on Diamond," 19 March 1911,
p. 7S.

E 554
"Drill Rustler Squad in New
Trick Play," 20 March 1911, p. 6.

E 555
"Rustlers Play for Fair Sex,"
21 March 1911, pp. 1, 8.

E 556
"Rustlers-Columbia Battle Called
Off," 22 March 1911, p. 10.

E 557
"Rustler Team in Sad Mixup,"
23 March 1911, p. 12.

E 558
"Hot Days Ahead for Rustlers,"
24 March 1911, p. 12.

E 559
"Rustlers Out to Win Series with
Yankees," 25 March 1911, p. 8.

E 560
"Too Much Chase Beats Rustlers
in Hot Game," 26 March 1911,
pp. 1S, 3S.

E 561
"Tenney Selects His Team of
Rustlers," 26 March 1911, p. 3S.

E 562
"Tenney Not to Trade Mattern to
Pirates," 27 March 1911, p. 6.

E 563
"Rustlers' Last Days of Spring
Training," 28 March 1911, p. 10.

E 564
"Rustlers Off for Columbia,"
29 March 1911, p. 9.

E 565
"Rustlers Play Columbia Team,"
30 March 1911, p. 11.

E 566
"Rustlers Again Play Columbias,"
31 March 1911, p. 14.

E 567
"Rustlers Play at Greensboro,"
1 April 1911, p. 8.

E 568
"Rustlers Smash Out 34–0
Victory at Greensboro," 2 April
1911, pp. 1S, 4S.

E 569
"Tenney Picks His Line-up Josh
Clarke Leads 'Em Off," 2 April
1911, p. 4S.

E 570
"Rustlers Now in Virginia,"
3 April 1911, p. 7.

E 571
"Rustlers Move to Richmond,"
4 April 1911, p. 11.

E 572
"Rustlers Play Norfolk Today,"
5 April 1911, p. 9.

E 573
"Tenney Confers with Hamilton,"
6 April 1911, p. 15.

E 574
"Rustlers Take on Lynchburg
To-Day," 7 April 1911, p. 15.

E 575
"New Catcher for Rustlers,"
8 April 1911, p. 7.

E 576
"Tenney Men Ready for First
Battle with Brooklyn," 9 April
1911, pp. 1S, 2S.

E 577
"Rustlers in Final Game with
Baltimore," 10 April 1911, p. 7.

E 578
"Rustlers Home for First Game,"
11 April 1911, p. 10.

E 579
"Rustlers Out To-Day for the
'Big Show'," 12 April 1911, p. 10.

E 580
"Rustlers Out for Brooklyn
Series," 13 April 1911, p. 13.

E 581
"Pick Curtis to Lead Rustlers to
Victory," 14 April 1911, p. 13.

E 582
"Rustlers After the First Game,"
15 April 1911, p. 1.

E 583
"Rustlers in Thrilling Finish Beat
Phillies in Tenth, 5–4," 16 April
1911, pp. 1S, 2S.

E 584
"Rustlers Play Fast Ball; Start in
a Rush," 16 April 1911, p. 2S.

E 585
"Rustlers Ready for the Phillies
Again," 17 April 1911, p. 7.

E 586
"Buster Brown Rustlers' Hope,"
18 April 1911, p. 6.

E 587
"Phillies Pile Up Big Lead in
Rustler Game," 19 April 1911, p.1.

E 588
"Rustlers' Busy Day with Two
Games On," 19 April 1911, p. 6.

E 589
"Red Sox at Home; Opening Is Put
Over," 20 April 1911, p. 12.

E 590
"Ray Collins Pitches Red Sox
Game Today," 22 April 1911, p. 8.

E 591
"Speaker Smashes Out 4–3
Victory for the Red Sox,"
23 April 1911, p. 1S.

E 592
"Red Sox Last with Athletics,"
24 April 1911, p. 6.

E 593
"Yankees in Series with Red Sox
Today," 25 April 1911, p. 11.

E 594
"Eddie Cicotte's Day to Do Stellar
Act," 26 April 1911, p. 9.

E 595
"Red Sox," 27 April 1911, p. 1.

E 596
"Red Sox Climbing Nearer to the
Top," 28 April 1911, p. 6.

E 597
"Bill Carrigan Hurt and Is Out of
Game," 28 April 1911, p. 14.

E 598
"Washington Opens Series with
Red Sox," 29 April 1911, p. 6.

E 599
"12,000 See Red Sox Beaten 4 to
3," 30 April 1911, pp. 1S, 2S.

E 600
"Red Sox Will Soon Leave Home
Grounds," 1 May 1911, p. 6.

E 601
"Red Sox," 2 May 1911, p. 1.

E 602
"Red Sox Near Finish of Home
Engagement," 2 May 1911, p. 10.

E 603
"Red Sox Last Home Game for
Month," 3 May 1911, p. 10.

E 604
"Rustlers Home to Make Spurt,"
4 May 1911, p. 15.

E 605
"Al Mattern Will Try to Win for
Rustlers," 5 May 1911, p. 13.

E 606
"Rustlers Can Land Top of 2d
Division," 6 May 1911, p. 8.

E 607
"Giants Win Weird South End
Game by a Huge Score," 7 May
1911, p. 1S.

E 608
"Lynch May Lay Off Rustlers
Players," 8 May 1911, p. 7.

E 609
"Rustlers Begin New Series with
the Reds," 9 May 1911, p. 10.

E 610
"Rustlers Will Try to Beat Reds
Today," 10 May 1911, p. 9.

E 611
"Buster Brown and George Suggs
Today," 11 May 1911, p. 13.

E 612
"Reds Must Face the Unbeaten
Pfeffer," 12 May 1911, p. 13.

E 613a
"Pirates Smash Out Victory from
Rustlers," 13 May 1911, pp. 1S, 2S.

E 613b
"Pirates Begin Series To–Day,"
13 May 1911, p. 9.

E 614
"Shortstop Is Hardest Job Herzog
Points Out Why," 14 May 1911,
p. 6S.

E 615
"Ill-Fated Rustlers Play Pirates
Again," 15 May 1911, p. 7.

E 616
"Pirates' Luck May Be Turned by
Rustlers," 16 May 1911, p. 10.

E 617
"Rustlers End with Pirates,"
17 May 1911, p. 1.

E 618
"17 Home Runs in Nine Games,"
17 May 1911, p. 9.

E 619
"Cardinals Just Beat Rustlers,"
18 May 1911, p. 1.

E 620
"Rustlers Won't Dally Long in
Last Place," 18 May 1911, p. 11.

E 621
"Another South Paw Pitches
Again Today," 9 May 1911, p. 13.

E 622
"Rustlers Try Again to Win,"
20 May 1911, p. 9.

E 623
"Cardinals Trim the Rustlers
Once More 4 to 1," 21 May
1911, pp. 1S, 2S.

E 624
"Doc and Scotty on 'Hitting' Hey,
Officer, He's In Again!" 21 May
1911, p. 3S.

E 625
"Rustlers Have One More Chance
to Win," 22 May 1911, p. 9.

E 626
"Cubs and Rustlers at South End
Park," 23 May 1911, p. 11.

E 627
"Red Sox," 24 May 1911, p. 1.

E 628
"Rustlers Have One More Game
with Cubs," 24 May 1911, p. 9,
10 O'clock Edition.

E 629
"Rustlers Doomed to Defeat Again
Today," 24 May 1911, p. 9,
5th Edition.

E 630
"Cubs Start Out West after
Today's Game," 25 May 1911,
p. 12.

E 631
"Steinfeldt in Rustler Game,"
26 May 1911, p. 13.

E 632
"Steinfeldt Is Rustler Hero,"
27 May 1911, p. 9.

E 633
"Dodgers Win Close Game from
Boston," 28 May 1911, pp. 1S, 2S.

E 634
"Graham Nine Men in One How
'Peaches' Won Out," 28 May
1911, p. 3S.

E 635
"Dodgers' Last with Rustlers,"
29 May 1911, p. 7.

E 636
"Two Games Today at So. End
Ball Grounds," 30 May 1911, p. 9,
First Extra Edition.

E 637
"Rustlers Lose First with
Philadelphia," 30 May 1911, p. 1,
Extra Home Edition.

E 638
"Rustlers Need Cecil Ferguson,"
30 May 1911, p. 9, Extra Home
Edition.

E 639
"Rustlers in Final Contest at
Home," 31 May 1911, p. 7.

E 640
"Red Sox Battle Chicago," 1 June
1911, pp. 1, 11.

E 641
"White Sox and Red Sox Again,"
2 June 1911, pp. 1, 13.

E 642
"Red Sox Go After 3rd Game,"
3 June 1911, pp. 1, 7.

E 643
"Speed Boys Bat Out Victory at
Last," 4 June 1911, pp. 1S, 2S.

E 644
"New Balls Beat 'Em All Perdue
Discovers a Few," 4 June 1911,
p. 3S.

E 645
"Red Sox Must Win to Quit Even
in Series," 5 June 1911, p. 7.

E 646
"Red Sox Game with Browns
Called Off," 6 June 1911, p. 9.

E 647
"St. Louis Browns Open Against
the Red Sox," 7 June 1911, p. 8.

E 648
"Browns Hard for Red Sox,"
8 June 1911, p. 10.

E 649
"Browns in Windup; Sox Laying
for Tigers," 9 June 1911, p. 11.

E 650
"Red Sox Play Mighty Tigers,"
10 June 1911, pp. 1, 7.

E 651
"27,000 See Red Sox Defeat the
Tigers in 10-Inning Game,"
11 June 1911, pp. 1S, 2S.

E 652
"Miller Champion Batter Rustler
Is 1911 Wonder," 11 June 1911,
p. 3S.

E 653
"Second Game with Tigers,"
12 June 1911, pp. 1, 7.

E 654
"Tigers Say Red Sox Don't Fit,"
13 June 1911, p. 11.

E 655
"Naps Open Series Against Red
Sox," 14 June 1911, p. 10.

E 656
"Tris Speaker Back in Sox Game
To-Day," 15 June 1911, p. 15.

E 657
"Big Cy Young on Job Today,"
16 June 1911, p. 6.

E 658
"Cy Young Still Is Much Alive,"
17 June 1911, p. 7.

E 659
"Speed Boys, in Fifth Place, Face
Some Hard Battles," 18 June
1911, p. 1S.

E 660
"Red Sox Lose Two to Naps and Drop Into Fifth Place," 18 June 1911, pp. 1S, 2S.

E 661
"Cobb's 'Inside' Baseball How It Wins the Game," 18 June 1911, p. 5S.

E 662
"Rustlers Home in Three Games," 19 June 1911, p. 6.

E 663
"Fans Can Now Decide on Merits of Swap," 20 June 1911, p. 8.

E 664
"Rustlers Not Pennant Stuff," 21 June 1911, p. 11.

E 665
"Rustlers End Short Series Here To-Day," 22 June 1911, p. 13.

E 666
"How 'Noisy John' Makes Good Kling's Tongue a Big Asset," 25 June 1911, p. 5S.

E 667
"Ingerton Back at Third Base," 7 July 1911, p. 6.

E 668
"Rustlers Try for the Third," 8 July 1911, pp. 1, 7.

E 669
"Reds Take Another from the Rustlers," 9 July 1911, pp. 1S, 2S.

E 670
"Rustlers Play Final with Reds To-Day," 10 July 1911, p. 6.

E 671
"St. Louis in Wreck Game Here is Called," 11 July 1911, p. 9.

E 672
"Rustlers Play Cards 2 Games," 12 July 1911, p. 1.

E 673
"Umpires and Players Even Up in Battles," 12 July 1911, p. 7.

E 674
"Tenney's Players in Fighting Spirit," 13 July 1911, p. 11.

E 675
"One Game Today with St. Louis," 14 July 1911, p. 8.

E 676
"Chicago Cubs Here to Play Rustlers," 15 July 1911, p. 7.

E 677
"Rustlers Walk Away with the Cubs in Opening Battle," 16 July 1911, pp. 1S, 2S.

E 678
"Rustler Rebels Out in Battle to Finish," 17 July 1911, pp. 1, 7, Last Home Edition.

E 679
"Rustlers Want to Show Cubs," 17 July 1911, p. 7, Last Home Edition.

E 680
"Rebel Players Standing Pat," 18 July 1911, p. 8.

E 681
"Sheckard Good for Many Years," 19 July 1911, p. 9.

E 682
"Pirates Are On Hand to Tackle Rustlers," 20 July 1911, p. 9.

E 683
"Herzog Goes for Bridwell," 21 July 1911, p. 1.

E 684
"Rustlers Must Have High-Class
Pitchers," 22 July 1911, p. 7.

E 685
"What! Baltimore Win the
Rustlers from Old Boston?"
23 July 1911, p. 1S.

E 686
"Rustlers Lose by Big Flock of
Seven Errors," 23 July 1911,
pp. 1S, 2S.

E 687
"Oddities of Bleacher 'Bugs' They
Err, but They're Happy," 23 July
1911, p. 4S.

E 688
"Red Sox Have Day's Rest; Then
Chicago," 24 July 1911, p. 7.

E 689
"Red Sox Begin Chicago Games,"
25 July 1911, p. 9.

E 690
"Hedges Anxious to Swap Ball
Players," 26 July 1911, p. 9.

E 691
"Red Sox Men Soon in Shape,"
27 July 1911, p. 8.

E 692
"Red Sox–Brown Game Called
Off," 28 July 1911, p. 5.

E 693
"Red Sox Have Fast Infield,"
29 July 1911, p. 6.

E 694
"No Hits or Runs and But Three
Browns Make First Base," 30 July
1911, pp. 1S, 2S.

E 695
"Jack Gleason Happy; He's in Big
League Baseball at Last," 30 July
1911, p. 3S.

E 696
"In the Press Box a Tragedy in
One Act," 30 July 1911.

E 697
"Red Sox in for a Busy Week,"
31 July 1911, p. 6.

E 698
"Fans on Edge to See Tigers,"
1 August 1911, p. 11.

E 699
"25,000 See Red Sox Play,"
2 August 1911, p. 1.

E 700
"Tigers, to Keep Lead, Must Win
Four Games," 2 August 1911,
p. 11.

E 701
"Tigers Battle Hard to Hold the
Red Sox," 3 August 1911, p. 11.

E 702
"Red Sox Victory Means Tigers'
Fall," 4 August 1911, p. 7.

E 703
"Detroit Team in Hard Luck,"
5 August 1911, p. 6.

E 704
"30,000 Look On While Tigers
Beat Red Sox," 6 August 1911,
pp. 1S, 2S.

E 705
"Naps Go After Sox in First,"
7 August 1911, p. 5.

E 706
"Sox Out to Get Even with Naps
in Second," 8 August 1911, p. 6.

E 707
"Sox Fight Hard for Odd Game,"
9 August 1911, p. 6.

E 708
"Both Baseball Teams Lay Off,"
10 August 1911, p. 6.

E 709
"Rustlers Open with Dodgers,"
11 August 1911, p. 6.

E 710
"Mike Donlin Here to Stay,"
12 August 1911, pp. 1, 2, Home
Edition.

E 711
"Rustlers Out to Win 40 Games in
Season," 12 August 1911, p. 5,
Home Edition.

E 712
"Rustlers Win One and Lose One
to Dodgers," 13 August 1911,
pp. 1S, 2S.

E 713
"German Rivals in Batting Duel
Both After Home-Run Records,"
13 August 1911, p. 5S.

E 714
"Rustlers Meet Dodgers in 4th,"
14 August 1911, p. 7.

E 715
"Rustlers Play Last Game with
Dodgers," 15 August 1911, p. 6.

E 716
"Cubs Here for Four Games with
Rustlers," 16 August 1911, p. 6.

E 717a
"Rustlers Go After Second Cubs'
Game," 17 August 1911, p. 8.

E 717b
"Rustlers Meet Cubs in Rubber,"
18 August 1911, p. 6.

E 718
"Rustlers Feel Sure of Crushing
Cubs," 19 August 1911, p. 5.

E 719
"10,000 See the Cubs Take
Revenge on Tenney's Rustlers,"
20 August 1911, pp. 1S, 2S.

E 720
"Big League Managers Well Paid,
but They Have a Big Problem,"
20 August 1911, p. 3S.

E 721
"Rustlers Have Very Busy Week,"
21 August 1911, p. 5.

E 722
" 'Old Cy' Young Day at So. End
Grounds," 22 August 1911, p. 7.

E 723
"Rustlers Play Reds Last Game
of Series," 23 August 1911, p. 7.

E 724
"Rustlers Have New Foe in
Cardinals," 24 August 1911, p. 10.

E 725
"2 Unfinished Series in Rustler
Schedule," 26 August 1911, p. 7.

E 726
"10,000 See 'Cy' Young Win One,
5 to 4," 27 August 1911, pp.
1S, 2S.

E 727
"Pirates Have a Chance to Battle
Again for World's Championship,"
27 August 1911, p. 3S.

E 728
"Pirates Open Here Against
Rustlers," 28 August 1911, p. 7.[5]

E 729
"Big Cy and O'Toole May Line Up
To-Day," 30 August 1911, p. 6,
Home Edition.

E 730
"Red Sox Home for Hard Games,"
31 August 1911, p. 10.

E 731
"Sun Welcome to Ball Fans,"
1 September 1911, p. 9.

E 732
"Detroit Must Hit to Capture
Title," 3 September 1911, pp.
1S, 5S.

E 733
"Rustlers' Revenge Prevented by
Rain," 10 September 1911, p. 5B.

E 734
"Lew Richie the Hope of the
Chicago Cubs in Big World's
Series," 10 September 1911, p. 6B.

E 735
"Baker's Hitting a Big Factor,"
14 September 1911, p. 11.[6]

E 736
"Doyle Is Sure a Flag Chaser,"
15 September 1911, p. 13.

E 737
"Rube Marquard Has the Goods,"
16 September 1911, p. 7.

E 738
"New York Giants Have Best
Chance to Take Honors from
Athletics," 17 September 1911,
p. 4S.

E 739
"Fred Snodgrass a Valuable Man,"
18 September 1911, p. 6.

E 740
"Coombs Not in Best of Shape,"
19 September 1911, p. 9.

E 741
"Giants Rely Chiefly on Meyers,"
20 September 1911, p. 8.

E 742
"Ames Now in Tip-Top Form,"
21 September 1911, p. 11.

E 743
"Strunk Ranks with Big Stars,"
22 September 1911, p. 10.

E 744
"Matty King of Pitchers,"
23 September 1911, p. 7.

E 745
"Coming World's Series Will Not
Be Frolic for Connie Mack's
Athletics," 24 September 1911,
p. 7S.

E 746
"Jack Murray a Hard Hitter,"
25 September 1911, p. 8.

E 747
"John M'Graw Wise Manager,"
26 September 1911, p. 8.

---

5. This article is signed 'R. N. Lardner'.
6. There was almost certainly an additional article between entries
E 734 and E 735.

E 748
"Lapp Partner of Jack Coombs,"
27 September 1911, p. 8.

E 749
"George Wiltse Has Control,"
28 September 1911, p. 11.

E 750
"Beals Becker a Speedy Man,"
29 September 1911, p. 12.

E 751
"Don Murphy Is Some Fielder,"
30 September 1911, p. 9.

E 752
"New York Giants Sure to Prove
Worthy Foes for World's
Champions," 1 October 1911,
pp. 5S, 6S.

E 753
"Rube Oldring a Classy Fielder,"
2 October 1911, p. 6.

E 754
"Wilson Is Weak on Foul Flies,"
3 October 1911, p. 7.

E 755
"Eddie Collins Is a Wonder,"
4 October 1911, p. 11.

E 756
"World's Series Primer,"
5 October 1911, p. 13.

E 757
"M'Innes Will Cover First,"
5 October 1911, p. 13.

E 758
"World's Series Primer,"
6 October 1911, p. 15.

E 759
"Bristol Lord, Speedy Fielder,"
6 October 1911, p. 15.

E 760
"World's Series Primer,"
7 October 1911, p. 6.

E 761
"Krause Sure to Work in Series,"
7 October 1911, p. 6.

E 762
"Fans Await Words of William
Klem," 8 October 1911, p. 3S.

E 763
"World's Series Primer,"
9 October 1911, p. 7.

E 764
"The World's Series the Big
Noise," 9 October 1911, p. 7.

E 765
"World's Series Primer,"
10 October 1911, p. 8.

E 766
"Matthewson May Fool
Dopesters," 11 October 1911, p. 7.

E 767
"World's Series Primer," 12
October 1911, p. 13.

E 768
"Giants Win by Hitting Bender at
Right Time," 15 October 1911,
p. 3S.

E 769
"Merkle Keeps at His Old Post on
First Base," 17 October 1911,
p. 10.

E 770
"4th Game Held Up by Rain,"
18 October 1911, p. 1.

E 771
"More Rain Rests Matty to Go In
Against Athletics," 19 October
1911, p. 12.

E 772
"Fourth Game Is All Off Again,"
20 October 1911, p. 14.

E 773
"Same Old Tale! Game Is Off!"
23 October 1911, p. 9.

CHICAGO EXAMINER[7]
(1912–1913)

E 774
"White Sox Here Ready to Start
Long Grind," 10 April 1912, p. 11.

E 775
"Baseball Eclipses Politics
To=Day; 170,000 Will See Open-
ing Games," 11 April 1912, p. 11.

E 776
"Mattick's First Hit in Majors
Decides Game," 13 April 1912,
p. 11.

E 777
"Sox Are Beaten, 2–0, by Browns,
in Battle of Pitching Recruits; Not
Peters' Fault, as Hits Show,"
14 April 1912, p. 1, sports section.

E 778
"Cubs Drub Cards, 5–2; Tie for
Fourth McIntire Good; Tinker
Stars at Bat," 26 April 1912, p. 9.

E 779
"Cubs Lambasted by Cards, 10–8,
on Lennox's 3 Errors; Cheney
Bad, Support Worse," 27 April
1912, p. 10.

E 780
"Cubs Smother Cards, 9 to 0, in
Batting Jamboree," 28 April 1912,
p. 1, sports section.

E 781
"Here's Frank Schulte's Woeful
Lay: Alas! We Play the Cards
To-Day Because It Rained All
Yesterday," 29 April 1912, p. 9.

E 782
"Pennant for the White Sox
Predicted By Murphy and P.L.;
Reulbach Will Pitch To-Day,"
30 April 1912, p. 9.

E 783
"Cubs, 4 Ahead, Lose to Reds,
7–5," 1 May 1912, p. 11.

E 784
"Cubs Whale Pittsburg, 7 to 2
Ritchie Is Great After First Inning
Hofman and Evers Glitter,"
2 May 1912, p. 11.

E 785
"Marty O'Toole Blanks Cubs
$22,500 Star Worth Weight in
Gold Ed Reulbach Shows Control,"
3 May 1912, p. 7.

E 786
"12 Cubs Whip 18 Pirates, 9 to 8,
in 11-Inning Battle," 4 May
1911, p. 3.

E 787
"O'Toole Beaten by Richie and
Zim, Who Didn't Cost $22,500,"
6 May 1912, p. 11.

---

7. All articles are signed 'R. W. Lardner'. The only located file of
the *Chicago Examiner* is at the Chicago Historical Society.

E 788
"Cubs Down Kling's Braves, 5–3
Climb to 500 and Third Place,"
7 May 1912, p. 13.

E 789
"Cubs Pummel Perdue and Beat
Boston, 9–4 Lavender Good for
7 Innings, Bad for Last 2,"
8 May 1912, p. 11.

E 790
"Zimmerman's Great Slugging
Beats Boston for Cubs 9–8,"
9 May 1912, p. 13.

E 791
"Hess, Nap Relic, Gives Cubs One
Hit, so Braves Win, 2–1,"
10 May 1912, p. 7.

E 792
"Cubs Shut Out by Giants, 4 to 0
Ames Excels Cheney in Pinches,"
11 May 1912, p. 7.

E 793
"Marquard Downs Cubs, 10 to 3
Giants Pound Richie and Cole,"
12 May 1912, p. 5, sports section.

E 794
"What Can Heine's Average Be?
Says Schulte, He's Hitting 1143,"
13 May 1912, p. 6.

E 795
"Cubs and Giants Play 4–4 Tie
Darkness Stops Game in Ninth,"
14 May 1912, p. 13.

E 796
"Cubs with New Lineup, Shut Out
Phillies, 2–0 Cheney Outpitches
Alexander, Quakers' Trump,"
15 May 1912, p. 13.

E 797
"Cubs Have a Class in Geography
They All Know the Way To
Louisville Too Wet to Play with
Phillies," 16 May 1912, p. 7.

E 798
"Zim Hitting .444 for 23 Games
at Least One Safety in Each Battle
Cubs and Phils Idle in Downpour,"
17 May 1912, p. 13.

E 799
"4 Cub Pitchers Fail Again
Phillies Cuff Them, 7 to 5,"
18 May 1912, p. 18.

E 800
"Zimmerman's Home Run and
Two Singles Help Cubs Trim
Dodgers, 5–4," 19 May 1912, p. 5.

E 801
"Cubs Get Trouncing from Dodgers, 6–2," 20 May 1912, p. 11.

E 802
"Chance's New Pitcher Wins;
Moroney Better Than Rucker, So
Cubs Trim Dodgers, 5 to 4," 22
May 1912, p. 11.

E 803
"Cubs Larrup Dodgers, 10 to 6
Zim Hits a Homer; Writes a Poem
Schulte Bunter Now, Says Heine,"
23 May 1912, p. 13.

E 804
"Cubs Battle in Pittsburg To-Day
Chance Grouchy About Weather,"
24 May 1912, p. 11.

E 805
"Pirates Slam Richie and Cole for
14 Hits, Whaling Cubs, 7–3;
Lavender and Reulbach Next,"
25 May 1912, p. 11.

E 806
"Pirate Horseshoe Beats Cubs, 4–2 Ousts Them from 3d Place, Too," 26 May 1912, p. 7, sports section.

E 807
"O'Toole Gets Revenge on Cubs Hurls Pirates to a 3–to–1 Win," 27 May 1912, p. 7.

E 808
"Ed Reulbach Holds Reds to Three Hits and Hurls Cubs Into Belated Win, 4–1," 28 May 1912, p. 13.

E 809
"Brown Comes Back as Did Reulbach, Beating Reds, 10–2; Mordecai Shows Old Skill," 29 May 1912, p. 11.

E 810
"Cubs Play 2 To-Day Harry M'Intire Sold," 30 May 1912, p. 11.

E 811
"Cubs Beat Reds 2, Schulte's 1st Homer Bagging the Opener," 31 May 1912, p. 9.

E 812
"Cubs in Boston, Saddened by Trade of Hofman and Cole; Schulte Poem Says Good-bye," 1 June 1912, p. 11.

E 813
"Cubs Get 7–5 Win Over Braves Saier's Homer Clinches Game," 2 June 1912, p. 6, sports section.

E 814
"Cubs Try Deep-Sea Fishing Cheney to Face the Braves To-Day Miller Keeps Leach on Beach," 3 June 1912, p. 15.

E 815
"Cubs Beat Dejected Braves, 4–3 Sheckard's Double Wins Game," 4 June 1912, p. 11.

E 816
"Braves Hand Cubs This One, 2–1 Kling and Tyler Generous Indeed Cheney Leads in 7th Win in Row," 5 June 1912, p. 17.

E 817
"Fickle Goddess Jilts the Cubs Dodgers' Win of 4–Leaf Clover Kind Zim Hits His Fifth Home Run," 6 June 1912, p. 11.

E 818
"Brooklyn Wet; Cubs Dry in N.Y. It's Lavender's Turn to Pitch To-Day Chance Praises Ward Miller," 7 June 1912, p. 11.

E 819
"Leifield Wins First Cub Game Holds Brooklyn to Four Hits," 8 June 1912, p. 11.

E 820
"Merciless Cubs Rout Dodgers Fifteen Hits Get a 10 to 2 Win," 9 June 1912, p. 4, sports section.

E 821
"Cubs Say They Are Giant Killers Profess No Fear of Rube Marquard Get Chance to Prove It To-Day," 10 June 1912, p. 11.

E 822
"Cubs Whip Giants in Ten Innings Heine's 2 Homers Take Melee, 9 to 8," 11 June 1912, p. 11.

E 823
"Cubs Outfinished by Giants, 8–3 Zim Hits His Ninth Home Run," 12 June 1912, p. 11.

E 824
"Cubs, with Tinker and Zim Out on Suspensions, Lose to Giants, 3–2, When L. Richie Is Injured," 13 June 1912, p. 11.

E 825
"Mathewson Tames Cubs, 3–2 in Bitter Battle With Cheney; J. Archer Clouts a Home Run," 14 June 1912, p. 11.

E 826
"Downs' Swats Score 5 Runs; Cubs Win, 7–5," 15 June 1912, p. 16.

E 827
"Cubs Just Can't Get Chance to Play with Regular Lineup," 18 June 1912, p. 11.

E 828
"Cheney Masters Phillies in Pitching Duel with Brennan," 19 June 1912, p. 17.

E 829
"Cubs Take Long Jump to Play Cards To-Day," 20 June 1912, p. 20.

E 830
"Cubs Beaten by Cardinals, 3–2, in 10th; Brown Weakens When Victory Seems Certain," 21 June 1912, p. 17.

E 831
"Cubs Win Nomination by a Small Majority at St. Louis," 22 June 1912, p. 11.

E 832
"Cubs Nominated by 10 to 2 Vote; Cards Play the Bull Moose," 23 June 1912, p. 3, sports section.

E 833
"Cleveland Gives Sox a Bump; Doc White Victim of Errors; Gregg Stingy; Gives 3 Hits," 24 June 1912, p. 7.

E 834
"Rollie Zeider Is a Sox Puzzle Coast Slugger Is Not in Form," 25 June 1912, p. 11.

E 835
"Browns Trim Walsh and Sox; E. Brown Is Felled with Ball," 26 June 1912, p. 17.

E 836
"Butcher Benz Has Good Day; Result Is, Sox Blank Browns," 27 June 1912, p. 11.

E 837
"Sox Drop One to the Tigers as Joe Benz' Meat Ball Fails," 29 June 1912, p. 11.

E 838
"Rain Halts the Sox; Play Tigers 2 To-Day," 30 June 1912, p. 4, sports section.

E 839
"Sox Divide with the Tigers; Walsh Pitches Shutout Game," 1 July 1912, p. 11.

E 840
"Rain Halts the Sox and Browns Double-Header Is Due To-Day," 2 July 1912, p. 11.

E 841
"Sox Get an Even Break, So Long Afternoon Is Wasted; Browns Grab First In Ninth," 3 July 1912, p. 11.

E 842
"Sox Here To-Day for 2 Battles with Naps," 4 July 1912, p. 10.

E 843
"Walsh Works Better Than Ralph
Works, so Sox Win," 6 July 1912,
p. 13.

E 844a
"Dubuc Blanks Sox with 1-Hit
Game, but Callahan Grabs the
Second in Ninth," 7 July 1912,
p. 3, sports section.

E 844b
"Stahl Is Pet of Boston Town
Puts Red Sox in Flag Race," 7
July 1912, p. 3, sports section.

E 845
"Sox Depart on Eastern Trip Rain
Permits Earlier Start," 8 July
1912, p. 7.

E 846
"Earth Is Wanted for Ty Cobb
'Eyah' and Cal Talk Trade," 9
July 1912, p. 11.

E 847
"Athletics Outfinish the Sox
Walsh and Coombs in Duel," 10
July 1912, p. 9.

E 848
"Sox Beat Athletics in the Ninth
Cut Down Big Lead to Win, Too,"
11 July 1912, p. 13.

E 849
"Sox and Athletics Have to Fly
for When One Inning Has Gone
by Water Issues from the Sky,"
12 July 1912, p. 11.

E 850
"Sox Lose Two to Athletics Get
Lone Run in Eighteenth," 13
July 1912, p. 11.

E 851
"Sox Help Senators' Advance
Cicotte's Debut a 4–2 Defeat," 14
July 1912, p. 2, sports section.

E 852
"Sox Dislike Washington Sunday
Doc White to Face Senators To-
Day Griffith Has a Great Ball
Club," 15 July 1912, p. 7.

E 853
"Bodie's 'Return to Life' Star Act
in Sox 4–2 Drama," 16 July 1912,
p. 13.

E 854
"Senators Whale Sox, 7 to 2 Too
Much Johnson, Reason," 17 July
1912, p. 13.

E 855
"24,000 See Sox Divide Honors
with Boston Walsh Blanks League
Leaders with 2 Hits," 18 July
1912, p. 3.

E 856
"Rain Saves Sox a Massacre
Boston Has 10 In, 2 Out, in First
Cicotte Is Easy for Old Mates,"
19 July 1912, p. 13.

E 857
"Sox Drop 2 to Boston; Get 1 Run
21 Innings Cicotte Makes Foe Go
12 Rounds in 2–1 Fray," 20 July
1912, p. 13.

E 858
"Stahl's Homer Helps Beat Walsh,
3–2," 21 July 1912, p. 1, sports
section.

E 859a
"Callahan Decides To Put Zeider
On First," 22 July 1912, p. 7.

E 859b
"How To Say == Cicotte," 22 July 1912, p. 7.

E 860
"Sox Keep Up the Losing Habit Drop One to Yankees, 13 to 3," 23 July 1912, p. 13.

E 861
"Sox Come Back, Beat Ford End Winning Streak of Yanks," 24 July 1912, p. 7.

E 862
"Walsh Disobeys Orders; Loses Pitcher in Row with Callahan," 25 July 1912, p. 13.

E 863
"Benz-Walsh Slab Combine Beats Yankees in 10 Innings, 6–4, and the Sox Start Home," 26 July 1912, p. 13.

E 864
"White and Red Sox Arrive Together for Fray To-Day," 27 July 1912, p. 13.

E 865
"Speaker, Held Hitless Until Tenth, Cracks Home Run Off Walsh Which Beats Sox, 5–3," 28 July 1912, p. 1, sports section.

E 866
"Stahl's Hitting Beats Our Sox Again, 5–4," 29 July 1912, p. 7.

E 867
"Red Sox Take 3d, This One 7–5 Prehistoric Trick Fools Benz," 30 July 1912, p. 13.

E 868
Headline unavailable, 31 July 1912, p. 13.

E 869
"Sox Have Contagion of Boots and Muffs Behind Cicotte, So Yankees Crumple Them, 12–3," 1 August 1912, p. 11.

E 870
"White's Rheumatic Delivery and a Homer by Callahan Get Revenge on Yankees, 2 to 1," 2 August 1912, p. 13.

E 871
"Chase Forces Cal to Chase Lange; Walsh Then Wins, 5–3; Sox Renew Pennant Chase," 3 August 1912, p. 11.

E 872
"Sox Fall Before Clever Hurling of Caldwell," 4 August 1912, p. 1, sports section.

E 873
"Senators Beat Sox in a Great Pitching Duel," 5 August 1912, p. 7.

E 874
"Sox Get 6 Runs Ahead, Then Lose in Tenth, 8–7 Pestiferous Mr. Johnson Again Saves Senators," 6 August 1912, p. 11.

E 875
"Doc White, Aged and Infirm, Resurrects His Jinx of Old to Trounce Senators, 2 to 1," 7 August 1912, p. 11.

E 876
"Walter Johnson Catches Sox Off Stride and Quits to Give New Senator Hurler a Test," 8 August 1912, p. 11.

E 877
"The Sox=Athletics' Fray, Which
Was Billed for Yesterday, Post-
poned Because It Was Too Wet to
Play," 9 August 1912, p. 11.

E 878
"Sox Trim Fading Athletics Walsh
Needs 7 Tallies to Win," 10 Au-
gust 1912, p. 11.

E 879
"Athletics Trim White Sox, 8–0,
in 5 Innings," 11 August 1912,
p. 1, sports section.

E 880
"Athletics in Stride; Beat the Sox
Twice," 12 August 1912, pp.
11–12.

E 881
"Sox Fall Before Cleveland, 3 to 1
Kahler Beats Walsh in a Duel,"
13 August 1912, pp. 5–6.

E 882
"President Taft Naps at Game in
Which Sox Beat the Senators, 5–
3," 14 August 1912, pp. 13–14.

E 883
"White Sox Blank Senators, 6–0
Only 28 Batters Face Cicotte,"
15 August 1912, p. 6.

E 884
"Lardner Writes Us a Letter
Telling How White Sox Lose to
the Senators in 10 Innings," 16
August 1912, pp. 5–6.

E 885
"Johnson Blanks Sox with 1 Hit;
Only 29 Bat," 17 August 1912, p.
5.

E 886
"Athletics Are Put Out of Race by
White Sox," 18 August 1912, p. 6,
sports section.

E 887
"The Sox Do Nothing but Wander
About and Wonder How the Cubs
and the Giants Came Out," 19
August 1912, p. 8.

E 888
"Sox-Athletics Game Put Off
Because Coombs Isn't Ready; So
They'll Play Twice To-Day," 20
August 1912, p. 5.

E 889
"Rath Does Not Get Due Credit
Brains of the Infield, Say White
Sox Lack of Weight, His Handi-
cap," 21 August 1912, p. 9.

E 890
"Sox Just Won't Win Against
Poor Team," 22 August 1912, p. 7.

E 891a
"Recruit Taylor in Sox Debut
Beats Yanks," 23 August 1912, p.
5.

E 891b
"Cicotte in His Third Straight
Win for Sox," 24 August 1912,
p. 7.

E 892
"N.Y. Fans Have Case of Ego
Think Cubs Are a Flash in the
Pan Can't See the Giants as
Losers," 24 August 1912, pp. 7–8.

E 893
"Doc White Bad Enough, but Ford
Is Worse, Still Yankees Trim Sox
in Final Game, 7–6," 25 August
1912, pp. 1–2, sports section.

E 894
"Dear Reader: The Sox Are Once
More in Boston by the Ocean's
Shore in Massachusetts' Famous
Town There Fish Is Fresh and
Bread Is Brown," 26 August 1912,
p. 7.

E 895
"Red Sox May Be Coming
Champs, but They Can't Beat
Walsh," 27 August 1912, p. 7.

E 896
"Sox and Boston Draw in 12th
Even Kid Gleason Gets in Game,"
28 August 1912, p. 6.

E 897
"White Sox Give Red Sox Big
Boost Toward a Pennant by
Losing Twice in a Day," 29
August 1912, pp. 7–8.

E 898
"Mattick Will Whip Gleason, Just
Once," 30 August 1912, p. 7.

E 899
"Sox Get Mastodon Who Loses to
Naps," 31 August 1912, pp. 5–6.

E 900
"Cicotte Trims Naps in Hot
Hurling Duel," 1 September 1912,
pp. 1–2, sports section.

E 901
"Wild Pitch by Dubuc Gives
Game to South Siders, 7–6," 2
September 1912, pp. 7–8.

E 902
"Tigers Beat Sox, 12–4, Then Rain
Wins, 100–0," 3 September 1912,
p. 9.

E 903
"Lardner About Ready to Write
Cubs' Obituary," 6 September
1912, pp. 5, 7.

E 904
"Cubs Defeat Reds by Rally in
Ninth; Eight Games Back," 7
September 1912, pp. 5–6.

E 905
"Cubs Beaten Again After Hot
Rally in the 9th Round," 8 September 1912, pp. 13–14, sports
section.

E 906
"Reds Use 2 1-2 Hours and Many
Recruits to Win in 7 Innings, 10–
8," 9 September 1912, pp. 7–8.

E 907
"Cubs Slipping, but Will Fight to
the End," 10 September 1912,
p. 5.

E 908
"Father Cheney Joins Team and
Beats Braves," 11 September
1912, pp. 5–6.

E 909
"Rain at Boston Robs Zim of
Homer No. 15; Heine Is Real
Angry," 12 September 1912, pp.
5–6.

E 910
"Cubs Not Sure Second Place Is
Secure," 13 September 1912, pp.
5–6.

E 911
"Cheney's Homer Starts Spurt of
West Siders," 14 September 1912,
p. 5.

E 912
"Tesreau Usurps Role of Cub Tamer, Giving But 3 Hits; Giants Whale Richie, 5 to 0," 15 September 1912, p. 13.

E 913
"Chance Yields Second Place to Pirates," 16 September 1912, p. 7.

E 914
"Reulbach Shows Giants Some Speed and Wins, 4 to 3," 17 September 1912, p. 5.

E 915
"Cubs Beat Giants in Farewell Combat, Getting 13 Victories Out of 22 During the Season," 18 September 1912, p. 5.

E 916
"Cubs Bill Two with Dodgers for To-Day," 19 September 1912, p. 5.

E 917
"Dodgers Divide Double Bill with Cubs," 20 September 1912, pp. 5–6.

E 918
"Cubs Champions at Finishing, Anyway," 21 September 1912, pp. 13–14.

E 919
"Phillies Break Cheney's String of Eight Straight Victories and Humiliate the Cubs Twice," 22 September 1912, p. 13, sports section.

E 920
"Cubs Are Coming Home to Stay Wednesday," 23 September 1912, pp. 5–6.

E 921
"Cubs Unable to Play Final Two with Phils," 25 September 1912, p. 5.

E 922
Headline unavailable, 26 September 1912, p. 15.

E 923
"Cubs Trample Reds Twice to Prove Condition," 27 September 1912, p. 13.

E 924
"Cubs Lose, Then Fight 10-Inning Tie to Hold Place No. 2," 28 September 1912, p. 13.

E 925
"Cubs Get One Hit and Lose 12–1 in Seven Innings," 29 September 1912, p. 15.

E 926
"Lardner Picks Boston to Beat Giants in Big Series 'Excel Mechanically, on Offense and Defense'," 29 September 1912, p. 15.

E 927
"Peerless Leader Denies That He Quit, but Says He'll Drink and Smoke When He So Wishes," 30 September 1912, p. 5.

E 928
"Hendrix Tames Cubs 9–3, As White Sox Look On," 1 October 1912, p. 5.

E 929
"Cubs, with Four Hits, Lose Third Straight to the Pirates," 2 October 1912, p. 13.

E 930
"World Series Primer," 3 October 1912, p. 15.

E 931
"Chance Admits Stock Sale
$40,000 Is in His Possession;
Willing to Boss Cubs Again," 4
October 1912, p. 13.

E 932
"Murphy, in Cincinnati, Silent on
Chance's $40,000 Stock Sale; P. L.
Directs Practice of Cubs," 5
October 1912, p. 13.

E 933
"9 Cub Twirlers Toiling Like Mad
to Beat the Sox," 5 October 1912,
p. 13.

E 934
"Lavender a Victor in His Trial
Gallop," 6 October 1912, p. 14.

E 935
"Lardner Says Cubs Are the
Better Team but Sox Have Edge
Because of Walsh," 6 October
1912, p. 16.

E 936
"M'Graw Puts Hope in His
Speedy Outfield," 7 October
1912, p. 5.

E 937
"World and City Baseball Wars
Start To-Day Matty vs. Wood
Before 40,000 Is Lardner's
Forecast," 8 October 1912, p. 13.

E 938
"Red Sox Beat Giants, 4–3,
Before 40,000 Fans," 9 October
1912, pp. 9–10.

E 939
"Lardner's World Series Sidelights," 9 October 1912, p. 10.

E 940
"Game Pitching of Mathewson
Saves Men of M'Graw in Battle
That Will Re-Echo in History,"
10 October 1912, pp. 13, 24.

E 941
"Marquard Beats Boston 2–1, and
Puts Giants on Even Terms
34,624 Groan as Devore's Great
Catch in Ninth Saves 'Rube'," 11
October 1912, pp. 5–6.

E 942
"Lardner's Big Series Sidelights,"
11 October 1912, p. 6.

E 943
"Men of M'Graw Unable to Hit
'Smoke Ball' of Hub Star," 12
October 1912, pp. 13–14.

E 944
"Lardner's Big Series Sidelights,"
12 October 1912, p. 13.

E 945
"Boston's Third Victory Is Won
After Bitter Struggle," 13 October
1912, pp. 13–14, sports section.

E 946
"Giants, in Last Ditch, Hope to
Stop Red Sox Rush To-Day," 14
October 1912, pp. 5, 7.

E 947
Headline unavailable, 15 October
1912, pp. 13–14.

E 948
"Red Sox in Panic As M'Grawites
Hammer Out 'Smokey Joe'," 16
October 1912, pp. 5–6.

E 949
"Lardner's Big Series Sidelights,"
16 October 1912, p. 6.

E 950
"Fatal Error by Snodgrass in
Final Round Loses Game," 17
October 1912, p. 13.

E 951
"Lardner's Big Series Sidelights,"
17 October 1912, p. 13.

E 952
"Sox Could Have Won World's
Series, Says Lardner," 19 October
1912, pp. 13–14.

E 953
"Maroons Smother Iowa, 34–14,
by Great Rally in Last Quarter;
Stagg Forced to Show Tricks," 20
October 1912, p. 5.

E 954
"Rube Marquard Surprise of
World Series Battles," 20 October
1912, p. 7, sports section.

E 955
"Murphy Still Refuses to Give
Name of New Cub Leader," 22
October 1912, p. 5.

E 956
"Murphy Tells Tinker to Seek Job
as Reds' Manager," 23 October
1912, pp. 5–6.

E 957
"Choice of Evers as Cubs' Next
Manager Is Verified," 24 October
1912, pp. 13–14.

E 958
"Pirates One Best Bet for Next
Year's Flag," 25 October 1912,
p. 14.

E 959
"The Giants and Pirates Will No
Longer Dance to Melody: 'Evers
to Tinker to Chance'," 26 October
1912, p. 13.

E 960
"Maroons Held to 7–0 Score by
Purdue," 27 October 1912, pp.
13–14.

E 961
"Garry Herrmann to Meet Joe
Tinker To-Morrow and Start
Three-Cornered Deal," 28 Oc-
tober 1912, p. 11.

E 962
"Herrmann Admits He May Sign
Joe Tinker," 29 October 1912, p.
11.

E 963
"Evers Pondering Over How to
Trade Tinker," 30 October 1912,
p. 11.

E 964
"Evers Refuses to Trade Tinker
Unless Herrmann Makes Him
Better Offer," 31 October 1912, p.
11.

E 965
"Illini in Practice at Sox Park See
Omen in 16 to 0 on Score Board
'We're Sure to Beat Gophers
Now'," 1 November 1912, p. 11.

E 966
"Badger Eleven in Row on Eve of
Chicago Struggle," 2 November
1912, p. 11.

E 967
"Wonderful Wisconsin Eleven
Batters Maroons to Defeat in
Desperate 30 to 12 Combat," 3
November 1912, pp. 17–18, sports
section.

E 968
"Lots of Fans Like Evers as Boss
but the Arbiters Gasp—Astounded
and Every Umpire Is Shaking," 4
November 1912, p. 11.

E 969
"Tinker Says Cub Demands Will
Spoil Deal," 5 November 1912,
p. 11.

E 970
"The Baseball Writer Finally
Bethinks Him of a Plan to Stand
Upon the Corner and Talk to
Every Fan," 6 November 1912, p.
17.

E 971
"Murphy Explains Delay on Park
Can Build Any Time, but Has
New Plans Cub Pitcher Goes to
Athletics," 7 November 1912, p. 8.

E 972
"Maroons Win Over Purple, 3–0,
in Desperate Gridiron Battle on
Sellers' Goal from Field," 10
November 1912, pp. 13, 15.

E 973
"Cubs Will Get 3 Players for
Tinker; Chance May Be Given
Release by Reds," 12 November
1912, p. 9.

E 974
"Deal with Reds May Cause Big
Shift in Cubs," 13 November
1912, p. 10.

E 975
"Evers Is Dined by 400 Fans of
West Side," 15 November 1912,
p. 11.

E 976
"Evers in Long Talk with
Huggins Murphy Also at 3-Hour
Conference but Hauser Is Still a
Cardinal," 16 November 1912,
p. 14.

E 977
"Fogel Explosion Is Due To-Day
Chicago Need Not Worry.—
Lardner Civil Court May Save
Horace," 26 November 1912,
p. 10.

E 978
"A Football Prayer," 26 November
1912, p. 11.

E 979
"Eichenlaub's Runs Give Notre
Dame Victory, 69–0," 29 Novem-
ber 1912, p. 17.

E 980
"Tinker Returns; Blames
Murphy," 30 November 1912,
p. 11.

E 981a
"Five Badgers Win Places on
All-Western Eleven; Des Jardien
Only Maroon," 1 December 1912,
p. 15, sports section.

E 981b
"Heine Zim Buys Neckties for
All Cub Players," 1 December
1912, p. 15, sports section.

E 982
"Murphy Picks Best Outfielder
Goes Out of Own League to Find
Him Speaker Is Choice of Cubs'
Head," 2 December 1912, p. 10.

E 983
"Come Back, Joe," 3 December
1912, p. 14.

E 984
"Jim Scott Just Hears That Sox
Beat the Cubs," 4 December
1912, p. 10.

E 985
"If Chance Quits Game Is a
Loser, Says Comiskey,"
5 December 1912, p. 14.

E 986
"Sox Trying Hard to Buy
Crawford," 6 December 1912,
p. 11.

E 987
"Callahan Has a Training
Scheme," 7 December 1912, p. 16.

E 988
"Introducing Mr. Shaughnessy,"
8 December 1912, p. 19,
sports section.

E 989
"Cheney Wins 26 of 36 Games;
Is 2nd to Hendrix,"
9 December 1912, p. 11.

E 990
"American League in Meeting
To-Day," 11 December 1912, p. 11.

E 991
"American League Does Its Part
in Tinker Deal," 12 December
1912, p. 18.

E 992
"Chance Is Coming East to Sign
Owner of Yankees Is Awaiting
Him Ban Johnson Praises the
P.L.," 13 December 1912, p. 16.

E 993
"Yankees to Pay Chance $20,000,"
14 December 1912, p. 16.

E 994
"Cubs Are Well Fortified on
Infield After Various Deals,"
15 December 1912, p. 17,
sports section.

E 995
"Murphy, Back, Pleased with
Tinker Trade," 16 December
1912, p. 14.

E 996
"Cub President Expects Evers to
Win Pennant," 17 December
1912, p. 10.

E 997
"Cub Park to Have a Bull Sign
Schulte Wants It in Right Field
He Gets $50 Each Time He Hits
It," 18 December 1912, p. 14.

E 998
"Comiskey Will Enlarge Park to
Seat 45,000," 19 December 1912,
p. 14.

E 999
"Schulte Is Writing Poetry Again
He Gets $1.65 a Week from
Lardner Brown in a Trade for
Two Reds?," 20 December 1912,
p. 15, sports section.

E 1000
" 'Bresnahan Goes to Reds.'—
Tinker," 21 December 1912, p. 13.

E 1001
"Evers Forced to Release 10 Cubs
to Reach League Limit,"
22 December 1912, p. 13,
sports section.

E 1002
"Baseball of 1912 Greatest in
History of the Sport Is Comment
of Lardner," 29 December 1912,
p. 11, sports section.

E 1003
"Joe Berger in Fight for Sox
Shortstop Job," 31 December
1912, p. 13.

E 1004
"Sox on the Wagon? No! Not This
Year," 1 January 1913, p. 16.

E 1005
"Evers Due in Chicago Next
Week Wants to Talk Trade with
Huggins Cal Prepares for
Training Trip," 2 January 1913,
p. 9.

E 1006
"P.L. Expected to Draw Big
Crowds," 4 January 1913, p. 13.

E 1007
"Murphy Asserts Bresnahan Will
Be a Cub When Season Starts,"
5 January 1913, pp. 13–14,
sports section.

E 1008
"Roger Bresnahan Will Catch for
Cubs Murphy Outbids Reds and
Pirates," 7 January 1913, p. 11.

E 1009
"Frank Chance Admits He May
Sign with Farrell To-Day,"
8 January 1913, p. 11.

E 1010
"Chance Signs for 3 Years with
Yanks at Big Salary,"
9 January 1913, p. 11.

E 1011
"Farrell's Deal Pleases Murphy;
Says Evers Is Equal of Frank
Chance," 10 January 1913, p. 11.

E 1012
"Chance Comes Back to Prove
He's P.L. of Old," 11 January
1913, p. 11.

E 1013
"Third League Holds Meeting in
Chicago to Fight Majors,"
12 January 1913, p. 13,
sports section.

E 1014
"Repartee," 12 January 1913,
p. 14, sports section.

E 1015
"M'Graw Says Cubs Will Be in
Fight," 14 January 1913, p. 11.

E 1016
"Cicotte Signs with Sox; Cubs
Let Downs Go," 15 January
1913, p. 13.

E 1017
"Baseball Rulers Meet Here
To-Day," 16 January 1913, p. 13.

E 1018
"White Sox Purchase Davy Jones
Herrmann Again Heads Commis-
sion Chicago Has Busy Baseball
Day," 17 January 1913, p. 11.

E 1019
"O'Day Refuses Job as Umpire,"
18 January 1913, p. 11.

E 1020
"White Sox Now Fastest Team
in the Majors, Says Lardner,"
19 January 1913, p. 13,
sports section.

E 1021
"The Veterans," 19 January 1913,
p. 15, sports section.

E 1022
"Herrmann Has Good Things to
Say of Tinker," 20 January
1913, p. 13.

E 1023
"Cubs Will Get Philly Pitchers
in Pending Deal," 21 January
1913, p. 11.

E 1024
"Art Hofman, in Town, Selects
Pirates to Win," 22 January
1913, p. 13.

E 1025
"Murphy Visits Huggins; Seeks
Koney in Trade?" 23 January
1913, p. 11.

E 1026
"Callahan Says Harry Lord Is Not
on Market," 24 January 1913,
p. 11.

E 1027
"Johnson Signs a Sox Contract
Tinker Gets Illini Pitcher for
Reds Callahan Relates Some
Stories," 25 January 1913, p. 11.

E 1028
"Murphy Denies He Got Chance
Wire Threatening Him,"
26 January 1913, p. 13,
sports section.

E 1029
"Parodies," 26 January 1913,
p. 15, sports section.

E 1030
"Chance Coming to Dicker with
Sox for Berger," 27 January 1913,
p. 13.

E 1031
"Bill Lange, Old Cub Star, to
Coach Sox Base Runners,"
28 January 1913, p. 13.

E 1032
"Callahan After Jim Thorpe for
the White Sox," 29 January
1913, p. 11.

E 1033
"Murphy Is Now in Race for
Thorpe," 30 January 1913, p. 13.

E 1034
"Thorpe May Not Be Free Agent
Indian on Fayetteville Reserve
List Cubs May Drink—a Little
Bit," 31 January 1913, p. 17.

E 1035
"Dinneen Wins Prize for Umpires
His Work Fastest in His League
Johnson Fights for Short Games,"
1 February 1913, p. 11.

E 1036
"Lardner Tells How Harry Lord
Became a Sock," 3 February 1913,
p. 11.

E 1037
"Evers? Why, He Is 'Keystone
King'," 4 February 1913, p. 9.

E 1038
"Murphy Sees a Box Office Gain
in 2 P.M. Start," 5 February
1913, p. 11.

E 1039
"Evers Now in Chicago to Take
Charge of Cubs," 6 February
1913, p. 15.

E 1040
"Del Howard to Be Cub Scout
in the Far West," 7 February
1913, p. 11.

E 1041
"Evers to Seek Good Pitchers at
N.Y. Confab," 8 February 1913,
p. 15.

E 1042
"Cubs to Start This Week on
Journey South," 9 February 1913,
pp. 17–18, sports section.

E 1043
" 'Ha! Ha!' Says Walsh,"
9 February 1913, p. 19,
sports section.

E 1044
"Chance in City; to Try Himself
for First Base," 10 February
1913, p. 11.

E 1045
"Sox to Open in Cleveland,"
11 February 1913, p. 11.

E 1046
"National League Schedule Is
Out Sox Are Certain to Tour
World," 13 February 1913, p. 17.

E 1047
"Evers Puts Foot Down on Murphy
Idea of 2 P.M. Games,"
14 February 1913, p. 10.

E 1048
"Evers Raps Tinker and Chance;
Cubs Start for Tampa To-Night,"
15 February 1913, p. 9.

E 1049
"Joe Benz Only Sock to Report
for Duty as Yet," 17 February
1913, p. 13.

E 1050
"Sox to Carry 4 Sets of Uniforms
on Coast Trip," 18 February
1913, p. 15.

E 1051
"Ed Walsh Arrives in Chicago
He's Going on the Stage Next
Winter Declines to Make World
Trip," 19 February 1913, p. 11.

E 1052
"90 on Sox Special to Leave on
California Trip To-Night,"
20 February 1913, p. 9.

E 1053
" 'White Sox' Dash to Coast Ends
at Oakland To-Day," 23 February
1913, pp. 17, 19, sports section.

E 1054
"Sox Have a Gay Day in Balmy
San Francisco," 24 February
1913, p. 11.

E 1055
"Rath Is Injured on First Day in
Sox Training Camp," 25 February
1913, p. 5.

E 1056
"Sox Players in Classy Practice
Despite Rains," 26 February
1913, p. 15.

E 1057
"Callahan Gives the Sox a Stiff
Drill in Sliding," 27 February
1913, p. 9.

E 1058
"Sox Put in Entire Day at Brisk
Work on Diamond," 28 February
1913, p. 9.

E 1059
"Blues Defeat Grays in First Sox
Game by 11 to 5 Score," 1 March
1913, p. 11.

E 1060
"A Mysterious New Twirler Seeks
Berth on Sox Squad," 2 March
1913, pp. 17–18, sports section.

E 1061
"The Busher's Son," 2 March
1913, p. 18, sports section.

E 1062
"Callahan Picks First Team;
Lord Is Back on Third Base,"
4 March 1913, p. 15.

E 1063
"Sox First Team in Oakland;
Squads Parted Until April,"
6 March 1913, p. 9.

E 1064
"Sox Wrest Coast Title from
Oakland Champs," 7 March
1913, p. 10.

E 1065
"Sox Defeat Del Howard's Seals,
5–4, After Hot Fight," 8 March
1913, p. 8.

E 1066
"White Sox Given a Surprise;
Get 2–1 Beating from Seals,"
9 March 1913, pp. 17–18,
sports section.

E 1067
"15,000 See White Sox Win 2
Games on Coast," 10 March
1913, p. 13.

E 1068
"Weaver's Hit Saves Sox Beating
by Collegians," 11 March 1913,
p. 9.

E 1069
"Sox Down Wolverton's
Sacramento Wolves, 7–3,"
12 March 1913, p. 11.

E 1070
"Sox Lose to Sacramento; Weaver
to Retain Place," 13 March
1913, p. 11.

E 1071
"Coast Champs Simply Can't Beat
the White Sox Oaks Explode in
Eighth and Cal's Men Win, 5–2,"
14 March 1913, p. 11.

E 1072
"Sox Take a Desperate Fight with
Seals, 3–2," 15 March 1913, p. 11.

E 1073
"Sox 4–3 Victors Over Seals on
7 Hits by Lord and Easterly,"
16 March 1913, pp. 17–18,
sports section.

E 1074
"Sox Regulars Divide Bill; Lose
in Oakland; Beat Seals,"
17 March 1913, p. 11.

E 1075
"White Sox Having Best Coast
Trip in History," 18 March 1913,
p. 11.

E 1076
"Police Force the White Sox to
Pitch Ed Walsh at Visalia,"
19 March 1913, p. 15.

E 1077
"Sox Drub Portland on Collins'
Hitting," 20 March 1913, pp. 5–6.

E 1078
"Song," 20 March 1913, p. 7.

E 1079
"Sox Trim Los Angeles, 6–3;
Borton Hits a Long Homer,"
21 March 1913, pp. 13–14.

E 1080
"Sox Drop a Game, Lose 2 Fly
Balls and an Infielder," 22 March
1913, p. 13.

E 1081
"Miller Has Been Sock Since
1908," 22 March 1913, p. 14.

E 1082
"Sox Encounter First Rainy Day
at Los Angeles," 23 March 1913,
p. 12, sports section.

E 1083
"Walsh Pitches and Sox Win;
Callahan and Lord Banished,"
24 March 1913, pp. 11–12.

E 1084
"Sox Make Trip to Catalina
Island; in Venice To-Day,"
25 March 1913, p. 13.

E 1085
"White Sox Beat Indian Nine in
a Farcical Combat, 14–3,"
26 March 1913, p. 13.

E 1086
"White Sox Get Hits in Clusters
and Beat Venice Before 5,000,"
27 March 1913, p. 16.

E 1087
"Sox Lose, 2–1, in 16 Innings
After Great Fight with Vernon
Tigers," 28 March 1913, p. 15.

E 1088
"Sox Drop Another Long One,
This Time in 11 Innings, 3–2,"
29 March 1913, p. 11.

E 1089
"A Plea," 30 March 1913, p. 14,
sports section.

E 1090
"Lardner Picks Pirates to Take
Pennant, with Giants 2d and Cubs
or Reds 3d," 30 March 1913, p. 15,
sports section.

E 1091
"Sox Win 2 Games and Quit
South California," 31 March
1913, p. 7.

E 1092
"Sox Loan Yuma 3 Men and Win
Anyway, 9 to 0," 1 April 1913, p. 9.

E 1093
"Sox Fool El Paso, 9–4, on April's
Foolish Day," 2 April 1913, p. 9.

E 1094
"Sox Scalp Amarillo Until Fans
End Game," 3 April 1913, p. 9.

E 1095
"Sox Find Batting Eyes in the
Bathtub League," 4 April 1913,
p. 11.

E 1096
"Omaha and a Balking Pitcher
Beat Sox, 3–1," 5 April 1913, p. 11.

E 1097
"Sox Have Fair Chance to Win
the Pennant, Says Lardner,"
6 April 1913, pp. 13–14,
sports section.

E 1098
"Song," 6 April 1913, p. 15,
sports section.

E 1099
"Mighty Walsh Beaten in Test
Game at St. Joe," 7 April
1913, p. 9.

E 1100
"Sox Get First Day Off; Benz to
Pitch Opener," 8 April 1913, p. 11.

E 1101
"White Sox Home Today; Cal to
Pick Regulars," 9 April 1913, p. 9.

E 1102
"Sox Play Naps To-Day; Benz
May Face Gregg," 10 April
1913, p. 9.

E 1103
"White Sox Balked, Too; Little
Chance To-Day," 11 April
1913, p. 11.

E 1104
"White Sox Lose Opener to Jackson, Gregg and Lajoie," 12 April 1913, p. 11.

E 1105
"Sox Give Naps Bad Lacing in Second Contest, 13 to 3," 13 April 1913, pp. 13–14, sports section.

E 1106
"Song," 13 April 1913, p. 14, sports section.

E 1107
"Walsh Fans 3 in Ninth to Save Game for Sox," 14 April 1913, p. 8.

E 1108
"Sox Lose to Browns, 2–1 and Blame Kid Gleason," 15 April 1913, p. 11.

E 1109
"Lardner's Sox Notes," 15 April 1913, p. 11.

E 1110
"Walsh Is Hit Hard in First Full Game, but Wins Anyway," 16 April 1913, p. 11.

E 1111
"Lardner's Sox Notes," 16 April 1913, p. 11.

E 1112
"Sox End Trip with Victory Beating Browns Out in 9th; Home to Play Naps To-Day," 17 April 1913, p. 11.

E 1113
"24,000 See Sox Beat Naps in First South Side Battle," 18 April 1913, p. 11.

E 1114
"Steen Battles White Sox; Naps Score 4 to 0 Victory," 19 April 1913, p. 11.

E 1115
"Sox Are Handed a Beating As Lange Explodes in Box," 20 April 1913, pp. 15–16, sports section.

E 1116
"Walsh Is Batted Out; Naps Win 3d Straight," 21 April 1913, p. 7.

E 1117
"Lardner's Sox Notes," 21 April 1913, p. 7.

E 1118
"Luckless Sox Whipped by Tyless Tigers, 3–2," 22 April 1913, p. 11.

E 1119
"White Sox Frustrate Tigers' Rally and Win," 23 April 1913, p. 9.

E 1120
"Doc White Tames Tigers, 2–1, Blocking a Rally in Ninth," 24 April 1913, p. 11.

E 1121
"Lardner's Sox Notes," 24 April 1913, p. 11.

E 1122
"Sox Winning Streak Ends; Cicotte Is Not Effective," 25 April 1913, p. 11.

E 1123
"Lardner's Sox Notes," 25 April 1913, p. 11.

E 1124
"There Weren't Any White Sox Left on Bases Yesterday," 26 April 1913, p. 11.

E 1125
"Russell Gives Browns 2 Hits and
Sox Win in the Ninth, 1–0,"
27 April 1913, pp. 13–14.

E 1126
"Song," 27 April 1913, p. 15.

E 1127
"Three Browns Bump Nine White
Sox, 3–0," 28 April 1913, p. 7.

E 1128
"C. Dryden of Mississippi Admits
to an Interview," 29 April 1913,
p. 11.

E 1129
"Sox Win in 12 Innings; Ty's
Throw Costs Game," 30 April
1913, p. 9.

E 1130
"Lardner's Sox Notes," 30 April
1913, p. 9.

E 1131
"Sox Show Up Tigers; Weaver
Has Great Day," 1 May 1913,
p. 11.

E 1132
"Sox Trim Tigers Again on Lord's
Four Bingles," 2 May 1913, p. 11.

E 1133
"Lardner's Sox Notes," 2 May
1913, p. 11.

E 1134
"Scott Keeps Sox Going; Detroit
Beaten, 2 to 1," 3 May 1913, p. 11.

E 1135
"Sox Beat Out Tigers in 11th 6–4
and Make It 5 Straight," 4 May
1913, pp. 16–17, sports section.

E 1136
"Tigers Imitate Worm and Turn
on Sox, 2–1," 5 May 1913, p. 9.

E 1137
"Lardner's Sox Notes," 5 April
1913, p. 9.

E 1138
"Walsh Is Ready to Stop March
of Easterners," 6 May 1913, p. 11.

E 1139
"C. Griffith and His Nationals
Arrive Some Games to Play,"
7 May 1913, p. 11.

E 1140
"Nationals Whale Sox, 3–2,
Without Johnson," 8 May
1913, p. 11.

E 1141
"Sox Show Home Folks How They
Hit, Routing Nationals 10 to 5
Mid Rain of Bingles," 9 May
1913, p. 11.

E 1142
"Lardner's Sox Notes," 9 May
1913, p. 11.

E 1143
"Sox Trim Nationals Again;
Fournier Is Pinch Hit Hero,"
10 May 1913, p. 11.

E 1144
"Athletics Look Great, but Walsh
and Sox Beat Them," 12 May
1913, p. 9.

E 1145
"Russell Gives Macks 3 Hits;
Still Bender Beats Him, 3–0,"
13 May 1913, p. 11.

E 1146
"Sox Thwarted by Rain, with
Macks Shy of Pitchers," 14 May
1913, p. 11.

CHICAGO TRIBUNE
"In the Wake of the News"[8] *(1913–1919)*

E 1147
3 June 1913, p. 13.

E 1148
4 June 1913, p. 15.

E 1149
5 June 1913, p. 13.

E 1150
6 June 1913, p. 15.

E 1151
7 June 1913, p. 10.

E 1152
8 June 1913, p. 1, pt. 3.

E 1153
9 June 1913, p. 13.

E 1154
10 June 1913, p. 11.

E 1155
11 June 1913, p. 15.

E 1156
12 June 1913, p. 13.

E 1157
13 June 1913, p. 15.

E 1158
14 June 1913, p. 15.

E 1159
15 June 1913, p. 1, pt. 3.

E 1160
16 June 1913, p. 13.

E 1161
17 June 1913, p. 13.

E 1162
18 June 1913, p. 13.

E 1163
19 June 1913, p. 13.

E 1164
20 June 1913, p. 13.

E 1165
21 June 1913, p. 13.

E 1166
22 June 1913, p. 1, pt. 3.

E 1167
23 June 1913, p. 13.

E 1168
24 June 1913, p. 13.

E 1169
25 June 1913, p. 13.

E 1170
26 June 1913, p. 13.

E 1171
27 June 1913, p. 13.

E 1172
28 June 1913, p. 13.

E 1173
29 June 1913, p. 1, pt. 3.

E 1174
30 June 1913, p. 13.

---

8. All columns to 5 June 1914 except one (E 1506) are signed 'R. W. Lardner'.

E 1175
1 July 1913, p. 15.

E 1176
2 July 1913, p. 13.

E 1177
3 July 1913, p. 13.

E 1178
4 July 1913, p. 9.

E 1179
5 July 1913, p. 10.

E 1180
6 July 1913, p. 1, pt. 3.
See C 57.

E 1181
7 July 1913, p. 9.

E 1182
8 July 1913, p. 11.
See C 57.

E 1183
9 July 1913, p. 13.

E 1184
10 July 1913, p. 13.

E 1185
11 July 1913, p. 13.

E 1186
12 July 1913, p. 13.

E 1187
13 July 1913, p. 1, pt. 3.

E 1188
14 July 1913, p. 9.

E 1189
15 July 1913, p. 12.

E 1190
16 July 1913, p. 13.

E 1191
17 July 1913, p. 13.

E 1192
18 July 1913, p. 9.

E 1193
19 July 1913, p. 13.

E 1194
20 July 1913, p. 1, pt. 3.

E 1195
21 July 1913, p. 9.

E 1196
22 July 1913, p. 13.

E 1197
23 July 1913, p. 13.

E 1198
24 July 1913, p. 13.

E 1199
25 July 1913, p. 8.

E 1200
26 July 1913, p. 13.

E 1201
27 July 1913, p. 1, pt. 3.

E 1202
28 July 1913, p. 12.

E 1203
29 July 1913, p. 13.

E 1204
30 July 1913, p. 13.

E 1205
31 July 1913, p. 13.

E 1206
1 August 1913, p. 11.

E 1207
2 August 1913, p. 9.

E 1208
3 August 1913, p. 1, pt. 3.

E 1209
4 August 1913, p. 9.

E 1210
5 August 1913, p. 11.

E 1211
6 August 1913, p. 13.

E 1212
7 August 1913, p. 15.

E 1213
8 August 1913, p. 11.

E 1214
9 August 1913, p. 11.

E 1215
10 August 1913, p. 1, pt. 3.

E 1216
11 August 1913, p. 12.

See *BB*.

E 1217
12 August 1913, p. 10.

E 1218
13 August 1913, p. 13.

E 1219
14 August 1913, p. 11.

E 1220
15 August 1913, p. 8.

E 1221
16 August 1913, p. 11.

E 1222
17 August 1913, p. 1, pt. 3.

E 1223
18 August 1913, p. 9.

E 1224
19 August 1913, p. 15.

E 1225
20 August 1913, p. 15.

E 1226
21 August 1913, p. 13.

E 1227
22 August 1913, p. 11.

E 1228
23 August 1913, p. 13.

E 1229
24 August 1913, p. 1, pt. 3.

E 1230
25 August 1913, p. 11.

E 1231
26 August 1913, p. 15.

E 1232
27 August 1913, p. 11.

E 1233
28 August 1913, p. 17.

E 1234
29 August 1913, p. 13.

E 1235
30 August 1913, p. 13.

E 1236
31 August 1913, p. 1, pt. 3.

E 1237
1 September 1913, p. 9.

E 1238
2 September 1913, p. 13.

E 1239
3 September 1913, p. 14.

E 1240
4 September 1913, p. 14.

E 1241
5 September 1913, p. 13.

E 1242
6 September 1913, p. 11.

E 1243
8 September 1913, p. 11.

E 1244
9 September 1913, p. 13.

E 1245
10 September 1913, p. 13.

E 1246
11 September 1913, p. 13.

E 1247
12 September 1913, p. 13.

E 1248
13 September 1913, p. 11.

E 1249
14 September 1913, p. 1, pt. 3.

E 1250
15 September 1913, p. 13.

E 1251
16 September 1913, p. 15.

E 1252
17 September 1913, p. 13.

E 1253
18 September 1913, p. 15.

E 1254
19 September 1913, p. 15.

E 1255
20 September 1913, p. 13.

E 1256
21 September 1913, p. 1, pt. 3.

E 1257
22 September 1913, p. 13.

E 1258
23 September 1913, p. 15.

E 1259
24 September 1913, p. 15.

E 1260
25 September 1913, p. 13.

E 1261
26 September 1913, p. 13.

E 1262
27 September 1913, p. 13.

E 1263
28 September 1913, p. 1, pt. 3.

E 1264
29 September 1913, p. 10.

E 1265
30 September 1913, p. 13.

E 1266
1 October 1913, p. 15.

E 1267
2 October 1913, p. 13.

E 1268
3 October 1913, p. 15.

E 1269
4 October 1913, p. 15.

E 1270
5 October 1913, p. 1, pt. 3.

E 1271
6 October 1913, p. 24.

E 1272
7 October 1913, p. 25.

E 1273
8 October 1913, p. 25.

E 1274
9 October 1913, p. 23.

E 1275
10 October 1913, p. 24.

E 1276
11 October 1913, p. 22.

E 1277
12 October 1913, p. 3, pt. 3.

E 1278
13 October 1913, p. 16.

E 1279
14 October 1913, p. 13.

E 1280
15 October 1913, p. 15.

E 1281
16 October 1913, p. 13.

E 1282
17 October 1913, p. 13.

E 1283
18 October 1913, p. 15.

E 1284
19 October 1913, p. 1, pt. 3.

E 1285
20 October 1913, p. 11.

E 1286
21 October 1913, p. 15.

E 1287
22 October 1913, p. 15.

E 1288
23 October 1913, p. 10.

E 1289
24 October 1913, p. 15.

E 1290
25 October 1913, p. 10.

E 1291
26 October 1913, p. 1, pt. 3.

E 1292
27 October 1913, p. 10.

E 1293
28 October 1913, p. 12.

E 1294
29 October 1913, p. 14.

E 1295
30 October 1913, p. 15.

E 1296
31 October 1913, p. 15.

E 1297
1 November 1913, p. 16.

E 1298
2 November 1913, p. 1, pt. 3.

E 1299
3 November 1913, p. 17.

E 1300
4 November 1913, p. 14.

E 1301
5 November 1913, p. 16.

E 1302
6 November 1913, p. 8.

E 1303
7 November 1913, p. 17.

E 1304
8 November 1913, p. 13.

E 1305
9 November 1913, p. 1, pt. 3.

E 1306
10 November 1913, p. 14.

E 1307
11 November 1913, p. 16.

E 1308
12 November 1913, p. 14.

E 1309
13 November 1913, p. 8.

E 1310
14 November 1913, p. 10.

E 1311
15 November 1913, p. 14.

E 1312
16 November 1913, p. 1, pt. 3.

E 1313
17 November 1913, p. 17.

E 1314
18 November 1913, p. 16.

E 1315
19 November 1913, p. 16.

E 1316
20 November 1913, p. 14.

E 1317
21 November 1913, p. 10.

E 1318
22 November 1913, p. 14.

E 1319
23 November 1913, p. 4, pt. 3.

E 1320
24 November 1913, p. 17.

E 1321
25 November 1913, p. 16.

E 1322
26 November 1913, p. 10.

E 1323
27 November 1913, p. 12.

E 1324
28 November 1913, p. 12.

E 1325
29 November 1913, p. 14.

E 1326
30 November 1913, p. 1, pt. 3.

E 1327
1 December 1913, p. 17.

E 1328
2 December 1913, p. 14.

E 1329
3 December 1913, p. 18.

E 1330
4 December 1913, p. 14.

E 1331
5 December 1913, p. 15.

E 1332
6 December 1913, p. 10.

E 1333
7 December 1913, p. 1, pt. 3.

E 1334
8 December 1913, p. 19.

E 1335
9 December 1913, p. 17.

E 1336
10 December 1913, p. 18.

E 1337
11 December 1913, p. 10.

E 1338
12 December 1913, p. 10.

E 1339
13 December 1913, p. 13.

E 1340
14 December 1913, p. 1, pt .3.

E 1341
15 December 1913, p. 17.

E 1342
16 December 1913, p. 16.

E 1343
17 December 1913, p. 16.

E 1344
18 December 1913, p. 10.

E 1345
19 December 1913, p. 14.

E 1346
20 December 1913, p. 14.

E 1347
21 December 1913, p. 1, pt. 3.

E 1348
22 December 1913, p. 18.

E 1349
23 December 1913, p. 14.

E 1350
24 December 1913, p. 8.

E 1351
25 December 1913, p. 18.

E 1352
26 December 1913, p. 6.

E 1353
27 December 1913, p. 4.

E 1354
28 December 1913, p. 1, pt. 3.

E 1355
29 December 1913, p. 12.

E 1356
30 December 1913, p. 6.

E 1357
31 December 1913, p. 12.

E 1358
1 January 1914, p. 20.

E 1359
2 January 1914, p. 10.

E 1360
3 January 1914, p. 13.

E 1361
4 January 1914, p. 1, pt. 3.

E 1362
5 January 1914, p. 14.

E 1363
6 January 1914, p. 14.

E 1364
7 January 1914, p. 14.

E 1365
8 January 1914, p. 8.

E 1366
9 January 1914, p. 8.

E 1367
10 January 1914, p. 14.

E 1368
11 January 1914, p. 1, pt. 3.

E 1369
12 January 1914, p. 10.

E 1370
13 January 1914, p. 14.

E 1371
14 January 1914, p. 8.

E 1372
15 January 1914, p. 14.

E 1373
16 January 1914, p. 14.

E 1374
17 January 1914, p. 14.

E 1375
18 January 1914, p. 1, pt. 3.

E 1376
19 January 1914, p. 12.

See *BB*.

E 1377
20 January 1914, p. 10.

E 1378
21 January 1914, p. 10.

E 1379
22 January 1914, p. 8.

E 1380
23 January 1914, p. 14.

E 1381
24 January 1914, p. 15.

E 1382
25 January 1914, p. 1, pt. 3.

E 1383
26 January 1914, p. 6.

See *BB*.

E 1384
27 January 1914, p. 13.

E 1385
28 January 1914, p. 18.

E 1386
29 January 1914, p. 8.

E 1387
30 January 1914, p. 14.

E 1388
31 January 1914, p. 14.

E 1389
1 February 1914, p. 1, pt. 3.

E 1390
2 February 1914, p. 14.

E 1391
3 February 1914, p. 10.

E 1392
4 February 1914, p. 10.

E 1393
5 February 1914, p. 14.

E 1394
6 February 1914, p. 10.

E 1395
7 February 1914, p. 14.

E 1396
8 February 1914, p. 1, pt. 3.

E 1397
9 February 1914, p. 14.

See *BB*.

E 1398
10 February 1914, p. 14.

E 1399
11 February 1914, p. 14.

E 1400
12 February 1914, p. 10.

E 1401
13 February 1914, p. 14.

E 1402
14 February 1914, p. 14.

E 1403
15 February 1914, p. 1, pt. 3.

E 1404
16 February 1914, p. 12.

E 1405
17 February 1914, p. 14.

E 1406
18 February 1914, p. 12.

E 1407
19 February 1914, p. 14.

E 1408
20 February 1914, p. 14.

E 1409
21 February 1914, p. 14.

E 1410
22 February 1914, p. 1, pt. 3.

E 1411
23 February 1914, p. 10.
See *BB*.

E 1412
24 February 1914, p. 15.

E 1413
25 February 1914, p. 14.

E 1414
26 February 1914, p. 10.

E 1415
27 February 1914, p. 8.

E 1416
28 February 1914, p. 14.

E 1417
1 March 1914, p. 1, pt. 3.

E 1418
2 March 1914, p. 14.
See *BB*.

E 1419
3 March 1914, p. 15.

E 1420
4 March 1914, p. 15.

E 1421
5 March 1914, p. 15.

E 1422
6 March 1914, p. 14.

E 1423
7 March 1914, p. 14.

E 1424
8 March 1914, p. 1, pt. 3.

E 1425
9 March 1914, p. 14.

E 1426
10 March 1914, p. 16.

E 1427
11 March 1914, p. 16.

E 1428
12 March 1914, p. 15.

E 1429
13 March 1914, p. 14.

E 1430
14 March 1914, p. 14.

E 1431
15 March 1914, p. 1, pt. 3.

E 1432
16 March 1914, p. 10.
See *BB*.

E 1433
17 March 1914, p. 13.

E 1434
18 March 1914, p. 12.

E 1435
19 March 1914, p. 11.

E 1436
20 March 1914, p. 15.

E 1437
21 March 1914, p. 14.

E 1438
22 March 1914, p. 1, pt. 3.

E 1439
23 March 1914, p. 10.

E 1440
24 March 1914, p. 11.

E 1441
25 March 1914, p. 14.

E 1442
26 March 1914, p. 13.

E 1443
27 March 1914, p. 13.

E 1444
28 March 1914, p. 15.

E 1445
29 March 1914, p. 1, pt. 3.

E 1446
30 March 1914, p. 14.

See *BB*.

E 1447
31 March 1914, p. 10.

E 1448
1 April 1914, p. 18.

E 1449
2 April 1914, p. 12.

E 1450
3 April 1914, p. 12.

E 1451
4 April 1914, p. 14.

E 1452
5 April 1914, p. 1, pt. 3.

E 1453
6 April 1914, p. 15.

E 1454
7 April 1914, p. 14.

E 1455
8 April 1914, p. 19.

E 1456
9 April 1914, p. 14.

E 1457
10 April 1914, p. 14.

E 1458
11 April 1914, p. 16.

E 1459
12 April 1914, p. 4, pt. 3.

E 1460
13 April 1914, p. 8.

E 1461
14 April 1914, p. 12.

E 1462
15 April 1914, p. 17.

E 1463
16 April 1914, p. 13.

E 1464
17 April 1914, p. 10.

E 1465
18 April 1914, p. 15.

E 1466
19 April 1914, p. 1, pt. 3.

E 1467
20 April 1914, p. 17.

E 1468
21 April 1914, p. 14.

E 1469
22 April 1914, p. 18.

E 1470
23 April 1914, p. 18.

E 1471
24 April 1914, p. 15.

E 1472
25 April 1914, p. 17.

E 1473
26 April 1914, p. 1, pt. 3.

E 1474
27 April 1914, p. 12.

E 1475
28 April 1914, p. 14.

E 1476
29 April 1914, p. 14.

E 1477
30 April 1914, p. 18.

E 1478
1 May 1914, p. 17.

E 1479
2 May 1914, p. 17.

E 1480
3 May 1914, p. 1, pt. 3.

E 1481
4 May 1914, p. 13.

E 1482
5 May 1914, p. 13.

E 1483
6 May 1914, p. 12.

E 1484
7 May 1914, p. 14.

E 1485
8 May 1914, p. 16.

E 1486
9 May 1914, p. 14.

E 1487
10 May 1914, p. 1, pt. 3.

E 1488
11 May 1914, p. 13.

E 1489
12 May 1914, p. 13.

E 1490
13 May 1914, p. 15.

E 1491
14 May 1914, p. 14.

E 1492
15 May 1914, p. 15.

E 1493
16 May 1914, p. 14.

E 1494
17 May 1914, p. 1, pt. 3.

E 1495
18 May 1914, p. 10.

E 1496
19 May 1914, p. 12.

E 1497
20 May 1914, p. 14.

E 1498
21 May 1914, p. 12.

E 1499
22 May 1914, p. 14.

E 1500
23 May 1914, p. 16.

E 1501
24 May 1914, p. 1, pt. 3.

E 1502
25 May 1914, p. 12.
See *BB*.

E 1503
26 May 1914, p. 16.

E 1504
27 May 1914, p. 19.

E 1505
28 May 1914, p. 14.

E 1506
29 May 1914, p. 16.[9]

E 1507
30 May 1914, p. 13.

E 1508
31 May 1914, p. 4, pt. 3.

E 1509
1 June 1914, p. 14.

E 1510
2 June 1914, p. 14.

E 1511
4 June 1914, p. 14.

E 1512
5 June 1914, p. 12.

E 1513
6 June 1914, p. 14.[10]

E 1514
7 June 1914, p. 4, pt. 3.

E 1515
8 June 1914, p. 11.

E 1516
9 June 1914, p. 12.

E 1517
10 June 1914, p. 15.

E 1518
11 June 1914, p. 16.

E 1519
12 June 1914, p. 15.

E 1520
13 June 1914, p. 18.

E 1521
14 June 1914, p. 1, pt. 3.

E 1522
15 June 1914, p. 14.

See *BB*.

E 1523
16 June 1914, p. 16.

E 1524
17 June 1914, p. 15.

E 1525
18 June 1914, p. 16.

E 1526
19 June 1914, p. 12.

E 1527
20 June 1914, p. 14.

E 1528
21 June 1914, p. 1, pt. 3.

E 1529
22 June 1914, p. 14.

E 1530
23 June 1914, p. 12.

E 1531
24 June 1914, p. 14.

E 1532
25 June 1914, p. 15.

E 1533
26 June 1914, p. 14.

E 1534
27 June 1914, p. 15.

9. Unsigned and headed "Sox–New York Score." Lardner refers to this misheading in 30 May 1914 column.

10. All columns beginning with this one are signed 'Ring W. Lardner'.

E 1535
28 June 1914, p. 4, pt. 3.

E 1536
29 June 1914, p. 12.

E 1537
30 June 1914, p. 12.

E 1538
1 July 1914, p. 18.

E 1539
2 July 1914, p. 15.

E 1540
3 July 1914, p. 13.

E 1541
4 July 1914, p. 13.

E 1542
5 July 1914, p. 4, pt. 3.

E 1543
6 July 1914, p. 13.

E 1544
7 July 1914, p. 16.

E 1545
9 July 1914, p. 15.

E 1546
10 July 1914, p. 10.

E 1547
11 July 1914, p. 14.

E 1548
12 July 1914, p. 1, pt. 3.

E 1549
13 July 1914, p. 15.
See *BB*.

E 1550
14 July 1914, p. 10.

E 1551
15 July 1914, p. 10.

E 1552
16 July 1914, p. 10.

E 1553
17 July 1914, p. 15.

E 1554
18 July 1914, p. 13.

E 1555
19 July 1914, p. 1, pt. 3.

E 1556
20 July 1914, p. 13.
See *BB*.

E 1557
21 July 1914, p. 10.

E 1558
22 July 1914, p. 14.

E 1559
23 July 1914, p. 14.

E 1560
24 July 1914, p. 9.

E 1561
25 July 1914, p. 15.

E 1562
26 July 1914, p. 1, pt. 3.

E 1563
27 July 1914, p. 12.
See *BB*.

E 1564
28 July 1914, p. 10.

E 1565
29 July 1914, p. 15.

E 1566
30 July 1914, p. 15.

E 1567
31 July 1914, p. 14.

E 1568
1 August 1914, p. 16.

E 1569
2 August 1914, p. 1, pt. 3.

E 1570
3 August 1914, p. 16.

E 1571
4 August 1914, p. 10.

E 1572
5 August 1914, p. 14.

E 1573
6 August 1914, p. 14.

E 1574
7 August 1914, p. 11.

E 1575
8 August 1914, p. 14.

E 1576
9 August 1914, p. 1, pt. 3.

E 1577
10 August 1914, p. 11.

E 1578
11 August 1914, p. 10.

E 1579
12 August 1914, p. 10.

E 1580
13 August 1914, p. 14.

E 1581
14 August 1914, p. 12.

E 1582
15 August 1914, p. 11.
See C 39.

E 1583
16 August 1914, p. 4, pt. 3.

E 1584
17 August 1914, p. 12.
See *BB*.

E 1585
23 August 1914, p. 4, pt. 3.

E 1586
24 August 1914, p. 13.

E 1587
30 August 1914, p. 4, pt. 3.

E 1588
31 August 1914, p. 14.
See *BB*.

E 1589
1 September 1914, p. 14.

E 1590
2 September 1914, p. 15.

E 1591
3 September 1914, p. 16.

E 1592
4 September 1914, p. 14.

E 1593
5 September 1914, p. 17.

E 1594
6 September 1914, p. 1, pt. 3.

E 1595
7 September 1914, p. 15.
See *BB*.

E 1596
8 September 1914, p. 13.

E 1597
9 September 1914, p. 10.

E 1598
10 September 1914, p. 16.

E 1599
11 September 1914, p. 11.

E 1600
12 September 1914, p. 11.

E 1601
13 September 1914, p. 1, pt. 3.

E 1602
14 September 1914, p. 14.

E 1603
18 September 1914, p. 11.

E 1604
19 September 1914, p. 14.

E 1605
20 September 1914, p. 1, pt. 3.

E 1606
21 September 1914, p. 11.

See *BB*.

E 1607
22 September 1914, p. 10.

E 1608
23 September 1914, p. 14.

E 1609
24 September 1914, p. 10.

E 1610
25 September 1914, p. 10.

E 1611
26 September 1914, p. 10.

E 1612
27 September 1914, p. 1, pt. 3.

E 1613
28 September 1914, p. 12.

E 1614
29 September 1914, p. 10.

E 1615
30 September 1914, p. 10.

E 1616
1 October 1914, p. 11.

E 1617
2 October 1914, p. 15.

E 1618
3 October 1914, p. 16.

E 1619
4 October 1914, p. 4, pt. 3.

E 1620
5 October 1914, p. 16.

E 1621
6 October 1914, p. 13.

E 1622
7 October 1914, p. 13.

E 1623
8 October 1914, p. 13.

E 1624
9 October 1914, p. 13.

E 1625
10 October 1914, p. 13.

E 1626
11 October 1914, p. 1, pt. 3.

E 1627
12 October 1914, p. 13.

E 1628
13 October 1914, p. 13.

E 1629
14 October 1914, p. 13.

E 1630
15 October 1914, p. 11.

E 1631
16 October 1914, p. 13.

E 1632
17 October 1914, p. 15.

E 1633
18 October 1914, p. 1, pt. 3.

E 1634
19 October 1914, p. 14.

E 1635
20 October 1914, p. 8.

E 1636
21 October 1914, p. 8.

E 1637
22 October 1914, p. 8.

E 1638
23 October 1914, p. 8.

E 1639
24 October 1914, p. 8.

E 1640
25 October 1914, p. 1, pt. 3.

E 1641
26 October 1914, p. 14.

E 1642
1 November 1914, p. 4, pt. 3.

E 1643
3 November 1914, p. 8.

E 1644
4 November 1914, p. 14.

E 1645
5 November 1914, p. 16.

E 1646
6 November 1914, p. 10.

E 1647
7 November 1914, p. 15.

E 1648
8 November 1914, p. 1, pt. 3.

E 1649
9 November 1914, p. 14.

E 1650
10 November 1914, p. 14.

E 1651
11 November 1914, p. 14.

E 1652
12 November 1914, p. 14.

E 1653
13 November 1914, p. 16.

E 1654
15 November 1914, p. 4, pt. 3.

E 1655
16 November 1914, p. 16.
See *BB*.

E 1656
17 November 1914, p. 11.

E 1657
18 November 1914, p. 11.

E 1658
19 November 1914, p. 9.

E 1659
20 November 1914, p. 14.

E 1660
21 November 1914, p. 14.

E 1661
22 November 1914, p. 4, pt. 3.

E 1662
23 November 1914, p. 16.
See *BB*.

E 1663
24 November 1914, p. 16.

E 1664
25 November 1914, p. 11.

E 1665
26 November 1914, p. 15.

E 1666
28 November 1914, p. 8.

E 1667
29 November 1914, p. 1, pt. 3.

E 1668
30 November 1914, p. 14.
See *BB*.

E 1669
1 December 1914, p. 16.

E 1670
2 December 1914, p. 16.

E 1671
3 December 1914, p. 11.

E 1672
4 December 1914, p. 11.

E 1673
5 December 1914, p. 16.

E 1674
6 December 1914, p. 1, pt. 3.

E 1675
7 December 1914, p. 18.
See *BB*.

E 1676
8 December 1914, p. 16.

E 1677
9 December 1914, p. 18.

E 1678
10 December 1914, p. 16.

E 1679
11 December 1914, p. 13.

E 1680
12 December 1914, p. 16.

E 1681
13 December 1914, p. 1, pt. 3.

E 1682
14 December 1914, p. 16.
See *BB*.

E 1683
15 December 1914, p. 14.

E 1684
16 December 1914, p. 13.

E 1685
17 December 1914, p. 16.

E 1686
18 December 1914, p. 13.

E 1687
19 December 1914, p. 8.

E 1688
20 December 1914, p. 1, pt. 3.

E 1689
21 December 1914, p. 13.
See *BB*.

E 1690
22 December 1914, p. 11.

E 1691
23 December 1914, p. 14.

E 1692
24 December 1914, p. 9.

E 1693
25 December 1914, p. 13.

E 1694
26 December 1914, p. 6.

E 1695
27 December 1914, p. 1, pt. 3.

E 1696
28 December 1914, p. 9.
See *BB*.

E 1697
29 December 1914, p. 12.

E 1698
30 December 1914, p. 12.

E 1699
31 December 1914, p. 11.

E 1700
1 January 1915, p. 15.

E 1701
2 January 1915, p. 9.

E 1702
3 January 1915, p. 1, pt. 3.

E 1703
4 January 1915, p. 16.
See *BB*.

E 1704
5 January 1915, p. 9.

E 1705
6 January 1915, p. 9.

E 1706
7 January 1915, p. 9.

E 1707
8 January 1915, p. 14.

E 1708
9 January 1915, p. 9.

E 1709
10 January 1915, p. 1, pt. 3.

E 1710
11 January 1915, p. 14.

E 1711
12 January 1915, p. 9.

E 1712
13 January 1915, p. 11.

E 1713
14 January 1915, p. 9.

E 1714
15 January 1915, p. 11.

E 1715
16 January 1915, p. 9.

E 1716
17 January 1915, p. 1, pt. 3.

E 1717
18 January 1915, p. 14.

E 1718
19 January 1915, p. 9.

E 1719
20 January 1915, p. 9.

E 1720
21 January 1915, p. 9.

E 1721
22 January 1915, p. 15.

E 1722
23 January 1915, p. 11.

E 1723
24 January 1915, p. 1, pt. 3.

E 1724
25 January 1915, p. 18.

E 1725
26 January 1915, p. 13.

E 1726
27 January 1915, p. 15.

E 1727
28 January 1915, p. 11.

E 1728
29 January 1915, p. 9.

E 1729
30 January 1915, p. 9.

E 1730
31 January 1915, p. 1, pt. 3.

E 1731
1 February 1915, p. 16.

E 1732
2 February 1915, p. 9.

E 1733
3 February 1915, p. 14.

E 1734
4 February 1915, p. 12.

E 1735
5 February 1915, p. 12.

E 1736
6 February 1915, p. 12.

E 1737
7 February 1915, p. 1, pt. 3.

E 1738
8 February 1915, p. 14.

E 1739
9 February 1915, p. 9.

E 1740
10 February 1915, p. 9.

E 1741
11 February 1915, p. 9.

E 1742
12 February 1915, p. 16.

E 1743
13 February 1915, p. 9.

E 1744
14 February 1915, p. 1, pt. 3.

E 1745
15 February 1915, p. 14.

E 1746
16 February 1915, p. 14.

E 1747
17 February 1915, p. 14.

E 1748
18 February 1915, p. 11.

E 1749
19 February 1915, p. 9.

E 1750
20 February 1915, p. 11.

E 1751
21 February 1915, p. 4, pt. 3.

E 1752
22 February 1915, p. 14.

E 1753
24 February 1915, p. 11.

E 1754
25 February 1915, p. 11.

E 1755
26 February 1915, p. 8.

E 1756
27 February 1915, p. 9.

E 1757
28 February 1915, p. 1, pt. 3.

E 1758
1 March 1915, p. 16.

E 1759
2 March 1915, p. 9.

E 1760
3 March 1915, p. 11.

E 1761
4 March 1915, p. 11.

E 1762
5 March 1915, p. 9.

E 1763
6 March 1915, p. 9.

E 1764
7 March 1915, p. 1, pt. 3.

E 1765
8 March 1915, p. 16.

E 1766
9 March 1915, p. 14.

E 1767
10 March 1915, p. 14.

E 1768
11 March 1915, p. 11.

E 1769
12 March 1915, p. 10.

E 1770
13 March 1915, p. 11.

E 1771
14 March 1915, p. 1, pt. 3.

E 1772
15 March 1915, p. 13.
See *BB*.

E 1773
16 March 1915, p. 9.

E 1774
17 March 1915, p. 10.

E 1775
18 March 1915, p. 10.

E 1776
19 March 1915, p. 12.

E 1777
20 March 1915, p. 11.

E 1778
21 March 1915, p. 1, pt. 3.

E 1779
22 March 1915, p. 11.

See *BB*.

E 1780
23 March 1915, p. 9.

E 1781
24 March 1915, p. 10.

E 1782
25 March 1915, p. 10.

E 1783
26 March 1915, p. 19.

E 1784
27 March 1915, p. 10.

E 1785
28 March 1915, p. 4, pt. 3.

E 1786
29 March 1915, p. 11.

E 1787
30 March 1915, p. 9.

E 1788
31 March 1915, p. 10.

E 1789
1 April 1915, p. 12.

E 1790
2 April 1915, p. 21.

E 1791
3 April 1915, p. 11.

E 1792
4 April 1915, p. 4, pt. 3.

E 1793
5 April 1915, p. 12.
See *BB*.

E 1794
6 April 1915, p. 13.

E 1795
7 April 1915, p. 11.

E 1796
8 April 1915, p. 10.

E 1797
9 April 1915, p. 15.

E 1798
10 April 1915, p. 8.

E 1799
11 April 1915, p. 4, pt. 3.

E 1800
12 April 1915, p. 9.
See *BB*.

E 1801
13 April 1915, p. 11.

E 1802
14 April 1915, p. 13.

E 1803
15 April 1915, p. 11.

E 1804
16 April 1915, p. 13.

E 1805
17 April 1915, p. 13.

E 1806
18 April 1915, p. 1, pt. 3.
See C 39.

E 1807
19 April 1915, p. 10.

E 1808
20 April 1915, p. 11.

E 1809
21 April 1915, p. 11.

E 1810
22 April 1915, p. 9.

E 1811
23 April 1915, p. 13.

E 1812
24 April 1915, p. 13.

E 1813
25 April 1915, p. 1, pt. 3.

E 1814
26 April 1915, p. 8.

E 1815
27 April 1915, p. 13.

E 1816
28 April 1915, p. 11.

E 1817
29 April 1915, p. 10.

E 1818
30 April 1915, p. 13.

E 1819
1 May 1915, p. 15.

E 1820
2 May 1915, p. 1, pt. 3.

E 1821
3 May 1915, p. 14.

E 1822
4 May 1915, p. 10.

E 1823
5 May 1915, p. 10.

E 1824
6 May 1915, p. 10.

E 1825
7 May 1915, p. 11.

E 1826
8 May 1915, p. 18.

E 1827
9 May 1915, p. 1, pt. 3.

E 1828
11 May 1915, p. 11.

E 1829
12 May 1915, p. 12.

E 1830
13 May 1915, p. 11.

E 1831
14 May 1915, p. 12.

E 1832
15 May 1915, p. 14.

E 1833
16 May 1915, p. 1, pt. 3.

E 1834
17 May 1915, p. 11.

E 1835
18 May 1915, p. 10.

E 1836
19 May 1915, p. 13.

E 1837
20 May 1915, p. 10.

E 1838
21 May 1915, p. 10.

E 1839
22 May 1915, p. 11.

E 1840
23 May 1915, p. 1, pt. 3.

E 1841
24 May 1915, p. 10.

E 1842
25 May 1915, p. 14.

E 1843
26 May 1915, p. 16.

E 1844
27 May 1915, p. 10.

E 1845
28 May 1915, p. 10.

E 1846
29 May 1915, p. 11.

E 1847
30 May 1915, p. 1, pt. 3.

E 1848
31 May 1915, p. 13.

E 1849
1 June 1915, p. 17.

E 1850
2 June 1915, p. 11.

E 1851
3 June 1915, p. 11.

E 1852
4 June 1915, p. 12.

E 1853
5 June 1915, p. 12.

E 1854
6 June 1915, p. 4, pt. 3.

E 1855
7 June 1915, p. 18.

E 1856
8 June 1915, p. 12.

E 1857
9 June 1915, p. 13.

E 1858
10 June 1915, p. 12.

E 1859
11 June 1915, p. 10.

E 1860
12 June 1915, p. 15.

E 1861
13 June 1915, p. 4, pt. 3.

E 1862
14 June 1915, p. 13.

E 1863
15 June 1915, p. 14.

E 1864
16 June 1915, p. 12.

E 1865
17 June 1915, p. 12.

E 1866
18 June 1915, p. 12.

E 1867
19 June 1915, p. 11.

E 1868
20 June 1915, p. 4, pt. 3.

E 1869
21 June 1915, p. 18.

E 1870
22 June 1915, p. 20.

E 1871
23 June 1915, p. 15.

E 1872
24 June 1915, p. 12.

E 1873
25 June 1915, p. 12.

E 1874
26 June 1915, p. 13.

E 1875
27 June 1915, p. 1, pt. 3.

E 1876
28 June 1915, p. 7.

E 1877
29 June 1915, p. 10.

E 1878
30 June 1915, p. 8.

E 1879
1 July 1915, p. 12.

E 1880
2 July 1915, p. 12.

E 1881
3 July 1915, p. 10.

E 1882
4 July 1915, p. 4, pt. 3.

E 1883
5 July 1915, p. 13.

E 1884
6 July 1915, p. 15.

E 1885
7 July 1915, p. 10.

E 1886
8 July 1915, p. 10.

E 1887
9 July 1915, p. 10.

E 1888
10 July 1915, p. 14.

E 1889
11 July 1915, p. 1, pt. 3.

E 1890
13 July 1915, p. 10.

E 1891
14 July 1915, p. 10.

E 1892
15 July 1915, p. 12.

E 1893
16 July 1915, p. 10.

E 1894
17 July 1915, p. 10.

E 1895
18 July 1915, p. 4, pt. 3.

E 1896
19 July 1915, p. 10.

E 1897
20 July 1915, p. 12.

E 1898
21 July 1915, p. 10.

E 1899
22 July 1915, p. 10.

E 1900
23 July 1915, p. 8.

E 1901
24 July 1915, p. 8.

E 1902
25 July 1915, p. 1, pt. 3.

E 1903
26 July 1915, p. 14.

E 1904
27 July 1915, p. 15.

E 1905
28 July 1915, p. 8.

E 1906
29 July 1915, p. 10.

E 1907
30 July 1915, p. 8.

E 1908
31 July 1915, p. 8.

E 1909
1 August 1915, p. 4, pt. 3.

E 1910
2 August 1915, p. 16.

E 1911
3 August 1915, p. 10.

E 1912
4 August 1915, p. 10.

E 1913
5 August 1915, p. 8.

E 1914
6 August 1915, p. 8.

E 1915
7 August 1915, p. 6.

E 1916
8 August 1915, p. 1, pt. 3.

E 1917
9 August 1915, p. 11.

E 1918
10 August 1915, p. 10.

E 1919
11 August 1915, p. 8.

E 1920
12 August 1915, p. 10.

E 1921
13 August 1915, p. 8.

E 1922
14 August 1915, p. 6.

E 1923
15 August 1915, p. 1, pt. 3.

E 1924
16 August 1915, p. 16.

E 1925
18 August 1915, p. 8.

E 1926
19 August 1915, p. 11.

E 1927
21 August 1915, p. 11.

E 1928
22 August 1915, p. 1, pt. 3.

E 1929
23 August 1915, p. 10.

E 1930
24 August 1915, p. 10.

E 1931
25 August 1915, p. 10.

E 1932
26 August 1915, p. 10.

E 1933
27 August 1915, p. 8.

E 1934
28 August 1915, p. 10.

E 1935
29 August 1915, p. 1, pt. 3.

E 1936
30 August 1915, p. 8.

E 1937
31 August 1915, p. 10.

E 1938
1 September 1915, p. 12.

E 1939
2 September 1915, p. 10.

E 1940
3 September 1915, p. 8.

E 1941
4 September 1915, p. 8.

E 1942
5 September 1915, p. 4, pt. 3.

E 1943
6 September 1915, p. 12.

E 1944
7 September 1915, p. 15.

E 1945
8 September 1915, p. 10.

E 1946
14 September 1915, p. 10.

E 1947
15 September 1915, p. 10.

E 1948
16 September 1915, p. 10.

E 1949
17 September 1915, p. 9.

E 1950
18 September 1915, p. 8.

E 1951
19 September 1915, p. 4, pt. 3.
See C 2.

E 1952
20 September 1915, p. 9.

E 1953
21 September 1915, p. 11.

E 1954
22 September 1915, p. 10.

E 1955
23 September 1915, p. 10.

E 1956
24 September 1915, p. 8.

E 1957
25 September 1915, p. 12.

E 1958
26 September 1915, p. 4, pt. 3.
See C 2.

E 1959
27 September 1915, p. 10.

E 1960
28 September 1915, p. 12.

E 1961
29 September 1915, p. 10.

E 1962
30 September 1915, p. 10.

E 1963
1 October 1915, p. 12.

E 1964
2 October 1915, p. 11.

E 1965
3 October 1915, p. 1, pt. 3.

E 1966
4 October 1915, p. 12.

E 1967
5 October 1915, p. 12.

E 1968
6 October 1915, p. 11.

E 1969
7 October 1915, p. 10.

E 1970
8 October 1915, p. 13.[11]

E 1971
9 October 1915, p. 15.

E 1972
10 October 1915, p. 1, pt. 3.

E 1973
11 October 1915, p. 13.

E 1974
12 October 1915, p. 11.

E 1975
13 October 1915, p. 13.

E 1976
14 October 1915, p. 9.

E 1977
15 October 1915, p. 11.

E 1978
16 October 1915, p. 11.

E 1979
17 October 1915, p. 4, pt. 3.

E 1980
18 October 1915, p. 10.

E 1981
19 October 1915, p. 11.

E 1982
20 October 1915, p. 10.

E 1983
21 October 1915, p. 10.

E 1984
22 October 1915, p. 10.

E 1985
23 October 1915, p. 8.

E 1986
24 October 1915, p. 4, pt. 3.

E 1987
25 October 1915, p. 10.

E 1988
26 October 1915, p. 10.

E 1989
27 October 1915, p. 8.

E 1990
28 October 1915, p. 9.

E 1991
29 October 1915, p. 11.

E 1992
31 October 1915, p. 1, pt. 3.

E 1993
1 November 1915, p. 13.

E 1994
2 November 1915, p. 13.

---

11. Columns from 8 October to 15 October are headed "Awake with the News."

E 1995
4 November 1915, p. 9.

E 1996
5 November 1915, p. 12.

E 1997
7 November 1915, p. 4, pt. 3.

E 1998
8 November 1915, p. 14.

E 1999
9 November 1915, p. 12.

E 2000
10 November 1915, p. 12.

E 2001
11 November 1915, p. 10.

E 2002
12 November 1915, p. 12.

E 2003
14 November 1915, p. 4, pt. 3.

E 2004
15 November 1915, p. 10.

E 2005
16 November 1915, p. 10.

E 2006
17 November 1915, p. 10.

E 2007
18 November 1915, p. 10.

E 2008
19 November 1915, p. 11.

E 2009
21 November 1915, p. 4, pt. 3.

E 2010
22 November 1915, p. 13.

E 2011
23 November 1915, p. 11.

E 2012
24 November 1915, p. 10.

E 2013
25 November 1915, p. 19.

E 2014
26 November 1915, p. 10.

E 2015
27 November 1915, p. 10.

E 2016
28 November 1915, p. 1, pt. 3.

E 2017
29 November 1915, p. 18.

E 2018
30 November 1915, p. 11.

E 2019
1 December 1915, p. 14.

E 2020
2 December 1915, p. 12.

E 2021
3 December 1915, p. 12.

E 2022
4 December 1915, p. 14.

E 2023
5 December 1915, p. 1, pt. 3.

E 2024
6 December 1915, p. 14.

E 2025
7 December 1915, p. 13.

E 2026
8 December 1915, p. 14.

E 2027
9 December 1915, p. 16.

E 2028
10 December 1915, p. 16.

E 2029
11 December 1915, p. 15.

E 2030
12 December 1915, p. 1, pt. 3.

E 2031
13 December 1915, p. 15.

E 2032
14 December 1915, p. 14.

E 2033
15 December 1915, p. 14.

E 2034
16 December 1915, p. 17.

E 2035
17 December 1915, p. 12.

E 2036
18 December 1915, p. 18.

E 2037
19 December 1915, p. 1, pt. 3.

E 2038
20 December 1915, p. 20.

E 2039
21 December 1915, p. 11.

E 2040
22 December 1915, p. 17.

E 2041
23 December 1915, p. 10.

E 2042
24 December 1915, p. 9.

E 2043
25 December 1915, p. 8.

E 2044
26 December 1915, p. 1, pt. 2.

E 2045
27 December 1915, p. 8.

E 2046
28 December 1915, p. 9.

E 2047
29 December 1915, p. 16.

E 2048
30 December 1915, p. 11.

E 2049
31 December 1915, p. 9.

E 2050
1 January 1916, p. 17.

E 2051
2 January 1916, p. 1, pt. 3.

E 2052
3 January 1916, p. 20.

E 2053
4 January 1916, p. 11.

E 2054
5 January 1916, p. 11.

E 2055
6 January 1916, p. 16.

E 2056
7 January 1916, p. 13.

E 2057
8 January 1916, p. 10.

E 2058
9 January 1916, p. 1, pt. 3.

E 2059
10 January 1916, p. 18.

E 2060
11 January 1916, p. 11.

E 2061
12 January 1916, p. 10.

E 2062
13 January 1916, p. 15.

E 2063
14 January 1916, p. 10.

E 2064
15 January 1916, p. 11.

E 2065
16 January 1916, p. 1, pt. 3.

E 2066
17 January 1916, p. 15.

E 2067
18 January 1916, p. 11.

E 2068
19 January 1916, p. 11.

E 2069
20 January 1916, p. 11.

E 2070
21 January 1916, p. 11.

E 2071
22 January 1916, p. 11.

E 2072
23 January 1916, p. 1, pt. 3.

E 2073
24 January 1916, p. 14.

E 2074
25 January 1916, p. 21.

E 2075
26 January 1916, p. 19.

E 2076
27 January 1916, p. 15.

E 2077
28 January 1916, p. 16.

E 2078
29 January 1916, p. 11.

E 2079
30 January 1916, p. 1, pt. 3.

E 2080
31 January 1916, p. 12.

E 2081
1 February 1916, p. 19.

E 2082
2 February 1916, p. 17.

E 2083
3 February 1916, p. 11.

E 2084
4 February 1916, p. 11.

E 2085
5 February 1916, p. 10.

E 2086
6 February 1916, p. 1, pt. 3.

E 2087
7 February 1916, p. 10.

E 2088
8 February 1916, p. 13.

E 2089
9 February 1916, p. 12.

E 2090
10 February 1916, p. 10.

E 2091
11 February 1916, p. 11.

E 2092
12 February 1916, p. 11.

E 2093
13 February 1916, p. 1, pt. 3.

E 2094
14 February 1916, p. 10.

E 2095
15 February 1916, p. 11.

E 2096
16 February 1916, p. 13.

E 2097
17 February 1916, p. 11.

E 2098
18 February 1916, p. 17.

E 2099
19 February 1916, p. 11.

E 2100
20 February 1916, p. 1, pt. 3.

E 2101
21 February 1916, p. 8.

E 2102
27 February 1916, p. 1, pt. 3.

E 2103
5 March 1916, p. 1, pt. 3.

E 2104
9 March 1916, p. 11.

E 2105
10 March 1916, p. 13.

E 2106
11 March 1916, p. 11.

E 2107
12 March 1916, p. 1, pt. 3.

E 2108
13 March 1916, p. 17.

E 2109
14 March 1916, p. 11.

E 2110
15 March 1916, p. 19.

E 2111
16 March 1916, p. 11.

E 2112
17 March 1916, p. 11.

E 2113
18 March 1916, p. 13.

E 2114
19 March 1916, p. 1, pt. 3.

E 2115
20 March 1916, p. 18.

E 2116
21 March 1916, p. 18.

E 2117
22 March 1916, p. 15.

E 2118
23 March 1916, p. 11.

E 2119
24 March 1916, p. 11.

E 2120
25 March 1916, p. 11.

E 2121
26 March 1916, p. 3, pt. 3.

E 2122
27 March 1916, p. 12.

E 2123
28 March 1916, p. 15.

E 2124
29 March 1916, p. 13.

E 2125
30 March 1916, p. 11.

E 2126
31 March 1916, p. 11.

E 2127
1 April 1916, p. 15.

E 2128
2 April 1916, p. 1, pt. 3.

E 2129
3 April 1916, p. 15.

E 2130
4 April 1916, p. 13.

E 2131
5 April 1916, p. 15.

E 2132
6 April 1916, p. 11.

E 2133
7 April 1916, p. 19.

E 2134
8 April 1916, p. 15.

E 2135
9 April 1916, p. 1, pt. 3.

E 2136
10 April 1916, p. 13.

E 2137
11 April 1916, p. 15.

E 2138
12 April 1916, p. 15.

E 2139
13 April 1916, p. 13.

E 2140
14 April 1916, p. 19.

E 2141
15 April 1916, p. 14.

E 2142
16 April 1916, p. 1, pt. 3.

E 2143
17 April 1916, p. 12.

E 2144
18 April 1916, p. 18.

E 2145
19 April 1916, p. 14.

E 2146
20 April 1916, p. 15.

E 2147
21 April 1916, p. 19.

E 2148
22 April 1916, p. 13.

E 2149
23 April 1916, p. 1, pt. 3.

E 2150
24 April 1916, p. 19.

E 2151
25 April 1916, p. 11.

E 2152
26 April 1916, p. 15.

E 2153
27 April 1916, p. 10.

E 2154
28 April 1916, p. 15.

E 2155
29 April 1916, p. 13.

E 2156
30 April 1916, p. 1, pt. 3.

E 2157
1 May 1916, p. 18.

E 2158
2 May 1916, p. 11.

E 2159
3 May 1916, p. 12.

E 2160
4 May 1916, p. 12.

E 2161
5 May 1916, p. 13.

E 2162
6 May 1916, p. 13.

E 2163
7 May 1916, p. 4, pt. 3.

E 2164
8 May 1916, p. 12.

E 2165
9 May 1916, p. 19.

E 2166
10 May 1916, p. 14.

E 2167
11 May 1916, p. 14.

E 2168
12 May 1916, p. 18.

E 2169
13 May 1916, p. 11.

E 2170
14 May 1916, p. 4, pt. 3.

E 2171
15 May 1916, p. 14.

E 2172
16 May 1916, p. 13.

E 2173
17 May 1916, p. 15.

E 2174
18 May 1916, p. 13.

E 2175
19 May 1916, p. 15.

E 2176
20 May 1916, p. 13.

E 2177
21 May 1916, p. 4, pt. 3.

E 2178
22 May 1916, p. 15.

E 2179
23 May 1916, p. 14.

E 2180
24 May 1916, p. 18.

E 2181
25 May 1916, p. 15.

E 2182
26 May 1916, p. 19.

E 2183
27 May 1916, p. 14.

E 2184
28 May 1916, p. 4, pt. 3.

E 2185
29 May 1916, p. 10.

E 2186
30 May 1916, p. 11.

E 2187
31 May 1916, p. 17.

E 2188
1 June 1916, p. 14.

E 2189
2 June 1916, p. 15.

E 2190
3 June 1916, p. 11.

E 2191
4 June 1916, p. 4, pt. 3.

E 2192
5 June 1916, p. 15.

E 2193
11 June 1916, p. 4, pt. 3.

E 2194
18 June 1916, p. 4, pt. 3.

E 2195
19 June 1916, p. 17.

E 2196
21 June 1916, p. 14.

E 2197
22 June 1916, p. 15.

E 2198
23 June 1916, p. 12.

E 2199
24 June 1916, p. 11.

E 2200
25 June 1916, p. 1, pt. 3.

E 2201
26 June 1916, p. 11.

E 2202
1 July 1916, p. 11.

E 2203
2 July 1916, p. 4, pt. 3.

E 2204
3 July 1916, p. 11.

E 2205
4 July 1916, p. 13.

E 2206
5 July 1916, p. 15.

E 2207
6 July 1916, p. 11.

E 2208
7 July 1916, p. 13.

E 2209
8 July 1916, p. 8.

E 2210
9 July 1916, p. 4, pt. 3.

E 2211
10 July 1916, p. 9.

E 2212
11 July 1916, p. 12.

E 2213
12 July 1916, p. 13.

E 2214
13 July 1916, p. 11.

E 2215
14 July 1916, p. 10.

E 2216
15 July 1916, p. 8.

E 2217
16 July 1916, p. 4, pt. 3.

E 2218
17 July 1916, p. 11.

E 2219
18 July 1916, p. 12.

E 2220
19 July 1916, p. 13.

E 2221
20 July 1916, p. 11.

E 2222
21 July 1916, p. 9.

E 2223
22 July 1916, p. 9.
See C 43.

E 2224
23 July 1916, p. 4, pt. 3.

E 2225
24 July 1916, p. 11.

E 2226
25 July 1916, p. 11.

E 2227
26 July 1916, p. 11.

E 2228
27 July 1916, p. 11.

E 2229
28 July 1916, p. 9.

E 2230
29 July 1916, p. 9.

E 2231
30 July 1916, p. 4, pt. 3.

E 2232
31 July 1916, p. 9.

E 2233
1 August 1916, p. 15.

E 2234
2 August 1916, p. 11.

E 2235
3 August 1916, p. 9.

E 2236
4 August 1916, p. 11.

E 2237
5 August 1916, p. 7.

E 2238
6 August 1916, p. 4, pt. 3.

E 2239
7 August 1916, p. 11.

E 2240
8 August 1916, p. 11.

E 2241
9 August 1916, p. 11.

E 2242
10 August 1916, p. 11.

E 2243
11 August 1916, p. 7.

E 2244
12 August 1916, p. 9.

E 2245
13 August 1916, p. 4, pt. 3.

E 2246
14 August 1916, p. 11.

E 2247
15 August 1916, p. 13.

E 2248
16 August 1916, p. 9.

E 2249
17 August 1916, p. 9.

E 2250
18 August 1916, p. 8.

E 2251
20 August 1916, p. 1, pt. 3.

E 2252
21 August 1916, p. 9.

E 2253
22 August 1916, p. 9.

E 2254
23 August 1916, p. 11.

E 2255
24 August 1916, p. 11.

E 2256
25 August 1916, p. 7.

E 2257
26 August 1916, p. 11.

E 2258
27 August 1916, p. 1, pt. 3.

E 2259
28 August 1916, p. 11.

E 2260
29 August 1916, p. 11.

E 2261
30 August 1916, p. 9.

E 2262
31 August 1916, p. 9.

E 2263
1 September 1916, p. 13.

E 2264
2 September 1916, p. 9.

E 2265
3 September 1916, p. 1, pt. 3.

E 2266
4 September 1916, p. 11.

E 2267
5 September 1916, p. 17.

E 2268
6 September 1916, p. 10.

E 2269
7 September 1916, p. 9.

E 2270
8 September 1916, p. 11.

E 2271
9 September 1916, p. 11.

E 2272
10 September 1916, p. 4, pt. 3.

E 2273
11 September 1916, p. 12.

E 2274
12 September 1916, p. 15.

E 2275
13 September 1916, p. 13.

E 2276
14 September 1916, p. 11.

E 2277
15 September 1916, p. 13.

E 2278
16 September 1916, p. 11.

E 2279
17 September 1916, p .1, pt. 3.

E 2280
18 September 1916, p. 11.

E 2281
19 September 1916, p. 15.

E 2282
20 September 1916, p. 11.

E 2283
21 September 1916, p. 11.

E 2284
22 September 1916, p. 13.

E 2285
23 September 1916, p. 11.

E 2286
24 September 1916, p. 4, pt. 3.

E 2287
25 September 1916, p. 13.

E 2288
26 September 1916, p. 15.

E 2289
27 September 1916, p. 13.

E 2290
28 September 1916, p. 11.

E 2291
29 September 1916, p. 11.

E 2292
30 September 1916, p. 13.

E 2293
1 October 1916, p. 4, pt. 3.

E 2294
2 October 1916, p. 15.

E 2295
3 October 1916, p. 13.

E 2296
4 October 1916, p. 14.

E 2297
8 October 1916, p. 4, pt. 3.

E 2298
15 October 1916, p. 4, pt. 3.

E 2299
16 October 1916, p. 19.

E 2300
17 October 1916, p. 13.

E 2301
21 October 1916, p. 11.

E 2302
22 October 1916, p. 4, pt. 3.

E 2303
23 October 1916, p. 12.

E 2304
24 October 1916, p. 13.

E 2305
25 October 1916, p. 13.

E 2306
26 October 1916, p. 13.

E 2307
27 October 1916, p. 13.

E 2308
28 October 1916, p. 11.

E 2309
29 October 1916, p. 4, pt. 3.

E 2310
30 October 1916, p. 14.

E 2311
31 October 1916, p. 13.

E 2312
1 November 1916, p. 19.

E 2313
2 November 1916, p. 13.

E 2314
3 November 1916, p. 13.

E 2315
4 November 1916, p. 13.

E 2316
5 November 1916, p. 4, pt. 3.

E 2317
6 November 1916, p. 21.

E 2318
7 November 1916, p. 11.

E 2319
8 November 1916, p. 12.

E 2320
9 November 1916, p. 11.

E 2321
10 November 1916, p. 15.

E 2322
11 November 1916, p. 11.

E 2323
12 November 1916, p. 4, pt. 3.

E 2324
13 November 1916, p. 14.

E 2325
14 November 1916, p. 15.

E 2326
15 November 1916, p. 15.

E 2327
16 November 1916, p. 13.

E 2328
17 November 1916, p. 13.

E 2329
18 November 1916, p. 9.

E 2330
19 November 1916, p. 1, pt. 3.

E 2331
20 November 1916, p. 16.

E 2332
21 November 1916, p. 11.

E 2333
22 November 1916, p. 13.

E 2334
23 November 1916, p. 11.

E 2335
24 November 1916, p. 15.

E 2336
25 November 1916, p. 11.

E 2337
26 November 1916, p. 3, pt. 3.

E 2338
27 November 1916, p. 12.

E 2339
28 November 1916, p. 14.

E 2340
29 November 1916, p. 11.

E 2341
30 November 1916, p. 19.

E 2342
1 December 1916, p. 15.

E 2343
2 December 1916, p. 15.

E 2344
3 December 1916, p. 1, pt. 3.

E 2345
4 December 1916, p. 21.

E 2346
5 December 1916, p. 19.

E 2347
6 December 1916, p. 15.

E 2348
7 December 1916, p. 13.

E 2349
8 December 1916, p. 15.

E 2350
9 December 1916, p. 13.

E 2351
10 December 1916, p. 1, pt. 3.

E 2352
11 December 1916, p. 19.

E 2353
12 December 1916, p. 15.

E 2354
13 December 1916, p. 19.

E 2355
14 December 1916, p. 13.

E 2356
15 December 1916, p. 13.

E 2357
16 December 1916, p. 13.

E 2358
17 December 1916, p. 1, pt. 3.

E 2359
18 December 1916, p. 15.

E 2360
19 December 1916, p. 11.

E 2361
20 December 1916, p. 15.

E 2362
21 December 1916, p. 11.

E 2363
22 December 1916, p. 13.

E 2364
23 December 1916, p. 12.

E 2365
24 December 1916, p. 1, pt. 2.

E 2366
25 December 1916, p. 18.

E 2367
26 December 1916, p. 9.

E 2368
27 December 1916, p. 9.

E 2369
28 December 1916, p. 12.

E 2370
29 December 1916, p. 11.

E 2371
30 December 1916, p. 11.

E 2372
31 December 1916, p. 1, pt. 3.

E 2373
1 January 1917, p. 24.

E 2374
2 January 1917, p. 15.

E 2375
3 January 1917, p. 13.

E 2376
4 January 1917, p. 9.

E 2377
5 January 1917, p. 11.

E 2378
6 January 1917, p. 9.

E 2379
7 January 1917, p. 1, pt. 3.

E 2380
8 January 1917, p. 11.

E 2381
9 January 1917, p. 13.

E 2382
10 January 1917, p. 16.

E 2383
11 January 1917, p. 8.

E 2384
12 January 1917, p. 13.

E 2385
13 January 1917, p. 14.

E 2386
14 January 1917, p. 1, pt. 3.

E 2387
15 January 1917, p. 11.

E 2388
16 January 1917, p. 16.

E 2389
17 January 1917, p. 8.

E 2390
18 January 1917, p. 9.

E 2391
19 January 1917, p. 14.

E 2392
20 January 1917, p. 9.

E 2393
21 January 1917, p. 1, pt. 2.

E 2394
22 January 1917, p. 14.

E 2395
23 January 1917, p. 16.

E 2396
24 January 1917, p. 8.

E 2397
25 January 1917, p. 7.

E 2398
26 January 1917, p. 14.

E 2399
27 January 1917, p. 11.

E 2400
28 January 1917, p. 1, pt. 2.

E 2401
29 January 1917, p. 18.

E 2402
30 January 1917, p. 22.

E 2417
14 February 1917, p. 14.

E 2403
31 January 1917, p. 22.

E 2418
15 February 1917, p. 12.

E 2404
1 February 1917, p. 19.

E 2419
16 February 1917, p. 9.

E 2405
2 February 1917, p. 15.

E 2420
17 February 1917, p. 9.

E 2406
3 February 1917, p. 14.

E 2421
18 February 1917, p. 1, pt. 2.

E 2407
4 February 1917, p. 1, pt. 2.[12]

E 2422
19 February 1917, p. 11.

E 2408
5 February 1917, p. 11.

E 2423
20 February 1917, p. 16.

E 2409
6 February 1917, p. 16.

E 2424
21 February 1917, p. 11.

E 2410
7 February 1917, p. 11.

E 2425
22 February 1917, p. 7.

E 2411
8 February 1917, p. 12.

E 2426
23 February 1917, p. 11.

E 2412
9 February 1917, p. 14.

E 2427
24 February 1917, p. 14.

E 2413
10 February 1917, p. 9.

E 2428
25 February 1917, p. 1, pt. 2.

E 2414
11 February 1917, p. 1, pt. 2.

E 2429
26 February 1917, p. 11.

E 2415
12 February 1917, p. 11.

E 2430
27 February 1917, p. 9.

E 2416
13 February 1917, p. 11.

E 2431
28 February 1917, p. 11.

---

12. From 4 February to 5 August 1917, Lardner's Sunday columns are headed "Crazy Kennedy, Detective." The "Crazy Kennedy" series ran from 7 January 1917 to 5 August 1917.

E 2432
1 March 1917, p. 13.

E 2433
2 March 1917, p. 16.

E 2434
3 March 1917, p. 12.

E 2435
4 March 1917, p. 1, pt. 2.

E 2436
5 March 1917, p. 16.

E 2437
6 March 1917, p. 16.

E 2438
7 March 1917, p. 14.

E 2439
8 March 1917, p. 12.

E 2440
9 March 1917, p. 9.

E 2441
10 March 1917, p. 14.

E 2442
11 March 1917, p. 1, pt. 2.

E 2443
12 March 1917, p. 11.

E 2444
13 March 1917, p. 11.

E 2445
14 March 1917, p. 14.

E 2446
15 March 1917, p. 12.

E 2447
16 March 1917, p. 9.

E 2448
17 March 1917, p. 14.

E 2449
18 March 1917, p. 1, pt. 2.

E 2450
19 March 1917, p. 16.

E 2451
20 March 1917, p. 13.

E 2452
21 March 1917, p. 11.

E 2453
22 March 1917, p. 12.

E 2454
23 March 1917, p. 14.

E 2455
24 March 1917, p. 11.

E 2456
25 March 1917, p. 1, pt. 2.

E 2457
26 March 1917, p. 11.

E 2458
27 March 1917, p. 14.

E 2459
28 March 1917, p. 13.

E 2460
29 March 1917, p. 14.

E 2461
30 March 1917, p. 16.

E 2462
31 March 1917, p. 11.

E 2463
1 April 1917, p. 1, pt. 2.

E 2464
2 April 1917, p. 14.

E 2465
3 April 1917, p. 11.

E 2466
4 April 1917, p. 10.

E 2467
5 April 1917, p. 9.

E 2468
6 April 1917, p. 16.

E 2469
7 April 1917, p. 16.

E 2470
8 April 1917, p. 1, pt. 2.

E 2471
9 April 1917, p. 16.

E 2472
10 April 1917, p. 12.

E 2473
11 April 1917, p. 18.

E 2474
12 April 1917, p. 10.

E 2475
13 April 1917, p. 13.

E 2476
14 April 1917, p. 13.

E 2477
15 April 1917, p. 1, pt. 2.

E 2478
16 April 1917, p. 16.

E 2479
17 April 1917, p. 14.

E 2480
18 April 1917, p. 11.

E 2481
19 April 1917, p. 9.

E 2482
20 April 1917, p. 10.

E 2483
21 April 1917, p. 11.

E 2484
22 April 1917, p. 1, pt. 2.

E 2485
23 April 1917, p. 18.

E 2486
24 April 1917, p. 14.

E 2487
25 April 1917, p. 13.

E 2488
26 April 1917, p. 17.

E 2489
27 April 1917, p. 11.

E 2490
28 April 1917, p. 11.

E 2491
29 April 1917, p. 1, pt. 2.

E 2492
30 April 1917, p. 13.

E 2493
1 May 1917, p. 18.

E 2494
2 May 1917, p. 16.

E 2495
3 May 1917, p. 13.

E 2496
4 May 1917, p. 14.
See C 39.

E 2497
5 May 1917, p. 11.

E 2498
6 May 1917, p. 1, pt. 2.

E 2499
7 May 1917, p. 20.

E 2500
8 May 1917, p. 18.

E 2501a
9 May 1917, p. 12.

E 2501b
10 May 1917, p. 13.

E 2502
11 May 1917, p. 18.

E 2503
12 May 1917, p. 13.

E 2504
13 May 1917, p. 1, pt. 2.

E 2505
15 May 1917, p. 13.

E 2506
16 May 1917, p. 14.

E 2507
17 May 1917, p. 13.

E 2508
18 May 1917, p. 10.

E 2509
19 May 1917, p. 13.

E 2510
20 May 1917, p. 1, pt. 2.

E 2511
23 May 1917, p. 12.

E 2512
24 May 1917, p. 12.

E 2513
25 May 1917, p. 13.

E 2514
26 May 1917, p. 13.

E 2515
27 May 1917, p. 1, pt. 2.

E 2516
29 May 1917, p. 16.

E 2517
30 May 1917, p. 10.

E 2518
31 May 1917, p. 12.

E 2519
1 June 1917, p. 12.

E 2520
2 June 1917, p. 10.

E 2521a
3 June 1917, p. 1, pt. 2.

E 2521b
5 June 1917, p. 10.

E 2521c
6 June 1917, p. 15.

E 2522
7 June 1917, p. 12.

E 2523
8 June 1917, p. 10.

E 2524
9 June 1917, p. 12.

E 2525
10 June 1917, p. 1, pt. 2.

E 2526
12 June 1917, p. 10.

E 2527
17 June 1917, p. 1, pt. 2.

E 2528
19 June 1917, p. 10.

E 2529
20 June 1917, p. 10.

E 2530
21 June 1917, p. 8.

E 2531
22 June 1917, p. 12.

E 2532
23 June 1917, p. 11.

E 2533
24 June 1917, p. 1, pt. 2.

E 2534
26 June 1917, p. 11.

E 2535
27 June 1917, p. 12.

E 2536
28 June 1917, p. 8.

E 2537
29 June 1917, p. 10.

E 2538
30 June 1917, p. 14.

E 2539
1 July 1917, p. 1, pt. 2.

E 2540
3 July 1917, p. 10.

E 2541
4 July 1917, p. 11.

E 2542
5 July 1917, p. 13.

E 2543
6 July 1917, p. 10.

E 2544
7 July 1917, p. 8.

E 2545
8 July 1917, p. 1, pt. 2.

E 2546
10 July 1917, p. 11.

E 2547
11 July 1917, p. 10.

E 2548
12 July 1917, p. 11.

E 2549
13 July 1917, p. 10.

E 2550
14 July 1917, p. 8.

E 2551
15 July 1917, p. 1, pt. 2.

E 2552
17 July 1917, p. 9.

E 2553
18 July 1917, p. 10.

E 2554
19 July 1917, p. 8.

E 2555
20 July 1917, p. 11.

E 2556
21 July 1917, p. 10.

E 2557
22 July 1917, p. 1, pt. 2.

E 2558
24 July 1917, p. 10.

E 2559
25 July 1917, p. 10.

E 2560
26 July 1917, p. 12.

E 2561
27 July 1917, p. 10.

E 2562
28 July 1917, p. 8.

E 2563
29 July 1917, p. 1, pt. 2.

E 2564
31 July 1917, p. 10.

E 2565
1 August 1917, p. 18.

E 2566
2 August 1917, p. 15.

E 2567
3 August 1917, p. 15.

E 2568
4 August 1917, p. 8.

E 2569
5 August 1917, p. 1, pt. 2.

E 2570
7 August 1917, p. 9.

E 2571
8 August 1917, p. 11.

E 2572
9 August 1917, p. 9.

E 2573
10 August 1917, p. 11.

E 2574
28 August 1917, p. 11.[13]

E 2575
29 August 1917, p. 13.

E 2576
11 September 1917, p. 13.

E 2577
12 September 1917, p. 11.

E 2578
14 September 1917, p. 13.[14]

E 2579
16 September 1917, p. 1, pt. 2.

E 2580
3 October 1917, p. 15.

E 2581
5 October 1917, p. 12.

E 2582
6 October 1917, p. 15.

E 2583
7 October 1917, p. 1, pt. 2.

E 2584
8 October 1917, p. 13.

E 2585
9 October 1917, p. 13.

E 2586
10 October 1917, p. 19.

E 2587
11 October 1917, p. 15.

E 2588
12 October 1917, p. 17.

E 2589
13 October 1917, p. 15.

E 2590
14 October 1917, p. 1, pt. 2.

E 2591
16 October 1917, p. 17.

E 2592
17 October 1917, p. 15.

E 2593
18 October 1917, p. 11.

---

13. From 28 August 1917 to 3 October 1917, Lardner's columns are headed "In the Wake of the War" except for the 14 September 1917 column (E 2578), which is headed "from the Front."

14. This column is headed "From the Front."

E 2594
19 October 1917, p. 15.

E 2595
20 October 1917, p. 19.

E 2596
21 October 1917, p. 1, pt. 2.

E 2597
23 October 1917, p. 15.

E 2598
24 October 1917, p. 13.

E 2599
27 October 1917, p. 13.

E 2600
28 October 1917, p. 1, pt. 2.

E 2601
29 October 1917, p. 13.

E 2602
30 October 1917, p. 13.

E 2603
31 October 1917, p. 11.

E 2604
1 November 1917, p. 21.

E 2605
2 November 1917, p. 13.

E 2606
3 November 1917, p. 13.

E 2607
4 November 1917, p. 1, pt. 2.

E 2608
6 November 1917, p. 11.

E 2609
7 November 1917, p. 15.

E 2610
8 November 1917, p. 11.

E 2611
9 November 1917, p. 13.

E 2612
10 November 1917, p. 15.

E 2613
11 November 1917, p. 1, pt. 2.

E 2614
13 November 1917, p. 13.

E 2615
14 November 1917, p. 13.

E 2616
15 November 1917, p. 13.

E 2617
16 November 1917, p. 11.

E 2618
17 November 1917, p. 13.

E 2619
18 November 1917, p. 1, pt. 2.

E 2620
20 November 1917, p. 11.

E 2621
21 November 1917, p. 13.

E 2622
22 November 1917, p. 11.

E 2623
23 November 1917, p. 13.

E 2624
24 November 1917, p. 13.

E 2625
25 November 1917, p. 1, pt. 2.

E 2626
27 November 1917, p. 16.

E 2627
28 November 1917, p. 18.

E 2628
29 November 1917, p. 20.

E 2629
30 November 1917, p. 11.

E 2630
1 December 1917, p. 18.

E 2631
2 December 1917, p. 1, pt. 2.

E 2632
4 December 1917, p. 13.

E 2633
6 December 1917, p. 11.

E 2634
7 December 1917, p. 22.

E 2635
8 December 1917, p. 15.

E 2636
9 December 1917, p. 1, pt. 2.

E 2637
11 December 1917, p. 18.

E 2638
12 December 1917, p. 15.

E 2639
13 December 1917, p. 21.

E 2640
14 December 1917, p. 15.

E 2641
15 December 1917, p. 15.

E 2642
16 December 1917, p. 1, pt. 2.

E 2643
18 December 1917, p. 15.

E 2644
19 December 1917, p. 21.

E 2645
20 December 1917, p. 15.

E 2646
21 December 1917, p. 15.

E 2647
22 December 1917, p. 11.

E 2648
23 December 1917, p. 1, pt. 2.

E 2649
25 December 1917, p. 21.

E 2650
26 December 1917, p. 9.

E 2651
27 December 1917, p. 14.

E 2652
29 December 1917, p. 14.

E 2653
30 December 1917, p. 1, pt. 2.

E 2654
1 January 1918, p. 21.

E 2655
2 January 1918, p. 13.

E 2656
3 January 1918, p. 7.

E 2657
4 January 1918, p. 13.

E 2658
5 January 1918, p. 9.

E 2659
6 January 1918, p. 1, pt. 2.

E 2660
8 January 1918, p. 11.

E 2661
9 January 1918, p. 11.

E 2662
10 January 1918, p. 11.

E 2663
11 January 1918, p. 11.

E 2664
12 January 1918, p. 16.

E 2665
13 January 1918, p. 1, pt. 2.

E 2666
15 January 1918, p. 9.

E 2667
16 January 1918, p. 13.

E 2668
17 January 1918, p. 12.

E 2669
18 January 1918, p. 13.

E 2670
19 January 1918, p. 12.

E 2671
20 January 1918, p. 2, pt. 2.

E 2672
22 January 1918, p. 15.

E 2673
23 January 1918, p. 14.

E 2674
24 January 1918, p. 9.

E 2675
25 January 1918, p. 11.

E 2676
26 January 1918, p. 14.

E 2677
27 January 1918, p. 1, pt. 2.

E 2678
29 January 1918, p. 15.

E 2679
30 January 1918, p. 18.

E 2680
1 February 1918, p. 13.

E 2681
2 February 1918, p. 12.

E 2682
3 February 1918, p. 1, pt. 2.

E 2683
5 February 1918, p. 16.

E 2684
6 February 1918, p. 14.

E 2685
7 February 1918, p. 9.

E 2686
8 February 1918, p. 11.

E 2687
9 February 1918, p. 9.

E 2688
10 February 1918, p. 1, pt. 2.

E 2689
12 February 1918, p. 14.

E 2690
13 February 1918, p. 13.

E 2691
14 February 1918, p. 9.

E 2692
15 February 1918, p. 9.

E 2693
16 February 1918, p. 14.

E 2694
17 February 1918, p. 1, pt. 2.

E 2695
19 February 1918, p. 14.

E 2696
20 February 1918, p. 14.

E 2697
21 February 1918, p. 12.

E 2698
22 February 1918, p. 14.

E 2699
23 February 1918, p. 14.

E 2700
24 February 1918, p. 1, pt. 2.

E 2701
26 February 1918, p. 18.

E 2702
27 February 1918, p. 11.

E 2703
28 February 1918, p. 14.

E 2704
1 March 1918, p. 18.

E 2705
2 March 1918, p. 11.

E 2706
3 March 1918, p. 1, pt. 2.

E 2707
5 March 1918, p. 11.

E 2708
6 March 1918, p. 11.

E 2709
7 March 1918, p. 11.

E 2710
9 March 1918, p. 14.

E 2711
10 March 1918, p. 1, pt. 2.

E 2712
11 March 1918, p. 13.

E 2713
12 March 1918, p. 14.

E 2714
13 March 1918, p. 13.

E 2715
14 March 1918, p. 9.

E 2716
15 March 1918, p. 11.

E 2717
16 March 1918, p. 16.

E 2718
17 March 1918, p. 1, pt. 2.

E 2719
19 March 1918, p. 16.

E 2720
20 March 1918, p. 18.

E 2721
21 March 1918, p. 16.

E 2722
22 March 1918, p. 18.

E 2723
23 March 1918, p. 11.

E 2724
24 March 1918, p. 1, pt. 2.

E 2725
26 March 1918, p. 13.

E 2726
27 March 1918, p. 13.

E 2727
28 March 1918, p. 16.

E 2728
29 March 1918, p. 18.

E 2729
30 March 1918, p. 13.

E 2730
31 March 1918, p. 1, pt. 2.

E 2731
2 April 1918, p. 13.

E 2732
3 April 1918, p. 13.

E 2733
4 April 1918, p. 13.

E 2734
5 April 1918, p. 16.

E 2735
6 April 1918, p. 18.

E 2736
7 April 1918, p. 1, pt. 2.

E 2737
9 April 1918, p. 13.

E 2738
11 April 1918, p. 11.

E 2739
12 April 1918, p. 9.

E 2740
13 April 1918, p. 9.

E 2741
14 April 1918, p. 1, pt. 2.

E 2742
16 April 1918, p. 11.

E 2743
17 April 1918, p. 12.

E 2744
18 April 1918, p. 11.

E 2745
19 April 1918, p. 9.

E 2746
20 April 1918, p. 13.

E 2747
21 April 1918, p. 1, pt. 2.

E 2748
23 April 1918, p. 13.

E 2749
24 April 1918, p. 13.

E 2750
25 April 1918, p. 12.

E 2751
26 April 1918, p. 10.

E 2752
27 April 1918, p. 11.

E 2753
28 April 1918, p. 1, pt. 2.

E 2754
30 April 1918, p. 12.

E 2755
1 May 1918, p. 19.

E 2756
2 May 1918, p. 11.

E 2757
5 May 1918, p. 1, pt. 2.

E 2758
7 May 1918, p. 12.

E 2759
8 May 1918, p. 14.

E 2760
9 May 1918, p. 8.

E 2761
10 May 1918, p. 13.

E 2762
11 May 1918, p. 9.

E 2763
12 May 1918, p. 1, pt. 2.

E 2764
14 May 1918, p. 14.

E 2765
15 May 1918, p. 12.

E 2766
16 May 1918, p. 11.

E 2767
17 May 1918, p. 13.

E 2768
18 May 1918, p. 12.

E 2769
19 May 1918, p. 1, pt. 2.

E 2770
21 May 1918, p. 12.

E 2771
22 May 1918, p. 12.

E 2772
23 May 1918, p. 10.

E 2773
24 May 1918, p. 12.

E 2774
25 May 1918, p. 12.

E 2775
26 May 1918, p. 1, pt. 2.

E 2776
28 May 1918, p. 12.

E 2777
29 May 1918, p. 11.

E 2778
30 May 1918, p. 11.

E 2779
31 May 1918, p. 13.

E 2780
1 June 1918, p. 11.

E 2781
2 June 1918, p. 1, pt. 2.

E 2782
4 June 1918, p. 10.

E 2783
5 June 1918, p. 10.

E 2784
6 June 1918, p. 9.

E 2785
7 June 1918, p. 12.

E 2786
8 June 1918, p. 11.

E 2787
9 June 1918, p. 1, pt. 2.

E 2788
11 June 1918, p. 9.

E 2789
12 June 1918, p. 10.

E 2790
13 June 1918, p. 9.

E 2791
14 June 1918, p. 15.

E 2792
15 June 1918, p. 11.

E 2793
16 June 1918, p. 1, pt. 2.

E 2794
18 June 1918, p. 13.

E 2795
19 June 1918, p. 10.

E 2796
20 June 1918, p. 11.

E 2797
21 June 1918, p. 11.

E 2798
22 June 1918, p. 8.

E 2799
23 June 1918, p. 3, pt. 2.

E 2800
25 June 1918, p. 9.

E 2801
26 June 1918, p. 10.

E 2802
27 June 1918, p. 14.

E 2803
28 June 1918, p. 8.

E 2804
29 June 1918, p. 9.

E 2805
30 June 1918, p. 1, pt. 2.

E 2806
2 July 1918, p. 8.

E 2807
3 July 1918, p. 13.

E 2808
4 July 1918, p. 12.

E 2809
5 July 1918, p. 8.

E 2810
6 July 1918, p. 9.

E 2811
7 July 1918, p. 1, pt. 2.

E 2812
9 July 1918, p. 11.

E 2813
10 July 1918, p. 10.

E 2814
11 July 1918, p. 8.

E 2815
12 July 1918, p. 9.

E 2816
13 July 1918, p. 8.

E 2817
14 July 1918, p. 1, pt. 2.

E 2818
16 July 1918, p. 10.

E 2819
17 July 1918, p. 10.

E 2820
18 July 1918, p. 8.

E 2821
19 July 1918, p. 8.

E 2822
20 July 1918, p. 8.

E 2823
21 July 1918, p. 1, pt. 2.

E 2824
23 July 1918, p. 10.

E 2825
24 July 1918, p. 13.

E 2826
25 July 1918, p. 9.

E 2827
26 July 1918, p. 8.

E 2828
27 July 1918, p. 8.

E 2829
28 July 1918, p. 1, pt. 2.

E 2830
30 July 1918, p. 11.

E 2831
31 July 1918, p. 11.

E 2832
1 August 1918, p. 12.

E 2833
2 August 1918, p. 8.

E 2834
3 August 1918, p. 6.

E 2835
4 August 1918, p. 1, pt. 2.

E 2836
6 August 1918, p. 15.

E 2837
7 August 1918, p. 8.

E 2838
8 August 1918, p. 15.

E 2839
9 August 1918, p. 9.

E 2840
10 August 1918, p. 15.

E 2841
11 August 1918, p. 1, pt. 2.

E 2842
13 August 1918, p. 9.

E 2843
14 August 1918, p. 9.

E 2844
15 August 1918, p. 9.

E 2845
16 August 1918, p. 7.

E 2846
17 August 1918, p. 7.

E 2847
18 August 1918, p. 1, pt. 2.

E 2848
20 August 1918, p. 11.

E 2849
21 August 1918, p. 11.

E 2850
22 August 1918, p. 9.

E 2851
23 August 1918, p. 9.

E 2852
24 August 1918, p. 10.

E 2853
25 August 1918, p. 1, pt. 2.

E 2854
27 August 1918, p. 9.

E 2855
28 August 1918, p. 7.

E 2856
29 August 1918, p. 9.

E 2857
31 August 1918, p. 9.

E 2858
1 September 1918, p. 1, pt. 2.

E 2859
3 September 1918, p. 13.

E 2860
4 September 1918, p. 11.

E 2861
5 September 1918, p. 13.

E 2862
6 September 1918, p. 9.

E 2863
7 September 1918, p. 7.

E 2864
8 September 1918, p. 4, pt. 2.

E 2865
Entry canceled.

E 2866
15 September 1918, p. 5, pt. 2.

E 2867
22 September 1918, p. 5, pt. 2.

E 2868
26 September 1918, p. 11.

E 2869
27 September 1918, p. 13.

E 2870
28 September 1918, p. 11.

E 2871
29 September 1918, p. 5, pt. 2.

E 2872
1 October 1918, p. 18.

E 2873
2 October 1918, p. 18.

E 2874
3 October 1918, p. 14.

E 2875
4 October 1918, p. 13.

E 2876
5 October 1918, p. 16.

E 2877
6 October 1918, p. 5, pt. 2.

E 2878
8 October 1918, p. 13.

E 2879
9 October 1918, p. 11.

E 2880
10 October 1918, p. 13.

E 2881
11 October 1918, p. 18.

E 2882
12 October 1918, p. 15.

E 2883
13 October 1918, p. 5, pt. 2.

E 2884
15 October 1918, p. 13.

E 2885
16 October 1918, p. 11.

E 2886
17 October 1918, p. 14.

E 2887
18 October 1918, p. 14.

E 2888
19 October 1918, p. 9.

E 2889
20 October 1918, p. 5, pt. 2.

E 2890
22 October 1918, p. 11.

E 2891
23 October 1918, p. 11.

E 2892
24 October 1918, p. 11.

E 2893
25 October 1918, p. 14.

E 2894
26 October 1918, p. 11.

E 2895
27 October 1918, p. 5, pt. 2.

E 2896
29 October 1918, p. 18.

E 2897
30 October 1918, p. 11.

E 2898
31 October 1918, p. 14.

E 2899
1 November 1918, p. 20.

E 2900
2 November 1918, p. 11.

E 2901
3 November 1918, p. 5, pt. 2.

E 2902
5 November 1918, p. 8.

E 2903
6 November 1918, p. 13.

E 2904
7 November 1918, p. 11.

E 2905
8 November 1918, p. 16.

E 2906
9 November 1918, p. 14.

E 2907
10 November 1918, p. 5, pt. 2.

E 2908
12 November 1918, p. 15.

E 2909
13 November 1918, p. 9.

E 2910
14 November 1918, p. 14.

E 2911
15 November 1918, p. 13.

E 2912
16 November 1918, p. 14.

E 2913
17 November 1918, p. 5, pt. 2.

E 2914
19 November 1918, p. 16.

E 2915
20 November 1918, p. 13.

E 2916
21 November 1918, p. 11.

E 2917
22 November 1918, p. 15.

E 2918
23 November 1918, p. 13.

E 2919
24 November 1918, p. 4, pt. 3.

E 2920
26 November 1918, p. 13.

E 2921
27 November 1918, p. 14.

E 2922
28 November 1918, p. 21.

E 2923
29 November 1918, p. 16.

E 2924
30 November 1918, p. 17.

E 2925
1 December 1918, p. 4, pt. 2.

E 2926
3 December 1918, p. 21.

E 2927
4 December 1918, p. 15.

E 2928
5 December 1918, p. 11.

E 2929
6 December 1918, p. 19.

E 2930
7 December 1918, p. 13.

E 2931
8 December 1918, p. 5, pt. 2.

E 2932
10 December 1918, p. 15.

E 2933
11 December 1918, p. 15.

E 2934
12 December 1918, p. 16.

E 2935
13 December 1918, p. 15.

E 2936
14 December 1918, p. 12.

E 2937
15 December 1918, p. 5, pt. 2.

E 2938
17 December 1918, p. 15.

E 2939
18 December 1918, p. 20.

E 2940
19 December 1918, p. 20.

E 2941a
20 December 1918, p. 20.

E 2941b
21 December 1918, p. 11.

E 2942
22 December 1918, p. 5, pt. 2.

E 2943
24 December 1918, p. 14.

E 2944
25 December 1918, p. 19.

E 2945
26 December 1918, p. 11.

E 2946
27 December 1918, p. 9.

E 2947
28 December 1918, p. 12.

E 2948
29 December 1918, p. 5, pt. 2.

E 2949
31 December 1918, p. 9.

E 2950
1 January 1919, p. 21.

E 2951
2 January 1919, p. 9.

E 2952
3 January 1919, p. 14.

E 2953
4 January 1919, p. 14.

E 2954
5 January 1919, p. 5, pt. 2.

E 2955
7 January 1919, p. 18.

E 2956
8 January 1919, p. 13.

E 2957
9 January 1919, p. 11.

E 2958
10 January 1919, p. 11.

E 2959
11 January 1919, p. 9.

E 2960
12 January 1919, p. 5, pt. 2.

E 2961
14 January 1919, p. 14.

E 2962
15 January 1919, p. 16.

E 2963
16 January 1919, p. 16.

E 2964
17 January 1919, p. 11.

E 2965
18 January 1919, p. 11.

E 2966
19 January 1919, p. 5, pt. 2.

E 2967
21 January 1919, p. 11.

E 2968
22 January 1919, p. 16.

E 2969
23 January 1919, p. 15.

E 2970
24 January 1919, p. 11.

E 2971
25 January 1919, p. 11.

E 2972
26 January 1919, p. 1, pt. 2.

E 2973
28 January 1919, p. 20.

E 2974
29 January 1919, p. 22.

E 2975
30 January 1919, p. 13.

E 2976
31 January 1919, p. 16.

E 2977
1 February 1919, p. 15.

E 2978
2 February 1919, p. 1, pt. 2.

E 2979
4 February 1919, p. 18.

E 2980
5 February 1919, p. 20.

E 2981
6 February 1919, p. 11.

E 2982
7 February 1919, p. 11.

E 2983
8 February 1919, p. 11.

E 2984
9 February 1919, p. 1, pt. 2.

E 2985
11 February 1919, p. 18.

E 2986
12 February 1919, p. 13.

E 2987
13 February 1919, p. 13.

E 2988
14 February 1919, p. 16.

E 2989
15 February 1919, p. 16.

E 2990
16 February 1919, p. 1, pt. 2.

E 2991
19 February 1919, p. 15.

E 2992
20 February 1919, p. 18.

E 2993
21 February 1919, p. 11.

E 2994
22 February 1919, p. 15.

E 2995
23 February 1919, p. 1, pt. 2.

E 2996
25 February 1919, p. 20.

E 2997
26 February 1919, p. 20.

E 2998
27 February 1919, p. 11.

E 2999
28 February 1919, p. 16.

E 3000
1 March 1919, p. 16.

E 3001
2 March 1919, p. 1, pt. 2.

E 3002
4 March 1919, p. 13.

E 3003
5 March 1919, p. 20.

E 3004
6 March 1919, p. 11.

E 3005
7 March 1919, p. 11.

E 3006
8 March 1919, p. 16.

E 3007
9 March 1919, p. 1, pt. 2.

E 3008
11 March 1919, p. 13.

E 3009
12 March 1919, p. 15.

E 3010
13 March 1919, p. 13.

E 3011
14 March 1919, p. 18.

E 3012
15 March 1919, p. 13.

E 3013
16 March 1919, p. 1, pt. 2.

E 3014
18 March 1919, p. 13.

E 3015
19 March 1919, p. 15.

E 3016
20 March 1919, p. 13.

E 3017
21 March 1919, p. 13.

E 3018
22 March 1919, p. 13.

E 3019
23 March 1919, p. 1, pt. 2.

E 3020
25 March 1919, p. 15.

E 3021
26 March 1919, p. 15.

E 3022
27 March 1919, p. 18.

E 3023
28 March 1919, p. 15.

E 3024
29 March 1919, p. 20.

E 3025
30 March 1919, p. 1, pt. 2.

E 3026
1 April 1919, p. 20.

E 3027
2 April 1919, p. 19.

E 3028
3 April 1919, p. 20.

E 3029
4 April 1919, p. 19.

E 3030
5 April 1919, p. 20.

E 3031
6 April 1919, p. 1, pt. 2.

E 3032
8 April 1919, p. 20.

E 3033
9 April 1919, p. 20.

E 3034
10 April 1919, p. 15.

E 3035
11 April 1919, p. 19.

E 3036
12 April 1919, p. 18.

E 3037
13 April 1919, p. 1, pt. 2.

E 3038
15 April 1919, p. 20.

E 3039
16 April 1919, p. 20.

E 3040
17 April 1919, p. 20.

E 3041
18 April 1919, p. 19.

E 3042
19 April 1919, p. 20.

E 3043
20 April 1919, p. 1, pt. 2.

E 3044
22 April 1919, p. 15.

E 3045
23 April 1919, p. 19.

E 3046
24 April 1919, p. 19.

E 3047
25 April 1919, p. 18.

E 3048
26 April 1919, p. 15.

E 3049
27 April 1919, p. 1, pt. 2.

E 3050
29 April 1919, p. 19.

E 3051
30 April 1919, p. 18.

E 3052
1 May 1919, p. 19.

E 3053
2 May 1919, p. 22.

E 3054
3 May 1919, p. 20.

E 3055
4 May 1919, p. 1, pt. 2.

E 3056
6 May 1919, p. 18.

E 3057
7 May 1919, p. 18.

E 3058
8 May 1919, p. 19.

E 3059
9 May 1919, p. 19.

E 3060
10 May 1919, p. 18.

E 3061
11 May 1919, p. 1, pt. 2.

E 3062
13 May 1919, p. 14.

E 3063
14 May 1919, p. 19.

E 3064
15 May 1919, p. 18.

E 3065
16 May 1919, p. 12.

E 3066
17 May 1919, p. 14.

E 3067
18 May 1919, p. 1, pt. 2.

E 3068
20 May 1919, p. 19.

E 3069
21 May 1919, p. 18.

E 3070
22 May 1919, p. 13.

E 3071
23 May 1919, p. 15.

E 3072
24 May 1919, p. 15.

E 3073
25 May 1919, p. 1, pt. 2.

E 3074
27 May 1919, p. 18.

E 3075
28 May 1919, p. 17.

E 3076
29 May 1919, p. 12.

E 3077
30 May 1919, p. 15.

E 3078
31 May 1919, p. 19.

E 3079
1 June 1919, p. 2, pt. 2.

E 3080
3 June 1919, p. 19.

E 3081
4 June 1919, p. 19.

E 3082
5 June 1919, p. 17.

E 3083
6 June 1919, p. 19.

E 3084
8 June 1919, p. 1, pt. 2.

E 3085
10 June 1919, p. 17.

E 3086
11 June 1919, p. 19.

E 3087
12 June 1919, p. 16.

E 3088
13 June 1919, p. 17.

E 3089
14 June 1919, p. 15.

E 3090
15 June 1919, p. 1, pt. 2.

E 3091
17 June 1919, p. 19.

E 3092
18 June 1919, p. 18.

E 3093
19 June 1919, p. 18.

E 3094
20 June 1919, p. 19.

CHICAGO TRIBUNE
By-lined articles (1913–1919)

While Lardner was conducting the "In the Wake of the News" column, he also wrote the following by-lined articles for the *Chicago Tribune*.

E 3095
"Here's Real Dope, by R. W. Lardner," 7 October 1913, p. 25.

E 3096
"Lardner's 'Dope' Proves Correct," 8 October 1913, p. 25.

E 3097
"Chappell Plays $18,000 Ball
Game," 9 October 1913, pp.
23–24.

E 3098
"Here's Real Yarn on Bodie's
Lapse," 10 October 1913, pp.
23–24.

See C 52.

E 3099
"Bert Fools Cals with Silent
Ball," 11 October 1913, pp. 21–
22.

E 3100a
"Cicotte Guilty of Fooling Evers,"
12 October 1913, pp. 1–2, pt. 3.

E 3100b
"Game Puts Towns on Baseball
Map," 13 October 1913, p. 15.

E 3101
"Calls White Sox Best Money
Team," 14 October 1913, pp. 13–
14.

E 3102
"Maroons Beat Hoosiers, 34–0,"
4 October 1914, pp. 1, 3, pt. 3.

E 3103
"Maroons Beat Purple Team by
28–0 Score," 11 October 1914,
pp. 1, 3, pt. 3.

E 3104
"Russell's Run for Maroons Defeats Iowa," 18 October 1914, pp.
1, 3, pt. 3.

E 3105
" 'Blue Monday' at Michigan, Says
Lardner," 27 October 1914, p. 11.

E 3106
"Wolverines Off for East Today;
Big Squad to Go," 28 October
1914, p. 14.

E 3107
"Yost Machine Reaches Camp in
East Today," 29 October 1914, p.
14.

E 3108
"Yost's Squad Loses Outfit; Also
Practice," 30 October 1914, p. 8.

E 3109
"Yost Cripples Meet Harvard in
East Today," 31 October 1914, p.
14.

E 3110
"Luck Favors Harvard in Beating
Michigan," 1 November 1914, pp.
1–2, pt. 3.

E 3111
"Michigan Team to Book
Harvard for 1915 Game," 2
November 1914, p. 18.

E 3112
"Illinois Fans Look for Win over
Maroons," 14 November 1914,
p. 8.

E 3113
"Illini by Late Attack Spill
Maroons, 21 to 7," 15 November
1914, pp. 1–2, pt. 3.

E 3114
"Assaults by Gophers Upset
Chicago, 13 to 7," 22 November
1914, pp. 1, 3, pt. 3.

E 3115
"Michigan Ties Maroons, 6–6;
Point Dispute," 27 November
1914, p. 15.

E 3116
"Factors in a Suburb's Sane
Fourth," 6 July 1915, p. 17.

E 3117
"Lardner in New York to Report
Big Battle," 9 September 1915,
p. 10.

E 3118
"Packey Looks like Battler, Says
Lardner," 10 September 1915,
p. 9.

E 3119
"Sure I'll Beat Gibbons, Packey
Tells Lardner," 11 September
1915, p. 9.

E 3120
"Lardner Gives Packey Fight by
Wide Margin," 12 September
1915, p. 1, pt. 3.

E 3121
"Wife to Decide Whether Packey
Shall Box Again," 13 September
1915, p. 9.

E 3122
"Lucky Victory for Alexander,
Says Lardner," 9 October 1915,
p. 15.

E 3123
"Lardner Gets an Earful of Post-
Mortems," 12 October 1915, p. 11.

E 3124
"Lardner Tells How Big Crisis
Worries Lewis," 13 October 1915,
p. 13.

E 3125
"Too Much Class Beats Phillies,
Declares Ring," 14 October 1915,
p. 9.

E 3126
"Illinois, Sans Pogue, Set for
Gopher Scrap," 30 October 1915,
p. 9.

E 3127
"Illinois Holds Gophers to Tie in
Great Battle, 6 to 6," 31 October
1915, pp. 1–2, pt. 3.

E 3128
"Lardner Says Michigan Has
Chance to Win," 6 November
1915, p. 13.

E 3129
"Michigan's Backs, Like Ring,
Want to Know: Why Is a Line?,"
7 November 1915, p. 1, pt. 3.

E 3130
"Maroon Hopes Placed in Line;
Gopher Choice," 13 November
1915, p. 10.

E 3131
"Gopher Steam Roller Crushes
Maroons, 20–7," 14 November
1915, p. 1, pt. 3.

E 3132
"Maroons Set for Illini; Badgers
Play Gophers," 20 November
1915, p. 11.

E 3133
"Gophers Beat Badgers; Tie
Illinois for Title," 21 November
1915, pp. 1–2, pt. 3.

E 3134
"Lardner Probes Giants' Scandal;
Finds 'Dodgers'," 5 October 1916,
p. 10.

E 3135
"Lardner Entertains for Hub
When Asked to Motor There,"
6 October 1916, p. 13.

E 3136
"Lardner Starts Story Verse,
Then Prose as Fattens Purse,"
7 October 1916, p. 13.

E 3137
"Let Ring Lardner Tell You
How Red Sox Beat Robins," 8
October 1916, p. 1, pt. 3.

E 3138
"Lardner Scoops the World!
Here's Story of Second Game,"
9 October 1916, p. 19.

E 3139
"Lardner Says Myers Nearly Lost
His Life," 10 October 1916, p. 12.

E 3140
"Bill Corrigan's Little Joke Costs
Contest, Lardner Says," 11
October 1916, p. 13.

E 3141
"Sun Robs Robins of Victory,
Lardner Says; So Does Larry
Gardner with Home Run," 12
October 1916, p. 13.

E 3142
"Now Mr. Lardner Knows How
Robins Won National Flag," 13
October 1916, p. 11.

E 3143
"Lardner Frames New Rules for
Future World's Series," 14 Oc-
tober 1916, p. 12.

E 3144
"Lardner Also Picks Stars; Differ
from Sanborn's Teams," 15
October 1916, p. 1, pt. 3.

E 3145
"Old Tricks and Boners Undoing
of Stagg Men," 29 October 1916,
pp. 1-2, pt. 3.

E 3146a
"Cornell's Rush at Finish Noses
Out Michigan, 23-20," 12
November 1916, pp. 1-2, pt. 3.

E 3146b
"Essential!" 8 September 1918,
p. 5, pt. 2.

E 3147
No headline, 17 April 1919, p. 19.

THE NEW YORK TIMES
Special article, 1917

E 3148
"Lardner Bends One Over for the Loan," *The New York Times,* 22
October 1917, p. 22.

Letter by Lardner in persona of Jack Keefe supporting Liberty Loan
campaign. The letter was released to newspapers by the U.S. Treasury
Department.

THE BELL SYNDICATE
"Ring Lardner's Weekly Letter"[15] *(1919–1927)*

Columns are listed as they appeared in the *San Francisco Examiner,*
with a few supplementary entries from the *Milwaukee Journal.*

E 3149
"Moving to the East," 2 November
1919, p. N6.

E 3150
"I'll Say I Won't Dance," 9
November 1919, p. E5.

E 3151
"Speaking of Strikes How About
One for Husbands on Christmas
Eve?," 16 November 1919, p. E5.

E 3152
"President Wilson Picks Thursday
for Thanksgiving Day This Year
in Spite of the Republicans," 23
November 1919, p. E5.

E 3153
"Picking the All-American Team,"
30 November 1919, p. E5.

E 3154
"On the Scarcity of Paper for
Newspapers," 7 December 1919,
p. E5.
See *F&L* ("On Newspapers").

E 3155
"How to Give Your Husband a
Merry Christmas on a Dime," 14
December 1919, p. E6.

E 3156
"Something Different for Christmas," 21 December 1919, p. E5.

E 3157
"I'll Go 50–50 on New Year's
Reforms," 28 December 1919, p.
E6.

E 3158
"Talking with Spirits at a
Seance," 4 January 1920, p. E4.

E 3159
"Lardner Comes Out for the
Nomination," 11 January 1920,
p. E4.

E 3160
"Telephone Directory vs.
Encyclopedia," 18 January 1920,
p. E5.

E 3161
"All Cleaned Up for an Interview," 25 January 1920, p. E6.

E 3162
"One Couldn't and the Other
Wouldn't," 1 February 1920, p.
E5.

E 3163
"Starve with Hoover or Feast with
Lardner," 8 February 1920, p. E6.

E 3164
"Madam Butterfly Was Some
Insect," 15 February 1920, p. E5.

E 3165
"Legal Tangles of Druids Make
Complications in Opera 'Norma',"
22 February 1920, p. E7.

E 3166
"Why I May Join Sir Oliver's
Lodge," 29 February 1920, p. E6.

---

15. All columns are signed 'Ring W. Lardner'. See Appendix 2.

E 3167
"I'll Have a Hand Picked Cabinet
——If Elected," 7 March 1920,
p. E7.

E 3168
"Are You a Hick?" 14 March
1920, p. E6.

E 3169
"Celebrities Shun New York as
Birthplace," 21 March 1920, p.
E6.

E 3170
"How to Dodge the Sheriff," 28
March 1920, p. E6.

E 3171
"Telephone Tragedies," 4 April
1920, p. E7.

E 3172
"Interviewing Carpentier with
and Without French," 11 April
1920, p. E5.

E 3173
"Some Recipes with Kicks," 18
April 1920, p. E4.

E 3174
"A Lesson in Natural History,"
25 April 1920, p. E4.

E 3175
"How About the Neglected Husband?," 2 May 1920, p. E6.

Reprinted in *Wheeler's Magazine*,
1 (October 1922), 9. *Wheeler's
Magazine* may have reprinted
other Bell columns by Lardner,
but none has been located. See
E 3236 (3 July 1921).

E 3176
"Limerick Contests Made Easy,"
9 May 1920, p. E6.

E 3177
"Dull Moments Have No Terror
for Ring; Visiting Philly, He Hits
on a New Plan," *Milwaukee
Journal*, 16 May 1920, p. 5, pt. 4.

E 3178
"Dark Horses and Platforms," 23
May 1920, p. E6.

E 3179
"I'll Be Satisfied with Second
Place," 30 May 1920, p. E4.

E 3180
" 'Every Good Speech Needs Some
Antidote'," 6 June 1920, p. E4.

E 3181
"First Aid to Tired Memories," 13
June 1920, p. E6.

E 3182
"Conventions Work Mostly One
Way—— Against the Boys," 20
June 1920, p. E6.

E 3183
"How to Keep a Party from Spoil-
ing: Lardner's Recipe," *Milwaukee Journal*, 27 June 1920, p. 5,
pt. 4.

E 3184
"Too Bad Women Miss Delights of
Barber Shops," 4 July 1920, p. E4.

E 3185
"Speed in Michigan," 11 July
1920, p. E4.

E 3186
"Our Own Upsetting Exercises,"
18 July 1920, p. E6.

E 3187
"Rough and Ready Taxicab–ing,"
25 July 1920, p. E6.

E 3188
"Short Cuts to Male Beauty," 1
August 1920, p. E5.

E 3189
"Ring Lardner Gives Advice on
Pitching to 'Babe' Ruth," 8
August 1920, p. E5.

E 3190
"Spare the Rough Stuff and Spoil
the Child," 15 August 1920, p. E5.

E 3191
"An Ounce of Preventions Is
Worth a Pt. of Hootch," 22
August 1920, p. E6.

E 3192
"Ring Lardner's Simple Course in
Character Reading," 29 August
1920, p. E5.

E 3193
"Eat and Save," 5 September
1920, p. E6.

E 3194
"Women's Styles Have Dire In-
fluence on Men's Fashions," 12
September 1920, p. E5.

E 3195
"If You're a Bachelor, You Must
Pay Your Way," 19 September
1920, p. E6.

E 3196
"Educational Opportunity: The
Ring School for Girls," 26 Sep-
tember 1920, p. E4.

E 3197
"Is Marriage a Success?," 3
October 1920, p. E5.

E 3198
"Rich but Not Idle," 10 October
1920, p. E5.

E 3199
"The Anatomy of a One-Reel
Comedy," 17 October 1920, p. E4.

E 3200
"How to Put the Throbs in Heart
Throb Movies," 24 October 1920,
p. E5.

E 3201
"To Know a Man, Marry Him or
Caddy for Him," 31 October
1920, p. E5.

E 3202
"At the Present Price of Coal, Be
an Eskimo," 7 November 1920, p.
E4.

E 3203
"Inside Facts of the Writing
Game," 14 November 1920, p. E4.

See C 7.

E 3204
"A Lot Depends on the Title," 21
November 1920, p. E6.

E 3205
"The Ten Full Counts in the Big
Quarrel," 28 November 1920, p.
E5.

See *F&L* ("Marriage Made
Easy").

E 3206
"Learn to Play Lip Golf," 5 December 1920, p. E5.

E 3207
"Why Xmas Shop at All?," 12
December 1920, p. E6.

E 3208
"Taking the Blue Out of Monday," 19 December 1920, p. E4.

E 3209
"I've Always Wanted to Live in a Cabinet," 26 December 1920, p. E4.

E 3210
"An Evening Accumulating Culture," 2 January 1921, p. E4.

E 3211
"Stamps Should Show What's Inside Letter," 9 January 1921, p. E4.

E 3212
"The Next Secretary of Agriculture Has Got to Be a Diplomat," 16 January 1921, p. E4.

E 3213
"Money Could Be Made to Talk Louder Than It Does," 23 January 1921, p. E4.

E 3214
"Keep the Reform Fires Burning," 30 January 1921, p. E4.

E 3215
"Automatic Writing Does Not Pay Interest on the Mortgage," 6 February 1921, p. E4.

E 3216
"If White House Needs a Master Mind——Well, You Know Me," 13 February 1921, p. E4.

E 3217
"Why Not Get Some Laughs in the Inauguration Speech?," 20 February 1921, p. E4.

E 3218
"Dressing for Inauguration Is Some Job," 27 February 1921, p. E4.

E 3219
"Othello Made Easy to Understand," 6 March 1921, p. E4.

E 3220
"The Art of Keeping a Dependent on $200 a Year," 13 March 1921, p. E4.

E 3221
"Your Apartment and Your Garden," 20 March 1921, p. E5.

E 3222
"How to Attain the Perfect Figure," 27 March 1921, p. E4.

E 3223
"Laws Could Add to Personal Comfort," 3 April 1921, p. E4.

E 3224
"An Ounce of Preventive Is Worth a Lot—But, Oh, You Cure!," 10 April 1921, p. E4.

E 3225
"It's a Good Thing Birthdays Don't Come Oftener," 17 April 1921, p. E4.

E 3226
"The Tribulations of a Comic Artist," 24 April 1921, p. E4.

E 3227
"The Presidential Golf Might Be Better," 1 May 1921, p. E4.

E 3228
"Open Air Is Still Within the Law," 8 May 1921, p. E4.

E 3229
"East Is Not West?," 15 May 1921, p. E4.

E 3230
"Why Is a Hotel Clerk?," 22 May 1921, p. E4.

E 3231
"Why Be a Joiner When You're a
Pastry Cook?," 29 May 1921, p.
E4.

E 3232
"Lardner Weekly Letter," 5
June 1921, p. E4.

E 3233
"Questioning as a Fine Art," 12
June 1921, p. E4.

E 3234
"How to Pick a Husband," 19
June 1921, p. E4.

E 3235
"How to Make Wedding Anni-
versaries Painless," 26 June 1921,
p. E4.

E 3236
"East Is East and Michigan Is
Michigan—When It Comes to
Dogs," 3 July 1921, p. E4.
See *F&L* ("Dogs"). Reprinted in
Wheeler's Magazine (February
1922). Not seen.

E 3237
"A Small Vocabulary May Have a
Big Kick," 10 July 1921, p. E4.
See C 7.

E 3238
"Catchers Have to Do Some
Guessing These Days," 17 July
1921, p. E4.
See C 54.

E 3239
"What Is George Ade?," 24 July
1921, p. E4.

E 3240
"A School of Matrimony," 31 July
1921, p. E4.

E 3241
"A School of Matrimony," 7
August 1921, p. E4.

E 3242
"We Live in the Age of Wonders,"
14 August 1921, p. E4.

E 3243
"Some Cigars Would Cure Any
Smoker," 21 August 1921, p. E4.

E 3244
"My Hat Is in the Mayoralty
Ring," 28 August 1921, p. E4.

E 3245
"Imaginary Vacations—
Roisterering with the Knockefel-
lers," 4 September 1921, p. E4.

E 3246
"It's a Wild Life If You Don't
Weaken," 11 September 1921, p.
E4.

E 3247
"Simplifying Simplicity," 18
September 1921, p. E4.

E 3248
"Cheese and Gifts," 25 September
1921, p. E4.

E 3249
"Love Letters Made Easy," 2
October 1921, p. E4.
See *F&L*.

E 3250
"Lardner Organizes the Ku Klux
Klan," 9 October 1921, p. E4.

E 3251
"Why Drug Clerks Go Wrong," 16
October 1921, p. E4.

E 3252
"Bathing Made Painless," 23
October 1921, p. E4.

E 3253
"Easy to Solve City Problems," 30
October 1921, p. E4.

E 3254
"Ring Lardner on Football," 6
November 1921, p. N14.

E 3255
"West Is West—And That Doesn't
Mean Pittsburgh," 13 November
1921, p. N14.

E 3256
"We'll Have to Change Life's
Schedule If We're Going to Live
300 Years," 20 November 1921,
p. E6.

E 3257
"The Australian Crawl Stroke Is
No Good in Tennis," 27 November
1921, p. E6.

E 3258
"The Best Part of Golf Is My
Opponents," 4 December 1921, p.
E7.

E 3259
"Make the Punishment Fit the
Crime," 11 December 1921, p. E5.

E 3260
"Speeding Up the Christmas
Shopping," 18 December 1921, p.
E7.

E 3261
"Why Not Declare a Marital
Holiday," 25 December 1921, p.
N5.

E 3262
"Don't Make New Year Resolu-
tions——Industry Is Bad Enough
Now," 1 January 1922, p. E5.

E 3263
"Have a Spelling of Your Own and
Save Time," 8 January 1922, p.
E5.

E 3264
"Gum Versus Nicotine," 15 January 1922, p. E8.

E 3265
"Another Joke on the Taxpayers,"
22 January 1922, p. E4.

E 3266
"Lardner's 1922 Rules for War,"
29 January 1922, p. E5.

E 3267
"The New Architecture," 5 January 1922, p. E7.

E 3268
"Give a Thought to City Nicknames," 12 January 1922, p. E6.

E 3269
"Explanations Are in Order," 19
February 1922, p. E7.

E 3270
"It's a Tough Year, Says the
Stars," 26 February 1922, p. E6.

E 3271
"Florida and the Ford," 5 March
1922, p. E7.

E 3272
"Brakes and Breaks——Both
Right," 12 March 1922, p. E6.

E 3273
"Are You in a Rut? Learn to
Teach Auction Bridge," 19 March
1922, p. E5.

E 3274
"A New Income Tax Scheme," 26
March 1922, p. E7.

E 3275
"More Amendments Coming. 'Our
Country May She Always Be
Right Irregardless of Congress',"
2 April 1922, p. E6.

E 3276
"Try Love Letters on Your
Creditors," 9 April 1922, p. E5.

E 3277
"Why Carry a Cane?," 16 April
1922, p. E8.

E 3278
"Maiden Names and the Lucy
Stoners," 23 April 1922, p. E6.

E 3279
"Sense and Southpaws," 30 April
1922, p. E6.

E 3280
"Divorces in the Disuniting
States," 7 May 1922, p. E6.

E 3281
"Got a Little Radio in Your
Home?," 14 May 1922, p. E6.

E 3282
"Shotguns, Razors, Chloroform vs.
Jack Dempsey——," 21 May
1922, p. E5.

E 3283
"Lure Social Upstagers Into
Home," 28 May 1922, p. E5.

E 3284
"Why Not a Peggy Hopkins
Week?," 4 June 1922, p. E7.

E 3285
"Ho for the Second Battle of the
Century!," 11 June 1922, p. E5.

E 3286
"Make Your Husband Laugh and
Aid His Digestion," 18 June 1922,
p. E5.

E 3287
"Passengers on the Hoof Gum Up
Traffic, Says Lardner," 25 June
1922, p. E5.

E 3288
"Rules for Commuting Boot-
leggers," 2 July 1922, p. E5.

E 3289
"Lardner Takes Up Oratory to
Escape Oblivion," 9 June 1922, p.
E5.

E 3290
"Try the Lie-Meter on Your
Friends," 16 July 1922, p. E4.

E 3291
" 'Kill the Umpire,' Is Cry East,
West and in Canada," 23 July
1922, p. E5.

E 3292
"Lardner Says: Move the Week-
End to the Middle of the Week,"
30 July 1922, p. E4.

E 3293
"Lardner a Terminus for Endless
Chain Letters," 6 August 1922, p.
E6.

See *F&L* ("On Chain Letters").

E 3294
"Highbrows Have Nothing on
Lardner," 13 August 1922, p. E6.

See *F&L* ("A Literary Diary");
C 10.

E 3295
"Lardner Suggests Jobs for Ex-Chorus Girls," 20 August 1922, p. E5.

See *F&L* ("On Jobs").

E 3296
"Lardner Solaces Fightless Chicago," 27 August 1922, p. E5.

E 3297
"Lardner Balks at Knickers for Women," 3 September 1922, p. E5.

See *F&L* ("Knickers for Women").

E 3298
"Lardner on Diet for Brain Workers Edison Practically Lives on Currents," 10 September 1922, p. E4.

E 3299
"Ring Lardner, Fisherman, Advises Issac 'Newtons'," 17 September 1922, p. E7.

E 3300
"Lardner Solves Fuel Problem," 24 September 1922, p. E4.

E 3301
"Lardner Discovers Origin of Football," 1 October 1922, p. E4.

See *F&L* ("The Origin of Football").

E 3302
"Lardner Saves Money on Motor Trip," 8 October 1922, p. E5.

E 3303
"Lardner Learns of Golf Amid the Pyramids," 15 October 1922, p. E4.

E 3304
"Lardner on Salt Water Fishing," 22 October 1922, p. E8.

See *F&L* ("Salt Water Fishing").

E 3305
"Lardner Finds Thrill in Football Guides," 29 October 1922, p. E4.

E 3306
"Lardner Describes Arctic Golf Club," 5 November 1922, p. E5.

E 3307
"Lardner Lays Out Life Schedule," 12 November 1922, p. E9.

E 3308
"Lardner to Stage a Benefit," 19 November 1922, p. E4.

E 3309
"Lardner Says You Must Have Police Dog to Belong," 26 November 1922, p. E6.

E 3310
"Lardner Tells How to Shoot Ducks," 3 December 1922, p. E8.

E 3311
"Lardner Would Try Coue on Beer, Beards, and Baseball," 10 December 1922, p. E9.

E 3312
"Lardner Suggests Winter Sports," 17 December 1922, p. E5.

E 3313
"Lardner on Quaint Xmas Customs Abroad," 24 December 1922, p. E8.

E 3314
"Lardner Describes Cross-Country Football," 31 December 1922, p. E6.

E 3315
"Lardner Would Keep Fat People at Home," 7 January 1923, p. E6.

E 3316
"Lardner Describes New Golf Accessories," 14 January 1923, p. E6.

See *F&L* ("New Golf Accessories").

E 3317
"Lardner Tells How to 'Stork' Big Game," 21 January 1923, p. E6.

See C 8 ("How to 'Stork' Big Game").

E 3318
"Lardner on Letters and Wasted Words," 28 January 1923, p. E6.

E 3319
"Lardner Gives Hints to Cold Weather Nimrods," 4 February 1923, p. E6.

E 3320
"Lardner Writes of the Lady in Upper 9," 11 February 1923, p. E6.

E 3321
"A Frolic at the Pinellas County Fair," 18 February 1923, p. E6.

E 3322
"New Ideas for the Host on Etiquette and Good Manners," 25 February 1923, p. E6.

E 3323
"Lardner Observes the Miami Mermaids," 4 March 1923, p. E6.

E 3324
"Lardner Writes of Jim Allison Who 'Knows Fish'," 11 March 1923, p. E6.

E 3325
" 'Anything on the Hip' Is Polite Question, Says Lardner, in Discussing Etiquette," 18 March 1923, p. E6.

See *F&L* ("Opening Remarks").

E 3326
" 'Signal It with Music,' New Bridge Idea," 25 March 1923, p. E7.

E 3327
" 'Don't Sleep,' Advises Lardner, Interpreting Dreams," 1 April 1923, p. E6.

E 3328
"Lardner Interviews Man 240 Years Old," 8 April 1923, p. E6.

E 3329
"Shoe Trees Feature Lardner's Garden," 15 April 1923, p. E11.

E 3330
"Lardner's Lawn Scene of an Auto Show," 22 April 1923, p. E6.

E 3331
"Sister or Elk? You Can't Tell by Looks, Complains Lardner," 29 April 1923, p. E4.

E 3332
"Lardner Says Jumping Bean Helps Alma Dance," 6 May 1923, p. E4.

E 3333
"Ring Writes of William, the Jap Chambermaid," 13 May 1923, p. E6.

E 3334
"Ring Describes Hot Dog, Iowa," 20 May 1923, p. E6.

E 3335
" 'Go South,' Cries Ring, As Old Sol Slows Down," 27 May 1923, p. E6.

E 3336
"Ring Opens War for New Etiquette Rules," 3 June 1923, p. E5.

See *F&L* ("Table Manners").

E 3337
"Lardner 'Exclaims' Patter Bridge," 17 June 1923, p. E5.

E 3338
"Life to Ring—Just One Jap After Another," 24 June 1923, p. E5.

E 3339
"Ring Writes of Golf Amid the Rhubarb," 1 July 1923, p. E5.

E 3340
"Ring Tells How Winners Quit Winners," 8 July 1923, p. E5.

See *F&L* ("How Winners Quit Winners").

E 3341
"Ring Reveals How He Won Tournament," 15 July 1923, p. E4.

E 3342
"Ring's Long Island Estate Open to Visitors," 22 July 1923, p. E4.

E 3343
"Ring Writes of Leviathan 'Incidence'," 29 July 1923, p. E6.

E 3344
"How to Get Rid of a Permanent Guest," 5 August 1923, p. E4.

E 3345
"Lardner Learns 'What to Talk About'," 12 August 1923, p. E5.

E 3346
"Ring Sees Why It's Called a Dog's Life," 19 August 1923, p. E4.

E 3347
" 'Go West, Democrats,' Advises Ring," 26 August 1923, p. E6.

E 3348
"Ring Reels Rhymes to Rout Rats," 2 September 1923, p. E5.

E 3349
"Ring Sings 'Perfect Day' at Saratoga," 9 September 1923, p. E6.

E 3350
"Ring Writes on Congressional Culture and Horse Sense," 16 September 1923, p. E4.

E 3351
"Ring Plans Amusement Park," 23 September 1923, p. E6.

E 3352
"Ring Writes of Summer Cottage Names," 30 September 1923, p. E4.

E 3353
"Try These Lardner Plays on Your Gridiron," 7 October 1923, p. E4.

E 3354
"Zoo Solves Caddie Problem for Ring," 14 October 1923, p. E6.

E 3355
"Ring Lardner Advises Investors," 21 October 1923, p. E5.

E 3356
"Ring Lardner Throws a Light on
Big Brawl," 28 October 1923, p.
E4.

E 3357
"Ring Tells Story of 'Snow
White'," 4 November 1923, p. E6.

See *F&L* ("A Bedtime Story").

E 3358
"Tricks That Have Win Games,"
11 November 1923, p. E6.

E 3359
"A Dog's Tale," 18 November
1923, p. E6.

See *WOI* ("Red Riding Hood").

E 3360
"As a 6-Footer, Ring Warns of
Thyroid Gland," 25 November
1923, p. E6.

See *WOI* ("Lay Off the Thyroid").

E 3361
"Ring Cheered When Notre
Dame 'Wan'," 2 December 1923,
p. E7.

E 3362
"Ring Gives a Brief History on the
Art of Dueling," 9 December
1923, p. E6.

E 3363
"Ring Gives Code for Lingo
Bridge," 23 December 1923, p.
E6.

See *WOI* ("Polyglot Bridge").

E 3364
"Ring Puts Dead Man on 'All-
World Team'," 30 December
1923, p. E5.

E 3365
"Diamond Ulsters Among 1924
Styles, Says Lardner," 6 January
1924, p. E5.

E 3366
"Short Story Writers Waste Time
in Barber Colleges, Says Ring," 13
January 1924, p. E6.

E 3367
"Ring's Water Bill $1643—
And Nobody Drinks It," 20
January 1924, p. E6.

E 3368
"Ring Recounts Benefits of
Prohibition," 27 January 1924, p.
E6.

See *WOI* ("Prohibition").

E 3369
"Another Subject of Moment
Reviewed by Ring," 3 February
1924, p. E5.

E 3370
"Ring Thinks Mr. Bok Pulled a
Bone," 10 February 1924, p. E5.

E 3371
"Ring Gives Correct Convention
Dope—Says Candidates Will
Appear When Heat Begins to
Take Effect," 17 February 1924,
p. E5.

E 3372
"Ring Favors Segregation of Fats
and Leans——Misery Loves
Company Basic Rule of New
Social Theory Invented by Great
Neck Sage," 24 February 1924,
p. E6.

See *WOI* ("Segregate the Fats").

E 3373
"Names Don't Mean Anything,
Says Ring," 2 March 1924, p. E5.

See *WOI* ("That Which We Call
a Rose").

E 3374
"Great Field for Specialist, Says
Ring; Suggests New University to
Teach How to Tame Rough
Pianos," 9 March 1924, p. E5.

See *WOI* ("Don't Be a Drudge").

E 3375
"No Manners in Mah Jong
Claims Ring," 16 March 1924,
p. E5.

E 3376
"New York Stations Sometimes
Heard As Far Away As Great
Neck, 14 Miles Off," 23 March
1924, p. E9.

E 3377
"Ring Has Innocent Flirtation
with Gal 55 Yrs. Old on Way to
Asheville," 30 March 1924, p. E6.

E 3378
"Asheville Hostelry Carries Milk-
Fed Prunes," 6 April 1924, p. E9.

E 3379
"Ring Discloses Plank in the
Lardner Presidential Platform,"
13 April 124, p. E4.

E 3380
"Ring Investigates Washington
Scandal Rumor," 20 April 1924,
p. E6.

See C 11.

E 3381
"Ring Exchanges Chatter with
Pres.," 27 April 1924, p. E4.

See C 11 ("Snappy Chatter with
President").

E 3382
"Ring Gives Suggestions to Bald
Headed Club," 4 May 1924, p. E6.

E 3383
"Ring Recommends Spulge Car as
Season's Best Buy," 11 May 1924,
p. E6.

See *WOI* ("The Spulge Nine").

E 3384
"Ring Drops Hints to Bobbed-
Hair Bandit," 18 May 1924, p. E6.

E 3385
"Large Doings Out at Great Neck
Orgy of Birthdays Keeps Ring
Busy," 25 May 1924, p. E5.

E 3386
"Ring Marvels at Neighbors'
Den," 1 June 1924, p. E4.

See *WOI* ("A Visit to the
Garrisons").

E 3387
"Treat Guests Rough, Says Ring,"
8 June 1924, p. E4.

See *WOI* ("Welcome to Our
Suburbs").

E 3388
"Ring Drops Hints to Honey-
mooners," 15 June 1924, p. E4.

E 3389
"Ring Lardner Gives Latest Dope
from Great Neck," 22 June 1924,
p. E4.

E 3390
"Lardner Maps Out Olympics
Program," 29 June 1924, p. E5.

See *WOI* ("Sane Olympics").

E 3391
"Lardner Recounts Sad Tale," 6
July 1924, p. E5.

See *WOI* ("Business Is Business").

E 3392
"Ring Frames Tax Bill to Include
Congressmen," 13 July 1924, p.
E6.

E 3393
"Ring Offers Substitute for Cross-
word Puzzle," 20 July 1924, p. E6.

See *WOI* ("Games for Smart
Alecks—I").

E 3394
"Ring Gives Vital Details of Convention Trip," 27 July 1924, p. E8.

E 3395
"Convention Had Vital Effect on
Great Neck, Says Ring," 3
August 1924, p. E4.

E 3396
"Convention Secrets Exposed by
Lardner," 10 August 1924, p. E4.

E 3397
"Ring Discloses His Own Beauty
Secrets," 17 August 1924, p. E6.

See *F&L* ("My Own Beauty
Secrets").

E 3398
"Ring and Extra Bright Friends
Convene Play Snappy Game In-
volving Capitals; a Good Time
Was Had by Nearly All," 24
August 1924, p. E6.

See *WOI* ("Games for Smart
Alecks—II").

E 3399
"Don't Weigh Your Rats in Beer,
Advises Doc Lardner; They Are
Apt to Reach Singing Stage," 31
August 1924, p. E9.

E 3400
"Ring Gets Shaved on Own Front
Porch," 7 September 1924, p. E6.

E 3401
"Ring Leaves Island to Give Prince
a Chance; Regrets He Must Dis-
appoint His Admirers," 14
September 1924, p. E4.

E 3402
"Budding Poet Discovered in
Great Neck and Proud Father
Publishes Offspring's Poem," 21
September 1924, p. E4.

E 3403
"How to Keep the Public Laughing, Fall Off a Train and You'll
Star as a Comedian, Says Ring,"
28 September 1924, p. E6.

E 3404
"Passport Boys Quiz Ring; Great
Neck Sage Before Sailing Fur-
nishes Custom House with Vital
Statistics," 5 October 1924, p. E9.

E 3405
"Ring Suggests 'Cable Tennis'
Would Save Forks and Give Give
[*sic*] Everybody Chance to Win;
Olympic Games Could Be Held
Same Way," 12 October 1924, p.
E5.

See *WOI* ("Tennis by Cable").

E 3406
"New Calendar System Has No
Appeal for Ring Floating New
Year's Eves Would Join Hospital
and Banish Small Talk——A
Poor Innovation," 26 October
1924, p. E6.

E 3407
"Ring Stumbles on Gwaffle, New Game," 7 December 1924, p. E4.

E 3408
"When the Wifes Get Together, Look Out, Says Ring," 14 December 1924, p. E4.

E 3409
"Prince Plays Tank Polo in Belgium," 21 December 1924, p. E5.

E 3410
"Ring Suggests Gilda Grey in Working Costume to Amuse Embarrassed Laborers," 28 December 1924, p. E7.

E 3411
"Ring Swears Off Betting and Princeton Games," 11 January 1925, p. E5.

E 3412
"Claims Recognition to Exclusive Rodent Societies," 1 February 1925, p. E12.

See *WOI* ("Who's Who").

E 3413
"If You Ain't in the Monday Club, You Don't Belong, Says Ring," 8 February 1925, p. E3.

See *F&L* ("Visiting Royalty").

E 3414
"Dorgan's Fire, Buck's New House and an Anonymous Cow Add Thrills," 15 February 1925, p. E3.

E 3415
"Ring Lardner," 22 February 1925, p. E4.

E 3416
"Ring Doesn't Want His Face Pruned," 1 March 1925, p. E4.

E 3417
"Ring Announces New Cure for Poets," 8 March 1925, p. E4.

E 3418
"Ring Lardner," 15 March 1925, p. E4.

E 3419
"Teeth and Hair Disappear, Notes Ring," 22 March 1925, p. E4.

E 3420
"Old Man Lardner Gives Secrets for Long Life," 29 March 1925, p. E4.

E 3421
"Ring's Friend, Harry Parks in Wrong Place," 5 April 1925, p. E3.

E 3422
"Ring Looks 'Em Over at the Race Tracks," 12 April 1925, p. E4.

E 3423
"Pajamas, Shimmy, Fish and Sharks Amuse Ring on Southern Isle," 19 April 1925, p. E4.

E 3424
"Ring Tries Golf and Roulette in Bermuda," 26 April 1925, p. E3.

E 3425
"Ring Drops Some Souvenir Hints," 3 May 1925, p. E4.

E 3426
"Ring Conducts Big Rat War," 10 May 1925, p. E4.

E 3427
"Ring Rakes Over Tender
Memories of Mah Jongg," 17 May
1925, p. E4.

E 3428
"Ring Hears of a Guy That Can
Do Anything," 24 May 1925, p.
E4.

E 3429
"Ring Receives Startling News
from Medicos," 31 May 1925, p.
E3.

E 3430
"All New Dope on Approaching
Customers Given by Ring," 7 June
1925, p. E3.

E 3431
"Ring Lardner," 14 June 1925,
p. E3.

E 3432
"Bevy of Birthdays Stir Lardner
Menage," 21 June 1925, p. E4.

E 3433
"Ring Lardner," 28 June 1925,
p. E4.

E 3434
"Ring Lardner," 5 July 1925,
p. E2.

See *F&L* ("Colleges for Cops").

E 3435
"Ring Has New System for
Running Newspapers," 12 July
1925, p. E4.

E 3436
"Ring Dopes Out New Golf
Lingo," 19 July 1925, p. E2.

E 3437
"Ring Reveals Interview with
Mysterious Southpaw Leonard,"
26 July 1925, p. E3.

See C 55 ("Watch Little Neck").

E 3438
" 'My Kingdom for a Horse,' but
Lardner Prefers a Bicycle," 2
August 1925, p. E4.

E 3439
"Ring Deplores Annoying Benefits
of Telephone," 9 August 1925,
p. E4.

E 3440
"Ring Lardner Runs Into Bril-
liant Pullman Talkers," 16
August 1925, p. E4.

See *F&L* ("On Conversation");
C 14 ("The Art of Keeping
Conversation Alive").

E 3441
"Ring Has One Idea About the
Acme of Golfdom," 23 August
1925, p. E4.

E 3442
"Ring Describes New Symptoms
of Nittiness," 30 August 1925, p.
E4.

E 3443
"Ring Submits Vital Suggestions
for Relief of Marriage Problems,"
6 September 1925, p. E4.

E 3444
"Ring Wouldn't Mind Being the
Last Guy on Earth," 13 September
1925, p. E4.

E 3445
"Ring Confused with Thunder
Shower by Radio Fans," 20 Sep-
tember 1925, p. E4.
See C 55 ("Weather Report").

E 3446
"Prof. Hare Gives Ring Advance Dope on Polar Trip," 27 September 1925, p. E4.

E 3447
"Ring Gives Examples of Guys Who Couldn't Forget Their Work," 4 October 1925, p. E4.

E 3448
"Ring Accepts Nomination for Mayor of New York," 11 October 1925, p. E4.

E 3449
"Ring Passes Up Male Beauty Contest for Men's Radio Event," 18 October 1925, p. E4.

E 3450
"Ring Covers Ladies and Gents Eyesore Exposition at Moomaw," 25 October 1925, p. E4.

E 3451
"Ring's Kid Stages Quick Tennis Comeback, Beats Bay State Star," 1 November 1925, p. E4.

E 3452
"Ring Explodes World-Wide Horse Prestige," 8 November 1925, p. E4.

See *F&L* ("Tips on Horses").

E 3453
"Numerology Dean Hands Ring the Inside Dope," 15 November 1925, p. E4.

See *F&L* ("On Names").

E 3454
"Prof. Gwatt Hands Ring the Cold Dope," 22 November 1925, p. E4.

E 3455
"Ring Hands Out Some Vital Thanksgiving Information," 29 November 1925, p. E4.

E 3456
"Ring Includes Grange and Self on All-American Team," 6 December 1925, p. E4.

E 3457
"Ring Replies to Report He Owes Chi $50," 13 December 1925, p. E4.

E 3458
"Wilbur the Wag Believes in a Merry Christmas," 20 December 1925, p. E4.

E 3459
"Ring Has Several Innovations for Household Equipment," 27 December 1925, p. E4.

E 3460
"Ring Interviews Himself and Reveals Unique Hobby," 3 January 1926, p. E4.

E 3461
" 'What's in a Name?'—A Lot of Argument, Says Ring," 10 January 1926, p. E4.

E 3462
"No Speaking at Vermillion Dinner for Ring," 17 January 1926, p. E4.

E 3463
"Ring Offers Name for Famous Niles Hostelry," 24 January 1926, p. E4.

E 3464
"Professor Gwatt Was Sick So Ring Got Wrong Dope," 31 January 1926, p. E4.

E 3465
"Waste Basket Oracle Slips Ring Strange Info," 7 February 1926, p. E4.

E 3466
"Gusto Tribe of South Algebra Scouted by Ring," 14 February 1926, p. E4.

E 3467
"Engineer in Business 'Pour le Sport' Only," 21 February 1926, p. E4.

E 3468
"Lardner Learns a Lot About Comical Writer," 28 February 1926, p. E4.

E 3469
"Ring Gives the Low-Down on Florida Etiquette," 7 March 1926, p. E4.

E 3470
"Ring Blows Will to Lunch and Then Sees His Act," 14 March 1926, p. E4.

E 3471
"Ivy Milton and Jack Surprise Ring in Fla.," 21 March 1926, p. E4.

E 3472
"Lardner Progeny Not Suffering from False Modesty," 28 March 1926, p. E4.

E 3473
"Ring Visits Way Down Yonder in New Orleans," 4 April 1926, p. E4.

E 3474
"Ring Never Saw Nome or Goldfield in the Old Days But ——," 11 April 1926, p. E4.

E 3475
"Loquacious Red, Taxi Pilot, Gives Ring Lowdown on Pasadena," 18 April 1926, p. E4.

E 3476
"Ring Gets Cordial Greeting from Pola," 25 April 1926, p. E4.

E 3477
"Ring, Mistaken for Harry Lauder, Sings 'Roaming'," 2 May 1926, p. E4.

E 3478
"Ring Thinks Grand Canyon Divot Should Be Covered," 9 May 1926, p. E4.

E 3479
"Ring Swamped with Still Life Photographers in San Francisco," 16 May 1926, p. E4.

E 3480
"Ring Reveals Startling Time-Saving Devices," 30 May 1926, p. E4.

E 3481
"Carpenter's Concert Mars Lardner's Slumber," 6 June 1926, p. E4.

E 3482
"Polar Secrets Divulged from Prof. Grottis Via Lardner," 13 June 1926, p. E4.

E 3483
"Sweet Potatoes, How Mrs. Ults Can Play Bridge!," 20 June 1926, p. E4.

E 3484
"Old Grad Lardner Had Hectic College Career," 27 June 1926, p. E4.

E 3485
"Ring Outlines Vacation with Subway Hamper," 4 July 1926, p. E4.

E 3486
"Ring Lardner," 11 July 1926, p. E4.

See *SWM.*

E 3487
"Ring Continues Story of a Wonder Man," 18 July 1926, p. E4.

See *SWM.*

E 3488
"Dolly Madison Danced with 6 Yr. Old Ring," 25 July 1926, p. E4.

See *SWM.*

E 3489
"Chapter IV of Ring Lardner's Autobiography," 1 August 1926, E3.

See *SWM.*

E 3490
"Gen. Lardner Tells How Spanish War Ended," 8 August 1926, p. E3.

See *SWM.*

E 3491
"Ring Threw Big Party for Jane Austen," 15 August 1926, p. E4.

See *SWM.*

E 3492
"Lily Langtry Shown Gotham by Lardner," 22 August 1926, p. E4.

See *SWM.*

E 3493
"Football Trick Uncorked at Yale by Lardner," 29 August 1926, p. E3.

See *SWM.*

E 3494
"Yale, Captained by Ring, Beaten by Blind Boys," 5 September 1926, p. E4.

See *SWM.*

E 3495
"Ring Has Gay Christmas Eve at Grudge's," 12 September 1926, p. E4.

See *SWM.*

E 3496
"History of When Lardner Swam the Hudson," 19 September 1926, p. E4.

See *SWM.*

E 3497
"Ring Transferred from Princeton to Medicine," 26 September 1926, p. E4.

See *SWM.*

E 3498
"Dr. Lardner Started Medical Career Auspiciously," 3 October 1926, p. E4.

See *SWM.*

E 3499
"2 Big Inventions Crowned Year 1899, Says Ring," 10 October 1926, p. E4.

See *SWM.*

E 3500
"Ring Accepts Job as Sport Writer on 'The Rabies'," 17 October 1926, p. E4.

See *SWM.*

E 3501
"Ring as Star Reporter for 'The Rabies' Covers Helsh Murder," 24 October 1926, p. E4.

See *SWM*.

E 3502
"Ring Is Promoted to Contest Editor of Rabies," 31 October 1926, p. E4.

See *SWM*.

E 3503
"Ring Spends Hallowe'en, 1896 in Polyandry Hospital," 7 November 1926, p. E4.

See *SWM*.

E 3504
"Quack Doc Puts Ring Hep to Soft Job," 14 November 1926, p. E4.

See *SWM*.

E 3505
"Dan Boone Resented Lardnerian Levity," 21 November 1926, p. E4.

See *SWM*.

E 3506
"Ring First Married in Central Park, N.Y.," 28 November 1926, p. E4.

See *SWM*.

E 3507
"Ring and Better Half Prefer to Be by Themselves on Honeymoon," 5 December 1926, p. E4.

See *SWM*.

E 3508
"Lardner Romance Blasted by Big Mail Magnate from Wash.," 12 December 1926, p. E4.

See *SWM*.

E 3509
"Ring Loses Divorce Case in Sensational Trial," 19 December 1926, p. E4.

See *SWM*.

E 3510
"Messrs. Dumb and Wheedle Battle Verbally at Lardner Trial," 26 December 1926, p. E4.

See *SWM*.

E 3511
"Idea Resulted in Antidote for Indecorous Nudity," 2 January 1927, p. E4.

See *SWM*.

E 3512
"Ring, in Post-Mortem Message, Describes His Death," 9 January 1927, p. E4.

See *SWM*.

E 3513
"Ring Has Rough Interview with Noted Prof.," 16 January 1927, p. E4.

E 3514
"Ring Returns from City of Flivers and Debutantes," 23 January 1927, p. E4.

E 3515
"Ring Bares More Baseball Scandals," 30 January 1927, p. E4.

E 3516
"Ring's Sensitive Nature Recoils
at Hockey," 6 February 1927,
p. E4.

E 3517
"Noted Rat Killer Tells His
System," 13 February 1927, p. E4.

E 3518
"Ring Lardner's World-Wide
Traffic Relief Information," 20
February 1927, p. E4.

E 3519
"Shark Alarms Ring's Rural
Community," 27 February 1927,
p. E4.

E 3520
"Pie-Eyed Piper Unable to Attend
Weird Spectacle," 6 March 1927,
p. E4.

E 3521
"Paper Cut-Outs of Stars Would
Animate Radio Programs," 13
March 1927, p. E4.

E 3522
"Ring Seeks to Enter Business
World," 20 March 1927, p. E4.

THE BELL SYNDICATE
Coverage of Special Events (1919–1927)

Articles are listed as they appeared in the *San Francisco Examiner*,
with supplementary entries from the *Milwaukee Journal*.

DEMPSEY–WILLARD, 1919

E 3523
"Jess' Stomach Shouldn't Be
Worried, Says Lardner," 22 June
1919, p. CC13.

E 3524
"Lardner Refuses to Be Third
Man in the Ring," 23 June 1919,
p. 15.

E 3525
"Lardner Discovers Both Jack and
Jess Can't Win," 24 June 1919,
p. 11.

E 3526
"Lardner Has a Hunch He
Ought to Stop the Fight," 25 June
1919, p. 9.

E 3527
"Lardner Thinks Big Jess Fast and
Dempsey Old," 26 June 1919,
p. 13.

E 3528
"Lardner Hears Peace Trio Will
Officiate at Bout," 27 June 1919,
p. 15.

E 3529
"After Seeing Jess in the Movies
Lardner Wonders How Jack Can
Win," 28 June 1919, p. 12.

E 3530
"Lardner Gets an Earful of Hot
Dogs; Learns Why Pecard Was
Chosen Referee," 29 June 1919,
p. R13.

E 3531
"In Lardner's Opinion Jess Is
Good Insurance Risk," 30 June
1919, p. 12.

E 3532
"Trick Watch Will Help Champion," 1 July 1919, p. C12.

E 3533
"Lardner Finds Souvenir Program
Illuminating," 2 July 1919, p.
C16.

E 3534
"Lardner Won on the Allies Gents
and Picks Jess Now," 4 July
1919, p. CC10.

E 3535
"Dempsey Upsets Experts'
Theory in Two Seconds," 5 July
1919, p. CC15.

WORLD SERIES, 1919

E 3536
"Gents: Lardner Says the Umpires Interfere with His 'Dope' on
Big Series," 28 September 1919,
p. 12, pt. 1.

E 3537
"Lardner Finds Cincinnati Baseball Mad, but Purse Is Out of
Danger," 29 September 1919,
p. 15.

E 3538
"Well Gents: The Chisox Won't
Forfeit the Series," 1 October
1919, p. 19.

E 3539
"Daubert Fools Lardner Sox Lack
'Strategem'," 2 October 1919,
p. 18.

E 3540
" 'Ballyhoo' Foils Gleason 'Happy'
Felsch Is Lucky," 3 October 1919,
p. 16.

E 3541
"Lardner Aids Chisox Little 'Dick'
Does Rest," 4 October 1919,
p. 16.

E 3542
"Rings Are Much Alike Nine
Games Hit Moran," 5 October
1919, p. 12, pt. 1.

E 3543
"Ring's Right on Rain Finds
Hurlers Immune," 6 October
1919, p. 15.

E 3544
"Ring Denies 'Hod' Rumor Moran
Meets Mr. Rigler," 7 October
1919, p. 16.

E 3545
"Ring Tells Umps' Secret Schalk
Right with Ban," 8 October 1919,
p. 16.

E 3546
"Lardner Has Shine Ball Kopf
Couldn't Hit It," 9 October 1919,
p. 16.

E 3547
"Pitchers Puzzle Lardner Ban
Suspends Flingers," 10 October
1919, p. 16.

REPUBLICAN CONVENTION, 1920

E 3548
"I'll Walk in While Delegates
Hunt Drug Stores, Says Ring,"
6 June 1920, p. 6.

E 3549
"Lardner Gives His Platform,"
7 June 1920, p. 6.

E 3550
"Candidates Enjoy Brisk Workout
Lowden Does Some Road Work
Hiram Johnson Punches the
Bag," 8 June 1920, p. 4.

E 3551
"Lodge Only One Who Speaks
English None Understand It, Says
Lardner Chairman Also Wore a
A.M. Coat," 9 June 1920, p. 6.

E 3552
"Lardner Solves Baffling Mystery
Gives All the Data on Sproul," 10
June 1920, p. 3.

E 3553
"Lardner Condenses G.O.P. Plat-
form He Who Has Time May
Now Read Peace Treaty
Postponed=Rain," 11 June 1920,
p. 5.

E 3554
"Ring Finds Fat Policemans
Plentiful No Use Trying to Reach
His Seat," 12 June 1920, p. 5.

E 3555
"Lardner Bolts the G. O. O. P. Is
Going to Join Federal League," 13
June 1920, p. 2.

DEMOCRATIC CONVENTION, 1920

E 3556
"Don't Nominate Cobb, Ring
Pleads President's Chair Ain't
Built for Him," 26 June 1920, p. 5.

E 3557
"Lardner Goes Cruising in S.F.
Taxi 'Chi' Boys Look like Hearse
Drivers," 27 June 1920, p. 6.

E 3558
"Vice=Presidency," 28 June
1920, p. 3.

E 3559
"Lardner Acts Noble to Sen. Reed
but Doesn't Like Bryan's Clothes
Latter Ain't Out for Anyone Yet,"
29 June 1920, p. 4.

E 3560
"M'Adoo Next Runner Up," 30
June 1920, p. 2.

E 3561
"Many Feet Slip, Says Lardner
Thinks City Could Stand Dry
Plank but He Missed Daniel's
Party," 1 July 1920, p. 8.

E 3562
"Lardner Proposes Woman's
Ticket Delegates Anxious About
Crops McAdoo Withdrawals
Losing Force," 2 July 1920, p. 3.

E 3563
"Name, Says Ring, Quite the
Thing; Label Might Win,"
Milwaukee Journal, 3 July 1920,
p. 2.[16]

E 3564
"Week Closes Like Camping Trip
All Friendship Ceases; No Smiles
Ring Dreads the Return Journey,"
4 July 1920, p. 6.

E 3565
"Ring Finds Deadlock Is Mere
Stall Embalmer Should Lead in
Prayer Hubbies Away from Home
Too Long," 5 July 1920, p. 3.

E 3566
"Candidate Ring to Sue for Libel
Glad to Give Half Vote to Cobb
Grateful to City, Climate of S.F.,"
6 July 1920, p. 4.

AMERICA'S CUP YACHT RACE, 1920

E 3567
"Many a Slipton Between the Cup
and the Lipton, As Ring Lardner
Sees It," 16 July 1920, p. 9.

See *F&L* ("Disaster").

E 3568
"Yachts Sail like Snail with
Paralysis, Says Ring," 18 July
1920, p. R11.

See *F&L* ("Lost Legs").

E 3569
"Lardner Stands by 'Cap'
Burton," 21 July 1920, p. 8.

See *F&L* ("A Delayed Start").

E 3570
"Lardner Sours on Yacht Races,"
22 July 1920, p. 9.

E 3571
"Resolute and Shamrock like
Snail and Hearse," 24 July 1920,
p. 12.

See *F&L* ("A Perfect Day").

E 3572
"Cup Yacht Races Easy to Call
Off, Says Lardner," 25 July 1920,
p. R13.

E 3573
"Too Many Waves, Not Enough
Wind," 27 July 1920, p. 8.

E 3574
"Boats Too Slow to Give a Kick,"
28 July 1920, p. 8.

See *F&L* ("The End of It").

WORLD SERIES, 1920

E 3575
"One Team Must Win Even
Lardner Says So," 5 October 1920,
p. 18.

E 3576
"Lardner Approached 'Master
Mind' Active," 6 October 1920,
p. 18.

---

16. Articles which did not appear in the *San Francisco Examiner*
are listed as they appeared in the *Milwaukee Journal.*

E 3577
"Ring's Serious Diary Doings of
Tough Day," 7 October 1920,
p. 16.

E 3578
"Defense of Ebbets Ring Gives
Him Credit," 8 October 1920,
p. 15.

E 3579
"Ring's in Cleveland and How He
Dreads It," 9 October 1920, p. 14.

E 3580
" 'Serious' Needs Pep Where's

Master Mind?," 10 October 1920,
p. W19.

E 3581
"Duel of Master Minds Lardner
Quits Cold," 11 October 1920,
p. 8.

E 3582
"Double-Header Played Lardner
Wins One," 12 October 1920,
p. 15.

E 3583
"Cleveland Day Now Columbus
Out of It," 13 October 1920, p. 15.

PRESIDENTIAL INAUGURATION, 1921

E 3584
"Simplicity Reigns at Washington
Lardner Finds Town Full of
Simps Cabinet Members Is
Moving In," 3 March 1921, p. 3.

E 3585
" 'Ring' Mourns at Ban on Jewels

He'll Have to Shed His First
Name," 4 March 1921, p. 3.

E 3586
"Simplicity Aplenty, Lardner
Finds Even Solons Look Simple
Minded Familiar Ring to Hard-
ing's Gags," 5 March 1921, p. 3.

DEMPSEY–CARPENTIER, 1921

E 3587
"I Will Bear Up, No Matter Who
Wins," 19 June 1921, p. W18.

E 3588
"Ring Discusses the 'Principles'
of July 2," 20 June 1921, p. 11.

E 3589
"Lardner Discovers What It's All
About," 21 June 1921, p. 15.

E 3590
"Ring Uses Strategy to Buzz
Frenchman," 22 June 1921, p. 13.

E 3591
"Lots of 'Trebles' at Carpentier's
Ringside," 23 June 1921, p. 14.

E 3592
"Everything Goes When You Hit
Dempsey Camp," 24 June 1921,
p. 13.

E 3593
"Ring Doesn't Savvy Why Is
Loving Cup," 25 June 1921, p. 12.

E 3594
"Dempsey Feeds Guests Fine,
Says Lardner," 26 June 1921,
p. W19.

E 3595
"Lardner Under Cover with the
Right Dope," 27 June 1921, p. 15.

E 3596
"Lardner 'Tumbles' Up Critics
from Europe," 28 June 1921,
p. 15.

E 3597
"Dempsey and Lardner Leaving
for Jersey," 29 June 1921, p. 16.

E 3598
"Experts Should Stick at Home,

Says Lardner," 30 June 1921,
p. 21.

E 3599
"Carp and Me Work in Secret,"
1 July 1921, p. 15.

E 3600
"Keep Cool Says Ring to the
General Public," 2 July 1921,
pp. 9, 11.

E 3601
"Lardner Is Glad He Wasn't in
the Ring," 3 July 1921, p. 12.

WORLD SERIES, 1921

E 3602
"Lively Ball Makes Task of
'Experting' Difficult," 3 October
1921, p. 13.

E 3603
"Lardner Looks for a Big Ticket
Scramble Scandal," 4 October
1921, p. 16.

E 3604
"Ring Lardner Is Much Mystified
Over 'Serious'," 5 October 1921,
p. 15.

E 3605
"Submarine Delivery Sunk 'Em,
Says Lardner," 6 October 1921,
p. 14.

E 3606
" 'Other Scribes Get the Breaks,'
Says Lardner," 7 October 1921,
p. 16.

E 3607
"Lardner Sees Pitchers Trot In
and Trot Out," 8 October 1921,
p. 15.

E 3608
"Rest Helps Yanks, but Not the
Visiting Gents," 9 October 1921,
p. W18.

E 3609
"Bill Lange's Big Nephew Made
Hero by Carl Mays," 10 October
1921, p. 14.

E 3610
"Please Go 'Way and Let Me Sleep
——R.W.L.," 11 October 1921,
p. 16.

E 3611
"You Have to Get There Early to
See Toney," 12 October 1921,
p. 14.

E 3612
"Mad Scramble of Cities for Last
'Serious' Game," 13 October 1921,
p. 17.

E 3613
"No Ninth Game for Yanks and
Giants, Decides Judge," 14
October 1921, p. 14.

DISARMAMENT CONFERENCE, 1921

E 3614
"No Navy=No Fight!," 13
November 1921, p. S3.

See *F&L* ("Disarmament in
1921").

E 3615
"If You Feel Like Scrapping—
Scrap Your Ships," 14 November
1921, p. CC3.

See *F&L* ("Disarmament in
1921").

E 3616
" 'Lowdown' on the Parley," 15
November 1921, p. R3.

See *F&L* ("Disarmament in
1921").

E 3617
"Show Is Losing Zip===
Lardner," 16 November 1921,
p. CC3.

See *F&L* ("Disarmament in
1921").

E 3618
"Hootch Reduction," 17 November 1921, p. R3.

See *F&L* ("Disarmament in
1921").

E 3619
"Honoring Foch by Degrees," 18
November 1921, p. R3.

See *F&L* ("Disarmament in
1921").

E 3620
"Hootch Holiday Approved," 19
November 1921, p. R2.

E 3621
"Out of Trenches by Xmas," 21
November 1921, p. CC2.

See *F&L* ("Disarmament in
1921").

WORLD SERIES, 1922

E 3622
" 'Ring' Lardner Hopes to Knock
Off Fur Benny," 3 October 1922,
p. P3.

See *F&L* ("Advance Notice").

E 3623
"That Fur Coat Is Already
Bought," 4 October 1922, p. P3.

E 3624
"Mr. Lardner Corrects a Wrong
Impression," 5 October 1922,
pp. P1–2.

See *F&L* ("The First Day"); C 10.

E 3625
"Lardner Feels His Way from
Park by Candle," 6 October 1922,
p. P1.

See *F&L* ("The Second Day").

E 3626
"3 Little Nice Kitties Is About to
Get Shot," 7 October 1922, pp.
P1, P3.

See *F&L* ("The Third Day").

E 3627
"Gamblers Flock to Lardner's
Standard," 8 October 1922, pp.
P1–2.

E 3628
"Yankees Need Cops to Direct
Traffic," 9 October 1922, pp.
P1–2.

See *F&L* ("The End").

WILLARD–FIRPO

E 3629
"Lardner Almost Put Out, Jess Is," 13 July 1923, p. P1.

DEMPSEY–FIRPO

E 3630
"They Ought to Spell It Furpo
Score Is 1–7 Against Wild Bull
Heaviest Beard Win Out," 3
September 1923, p. P2.

See *F&L* ("A Prize Fight").

E 3631
"Luis Angel Firpo to Run Thinks
It May Come in Handy,"
4 September 1923, p. P3.

See *F&L* ("A Prize Fight").

E 3632
"Lardner Sees the Wild Bull
'Buenavista!' Burbles Luis,"
5 September 1923, p. P3.

See *F&L* ("A Prize Fight").

E 3633
"Luis Tough with Scribe,"
6 September 1923, pp. P1, P3.

E 3634
"Firpo Sleeps on Bare Floor Dines
on Half a Cow at Lunch Plays
Leapfrog for Exercise,"
7 September 1923, pp. P1–2.

See *F&L* ("A Prize Fight").

E 3635
"Firpo Submits to Inspection
Luis Has Full House, Loses $2,"
8 September 1923, pp. P1, P4.

See *F&L* ("A Prize Fight").

E 3636
"Luis Gets Coaching by Cable
Tutor Is in 'Brainless Aires' No
Place for Gentle Referee,"
9 September 1923, p. P4.

See *F&L* ("A Prize Fight").

E 3637
"Firpo Gets Real Wild if Hit Has
Wicked Wallop When Mad,"
10 September 1923, p. P2.

See *F&L* ("A Prize Fight").

E 3638
"Dempsey Supremely Confident
Eager to Hook Up with Firpo,"
11 September 1923, p. P2.

See *F&L* ("A Prize Fight").

E 3639
"Jack's Left Will Bother Luis
Firpo Lacks Real Defense,"
12 September 1923, pp. P1, P3.

E 3640
"Camp Full of Sponges If Jack
Feels the Need," *Milwaukee
Journal,* 12 September 1923, p. 20.

See *F&L* ("A Prize Fight").

E 3641
"Lardner in Great Shape for
Wordy Battle Does Shadow
Boxing with His Typewriter,"
13 September 1923, p. P1.

See *F&L* ("A Prize Fight").

E 3642
"G.B.S. Tells Lardner Luis Angel
Will Win," 14 September 1923,
pp. P1–2.

See *F&L* ("A Prize Fight").

E 3643
"Lardner Has Tough Time
Getting In to See Battlers,"
15 September 1923, pp. P1, P4.

See *F&L* ("A Prize Fight").

WORLD SERIES, 1923

E 3644
"Lardner Banks on New York to
Win," 10 October 1923, p. P4.

E 3645
"Only One Team Could Lose That
Game = the Yanks," 11 October
1923, pp. P1, P3.

E 3646
"Feats of Pennock Defeated
Giants," 12 October 1923,
pp. P1–2.

E 3647
"Stengel Has Made Good Recruit
Showed Iron Nerve," 13 October
1923, pp. P1, P3.

E 3648
"Yanks Roll Up Grid Score Make
Two Goals and Safety,"
14 October 1923, pp. P1, P3.

E 3649
"Giants Kept Chasing Pellet but
Where Was the 19th Hole?"
15 October 1923, p. P4.

E 3650
"Meusel's Hit in 8th Puts Jinx
on Brains," 16 October 1923,
pp. P1, P4.

REPUBLICAN CONVENTION, 1924

E 3651
"Coolidge May Win: Lardner,"
10 June 1924, p. 3.

E 3652
"Coolidge Is 'Dark Horse,' Says
Lardner," 11 June 1924, p. 3.

E 3653
" 'Twin Bill' Bleachers Go
Begging," 12 June 1924, p. 2.

E 3654
" 'Big Surprise,' Says Lardner,"
13 June 1924, p. 3.

DEMOCRATIC CONVENTION, 1924

E 3655
"Ring Lardner Will Run If
Coolidge Withdraws," *Milwaukee
Journal*, 24 June 1924, p. 2.

See *F&L* ("The Democrats in
1924").

E 3656
"Ring Refuses to Run; 'Bugs'
Baer Boosted," 25 June 1924, p. 2.

See *F&L* ("The Democrats in
1924").

E 3657
"Ring Lardner Plays Safe with
Police," 26 June 1924, p. 3.

See *F&L* ("The Democrats in
1924").

E 3658
"Lardner Sees Windup by
September 1," 27 June 1924, p. 3.

See *F&L* ("The Democrats in
1924").

E 3659
"Try and Find Parley Hall, Ring
Advises," 28 June 1924, p. 3.

See *F&L* ("The Democrats in
1924").

E 3660
"Why Not a Girl? Asks Delegate
Woose," *Milwaukee Journal*,
29 June 1924, p. 4, pt. 1.

See *F&L* ("The Democrats in
1924").

E 3661
"Women Held to Blame for Long
Session," 30 June 1924, p. 3.

See *F&L* ("The Democrats in
1924").

E 3662
"Zev Heads Ring's Dark Horse
List," 1 July 1924, p. 4.

See *F&L* ("The Democrats in
1924").

E 3663
"Davis Should Win on 41st, Says
Lardner," 2 July 1924, p. 4.

E 3664
"Ring Defends Criticism of Misfit
Socks," 3 July 1924, p. 3.

E 3665
"Ring Wants Bryan Lured
Away," 4 July 1924, p. 2.

E 3666
"Conclave Program for October
Set by Ring Lardner," 5 July
1924, p. 2.

E 3667
"It Looks Like All Summer, Says
Lardner," 6 July 1924, p. 3.

E 3668
"Democrats Out for New Records,
Ring," 8 July 1924, p. 2.

E 3669
"Ring Covers Convention by
Telephone," 9 July 1924, p. 2.

WORLD SERIES, 1925

E 3670
"Lardner Bares Series Secrets
Lowdown on Nicknames,"
7 October 1925, pp. P1, P4.

E 3671
"Deep Scandal in Pittsburgh, Says
Lardner," 8 October 1925,
pp. P1, P3.

E 3672
"Sing Fat Won Contest for the
Pirates," 9 October 1925,
pp. P1, P4.

E 3673
"Rain All for Best==Lardner
Refreshments Not So Good,"
10 October 1925, p. P4.

E 3674
"Blizzards 'n Politics Hit Pirate

Punch," 11 October 1925,
pp. P1–2.

E 3675
"The Goose-Goslin Flys High
Barney Causes Much Illness,"
12 October 1925, pp. P1, P4.

E 3676
"Ring Lardner on Trail of Missing
Shirt," 13 October 1925,
pp. P1, P4.

E 3677
"Lardner Gets More Time to
Locate Shirt," 14 October
1925, pp. P1–2.

E 3678
"Start Serious Xmas: Lardner,"
15 October 1925, pp. P1, P4.

DEMPSEY–TUNNEY, 1926

E 3679
"Lardner Bets Dempsey, Wife Out
Mink Coat Tunney Used

Monosyllables to Jack's Jaw,"
24 September 1926, p. P5.

WORLD SERIES, 1927

E 3680
"Pirates Rate Handicap, Says
Ring Lardner," 5 October 1927,
pp. P1, P6.

E 3681
" 'Ducky' Girl and Radio Handicap
to Lardner," 6 October 1927,
pp. P1, P3.

E 3682
"Miss Thoke Fears Pirates Are

Throwing Her Down,"
7 October 1927, pp. P1, P6.
See C 36.

E 3683
"Lardner Finds Yank Pitchers
Slow Up Game," 8 October 1927,
pp. P1–2.

E 3684
"Terrible Thoke Woman Still
Pursues Ring," 9 October
1927, p. CC 33.

THE BELL SYNDICATE
"You Know Me Al" Comic Strip[17] *(1922–1925)*

The comic strip "You Know Me Al" appeared Monday through Saturday from 26 September 1922 to 26 September 1925 under Lardner's by-line. Continuity was written by Lardner; drawing was done by Will B. Johnstone and, later, Dick Dorgan. The strip continued after 26 September 1925 signed by Dick Dorgan, who wrote continuity himself after Lardner gave it up. Lardner actually severed connections with the strip in January of 1925 (see Caruthers, p. 45, and Elder, p. 197) but had apparently completed continuity through September of that year.

Strips are listed as they appeared in the *Milwaukee Journal*.

E 3685
26 September 1922, p. 26.

E 3694
6 October 1922, p. 46.

E 3686
27 September 1922, p. 28.

E 3695
7 October 1922, p. 14.

E 3687
28 September 1922, p. 30.

E 3696
9 October 1922, p. 22.

E 3688
29 September 1922, p. 44.

E 3697
10 October 1922, p. 30.

E 3689
30 September 1922, p. 14.

E 3698
11 October 1922, p. 28.

E 3690
2 October 1922, p. 22.

E 3699
12 October 1922, p. 32.

E 3691
3 October 1922, p. 26.

E 3700
13 October 1922, p. 48.

E 3692
4 October 1922, p. 28.

E 3701
14 October 1922, p. 12.

E 3693
5 October 1922, p. 32.

E 3702
16 October 1922, p. 22.

---

17. All listed strips carry the by-line 'Ring Lardner'. Drawings are signed 'Will B. Johnstone' from beginning to 24 February 1923. The drawings are unsigned from 25 February 1923 to 25 March 1923. They are signed 'Dick Dorgan' after 26 March 1923.

E 3703
17 October 1922, p. 28.

E 3704
18 October 1922, p. 30.

E 3705
19 October 1922, p. 34.

E 3706
20 October 1922, p. 46.

E 3707
21 October 1922, p. 14.

E 3708
23 October 1922, p. 24.

E 3709
24 October 1922, p. 32.

E 3710
25 October 1922, p. 32.

E 3711
26 October 1922, p. 38.

E 3712
27 October 1922, p. 44.

E 3713
28 October 1922, p. 14.

E 3714
30 October 1922, p. 20.

E 3715
31 October 1922, p. 26.

E 3716
1 November 1922, p. 32.

E 3717
2 November 1922, p. 32.

E 3718
3 November 1922, p. 46.

E 3719
4 November 1922, p. 14.

E 3720
6 November 1922, p. 26.

E 3721
7 November 1922, p. 24.

E 3722
8 November 1922, p. 32.

E 3723
9 November 1922, p. 32.

E 3724
10 November 1922, p. 44.

E 3725
11 November 1922, p. 14.

E 3726
13 November 1922, p. 22.

E 3727
14 November 1922, p. 28.

E 3728
15 November 1922, p. 28.

E 3729
16 November 1922, p. 34.

E 3730
17 November 1922, p. 44.

E 3731
18 November 1922, p. 12.

E 3732
20 November 1922, p. 24.

E 3733
21 November 1922, p. 28.

E 3734
22 November 1922, p. 30.

E 3735
23 November 1922, p. 36.

E 3736
24 November 1922, p. 48.

E 3737
25 November 1922, p. 12.

E 3738
27 November 1922, p. 24.

E 3739
28 November 1922, p. 28.

E 3740
29 November 1922, p. 20.

E 3741
30 November 1922, p. 28.

E 3742a
1 December 1922, p. 46.

E 3742b
2 December 1922, p. 12.

E 3743
4 December 1922, p. 22.

E 3744
5 December 1922, p. 26.

E 3745
6 December 1922, p. 30.

E 3746
7 December 1922, p. 30.

E 3747
8 December 1922, p. 46.

E 3748
9 December 1922, p. 12.

E 3749
11 December 1922, p. 22.

E 3750
12 December 1922, p. 30.

E 3751
13 December 1922, p. 26.

E 3752
14 December 1922, p. 36.

E 3753
15 December 1922, p. 48.

E 3754
16 December 1922, p. 12.

E 3755
18 December 1922, p. 22.

E 3756
19 December 1922, p. 30.

E 3757
20 December 1922, p. 28.

E 3758
21 December 1922, p. 30.

E 3759
22 December 1922, p. 28.

E 3760
23 December 1922, p. 12.

E 3761
26 December 1922, p. 22.

E 3762
27 December 1922, p. 22.

E 3763
28 December 1922, p. 26.

E 3764
29 December 1922, p. 26.

E 3765
30 December 1922, p. 12.

E 3766
2 January 1923, p. 24.

E 3767
3 January 1923, p. 24.

E 3768
4 January 1923, p. 26.

E 3769
5 January 1923, p. 32.

E 3770
6 January 1923, p. 12.

E 3771
8 January 1923, p. 20.

E 3772
9 January 1923, p. 24.

E 3773
10 January 1923, p. 24.

E 3774
11 January 1923, p. 30.

E 3775
12 January 1923, p. 38.

E 3776
13 January 1923, p. 14.

E 3777
15 January 1923, p. 20.

E 3778
16 January 1923, p. 24.

E 3779
17 January 1923, p. 26.

E 3780
18 January 1923, p. 28.

E 3781
19 January 1923, p. 38.

E 3782
20 January 1923, p. 12.

E 3783
22 January 1923, p. 22.

E 3784
23 January 1923, p. 28.

E 3785
24 January 1923, p. 28.

E 3786
25 January 1923, p. 30.

E 3787
26 January 1923, p. 40.

E 3788
27 January 1923, p. 12.

E 3789
29 January 1923, p. 22.

E 3790
30 January 1923, p. 24.

E 3791
31 January 1923, p. 24.

E 3792
1 February 1923, p. 32.

E 3793
2 February 1923, p. 42.

E 3794
3 February 1923, p. 12.

E 3795
5 February 1923, p. 22.

E 3796
6 February 1923, p. 26.

E 3797
7 February 1923, p. 26.

E 3798
8 February 1923, p. 30.

E 3799
9 February 1923, p. 40.

E 3800
10 February 1923, p. 14.

E 3801
12 February 1923, p. 20.

E 3802
13 February 1923, p. 26.

E 3803
14 February 1923, p. 26.

E 3804
15 February 1923, p. 28.

E 3805
16 February 1923, p. 30.

E 3806
17 February 1923, p. 12.

E 3807
19 February 1923, p. 24.

E 3808
20 February 1923, p. 30.

E 3809
21 February 1923, p. 28.

E 3810
22 February 1923, p. 26.

E 3811
23 February 1923, p. 38.

E 3812
24 February 1923, p. 12.

E 3813
26 February 1923, p. 22.

E 3814
27 February 1923, p. 28.

E 3815
28 February 1923, p. 24.

E 3816
1 March 1923, p. 30.

E 3817
2 March 1923, p. 44.

E 3818
3 March 1923, p. 14.

E 3819
5 March 1923, p. 22.

E 3820
6 March 1923, p. 32.

E 3821
7 March 1923, p. 28.

E 3822
8 March 1923, p. 32.

E 3823
9 March 1923, p. 44.

E 3824
10 March 1923, p. 12.

E 3825
12 March 1923, p. 22.

E 3826
13 March 1923, p. 28.

E 3827
14 March 1923, p. 28.

E 3828
15 March 1923, p. 34.

E 3829
16 March 1923, p. 42.

E 3830
17 March 1923, p. 12.

E 3831
19 March 1923, p. 24.

E 3832
20 March 1923, p. 28.

E 3833
21 March 1923, p. 28.

E 3834
22 March 1923, p. 36.

E 3835
23 March 1923, p. 46.

E 3836
24 March 1923, p. 12.

E 3837
26 March 1923, p. 26.

E 3838
27 March 1923, p. 28.

E 3839
28 March 1923, p. 32.

E 3840
29 March 1923, p. 36.

E 3841
30 March 1923, p. 48.

E 3842
31 March 1923, p. 12.

E 3843
2 April 1923, p. 26.

E 3844
3 April 1923, p. 26.

E 3845
4 April 1923, p. 32.

E 3846
5 April 1923, p. 36.

E 3847
6 April 1923, p. 44.

E 3848
7 April 1923, p. 14.

E 3849
9 April 1923, p. 26.

E 3850
10 April 1923, p. 28.

E 3851
11 April 1923, p. 32.

E 3852
12 April 1923, p. 36.

E 3853
13 April 1923, p. 48.

E 3854
14 April 1923, p. 14.

E 3855
16 April 1923, p. 26.

E 3856
17 April 1923, p. 28.

E 3857
18 April 1923, p. 34.

E 3858
19 April 1923, p. 38.

E 3859
20 April 1923, p. 50.

E 3860
21 April 1923, p. 14.

E 3861
23 April 1923, p. 24.

E 3862
24 April 1923, p. 28.

E 3863
25 April 1923, p. 34.

E 3864
26 April 1923, p. 36.

E 3865
27 April 1923, p. 50.

E 3866
28 April 1923, p. 14.

E 3867
30 April 1923, p. 26.

E 3868
1 May 1923, p. 36.

E 3869
2 May 1923, p. 34.

E 3870
3 May 1923, p. 36.

E 3871
4 May 1923, p. 52.

E 3872
5 May 1923, p. 14.

E 3873
7 May 1923, p. 26.

E 3874
8 May 1923, p. 30.

E 3875
9 May 1923, p. 34.

E 3876
10 May 1923, p. 40.

E 3877
11 May 1923, p. 48.

E 3878
12 May 1923, p. 14.

E 3879
14 May 1923, p. 24.

E 3880
15 May 1923, p. 32.

E 3881
16 May 1923, p. 30.

E 3882
17 May 1923, p. 34.

E 3883
18 May 1923, p. 48.

E 3884
19 May 1923, p. 14.

E 3885
21 May 1923, p. 24.

E 3886
22 May 1923, p. 30.

E 3887
23 May 1923, p. 32.

E 3888
24 May 1923, p. 34.

E 3889
25 May 1923, p. 48.

E 3890
26 May 1923, p. 14.

E 3891
28 May 1923, p. 26.

E 3892
29 May 1923, p. 22.

E 3893
30 May 1923, p. 20.

E 3894
31 May 1923, p. 36.

E 3895
1 June 1923, p. 48.

E 3896
2 June 1923, p. 14.

E 3897
4 June 1923, p. 22.

E 3898
5 June 1923, p. 30.

E 3899
6 June 1923, p. 30.

E 3900
7 June 1923, p. 36.

E 3901
8 June 1923, p. 48.

E 3902
9 June 1923, p. 14.

E 3903
11 June 1923, p. 24.

E 3904
12 June 1923, p. 28.

E 3905
13 June 1923, p. 28.

E 3906
14 June 1923, p. 32.

E 3907
15 June 1923, p. 44.

E 3908
16 June 1923, p. 14.

E 3909
18 June 1923, p. 22.

E 3910
19 June 1923, p. 28.

E 3911
20 June 1923, p. 28.

E 3912
21 June 1923, p. 32.

E 3913
22 June 1923, p. 48.

E 3914
23 June 1923, p. 14.

E 3915
25 June 1923, p. 20.

E 3916
26 June 1923, p. 26.

E 3917
27 June 1923, p. 26.

E 3918
28 June 1923, p. 34.

E 3919
29 June 1923, p. 44.

E 3920
30 June 1923, p. 12.

E 3921
2 July 1923, p. 22.

E 3922
3 July 1923, p. 18.

E 3923
5 July 1923, p. 34.

E 3924
6 July 1923, p. 36.

E 3925
7 July 1923, p. 12.

E 3926
9 July 1923, p. 22.

E 3927
10 July 1923, p. 24.

E 3928
11 July 1923, p. 26.

E 3929
12 July 1923, p. 30.

E 3930
13 July 1923, p. 40.

E 3931
14 July 1923, p. 12.

E 3932
16 July 1923, p. 24.

E 3933
17 July 1923, p. 24.

E 3934
18 July 1923, p. 24.

E 3935
19 July 1923, p. 30.

E 3936
20 July 1923, p. 36.

E 3937
21 July 1923, p. 12.

E 3938
23 July 1923, p. 22.

E 3939
24 July 1923, p. 28.

E 3940
25 July 1923, p. 26.

E 3941
26 July 1923, p. 26.

E 3942
27 July 1923, p. 40.

E 3943
28 July 1923, p. 12.

E 3944
30 July 1923, p. 22.

E 3945
31 July 1923, p. 26.

E 3946
1 August 1923, p. 22.

E 3947
2 August 1923, p. 26.

E 3948
3 August 1923, p. 38.

E 3949
4 August 1923, p. 12.

E 3950
6 August 1923, p. 22.

E 3951
7 August 1923, p. 22.

E 3952
8 August 1923, p. 24.

E 3953
9 August 1923, p. 24.

E 3954
10 August 1923, p. 38.

E 3955
11 August 1923, p. 12.

E 3956
13 August 1923, p. 20.

E 3957
14 August 1923, p. 24.

E 3958
15 August 1923, p. 22.

E 3959
16 August 1923, p. 28.

E 3960
17 August 1923, p. 38.

E 3961
18 August 1923, p. 12.

E 3962
20 August 1923, p. 20.

E 3963
21 August 1923, p. 26.

E 3964
22 August 1923, p. 22.

E 3965
23 August 1923, p. 28.

E 3966
24 August 1923, p. 40.

E 3967
25 August 1923, p. 12.

E 3968
27 August 1923, p. 22.

E 3969
28 August 1923, p. 26.

E 3970
29 August 1923, p. 24.

E 3971
30 August 1923, p. 30.

E 3972
31 August 1923, p. 40.

E 3973
1 September 1923, p. 14.

E 3974
4 September 1923, p. 28.

E 3975
5 September 1923, p. 26.

E 3976
6 September 1923, p. 28.

E 3977
7 September 1923, p. 46.

E 3978
8 September 1923, p. 14.

E 3979
10 September 1923, p. 24.

E 3980
11 September 1923, p. 26.

E 3981
12 September 1923, p. 28.

E 3982
13 September 1923, p. 32.

E 3983
14 September 1923, p. 52.

E 3984
15 September 1923, p. 14.

E 3985
17 September 1923, p. 24.

E 3986
18 September 1923, p. 28.

E 3987
19 September 1923, p. 28.

E 3988
20 September 1923, p. 32.

E 3989
21 September 1923, p. 48.

E 3990
22 September 1923, p. 14.

E 3991
24 September 1923, p. 24.

E 3992
25 September 1923, p. 28.

E 3993
26 September 1923, p. 30.

E 3994
27 September 1923, p. 38.

E 3995
28 September 1923, p. 56.

E 3996
29 September 1923, p. 14.

E 3997
1 October 1923, p. 24.

E 3998
2 October 1923, p. 32.

E 3999
3 October 1923, p. 30.

E 4000
4 October 1923, p. 36.

E 4001
5 October 1923, p. 54.

E 4002
6 October 1923, p. 14.

E 4003
8 October 1923, p. 24.

E 4004
9 October 1923, p. 30.

E 4005
10 October 1923, p. 32.

E 4006
11 October 1923, p. 32.

E 4007
12 October 1923, p. 54.

E 4008
13 October 1923, p. 14.

E 4009
15 October 1923, p. 24.

E 4010
16 October 1923, p. 30.

E 4011
17 October 1923, p. 32.

E 4012
18 October 1923, p. 38.

E 4013
19 October 1923, p. 52.

E 4014
20 October 1923, p. 14.

E 4015
22 October 1923, p. 24.

E 4016
23 October 1923, p. 26.

E 4017
24 October 1923, p. 30.

E 4018
25 October 1923, p. 36.

E 4019
26 October 1923, p. 56.

E 4020
27 October 1923, p. 14.

E 4021
29 October 1923, p. 24.

E 4022
30 October 1923, p. 26.

E 4023
31 October 1923, p. 28.

E 4024
1 November 1923, p. 36.

E 4025
2 November 1923, p. 52.

E 4026
3 November 1923, p. 12.

E 4027
5 November 1923, p. 24.

E 4028
6 November 1923, p. 28.

E 4029
7 November 1923, p. 32.

E 4030
8 November 1923, p. 36.

E 4031
9 November 1923, p. 54.

E 4032
10 November 1923, p. 12.

E 4033
12 November 1923, p. 24.

E 4034
13 November 1923, p. 32.

E 4035
14 November 1923, p. 34.

E 4036
15 November 1923, p. 36.

E 4037
16 November 1923, p. 52.

E 4038
17 November 1923, p. 14.

E 4039
19 November 1923, p. 24.

E 4040
20 November 1923, p. 30.

E 4041
21 November 1923, p. 32.

E 4042
22 November 1923, p. 34.

E 4043
23 November 1923, p. 56.

E 4044
24 November 1923, p. 14.

E 4045
26 November 1923, p. 28.

E 4046
27 November 1923, p. 30.

E 4047
28 November 1923, p. 18.

E 4048
29 November 1923, p. 30.

E 4049
1 December 1923, p. 12.

E 4050
3 December 1923, p. 24.

E 4051
4 December 1923, p. 32.

E 4052
5 December 1923, p. 32.

E 4053
6 December 1923, p. 32.

E 4054
7 December 1923, p. 52.

E 4055
8 December 1923, p. 12.

E 4056
10 December 1923, p. 26.

E 4057
11 December 1923, p. 32.

E 4058
12 December 1923, p. 32.

E 4059
13 December 1923, p. 34.

E 4060
14 December 1923, p. 56.

E 4061
15 December 1923, p. 14.

E 4062
17 December 1923, p. 24.

E 4063
18 December 1923, p. 32.

E 4064
19 December 1923, p. 32.

E 4065
20 December 1923, p. 36.

E 4066
21 December 1923, p. 48.

E 4067
22 December 1923, p. 14.

E 4068
24 December 1923, p. 24.

E 4069
26 December 1923, p. 26.

E 4070
27 December 1923, p. 24.

E 4071
28 December 1923, p. 36.

E 4072
29 December 1923, p. 12.

E 4073
31 December 1923, p. 22.

E 4074
2 January 1924, p. 28.

E 4075
3 January 1924, p. 28.

E 4076
4 January 1924, p. 38.

E 4077
5 January 1924, p. 12.

E 4078
7 January 1924, p. 20.

E 4079
8 January 1924, p. 26.

E 4080
9 January 1924, p. 24.

E 4081
10 January 1924, p. 26.

E 4082
11 January 1924, p. 40.

E 4083
12 January 1924, p. 12.

E 4084
14 January 1924, p. 24.

E 4085
15 January 1924, p. 24.

E 4086
16 January 1924, p. 26.

E 4087
17 January 1924, p. 26.

E 4088
18 January 1924, p. 42.

E 4089
19 January 1924, p. 12.

E 4090
21 January 1924, p. 22.

E 4091
22 January 1924, p. 28.

E 4092
23 January 1924, p. 30.

E 4093
24 January 1924, p. 28.

E 4094
25 January 1924, p. 42.

E 4095
26 January 1924, p. 12.

E 4096
28 January 1924, p. 22.

E 4097
29 January 1924, p. 24.

E 4098
30 January 1924, p. 26.

E 4099
31 January 1924, p. 32.

E 4100
1 February 1924, p. 44.

E 4101
2 February 1924, p. 12.

E 4102
4 February 1924, p. 24.

E 4103
5 February 1924, p. 26.

E 4104
6 February 1924, p. 24.

E 4105
7 February 1924, p. 30.

E 4106
8 February 1924, p. 42.

E 4107
9 February 1924, p. 12.

E 4108
11 February 1924, p. 20.

E 4109
12 February 1924, p. 24.

E 4110
13 February 1924, p. 24.

E 4111
14 February 1924, p. 28.

E 4112
15 February 1924, p. 44.

E 4113
16 February 1924, p. 12.

E 4114
18 February 1924, p. 20.

E 4115
19 February 1924, p. 26.

E 4116
20 February 1924, p. 26.

E 4117
21 February 1924, p. 30.

E 4118
22 February 1924, p. 40.

E 4119
23 February 1924, p. 12.

E 4120
25 February 1924, p. 22.

E 4121
26 February 1924, p. 24.

E 4122
27 February 1924, p. 26.

E 4123
28 February 1924, p. 34.

E 4124
29 February 1924, p. 46.

E 4125
1 March 1924, p. 14.

E 4126
3 March 1924, p. 22.

E 4127
4 March 1924, p. 24.

E 4128
5 March 1924, p. 26.

E 4129
6 March 1924, p. 32.

E 4130
7 March 1924, p. 42.

E 4131
8 March 1924, p. 12.

E 4132
10 March 1924, p. 22.

E 4133
11 March 1924, p. 28.

E 4134
12 March 1924, p. 26.

E 4135
13 March 1924, p. 30.

E 4136
14 March 1924, p. 46.

E 4137
15 March 1924, p. 14.

E 4138
17 March 1924, p. 24.

E 4139
18 March 1924, p. 28.

E 4140
19 March 1924, p. 32.

E 4141
20 March 1924, p. 32.

E 4142
21 March 1924, p. 52.

E 4143
22 March 1924, p. 12.

E 4144
24 March 1924, p. 22.

E 4145
25 March 1924, p. 26.

E 4146
26 March 1924, p. 26.

E 4147
27 March 1924, p. 36.

E 4148
28 March 1924, p. 48.

E 4149
29 March 1924, p. 14.

E 4150
31 March 1924, p. 24.

E 4151
1 April 1924, p. 28.

E 4152
2 April 1924, p. 32.

E 4153
3 April 1924, p. 36.

E 4154
4 April 1924, p. 48.

E 4155
5 April 1924, p. 14.

E 4156
7 April 1924, p. 24.

E 4157
8 April 1924, p. 32.

E 4158
9 April 1924, p. 32.

E 4159
10 April 1924, p. 38.

E 4160
11 April 1924, p. 54.

E 4161
12 April 1924, p. 14.

E 4162
14 April 1924, p. 24.

E 4163
15 April 1924, p. 34.

E 4164
16 April 1924, p. 32.

E 4165
17 April 1924, p. 36.

E 4166
18 April 1924, p. 46.

E 4167
19 April 1924, p. 14.

E 4168
21 April 1924, p. 22.

E 4169
22 April 1924, p. 32.

E 4170
23 April 1924, p. 32.

E 4171
24 April 1924, p. 34.

E 4172
25 April 1924, p. 48.

E 4173
26 April 1924, p. 14.

E 4174
28 April 1924, p. 24.

E 4175
29 April 1924, p. 32.

E 4176
30 April 1924, p. 34.

E 4177
1 May 1924, p. 42.

E 4178
2 May 1924, p. 48.

E 4179
3 May 1924, p. 14.

E 4180
5 May 1924, p. 26.

E 4181
6 May 1924, p. 32.

E 4182
7 May 1924, p. 32.

E 4183
8 May 1924, p. 36.

E 4184
9 May 1924, p. 52.

E 4185
10 May 1924, p. 14.

E 4186
12 May 1924, p. 24.

E 4187
13 May 1924, p. 32.

E 4188
14 May 1924, p. 32.

E 4189
15 May 1924, p. 36.

E 4190
16 May 1924, p. 48.

E 4191
17 May 1924, p. 14.

E 4192
19 May 1924, p. 22.

E 4193
20 May 1924, p. 30.

E 4194
21 May 1924, p. 30.

E 4195
22 May 1924, p. 34.

E 4196
23 May 1924, p. 50.

E 4197
24 May 1924, p. 14.

E 4198
26 May 1924, p. 22.

E 4199
27 May 1924, p. 30.

E 4200
28 May 1924, p. 32.

E 4201
29 May 1924, p. 24.

E 4202
30 May 1924, p. 36.

E 4203
31 May 1924, p. 12.

E 4204a
2 June 1924, p. 24.

E 4204b
3 June 1924, p. 28.

E 4205
4 June 1924, p. 28.

E 4206
5 June 1924, p. 32.

E 4207
6 June 1924, p. 44.

E 4208
7 June 1924, p. 14.

E 4209
9 June 1924, p. 24.

E 4210
10 June 1924, p. 30.

E 4211
11 June 1924, p. 34.

E 4212
12 June 1924, p. 36.

E 4213
13 June 1924, p. 48.

E 4214
14 June 1924, p. 14.

E 4215
16 June 1924, p. 24.

E 4216
17 June 1924, p. 28.

E 4217
18 June 1924, p. 28.

E 4218
19 June 1924, p. 32.

E 4219
20 June 1924, p. 46.

E 4220
21 June 1924, p. 14.

E 4221
23 June 1924, p. 24.

E 4222
24 June 1924, p. 26.

E 4223
25 June 1924, p. 26.

E 4224
26 June 1924, p. 32.

E 4225
27 June 1924, p. 42.

E 4226
28 June 1924, p. 14.

E 4227
30 June 1924, p. 22.

E 4228
1 July 1924, p. 28.

E 4229
2 July 1924, p. 28.

E 4230
3 July 1924, p. 22.

E 4231
5 July 1924, p. 14.

E 4232
7 July 1924, p. 20.

E 4233
8 July 1924, p. 26.

E 4234
9 July 1924, p. 28.

E 4235
10 July 1924, p. 28.

E 4236
11 July 1924, p. 34.

E 4237
12 July 1924, p. 12.

E 4238
14 July 1924, p. 18.

E 4239
15 July 1924, p. 22.

E 4240
16 July 1924, p. 26.

E 4241
17 July 1924, p. 26.

E 4242
18 July 1924, p. 34.

E 4243
19 July 1924, p. 12.

E 4244
21 July 1924, p. 20.

E 4245
22 July 1924, p. 22.

E 4246
23 July 1924, p. 24.

E 4247
24 July 1924, p. 24.

E 4248
25 July 1924, p. 32.

E 4249
26 July 1924, p. 12.

E 4250
28 July 1924, p. 20.

E 4251
29 July 1924, p. 24.

E 4252
30 July 1924, p. 22.

E 4253
31 July 1924, p. 26.

E 4254
1 August 1924, p. 36.

E 4255
2 August 1924, p. 12.

E 4256
4 August 1924, p. 20.

E 4257
5 August 1924, p. 24.

E 4258
6 August 1924, p. 22.

E 4259
7 August 1924, p. 28.

E 4260
8 August 1924, p. 34.

E 4261
9 August 1924, p. 12.

E 4262
11 August 1924, p. 20.

E 4263
12 August 1924, p. 24.

E 4264
13 August 1924, p. 24.

E 4265
14 August 1924, p. 26.

E 4266
15 August 1924, p. 36.

E 4267
16 August 1924, p. 12.

E 4268
18 August 1924, p. 18.

E 4269
19 August 1924, p. 24.

E 4270
20 August 1924, p. 22.

E 4271
21 August 1924, p. 28.

E 4272
22 August 1924, p. 36.

E 4273
23 August 1924, p. 12.

E 4274
25 August 1924, p. 20.

E 4275
26 August 1924, p. 28.

E 4276
27 August 1924, p. 30.

E 4277
28 August 1924, p. 30.

E 4278
29 August 1924, p. 40.

E 4279
30 August 1924, p. 14.

E 4280
2 September 1924, p. 26.

E 4281
3 September 1924, p. 26.

E 4282
4 September 1924, p. 28.

E 4283
5 September 1924, p. 42.

E 4284
6 September 1924, p. 12.

E 4285
8 September 1924, p. 20.

E 4286
9 September 1924, p. 30.

E 4287
10 September 1924, p. 30.

E 4288
11 September 1924, p. 32.

E 4289
12 September 1924, p. 48.

E 4290
13 September 1924, p. 14.

E 4291
15 September 1924, p. 24.

E 4292
16 September 1924, p. 32.

E 4293
17 September 1924, p. 30.

E 4294
18 September 1924, p. 32.

E 4295
19 September 1924, p. 48.

E 4296
20 September 1924, p. 14.

E 4297
22 September 1924, p. 24.

E 4298
23 September 1924, p. 28.

E 4299
24 September 1924, p. 26.

E 4300
25 September 1924, p. 32.

E 4301
26 September 1924, p. 54.

E 4302
27 September 1924, p. 14.

E 4303
29 September 1924, p. 20.

E 4304
30 September 1924, p. 28.

E 4305
1 October 1924, p. 30.

E 4306
2 October 1924, p. 32.

E 4307
3 October 1924, p. 54.

E 4308
4 October 1924, p. 14.

E 4309
6 October 1924, p. 22.

E 4310
7 October 1924, p. 30.

E 4311
8 October 1924, p. 32.

E 4312
9 October 1924, p. 30.

E 4313
10 October 1924, p. 54.

E 4314
11 October 1924, p. 14.

E 4315
13 October 1924, p. 24.

E 4316
14 October 1924, p. 28.

E 4317
15 October 1924, p. 28.

E 4318
16 October 1924, p. 30.

E 4319
17 October 1924, p. 50.

E 4320
18 October 1924, p. 12.

E 4321
20 October 1924, p. 24.

E 4322
21 October 1924, p. 28.

E 4323
22 October 1924, p. 36.

E 4324
24 October 1924, p. 52.

E 4325
25 October 1924, p. 12.

E 4326
27 October 1924, p. 24.

E 4327
28 October 1924, p. 28.

E 4328
29 October 1924, p. 26.

E 4329
30 October 1924, p. 32.

E 4330
31 October 1924, p. 32.

E 4331
1 November 1924, p. 12.

E 4332
3 November 1924, p. 24.

E 4333
4 November 1924, p. 22.

E 4334
5 November 1924, p. 36.

E 4335
6 November 1924, p. 36.

E 4336
7 November 1924, p. 50.

E 4337
8 November 1924, p. 12.

E 4338
10 November 1924, p. 22.

E 4339
11 November 1924, p. 32.

E 4340
12 November 1924, p. 30.

E 4341
13 November 1924, p. 34.

E 4342
14 November 1924, p. 52.

E 4343
15 November 1924, p. 12.

E 4344
17 November 1924, p. 24.

E 4345
18 November 1924, p. 32.

E 4346
19 November 1924, p. 34.

E 4347
20 November 1924, p. 30.

E 4348
21 November 1924, p. 46.

E 4349
22 November 1924, p. 14.

E 4350
24 November 1924, p. 26.

E 4351
25 November 1924, p. 30.

E 4352
26 November 1924, p. 22.

E 4353
27 November 1924, p. 28.

E 4354
28 November 1924, p. 44.

E 4355
29 November 1924, p. 14.

E 4356
1 December 1924, p. 22.

E 4357
2 December 1924, p. 32.

E 4358
3 December 1924, p. 36.

E 4359
4 December 1924, p. 34.

E 4360
5 December 1924, p. 52.

E 4361
6 December 1924, p. 12.

E 4362
8 December 1924, p. 24.

E 4363
9 December 1924, p. 32.

E 4364
10 December 1924, p. 32.

E 4365
11 December 1924, p. 36.

E 4366
12 December 1924, p. 58.

E 4367
13 December 1924, p. 12.

E 4368
15 December 1924, p. 24.

E 4369
16 December 1924, p. 32.

E 4370
17 December 1924, p. 32.

E 4371
18 December 1924, p. 32.

E 4372
19 December 1924, p. 50.

E 4373
20 December 1924, p. 12.

E 4374
22 December 1924, p. 28.

E 4375
23 December 1924, p. 26.

E 4376
24 December 1924, p. 26.

E 4377
26 December 1924, p. 34.

E 4378
27 December 1924, p. 12.

E 4379
29 December 1924, p. 20.

E 4380
30 December 1924, p. 22.

E 4381
31 December 1924, p. 26.

E 4382
2 January 1925, p. 32.

E 4383
3 January 1925, p. 12.

E 4384
5 January 1925, p. 20.

E 4385
6 January 1925, p. 28.

E 4386
7 January 1925, p. 26.

E 4387
8 January 1925, p. 28.

E 4388
9 January 1925, p. 36.

E 4389
10 January 1925, p. 12.

E 4390
12 January 1925, p. 20.

E 4391
13 January 1925, p. 26.

E 4392
14 January 1925, p. 28.

E 4393
15 January 1925, p. 30.

E 4394
16 January 1925, p. 36.

E 4395
17 January 1925, p. 14.

E 4396
19 January 1925, p. 22.

E 4397
20 January 1925, p. 28.

E 4398
21 January 1925, p. 30.

E 4399
22 January 1925, p. 30.

E 4400
23 January 1925, p. 38.

E 4401
24 January 1925, p. 14.

E 4402
26 January 1925, p. 22.

E 4403
27 January 1925, p. 26.

E 4404
28 January 1925, p. 24.

E 4405
29 January 1925, p. 28.

E 4406
30 January 1925, p. 36.

E 4407
31 January 1925, p. 12.

E 4408
2 February 1925, p. 22.

E 4409
3 February 1925, p. 26.

E 4410
4 February 1925, p. 26.

E 4411
5 February 1925, p. 26.

E 4412
6 February 1925, p. 38.

E 4413
7 February 1925, p. 12.

E 4414
9 February 1925, p. 22.

E 4415
10 February 1925, p. 26.

E 4416
11 February 1925, p. 28.

E 4417
12 February 1925, p. 28.

E 4418
13 February 1925, p. 38.

E 4419
14 February 1925, p. 14.

E 4420
16 February 1925, p. 22.

E 4421
17 February 1925, p. 24.

E 4422
18 February 1925, p. 26.

E 4423
19 February 1925, p. 30.

E 4424
20 February 1925, p. 38.

E 4425
21 February 1925, p. 12.

E 4426
23 February 1925, p. 20.

E 4427
24 February 1925, p. 30.

E 4428
25 February 1925, p. 30.

E 4429
26 February 1925, p. 26.

E 4430
27 February 1925, p. 40.

E 4431
28 February 1925, p. 14.

E 4432
2 March 1925, p. 22.

E 4433
3 March 1925, p. 28.

E 4434
4 March 1925, p. 26.

E 4435
5 March 1925, p. 28.

E 4436
6 March 1925, p. 40.

E 4437
7 March 1925, p. 12.

E 4438
9 March 1925, p. 20.

E 4439
10 March 1925, p. 28.

E 4440
11 March 1925, p. 28.

E 4441
12 March 1925, p. 28.

E 4442
13 March 1925, p. 46.

E 4443
14 March 1925, p. 12.

E 4444
16 March 1925, p. 24.

E 4445
17 March 1925, p. 28.

E 4446
18 March 1925, p. 26.

E 4447
19 March 1925, p. 30.

E 4448
20 March 1925, p. 46.

E 4449
21 March 1925, p. 12.

E 4450
23 March 1925, p. 24.

E 4451
24 March 1925, p. 28.

E 4452
25 March 1925, p. 26.

E 4453
26 March 1925, p. 30.

E 4454
27 March 1925, p. 46.

E 4455
28 March 1925, p. 14.

E 4456
30 March 1925, p. 24.

E 4457
31 March 1925, p. 28.

E 4458
1 April 1925, p. 32.

E 4459
2 April 1925, p. 32.

E 4460
3 April 1925, p. 48.

E 4461
4 April 1925, p. 14.

E 4462
6 April 1925, p. 24.

E 4463
7 April 1925, p. 32.

E 4464
8 April 1925, p. 32.

E 4465
9 April 1925, p. 36.

E 4466
10 April 1925, p. 46.

E 4467
11 April 1925, p. 14.

E 4468
13 April 1925, p. 26.

E 4469
14 April 1925, p. 30.

E 4470
15 April 1925, p. 32.

E 4471
16 April 1925, p. 30.

E 4472
17 April 1925, p. 48.

E 4473
18 April 1925, p. 14.

E 4474
20 April 1925, p. 26.

E 4475
21 April 1925, p. 30.

E 4476
22 April 1925, p. 32.

E 4477
23 April 1925, p. 30.

E 4478
24 April 1925, p. 46.

E 4479
25 April 1925, p. 14.

E 4480
27 April 1925, p. 24.

E 4481
28 April 1925, p. 32.

E 4482
29 April 1925, p. 32.

E 4483
30 April 1925, p. 36.

E 4484
1 May 1925, p. 48.

E 4485
2 May 1925, p. 14.

E 4486
4 May 1925, p. 24.

E 4487
5 May 1925, p. 32.

E 4488
6 May 1925, p. 32.

E 4489
7 May 1925, p. 34.

E 4490
8 May 1925, p. 48.

E 4491
9 May 1925, p. 14.

E 4492
11 May 1925, p. 26.

E 4493
12 May 1925, p. 32.

E 4494
13 May 1925, p. 32.

E 4495
14 May 1925, p. 32.

E 4496
15 May 1925, p. 46.

E 4497
16 May 1925, p. 14.

E 4498
18 May 1925, p. 26.

E 4499
19 May 1925, p. 28.

E 4500
20 May 1925, p. 32.

E 4501
21 May 1925, p. 36.

E 4502
22 May 1925, p. 46.

E 4503
23 May 1925, p. 14.

E 4504
25 May 1925, p. 26.

E 4505
26 May 1925, p. 32.

E 4506
27 May 1925, p. 34.

E 4507
28 May 1925, p. 38.

E 4508
29 May 1925, p. 24.

E 4509
30 May 1925, p. 14.

E 4510
1 June 1925, p. 18.

E 4511
2 June 1925, p. 18.

E 4512
3 June 1925, p. 22.

E 4513
4 June 1925, p. 24.

E 4514
5 June 1925, p. 42.

E 4515
6 June 1925, p. 6.

E 4516
8 June 1925, p. 18.

E 4517
9 June 1925, p. 21.

E 4518
10 June 1925, p. 23.

E 4519
11 June 1925, p. 22.

E 4520
12 June 1925, p. 44.

E 4521
13 June 1925, p. 6.

E 4522
15 June 1925, p. 17.

E 4523
16 June 1925, p. 19.

E 4524
17 June 1925, p. 21.

E 4525
18 June 1925, p. 22.

E 4526
19 June 1925, p. 40.

E 4527
20 June 1925, p. 6.

E 4528
22 June 1925, p. 17.

E 4529
23 June 1925, p. 19.

E 4530
24 June 1925, p. 23.

E 4531
25 June 1925, p. 31.

E 4532
26 June 1925, p. 41.

E 4533
27 June 1925, p. 6.

E 4534
29 June 1925, p. 12.

E 4535
30 June 1925, p. 25.

E 4536
1 July 1925, p. 25.

E 4537
2 July 1925, p. 25.

E 4538
3 July 1925, p. 9.

E 4539
6 July 1925, p. 17.

E 4540
7 July 1925, p. 21.

E 4541
8 July 1925, p. 23.

E 4542
9 July 1925, p. 25.

E 4543
10 July 1925, p. 25.

E 4544
11 July 1925, p. 6.

E 4545
13 July 1925, p. 15.

E 4546
14 July 1925, p. 17.

E 4547
15 July 1925, p. 21.

E 4548
16 July 1925, p. 23.

E 4549
17 July 1925, p. 21.

E 4550
18 July 1925, p. 6.

E 4551
20 July 1925, p. 15.

E 4552
21 July 1925, p. 17.

E 4553
22 July 1925, p. 17.

E 4554
23 July 1925, p. 19.

E 4555
24 July 1925, p. 23.

E 4556
25 July 1925, p. 6.

E 4557
27 July 1925, p. 17.

E 4558
28 July 1925, p. 17.

E 4559
29 July 1925, p. 21.

E 4560
30 July 1925, p. 23.

E 4561
31 July 1925, p. 20.

E 4562
1 August 1925, p. 6.

E 4563
3 August 1925, p. 15.

E 4564
4 August 1925, p. 16.

E 4565
5 August 1925, p. 19.

E 4566
6 August 1925, p. 23.

E 4567
7 August 1925, p. 23.

E 4568
8 August 1925, p. 6.

E 4569
10 August 1925, p. 11.

E 4570
11 August 1925, p. 17.

E 4571
12 August 1925, p. 19.

E 4572
13 August 1925, p. 21.

E 4573
14 August 1925, p. 25.

E 4574
15 August 1925, p. 6.

E 4575
17 August 1925, p. 19.

E 4576
18 August 1925, p. 17.

E 4577
19 August 1925, p. 19.

E 4578
20 August 1925, p. 21.

E 4579
21 August 1925, p. 23.

E 4580
22 August 1925, p. 6.

E 4581
24 August 1925, p. 15.

E 4582
25 August 1925, p. 19

E 4583
26 August 1925, p. 23.

E 4584
27 August 1925, p. 21.

E 4585
28 August 1925, p. 25.

E 4586
29 August 1925, p. 6.

E 4587
31 August 1925, p. 11.

E 4588
1 September 1925, p. 19.

E 4589
2 September 1925, p. 21.

E 4590
3 September 1925, p. 19.

E 4591
4 September 1925, p. 39.

E 4592
5 September 1925, p. 6.

E 4593
8 September 1925, p. 23.

E 4594
9 September 1925, p. 19.

E 4595
10 September 1925, p. 23.

E 4596
11 September 1925, p. 45.

E 4597
12 September 1925, p. 8.

E 4598
14 September 1925, p. 18.

E 4599
15 September 1925, p. 23.

E 4600
16 September 1925, p. 32.

E 4601
17 September 1925, p. 23.

E 4602
18 September 1925, p. 47.

E 4603
19 September 1925, p. 6.

E 4604
21 September 1925, p. 17.

E 4605
22 September 1925, p. 23.

E 4606
23 September 1925, p. 23.

E 4607
24 September 1925, p. 21.

E 4608
25 September 1925, p. 48.

E 4609
26 September 1925, p. 6.

MISCELLANEOUS
(1922–1928)

The following entries (E 4610 to E 4628) appeared during the course of "Ring Lardner's Weekly Letter." They are grouped here for convenience.

E 4610
Heywood Broun, "It Seems to Me," *New York World*, 9 March 1922, p. 11.

Contains a letter from Lardner. Reprinted in Elder, pp. 247–248.

E 4611
"10 Books I Have Enjoyed Most," *Scranton* (Pa.) *Times*, 10 July 1923, p. 25.

Syndicated by North American Newspaper Alliance.

E 4612
Franklin P. Adams, "The Conning Tower," *New York World*, 5 July 1924, p. 11.[18]

E 4613
Franklin P. Adams, "The Conning Tower," *New York World*, 4 December 1924, p. 13.

Contains a letter from Lardner.

E 4614
Franklin P. Adams, "The Conning Tower," *New York World*, 9 December 1924, p. 13.

Contains a letter from Lardner.

E 4615
"Confessions," *Chicago Tribune*, 3 January 1925, p. 9.

Letter to Fanny Butcher.

E 4616
Grantland Rice, "Sportlight: Grantland Rice Lets Ring Lardner Tell Him About Baseball," *New York Herald Tribune*, 19 June 1925, p. 16.
See C 42.

E 4617
Franklin P. Adams, "The Conning Tower," *New York World*, 5 October 1925, p. 5.

Contains a letter from Lardner.

E 4618
"Ring Lardner Writes Way Into Our Paper," *Great Neck* (N.Y.) *News*, 28 November 1925, p. 3.

E 4619
Franklin P. Adams, "The Conning Tower," *New York World*, 29 December 1925, p. 13.

Contains a letter from Lardner.

E 4620
Grantland Rice, "Tunney Defeats Dempsey and Becomes Champion As 135,000 Cheer Him," *New York Herald Tribune*, 24 September 1926, p. 1.

Can be attributed to Lardner on the basis of Rice's autobiography *The Tumult and the Shouting* (New York: A. S. Barnes, 1954), p. 150.

---

18. Lardner appears to have been a frequent contributor to "The Conning Tower." The compilers are by no means confident that all of Lardner's appearances in that column have been identified.

E 4621
"Ring (Side) Lardner Sees 'Em Through," *New York World*, 24 September 1926, p. 21.

Lardner's coverage of Dempsey-Tunney fight. See Elder, p. 294.

E 4622
Alexander Woollcott, "The Stage," *New York World*, 31 January 1927, p. 11.

Letter from Lardner.

E 4623
"Ring Lardner, Jr.'s Old Man Glories That Kids Put It Over," *Great Neck* (N.Y.) *News*, 2 April 1927, p. 5.

E 4624
"Lambs' Public Gambol Comes April 24," *Great Neck* (N.Y.) *News*, 16 April 1927, p. 10.

Includes Lardner poem, "The Birth of the Lambs."

E 4625
Percy Hammond, "The Theaters," *New York Herald Tribune*, 24 April 1927, p. 7, section 6.

Letter from Lardner.

E 4626
"Ring W. Pays 25 Cents for Skating on Jack Curley's Rink," *Great Neck* (N.Y.) *News*, 31 December 1927, p. 20.

E 4627
"Words That Ring from Our Coach, Mr. Lardner," *Indianapolis News*, 2 January 1928, p. 24.

E 4628
"Letter from an Author," *Chicago Tribune*, 17 June 1928, p. 3, pt. 7.

Letter from Lardner about Chicago opening of *Elmer the Great*.

(NEW YORK) MORNING TELEGRAPH
"Ring's Side"[19] (1928–1929)

"Ring's Side" was probably syndicated.

E 4629
"Preface," 4 December 1928, p. 1.

E 4630
"Vox Populi," 5 December 1928, p. 1.

E 4631
"Yesterday in New York Society," 6 December 1928, p. 1.

E 4632
"Victim of Poisoned Liquor," 9 December 1928, p. 1.

E 4633
11 December 1928, p. 1.

E 4634
"Situations Wanted—Male," 12 December 1928, p. 1.

19. All columns are signed 'Ring Lardner'. Fourteen of the "Ring's Side" columns appear in the *Pittsburgh Post-Gazette* between 21 January and 6 February 1929. The column was announced on 19 January 1929, p. 6, as appearing 'exclusively in *Pittsburgh Post-Gazette*'.

E 4635
13 December 1928, p. 1.

E 4636
"H. Jolson Et Al," 16 December
1928, p. 1.

E 4637
18 December 1928, p. 1.

E 4638
"Yesterday," 19 December 1928,
p. 1.

E 4639
20 December 1928, p. 1.

E 4640
"Christmas Card," 23 December
1928, p. 1.

E 4641
25 December 1928, p. 1.

E 4642
"The Morning After," 26 December 1928, p. 1.

E 4643
27 December 1928, p. 1.

E 4644
"Abend di Anni Nouveau," 30
December 1928, p. 1.

E 4645
1 January 1929, p. 1.

E 4646
2 January 1929, p. 1.

E 4647
"Confidential," 3 January 1929,
p. 1.

E 4648
"Elle Stoop S'Amuser," 6 January
1929, p. 1.

E 4649
8 January 1929, p. 1.

E 4650
9 January 1929, p. 1.

E 4651
10 January 1929, p. 1.

E 4652
"Lapsus Lazuli," 13 January
1929, p. 3.

E 4653
15 January 1929, p. 3.

E 4654
"To Producers, Authors, Actors,
Etc.," 16 January 1929, p. 3.

See C 50.

E 4655
17 January 1929, p. 3.

E 4656
"Strange Intermission," 20
January 1929, p. 3.

E 4657
"Your Broadway, Beau, and You
Can Have It," 22 January 1929,
p. 3.

See *F&L*

E 4658
"Diff'rent," 23 January 1929, p. 3.

E 4659
"Bahamas Bound," 24 January
1929, p. 3.

E 4660
27 January 1929, p. 3.

See *F&L* ("To Nassau").

E 4661
29 January 1929, p. 3.

E 4662
"Immune," 30 January 1929, p. 3.

E 4663
31 January 1929, p. 3.

See *F&L* ("Brief Baedeker").

E 4664
3 February 1929, p. 3.

E 4665
6 February 1929, p. 2.

MISCELLANEOUS
(*1929–1933*)

The following items (E 4666 to E 4676) appeared during the course of "Ring's Side." They are grouped here for convenience.

E 4666
Franklin P. Adams, "The Conning Tower," *New York World*, 20 June 1929, p. 15.

Contains Lardner letter.

E 4667
" 'Let George Do It,' " *Atlantic City Press*, 31 July 1929.

See A 23.

E 4668
"The Marvelous Lardner Method in Playwriting," *New York World*, 6 October 1929, p. 3M.

E 4669
"Mr. Lardner Has His Fun," *The New York Times*, 6 October 1929, p. 4, section 9.

See A 23.

E 4670
"Mr. Lardner Appears in Person, In So Far As Type Is Concerned," *New York Herald Tribune*, 6 October 1929, p. 2, section 8.

E 4671
"The Addison Sims of 44th Street," *The New York Times*, 16 March 1930, p. 4, section 9.

E 4672
Gladys Baker, "An Eye on Father," *Birmingham* (Ala.) *News*, 29 July 1930.

Lardner letter quoted.

E 4673
"Jack Donahue," *The New York Times*, 5 October 1930, p. 1, section 9.

E 4674
"The Slave's Lament," *The New York Times*, 16 November 1930, p. 2, section 8.

E 4675
Franklin P. Adams, "The Conning Tower," *New York Herald Tribune*, 23 October 1931, p. 17.

'Brief Admonition from Daddams to Daddams: DON'T VISIT HERE WITH PERSEPHONE ADAMS!
        MR. LARDNER'

E 4676
Franklin P. Adams, "The Conning Tower," *New York Herald Tribune*, 30 September 1933, p. 9.

Contains Lardner letter.
See C 34.

THE BELL SYNDICATE
"A Night Letter from Ring Lardner"[20] *(1931)*

Columns were syndicated by Bell in association with the *Chicago Tribune* and the *New York Daily News*. They are listed as they appeared in the *Chicago Tribune*.

E 4677
2 February 1931, p. 1.

E 4690
17 February 1931, p. 3.

E 4678
3 February 1931, p. 1.

E 4691
18 February 1931, p. 3.

E 4679
4 February 1931, p. 1.

E 4692
19 February 1931, p. 3.

E 4680
5 February 1931, p. 1.

E 4693
20 February 1931, p. 3.

E 4681
6 February 1931, p. 1.

E 4694
21 February 1931, p. 3.

E 4682
7 February 1931, p. 1.

E 4695
23 February 1931, p. 3.

E 4683
9 February 1931, p. 1.

E 4696
24 February 1931, p. 3.

E 4684
10 February 1931, p. 3.

E 4697
25 February 1931, p. 3.

E 4685
11 February 1931, p. 3.

E 4698
26 February 1931, p. 3.

E 4686
12 February 1931, p. 3.

E 4699
27 February 1931, p. 3.

E 4687
13 February 1931, p. 3.

E 4700
28 February 1931, p. 3.

E 4688
14 February 1931, p. 3.

E 4701
2 March 1931, p. 3.

E 4689
16 February 1931, p. 3.

E 4702
3 March 1931, p. 3.

---

20. All columns are signed 'Ring Lardner'.

E 4703
4 March 1931, p. 3.

E 4704
6 March 1931, p. 3.

E 4705
7 March 1931, p. 3.

E 4706
9 March 1931, p. 3.

E 4707
10 March 1931, p. 3.

E 4708
12 March 1931, p. 3.

E 4709
14 March 1931, p. 3.

E 4710
16 March 1931, p. 3.

E 4711
17 March 1931, p. 3.

E 4712
18 March 1931, p. 3.

E 4713
19 March 1931, p. 3.

E 4714
20 March 1931, p. 3.

E 4715
21 March 1931, p. 3.

E 4716
23 March 1931, p. 3.

E 4717
24 March 1931, p. 3.

E 4718
25 March 1931, p. 3.

E 4719
26 March 1931, p. 3.

E 4720
27 March 1931, p. 4.

E 4721
28 March 1931, p. 3.

E 4722
30 March 1931, p. 3.

E 4723
31 March 1931, p. 4.

E 4724
1 April 1931, p. 3.

E 4725
2 April 1931, p. 3.

E 4726
3 April 1931, p. 38.

E 4727
4 April 1931, p. 21.

E 4728
6 April 1931, p. 29.

E 4729
7 April 1931, p. 27.

E 4730
8 April 1931, p. 29.

E 4731
9 April 1931, p. 29.

E 4732
10 April 1931, p. 29.

E 4733
11 April 1931, p. 19.

E 4734
13 April 1931, p. 27.

E 4735
14 April 1931, p. 30.

E 4736
15 April 1931, p. 26.

Beginning 16 April 1931 this
column ("A Night Letter from
Ring Lardner") was retitled "Ring
Lardner Hears from Willis
Clough."

E 4737
16 April 1931, p. 24.

E 4738
17 April 1931, p. 31.

E 4739
18 April 1931, p. 23.

E 4740
20 April 1931, p. 29.

E 4741
21 April 1931, p. 27.

E 4742
22 April 1931, p. 24.

E 4743
23 April 1931, p. 27.

E 4744
24 April 1931, p. 28.

E 4745
25 April 1931, p. 21.

PITTSBURGH POST-GAZETTE

E 4746
"Ring Lardner's Autobiography,"
Pittsburgh Post-Gazette.

Unidentified clipping. Apparently
an advertisement for "Ring's

Side" in *Pittsburgh Post-Gazette*
(see n. 19 to "Ring's Side" on
p. 375). A search of the
Post-Gazette has not located
this poem.

*   *   *

Note 1:   See "Addenda" on p. 198 for entries E 4747 through E 4756,
which were added in proof.

Note 2:   See D 245 for the Lardner story "Via the Canal" in the *New
York Sunday News*, 7 January 1934.

F. Movie Work

Movies to which Lardner contributed script material or which were made from his work, arranged chronologically.

F 1

Serial of baseball humor. 1915. Produced in Chicago by Hans Moss.

Lardner wrote scenarios. See "In the Wake of the News," 22 June 1915, E 1870. Title of serial unknown; no print located.

F 2

The New Klondike. Paramount, 1926. Produced by Adolph Zukor and Jesse L. Lasky; directed by Lewis Milestone.

Copyright 15 March 1926. Lardner wrote special story adapted by Thomas J. Geraghty and J. Clarkson Miller. The film story was made into a book *The New Klondike*, by Peggy Griffith (New York: Jacobsen-Hodgkinson, [1926])—which does not credit Lardner.

F 3

Fast Company. Paramount, 1929. Directed by A. Edward Sutherland; adapted by Patrick J. Kearney and Walton Butterfield; screenplay by Florence Ryerson.

Copyright 13 September 1929. From *Elmer the Great,* by Lardner and George M. Cohan. See F 6; F 9; G 8.

F 4

The Fight. Vitaphone Varieties, 1930. 1 reel.

Copyright 9 June 1930. From an original scenario, "Round One," by Lardner.

F 5

June Moon. Paramount, 1931. Directed by A. Edward Sutherland; screenplay by Keene Thompson and Joseph A. Mankiewicz.

Copyright 20 March 1931. From the play by Lardner and George S. Kaufman. See A 24; F 8; G 10.

F 6
Elmer the Great. First National Pictures, 1933. Directed by Mervin LeRoy; screenplay by Thomas J. Geraghty.

Copyright 13 April 1933. From the play by Lardner and George M. Cohan. See F 3; F 9; G 8.

F 7
Alibi Ike. Warner Brothers, 1935. Directed by Raymond Enright; screenplay by William Wister Haines.

Released 7 June 1935. From the story by Lardner. See A 16. "Rev. Temp." script dated 31 January 1935 in Bruccoli collection.

F 8
Blonde Trouble. Paramount, 1937. Produced by Adolph Zukor; directed by George Archainbaud; screenplay by Lily Hayward.

Copyright 6 August 1937. from *June Moon,* by Lardner and George S. Kaufman. See A 24; F 5; G 10.

F 9
The Cowboy Quarterback. First National Pictures, 1939. Directed by Noel Smith; screenplay by Fred Niblo.

Copyright 29 July 1939. From *Elmer the Great,* by Lardner and George M. Cohan. See F 3; F 6; G 8.

F 10
So This Is New York. Screen Plays Inc., Enterprise Production, released through United Artists, 1948. Produced by Stanley Kramer; directed by Richard O. Fleischer; screenplay by Carl Foreman.

Copyright 25 June 1948. From *The Big Town,* by Lardner. See A 14.

F 11
Champion. Screen Plays Inc, released through United Artists, 1949. Produced by Stanley Kramer; directed by Mark Robson; screenplay by Carl Foreman.

Copyright 9 February 1949. From the story by Lardner.

*   *   *

Note 1: There is a letter dated 10 April 1916 from Lardner to one identified only as Mr. Griffen that reads as follows: "In reply to your letter of the first, which I should have answered before, I will write the scenarios you desire (twelve in all, delivered one per month) at $250 apiece and an advance of $250." These "scenarios" have not been identified.

Note 2:   RWL Jr. has retained a contract between Lardner and Lee Moran dated 12 December 1922 in which "all motion picture rights in and to the said series of stories entitled 'You Know Me Al' " were assigned to Moran, who then had the right "to make and release not more than fifteen (15) motion picture comedies, each of which shall not be longer than two (2) standard reels, and that the said comedies shall be released, the first one on or before June first, Nineteen hundred and twenty-three." A second contract dated 22 June 1923 extended the deadline for the release of the motion pictures. There is a hand-written note attached to the second contract which reads: "Hammons says only one picture was released: the movie of it is 'The Busher.' He says the picture made by Moran was so bad he had the whole thing remade so that no one could tell any of Lardner's stuff was in it. McKern [?]" The note is dated 29 February 1924. The only movie located entitled "The Busher" was released in mid-1919 and on the basis of a review cannot be related to "The Busher" referred to above.

Note 3:   An article in *The Great Neck News*, 24 April 1926, p. 26, states that "Ring Lardner's series, 'You Know Me Al' will be produced in fifty-two pictures by Century Comedies." Lardner's record of his income, held by RWL Jr., indicates he received $7,500 from "Century Films Corp." in 1926. No copyright information has been found for the serial, and there is no evidence that it was actually produced.

Note 4:   The following is a television adaptation.

"Zone of Quiet." 1949.

TV screenplay by David Shaw; produced on *Actor's Studio*, ABC Television, 13 February 1949. Screenplay published in *The Best Television Plays of the Year*, ed. William I. Kaufman (New York: Merlin Press, 1950). See D 116.

G. Dramatic Work

Dramatic productions to which Lardner contributed, arranged chronologically. Only plays, revues, and sketches that were performed are listed.

G 1
Zanzibar. 1903.

Produced by The American Minstrels at the Opera House in Niles, Mich.; book by Harry Schmidt; lyrics and music by Ring Lardner. This was a local production staged on 14 April 1903. See A 1.

G 2
"A Soldier's Mother." 1919.

Nine-minute skit produced at Chicago theatres as an advertisement for the Liberty Loan campaign. See *Chicago Tribune,* 19 April 1919, p. 19.

G 3
According to Elder (p. 252), Lardner collaborated with Charles Washburn on a sketch for the 1920 (?) burlesque revue *Joy Belles.*

G 4
The Ziegfeld Follies. 1922.

Produced by Florenz Ziegfeld at the New Amsterdam Theatre in New York; opened 5 June 1922. Lardner contributed two sketches: "The Bull Pen" and "Rip van Winkle, Jr." See A 26; D 83.

G 5
The 49ers. 1922.

Produced at the Punch and Judy Theatre in New York; opened 7 November 1922. Lardner contributed "The Tridget of Greva," one of eleven sketches. See C 28; AA 8.

389

G 6
The D T's of 1925. 1925.

Produced "by the various authors" at the Dutch Treat Club Dinner
held on 27 March 1925 at the Waldorf-Astoria Hotel in New York.
Lardner contributed " 'In Conference'," one of ten sketches. See
A 17; D 106.

G 7
D. T Show 1927. 1927.

Produced at the Dutch Treat Club Dinner held on 25 March 1927.
Lardner contributed "Dinner & Bridge" produced by Joseph M.
Kerrigan, one of five sketches. See A 26; D 131.

G 8
Elmer The Great, with George M. Cohan. 1928.

Produced by George M. Cohan at the Lyceum Theatre, New York;
staged by Sam Forrest; opened 24 September 1928. See F 3; F 6;
F 9.

G 9
"Game Called Off." 1929.

Performed 6 October 1929 on the CBS radio program "Majestic
Theatre of the Air." The sketch was reported to be a "radio drama
with a background of a world series baseball game" written by
Lardner expressly for the "Majestic Theatre of the Air." See *Hot
Springs National Park, Arkansas Sentinel* (6 October 1929).

G 10
June Moon, with George S. Kaufman. 1929.

Produced by Sam H. Harris at the Broadhurst Theatre, New York;
opened 9 October 1929. See A 24; F 5; F 8.

G 11
Ruth Selwyn's Nine Fifteen Revue. 1930.

Produced by Ruth Selwyn at the George M. Cohan Theatre, New
York; directed by Earl Carroll; opened 11 February 1930. Lardner
contributed one of thirty-six sketches.

G 12
Smiles. 1930.

Produced by Florenz Ziegfeld at the Ziegfeld Theatre, New York; book and direction by William Anthony McGuire; opened 18 November 1930. Lardner contributed lyrics for eight songs with music by Vincent Youmans. See B 8; B 9.

G 13
A Round with Ring. 1969.

Produced by American National Theatre and Academy at the Theatre de Lys, New York; adapted by Nathan R. Teitel and Haila Stoddard from the works of Lardner; opened 28 October 1969.

* * *

Note 1: The Lardner papers at The Newberry Library include a contract dated 14 February 1919 between Lardner and Morris Gest of the Century Theatre in New York for "not less than two plays (comedies or dramas) and one libretto and lyrics of a musical play." No copyright record or other evidence of production has been found for any of these works.

Note 2: The Lardner papers at The Newberry Library include a review by the A. L. Erlanger play review department dated 29 April 1921 of a play by Lardner, "The Banker." The play was strongly recommended by the reviewer. No other record of "The Banker" has been located.

Note 3: The following quote is in "From Vaudeville," by Joe Laurie, Jr., in *The Third Fireside Book of Baseball*, edited by Charles Einstein (New York: Simon & Schuster, 1968), pp. 260–261: "Capt. Adrian C. 'Pop' Anson, the dean of baseball, went into vaude about 1913 and did a monologue, finishing up with a short dance. He liked vaude, because he came back in 1921 with his two beautiful daughters in a skit written for them by Ring Lardner with songs by Herman Timberg." This skit has not been identified.

H. Interviews

Interviews with Lardner, arranged chronologically.

H 1
"Three Stories a Year Are Enough for a Writer," *The New York Times*, 25 March 1917, p. 14, section 6.

H 2
Flora Merrill, "There's a Lot of Laughing Done by People Who Are Afraid Not to, Says Ring Lardner," *New York World*, 10 May 1925, pp. 1, 8, section 3.

H 3
W. Tittle, "Glimpses of Interesting Americans," *The Century Magazine*, 110 (July 1925), 313–317.

H 4
Grant Overton, "Ring W. Lardner's Bell Lettres," *The Bookman*, 62 (September 1925), 44–49.

H 5
"Ring Lardner Hunts for a Lead," *The American Press* (August 1929) p. 23.

H 6
Bozeman Bulger, "Giants Hope to Even Count Over Season with Braves," *New York Evening World*, 30 July 1930.

H 7
"Grantland Rice and Lardner Exchange Roles for a Day," *Boston Post*, 17 August 1930.

H 8
"Ring Lardner Visits Boston," *Boston Herald*, 31 October 1930.

H 9
"Why Try to Make Presidents Funny? Asks Ring Lardner Sorrowfully," *Boston Herald*, 9 November 1930.

H 10
"Spacious Justification," *Detroit Free Press*, 6 December 1930.

H 11
George Britt, "Lardner, Ill, Gazes Long at Typewriter, but May Only Talk of What Others Write," *New York World-Telegram*, 29 October 1931, p. 3.

H 12
Louis Reed, "The Loudspeaker," *New York American*, 15 December 1931.

H 13
Dana Tiverton, "Ring Lardner Writes a Story," *The Writer*, 46 (January 1933), 8–9.

H 14
John E. Hazzard, "Few Kind Words!," *Great Neck News*, 6 October 1933, p. 4.

I. Dust-Jacket Blurbs

Blurbs (statements by Lardner on dust jackets of books by other authors), arranged chronologically.

I 1
Charles E. Van Loan. *Taking the Count.* New York: Doran, [1915].

Lardner statement on back of dust jacket:

'*Says Ring W. Lardner:* "The best sport fiction I | know of, practically the only | sport fiction that an adult | may read without fear of | stomach trouble, is con- | tained in the collected works | of Charles E. Van Loan." '

Location: MJB.

I 2
Eugene O'Neill. *Desire Under the Elms.* New York: Boni & Liveright, 1925.

Lardner statement on back of dust jacket:

' "Have not seen 'Desire Un- | der the Elms' yet, but under- | stand that the sinners in it | get hell, which is moral. If | not, why don't they pick on | 'Hamlet'?"   —*Ring W. Lardner*'

Location: MJB.

I 3
Josephine Herbst. *Nothing Is Sacred.* New York: Coward-McCann, 1928.

Lardner statement appears twice on wraparound band: " 'A swell book.' "

Location: MdU.

399

Appendices / Index

Appendix 1

Newspapers Subscribing to the Bell Syndicate
Column, "Ring Lardner's Weekly Letter"

The following list of newspapers subscribing to "Ring Lardner's Weekly Letter," distributed by the Bell Syndicate, is derived from two Bell promotional brochures which advertised his column and listed the papers that carried it. These brochures are apparently from different time periods, one about 1920 and the other about 1925. The list is probably incomplete, and it should not be inferred that all of the newspapers listed subscribed to the column for its duration.

Akron, Ohio, *Times*
Albany, N.Y., *Argus*
Anaconda, Mont., *Standard*
Asheville, N.C., *Citizen*
Atlanta, Ga., *Journal*
Augusta, Ga., *Chronicle*
Austin, Tex., *American*
Baltimore, Md., *American*
Baltimore, Md., *Sun*
Beaumont, Tex., *Enterprise*
Bethlehem, Pa., *Globe*
Binghamton, N.Y., *Sun*
Birmingham, Ala., *News*
Boise, Idaho, *Statesman*
Boston, Mass., *Globe*
Bridgeport, Conn., *Herald*
Bridgeport, Conn., *Post*
Buffalo, N.Y., *Courier*
Butte, Mont., *Miner*
Canton, Ohio, *News*
Casper, Wyo., *Herald*
Charleston, S.C., *News & Courier*
Charlotte, N.C., *News*
Chattanooga, Tenn., *Times*
Chicago, Ill., *Herald Examiner*

Cincinnati, Ohio, *Commercial Tribune*
Clarksville, Tenn., *Leaf Chronicle*
Cleveland, Ohio, *News Leader*
Cleveland, Ohio, *Times*
Colorado Springs, Colo., *Telegraph*
Columbia, S.C., *State*
Columbus, Ga., *Enquirer Sun*
Corpus Christi, Tex., *Caller*
Dallas, Tex., *Beau Monde*
Davenport, Iowa, *Democrat*
Dayton, Ohio, *News*
Denver, Colo., *Rocky Mountain News*
Des Moines, Iowa, *Capital*
Des Moines, Iowa, *Register & Tribune*
Detroit, Mich., *News*
Dubuque, Iowa, *Daily News*
Duluth, Minn., *News Tribune*
Elkhart, Ind., *Truth*
El Paso, Tex., *Herald*
Enid, Okla., *Eagle & News*
Evansville, Ind., *Courier*

Ft. Worth, Tex., *Star Telegram*
Fresno, Calif., *Republican*
Goshen, Ind., *Democrat*
Greenville, S.C., *News*
Halifax, Nova Scotia, *Herald*
Hartford, Conn., *Courant*
Houston, Tex., *Chronicle*
Houston, Tex., *Saturday Night Review*
Huntington, Ind., *Press*
Huntington, W.Va., *Herald Dispatch*
Hutchinson, Kans., *News*
Indianapolis, Ind., *Star*
Jackson, Mich., *News*
Jacksonville, Fla., *Journal*
Johnson City, Tex., *Chronicle*
Joplin, Mo., *Globe*
Kansas City, Mo., *Star*
Little Rock, *Arkansas Democrat*
Los Angeles, Calif., *Examiner*
Louisville, Ky., *Courier Journal*
Marion, Ohio, *Star*
Memphis, Tenn., *Commercial Appeal*
Miami, Fla., *Metropolis*
Milwaukee, Wis., *Journal*
Montgomery, Ala., *Journal*
Montreal, Quebec, *Star*
Muskogee, Okla., *Daily News*
Muskogee, Okla., *Phoenix*
Nashville, Tenn., *Tennessean*
Newark, N.J., *Advocate*
New Haven, Conn., *Register*
New Orleans, La., *Item*
New York, N.Y., *American*
New York, N.Y., *World*
Norfolk, Va., *Ledger Dispatch*
Oklahoma City, Okla., *Oklahoman*
Okmulgee, Okla., *Daily Times*
Omaha, Nebr., *World-Herald*
Pensacola, Fla., *Journal*
Peoria, Ill., *Journal*

Philadelphia, Pa., *Bulletin*
Philadelphia, Pa., *Public Ledger*
Pittsburgh, Pa., *Gazette Times*
Pocatello, Idaho, *Herald*
Portland, Oreg., *Journal*
Pueblo, Colo., *Star Journal*
Raleigh, N.C., *News & Observer*
Raleigh, N.C., *Times*
Reading, Pa., *Tribune*
Richmond, Va., *News Leader*
Rochester, N.Y., *Herald*
St. John, New Brunswick, *Standard*
St. Joseph, Mo., *News Press*
St. Louis, Mo., *Post Dispatch*
St. Paul, Minn., *Dispatch*
St. Paul, Minn., *Dispatch Pioneer Press*
Salt Lake City, Utah, *Tribune*
San Antonio, Tex., *Light*
San Bernardino, Calif., *Sun*
San Diego, Calif., *Union*
San Francisco, Calif., *Examiner*
Saskatoon, Saskatchewan, *Star*
Scranton, Pa., *Telegram*
Seattle, Wash., *Post Intelligencer*
Seattle, Wash., *Times*
Shreveport, La., *Times*
Sioux City, Iowa, *Journal*
Springfield, Illinois *State Journal*
Springfield, Mass., *Union*
Springfield, Ohio, *News*
Syracuse, N.Y., *Herald*
Tarrytown, N.Y., *News*
Terre Haute, Ind., *Tribune*
Toledo, Ohio, *Times*
Tokyo, Japan, *Advertiser*
Toronto, Ontario, *Star Weekly*
Trenton, N.J., *Times*
Tulsa, Okla., *World*

Utica, N.Y., *Saturday Globe*

Vancouver, British Columbia,
  Sun

Waco, Tex., *News Tribune*

Washington, D.C., *Star*

Waterbury, Conn., *Republican*

Wheeling, W.Va., *News*

Wichita, Kans., *Eagle*

Wichita Falls, Tex., *Record
  News*

Wilkes Barre, Pa., *Times
  Leader*

Wilmington, Del., *Star*

Winnipeg, Ontario, *Free Press*

Winston-Salem, N.C., *Sentinel*

Yakima, Wash., *Herald*

Youngstown, Ohio, *Vindicator*

Zanesville, Ohio, *Times Signal*

Appendix 2

Bell Syndicate Re-releases

Between March 1928 and November 1933 the Bell Syndicate distributed on a weekly basis previously printed Lardner pieces. Most were resyndications of Bell Syndicate columns; but some had been published in magazines, and some were from the "Ring's Side" series in the New York *Morning Telegraph*. All of these columns had been previously published. A number of these Bell re-releases were edited or updated by an unknown hand.

In 1968 Bruccoli purchased from the Scribner Rare Book Department a carton containing 241 dated mimeographed re-releases from the Bell Syndicate, covering the 1928–1933 period, that had apparently been assembled by Gilbert Seldes in compiling *First and Last*. The re-releases have been located in the Binghamton (N.Y.) *Press*, the Flint (Mich.) *Journal*, and the Mobile (Ala.) *Press*.

Appendix 3

Principal Works About Ring W. Lardner

Caruthers, Clifford M., ed. *Ring Around Max: The Correspondence of Ring Lardner & Max Perkins*. DeKalb: Northern Illinois University Press, 1973.

Elder, Donald. *Ring Lardner: A Biography*. Garden City, N.Y.: Doubleday, 1956.

Frakes, James R. "Ring Lardner: A Critical Survey." Unpub. diss., University of Pennsylvania, 1953.

Friedrich, Otto. *Ring Lardner*. Minneapolis: University of Minnesota Press, 1965.

Geismar, Maxwell. *Ring Lardner and the Portrait of Folly*. New York: Crowell, 1972.

Layman, Richard. "Bibliographical Information for a Life of Ring Lardner." Unpub. diss., University of South Carolina, 1975.

Patrick, Walton R. *Ring Lardner*. New York: Twayne, 1963.

Webb, Howard W. "Ring Lardner's Conflict and Reconciliation with American Society." Unpub. diss., University of Iowa, 1953.

Index

409

DATE DUE